Speaking Culturally

Language Diversity in the United States

Fern L. Johnson

 Sage Publications, Inc.
International Educational and Professional Publisher
Thousand Oaks ▪ London ▪ New Delhi

For information:

Sage Publications, Inc.
2455 Teller Road
Thousand Oaks, California 91320
E-mail: order@sagepub.com

Sage Publications Ltd.
6 Bonhill Street
London EC2A 4PU
United Kingdom

Sage Publications India Pvt. Ltd.
M-32 Market
Greater Kailash I
New Delhi 110 048 India

Printed in the United States of America

Library of Congress Cataloging-in-Publication Data

Johnson, Fern L.
    Speaking culturally: Language diversity in the United States /
by Fern L. Johnson.
        p. cm.
    Includes bibliographical references and index.
    ISBN 0-8039-5911-7 (alk. paper)—ISBN 0-8039-5912-5 (alk. paper)
    1. Language and culture—United States. 2. Linguistic minorities—
United States. 3. Language and languages—Variation—United States.
4. Multilingualism—United States. I. Title.
    P35.5U6 J64 2000
    306.44′0973—dc21   99-006890

This book is printed on acid-free paper.

00   01   02   03   04   05   10   9   8   7   6   5   4   3   2   1

Acquiring Editor:	Margaret H. Seawell
Production Editor:	Astrid Virding
Editorial Assistant:	Karen Wiley
Designer/Typesetter:	Janelle LeMaster
Cover Designer:	Candice Harman

For my mother—who throughout her life
opened herself to difference.

Contents

II. Locating Cultural Discourses

III. Language Consequences and Controversies

Preface

Over the past decade, I have become increasingly aware that the typical ways in which we tend to talk about diversity and communication barely skim the surface of the rich cultural underpinnings of all discourse. In the United States, we still operate too often on tenuous assumptions that a common culture exists for most citizens and that cultural assimilation for "others" (minorities, immigrants, speakers of languages other than English) pivots only on their will to fit in. Cultural explanations for language differences certainly occur in scholarly analyses, but the more common approaches use relatively conventional sociolinguistic concepts, which have never been as fully developed on the social theory side as on the linguistic side, or they draw on concepts in the analysis of communication that help give a sense of understanding to language behavior but delve little into the cultural foundations of communication. Even in the field of intercultural communication, considerations of cultural diversity *within* the United States become easily overwhelmed by international and global perspectives. Only recently have we begun to see more attention given to communication within the United States as an intercultural phenomenon; scholarship on discourse dimensions associated with African Americans, Asian Americans, and Hispanics usually emerges, rather, within specialized literatures focused on these groups.

About 15 years ago, I began to think about the ways in which culture as a model would be helpful to making sense of the ways in which women and men use language in everyday life. I was thinking at that time about culture as a metaphor to enrich explanations for why women and men often approached communicative situations so very differently. After much reading in texts from cultural anthropology (a project aided by Sylvia Forman, who was a faculty member in the anthropology department at the University of Massachusetts at Amherst until her untimely death from cancer in 1991), I became convinced that culture served more than metaphorical purposes in understanding gender. I saw culture as a crucial way to bring a kind of "deep structure substance" to questions not easily answered through traditional sociolinguistic analysis. In that context, I lectured and wrote about gender cultures in the mid- and late 1980s. What I said then about culture and the role of culture in gender appears now to be overly simplistic, but the formulation of ideas proved critical to what I believe today about the broader perspective of culture as an explanatory system for discourse.

My long-standing interest in culture and language in the United States frames the project I undertook in *Speaking Culturally.* Using a view that I term the *Language-Centered Perspective on Culture,* the book aims to provide culture-based interpretations for language-in-use and for broader discourse issues. I wanted to bring together in one volume a connected discussion of how language works among various groups of people in the United States—culturally founded groups with histories, traditions, and ever-changing patterns of life brought about through the culturally complex circumstances of living in the United States. I wanted also to grapple with how cultural identity relates to communicative conduct and how dominant ideology can erase that connection. And I wanted to profile the ideas of what I call *cultural mindedness* and *cultural linguistics* at the symbolically significant juncture of the millennium.

As the new century begins, we are living a kind of cultural revolution in the United States. I sense more and more that everyday life consists of many different cultural discourses, that we all speak culturally even when unaware of how our language both carries and creates the world(s) we inhabit and think we know to exist. The 1960s proved to be a turning point in many ways for the cultural diversity of today. The Civil Rights Movement forced greater recognition of the two worlds of black and white and fostered a black pride movement that would become the energizing force behind many ethnic pride movements to follow. Immigration reforms in 1965 opened the United States to peoples from other countries and with native languages other than English.

Yet, many of us who are white, of U.S. birth, native speakers of American English, and of European ancestry (what I will call *Eurowhites* in this book) rarely think about the cultural dimensions of discourse except in relation to foreign countries and people in the United States who are identified as foreign. We may think about and even take action to assist and support peoples from cultural groups unlike our own, but even then, we usually do so acting and speaking out of the tacit assumptions of our cultural system. Another way of putting this is to say that culture exists for many Eurowhites as something someone else has, with the possible exception of thinking of an aggregate "American culture." In my teaching, however, I have found that, with some initial facilitation, students of different races, nationalities, ethnicities, social classes, gender identities, and generations find the concept of cultural patterns helpful in making sense of a range of language and communication difference they experience and in understanding why communication across groups identified as "different" from one another can be so difficult. One advantage that students have at the university where I teach is that close to one fifth of the undergraduate population comes from other countries. U.S. students, who often experience difficulty, anger, guilt, awkwardness, and so forth, when talking about language and culture in their own country, seem better able to do so once they've engaged with peers from other countries and languages. My hope is that the intermingling of cultural groups within the framework of this book will similarly facilitate cultural understanding.

The book is organized into three sections. The first three chapters present an overview of language and culture in the United States and introduce a set of concepts and vocabulary for understanding language and cultural complexity. In Chapter 1, the importance of thinking about language from a cultural perspective—what I term *cultural linguistics*—is introduced, and an overview of U.S. demographics is presented. I also provide a brief historical overview of American English as a way of putting the language many people take for granted into the context of both cultural diversity and a linguistic perspective. Chapter 2 is a kind of primer—although selectively focused—in how to understand and analyze language. A number of concepts and terms are introduced that recur throughout the book. Chapter 3 provides exposition of the Language-Centered Perspective on Culture.

The second section (Chapters 4-7) consists of specific applications of the Language-Centered Perspective on Culture. Each chapter can be thought of as a kind of case study for what a cultural approach to language and discourse reveals. Chapter 4 deals with gender and discourse, Chapter 5 with African

American discourse, Chapter 6 with Hispanic discourse, and Chapter 7 with Asian American discourse. None of these chapters is in any sense exhaustive, but, rather, representative of how one might think through a cultural analysis of language. These chapters are not developed in precisely the same way, although I have tried to place salient aspects of cultural systems at the beginning of each chapter so that what follows regarding language is illuminated by the cultural explication.

Writing the book as I have by designating certain groups as focal points— African Americans, Mexican Americans, Puerto Ricans, Cuban Americans, Chinese Americans, Filipino Americans, Japanese Americans, and so on— opens treacherous terrain. Treacherous because the analysis could be misunderstood as simplifying and essentializing cultural identities. This is absolutely not my intention. Every cultural group evidences complexity, just as every person's identity pivots on more than one social or cultural marker. It is the case, however, that, in the United States, cultural identity matters greatly: to those who identity with one culture or another, to those who identify others as having one or another cultural identity, and to public discourse and public policy, which incorporate the terminology of cultural groupings into the symbolic "reality" of the country. In all of these matters, cultural identity positions people and ideas rather than conveying some indelible essence. I am guided here by Gayatri Chakravorty Spivak (1985/1996), a cultural critic and theorist, who uses the term *strategic essentialism* to describe those endeavors in which identifying groups is important for political reasons and to ensure that the consciousness of these groups is not undermined by either their erasure or by rendering them only with concepts elaborated through dominant ideology. In sum, it is strategic (both politically and linguistically) to identify those cultural groups not in the mainstream of American life so that significant aspects of discourses also not in the mainstream of American life can be better understood.

The third section consists of two chapters in which I explore applied aspects of cultural linguistics. In Chapter 8, several significant contexts in which language diversity has consequences are examined and suggestions offered for how cultural matters related to and manifest in discourse might be better handled. Chapter 9 takes up the current debates over bilingual education and Ebonics. I argue that the controversies have common roots in U.S. ideology regarding "standard" American English and monolingualism, concluding with a proposal for how to make bilingual education a priority for all students, not just for those whose native language is not English.

Finally, a comment about terms and consistency is in order. Language is symbolic, and terms change—not only over time but depending on context. I have not pledged allegiance to consistency in my use of terms. In using terms like *black* and *African American,* I have sometimes used them in a technical sense (that is, not all blacks are African Americans) but often in keeping with the particular context of what is being discussed, how the voices of expertise name a group of people, and so on. *Asian American* and *Hispanic* are sweepingly broad terms belying the diversity they encompass, yet these terms are meaningful in some contexts while in others it is important to specify with terms such as *Asian American Indian* or *Mexican-American,* or *Chicana.* The hyphen mark as symbolic for "hyphenated identity" is also not used consistently. I sense that the hyphen mark appears more often among Hispanic writers and scholars than those who are African American or Asian American, so I regularized that sense in my writing. I also use an elaborate vocabulary for sex and gender and have tried to avoid patterns of male priority usage even in terms like *boys and girls* and *men and women,* alternating with *girls and boys* and *women and men.* And last, the term *American* is one that gives me pause every time I write or speak it. The term appropriates two continents for the convenience of one country, symbolically excluding all those from the Americas who are not of the United States. But the term also carries meaning as part of a global language-in-use designation for a cultural as well as a national site. Because my attempt to purge *American* from my own vocabulary has been a failure, I use the term when it seems right, intending no U.S.-centric offense.

Throughout the book, substantial emphasis is given to the negative impacts of dominant ideology on marginalized peoples and language varieties. For those more in the mainstream, these negative impacts can go unnoticed and sometimes even be hostilely motivated. For those who are marginalized, the impacts can be both symbolic and material. As stressful as diversity may be, however, thinking more deeply about the cultural roots of diversity may be the best tool we have for constructively engaging our changing demographics. My hope is that readers of *Speaking Culturally* will gain a sense of the rich cultural resource our language diversity offers.

Acknowledgments

The project of writing *Speaking Culturally* brought me back to faculty and intellectual life after a decade of academic administration. Many of the ideas for the book took shape, however, while I was Provost at Clark University—a 5-year period from 1988 to 1993, during which time I developed and taught a course titled "Language Diversity in the United States." The course, originally conceived as a sociolinguistic perspective on contemporary language diversity in the United States, evolved over time into a deeper cultural examination of the complexities of language-in-use and of the growing policy debates related to language issues. To the students who took my class during that period, thanks are due. Many asked intelligent and probing questions, offered their perspectives as people socialized in different cultural places and spaces and with a range of languages, and thoughtfully connected their learning in my course to ideas and materials encountered in other courses and in their daily interactions. Their collective role in my thinking demonstrates why teaching and scholarship are interrelated.

I feel especially grateful to Howard Giles, the editor for Sage's **Language and Language Behaviors Series**. Howie had confidence in my project, was patient and encouraging throughout, and each time I missed the (revised) deadline for the project, responded with the kind of optimism and continued

xviii SPEAKING CULTURALLY

interest that gave me the spark to push forward. Margaret Seawell, Sage's editor with whom I worked, was also extraordinarily encouraging about the project. Her suggestions and patience helped me produce a more focused manuscript. I also thank Astrid Virding (production editor) and Jacqueline Tasch (copy editor) who made working with Sage a positive experience.

Many friends and colleagues offered support during the various stages of my work. Serena Hilsinger, Chair of the English Department at Clark and good friend, had a way of knowing just when to "protect" me from those little chores and commitments that mount up to make research and writing difficult. Others made suggestions, provided leads on good materials to incorporate into my thinking, offered comments that jarred my thinking, and kept me going through their encouragement: Carolyn Anderson, Michael Bamberg, Parminder Bhachu, Nancy Budwig, Karen Foss, Stephen Littlejohn, Sarah Michaels, Winston Napier, Barb Sharf, Orlando Taylor, Ginger Vaughan, Maury Weinrobe, Julia Wood, and many others who showed interest in my project.

I want to thank the good colleagues and friends (some old, some new) who reviewed drafts of various chapters: Rick Arons, Jim Gee, Marsha Houston, Aimin Li, Don Rubin, and Aki Uchida not only took the time to read chapters in draft form but in many cases wrote copious comments.

My sons William and Julius inspired me because they will be the adults in the changed world that is the horizon for this book. There were times when I'm sure they thought I never left the study because I was there when they went to sleep and there when they awoke. There were too many times when they were told not to interrupt me and times when they occupied themselves quietly so that I could get something written. Their pride in telling friends and teachers about my book has been the most important "review" that I will get.

To Marlene Fine—my partner, colleague, and friend—I owe so very much. She pored over manuscripts, serving as my toughest but most helpful critic. She reminded me many times not to be impatient, to remember back a few years to when she was struggling to complete a book by squeezing it in along with a busy professional life and small children. She put up with more than any person should and was infinitely creative in figuring out ways for me to get some work time. Our conversations over the years about much of the material in the book are central to what I think and have helped me work through my ideas.

Language in Demographic and Cultural Perspective

1

The Linguistic Environment of the United States

We live in an age of bilingual baseball cards, television programming in Spanish, and election ballots available in many different languages. Super Bowl Sunday debuted in the Navaho language in 1995. A major bank in the Boston area advertises the availability of its services in 36 languages. Fannie Mae publishes a consumer guide to home ownership in Spanish, Chinese, Korean, Vietnamese (and English). We can hear some authentic sounds of African American English on television, and depending on where you live, you are just as likely to hear a language other than English as to hear English. National newscasters are no longer prohibited from using regional accents. These indicators all point to a society of increasing linguistic complexity. Yet, along with the many voices that now characterize the sounds of the United States, we find disturbing evidence of linguistic intolerance. Consider the three examples that follow.

• Two Puerto Rican women in middle management positions at a large insurance company happened to be in the women's lavatory at the same time. As they often did when meeting informally, they spoke to one another in Spanish. To their shock, a woman in a lavatory stall hollered out to them,

"You should speak English! If you don't want to speak English, go back to your own country!"

- The scene was a meeting of the Board of Trustees at a small, selective liberal arts college. African American students and their supporters were holding a demonstration at the meeting to protest recent decreases in African American faculty and staff at their college. A male leader in the group addressed a Trustee committee in impassioned, eloquent style, making the case for the group's cause. He spoke forcefully without notes and used a style that was marked by some of the rhetorical and dialect features of African American communication. Later that day, a white trustee of substantial economic means and in his early 50s emphatically noted in reference to this young man that "students who cannot speak proper English should not be admitted to this college." Ironically, the trustee speaks with a marked regional dialect that many would say sounds "uneducated."

- A young Japanese American faculty member tells the story of his first faculty meeting. Among those who approached him after the meeting was a faculty member from another department who welcomed him to the university and asked how long he has been living in the United States. He responded only by saying "forever." He was born and raised in California, learned English as his native language, but is often asked questions based on the assumption that he is a foreigner who speaks English as a second language.

These three examples all point to the power and influence of language as a symbol of social and cultural background. They also misrepresent the United States as a monolingual, monocultural society.

The Need for Cultural Linguistics

Both the patterns of language use and the ways in which people respond to the social overtones embedded in language use are subject matter for the field of *sociolinguistics,* which is devoted to the study of the relationship between language and society. Sociolinguistics deals with a broad range of concerns touching on the ways in which language is intertwined with the social context surrounding its use. Although much of sociolinguistics rests on conventional sociological concepts such as social class, race, ethnicity, and gender, the examples above and the discussion that unfolds in this book reveal the close bond between language behavior and the cultural framework from which it arises and is interpreted. In this book, then, *culture* rather than *society* is the prominent concept through which we interpret and explain patterned differences in language use within the U.S. context. *Cultural linguistics,* in contrast to sociolinguistics, better describes many of the language issues in the United States because they arise not just from social differentiation but from the larger cultural multiplicity of the country. My focus throughout the book brings a cultural linguistic perspective to bear on the realities of U.S. demographics and, in so doing, shows that ideals about a monocultural nation are fictions that create obstacles to informed public policy debate about language.

In each of the three preceding examples, the individuals involved communicate in a manner that is tied to their cultural identities; when judgments about either the language use or its users are made, these judgments emanate from cultural criteria, albeit different ones in each case. Something is also revealed about that mysterious brand of English known as the "standard." As illusive as Standard English may be to define, there is a stubborn persistence of the idea that one way of speaking English in the United States is correct, expected, and preferred, whereas other versions fall short of this ideal perfection. Furthermore, the example of the college trustee with the marked socioregional accent reveals an oddity about linguistic perceptions and judgments: How a person speaks may have little to do with that person's willingness to judge another's language as improper or inferior—a linguistic twist on the old adage that "people who live in glass houses shouldn't throw stones." Each example also points to the importance of *cultural mindedness,* or the ability to understand that cultural systems play a major role in communicative conduct and symbolic interpretation. In each example, cultural mindedness is breached: The woman in the lavatory is disrespectful of the importance of Spanish to Puerto Ricans; the trustee errs in thinking that African American speech is defective rather than different from mainstream speech; the faculty member is oblivious to the fact that English is the native language of many Asian Americans, especially Japanese Americans—the Asian American group with the greatest number of native English speakers.

Language in the United States: Melting Pot or Mosaic and Kaleidoscope?

The United States is a multilingual nation in many different ways. American English as spoken by the peoples of this country is thought to be a common language, and it definitely functions as such for purposes of public discourse.

This view mirrors the idea of a country where peoples of different backgrounds mix to form a melting pot where "one people = one language." Yet, the commonality is by no means absolute or unambiguous. Varied cultural backgrounds, racial groupings, ethnic identities, and regional origins of the nation's citizens all produce important differences in the ways in which English is spoken, understood, and made meaningful. Rather than a melting pot, the mosaic with its multitude of colors and shapes offers a more vivid image of the reality of cultural diversity at any given moment, and the kaleidoscope better represents the ever-changing realities of the late 20th century and millennium.

Add to this diversity the broad range of languages and cultures other than English and American that are present in the country, and the result challenges the idea of one people = one language. Although it is not a new phenomenon, the recent growth in the population of non-English speakers and speakers with limited English proficiency (LEP), as well as the educational programs that mushroomed since the 1960s to teach English to non-native speakers, have created public tensions over both the role of English as *the national language* and the appropriate approach for educating a literate English-speaking population.

In discussing the history of language use in the United States, Jean Molesky (1988) points out that "throughout U.S. history, periods of tolerance for linguistic diversity have alternated with periods of linguistic restrictions on or even persecution of 'newcomers,' especially if the 'newcomers' are visibly 'different,' non-Anglophone, non-Northwest-European immigrants" (p. 35). Shirley Brice Heath (1981) characterizes the language history in the United States as closely related to the degree to which languages other than English "have been viewed as politically, socially, or economically threatening" (p. 10). The present day volatility about language diversity places us in a period of great national conflict over whether this diversity should not only be tolerated but embraced or whether English, especially in its standard form, is under threat and must be protected. The rise of Spanish as a sizable minority language undoubtedly anchors the conflict, but as we shall see, Spanish language use is only the tip of the proverbial iceberg.

Demography in Linguistic Perspective

The nation's cultural complexity and linguistic composition can be best understood by looking at the population characteristics of the present-day United States, along with projections for how the mix of ethnicities will

TABLE 1.1   Population of the United States, by Race and Ethnicity:
1990 to 1997 Comparison

Group	1990	1997
White non-Hispanic	188,307,000 (75.7%)	194,751,000 (72.7%)
American Indian, non-Hispanic	1,796,000 (.7%)	1,977,000 (.7%)
Asian and Pacific Islander	7,462,000 (3.0%)	10,130,000 (3.8%)
Black non-Hispanic	29,299,000 (11.8%)	32,324,000 (12.1%)
Hispanic	22,372,000 (9.0%)	29,160,000 (10.9%)

SOURCE: U.S. Bureau of the Census (1999).

change over the next half century. The shifting ethnic, cultural, and language backgrounds and practices of U.S. residents invite rethinking of many of the assumptions about language and culture that have been prevalent during the 20th century.

Demographic Dimensions of Race and Ethnicity

The official population count in April 1999 was 272,190,000 (U.S. Bureau of the Census, 1999). Of that number, less than three quarters (72.7%) are non-Hispanic Whites (U.S. Bureau of the Census, 1999), an aggregate containing significant ethnic diversity that is nowhere captured in the census methodology. Italians, Norwegians, Irish, Armenians, and Germans alike often celebrate and take great pride in their ancestral heritage. Just over one quarter of the population is characterized as "minority" by the Census Bureau: 12.1% of the entire population is black; 10.9% is of Hispanic origin (including Mexican-Americans, Puerto Ricans, Cubans, Central and South Americans, and miscellaneous others); 3.8% is Asian or Pacific Islander (including a broad range of people but dominated by Chinese, Filipino, and Japanese); and less than 1% (.9) is American Indian, Eskimo, and Aleut. Population numbers for 1997 for each group represented in the census methodology are presented in Table 1.1. In this table, comparisons are shown with 1990 to demonstrate the population shifts already occurring. The number of non-Hispanic whites has decreased by 3% over the 7-year period.

Added to the groups officially counted in the U.S. population are the growing number of illegal immigrants, now estimated at about 5 million people (U.S. Immigration and Naturalization Service, 1998). Furthermore, the official counts do not reflect the growing number of *multiracial* individuals in the United States simply because no census category exists. As of this writing, attention to the legitimacy of multiracial and multicultural identities

TABLE 1.2   Projected Population of the United States: Year 2050

White non-Hispanic	205,849,000 (52.5%)
American Indian	3,701,000 (1.0%)
Asian American	38,064,000 (9.7%)
Black	56,346,000 (14.4%)
Hispanic	88,071,000 (22.5%)

SOURCE: Day (1993).

is growing. The U.S. Bureau of the Census studied the option of a *multicultural* category for the year 2000 census, and at about the same time it was decided not to use such a category, a young golfer named Tiger Woods burst onto the scene. The son of an African American father (whose ancestry includes Native American) and a Thai mother, Woods won the Masters Tournament in 1997 at age 21, drawing international attention never before given to a golfer. *Time* magazine (April 21, 1997) described Woods as drawing spectators partly "because of . . . the blood (Asian, African, American Indian" (p. 41). Woods is one of many: Census Bureau data indicate that there are now about 2 million multiracial children in the United States (Edwards, Lafferty, Monroe, & Rainert, 1997)—children whose lineage might be Japanese and Polish, African American and Navajo, Filipino and Mexican-American, and Eurowhite and Puerto Rican, to name only a few of the possible combinations.

The two population segments experiencing the fastest rate of growth are Asian and Hispanic. From 1980 to 1990, the proportion of Asian and Pacific Islanders in the population doubled from 1.5% to 3%, and the proportion of all Hispanics increased from 6.4% to 10%; both represent growth trends that will continue into the future and substantially change the face and sound of the populace. These growth trends, when modeled into population projections for the middle of the 21st century, indicate that dramatic changes in the proportion of non-Hispanic whites will occur. The population of the United States is projected to grow to about 394 million by 2050 (U.S. Bureau of the Census, 1996c), an increase from 1998 of 125 million. The percentage of non-Hispanic whites will decrease to little more than 50% while the proportion of all other segments, even Native Americans, increases. The projections for the year 2050 are shown in Table 1.2. Pie charts comparing the race and ethnic composition of the 1997 population with projections for the year 2050 are displayed in Figure 1.1. These same comparisons appear in bar graph form in Figure 1.2.

1997   2050

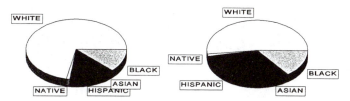

Figure 1.1. U.S. Race and Ethnicity: 1997 Actual and 2050 Projection

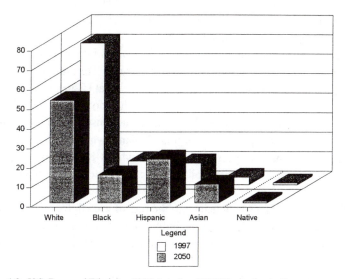

Figure 1.2. U.S. Race and Ethnicity: 1997 Actual and 2050 Projection in Percentages

The projected population growth shows dramatic increases for the Hispanic and Asian groups. Both Hispanics and Asians will be added to the population at rates far surpassing any other group. The factors directly influencing the differential growth rates for the various population segments are (a) fertility (birth) rate, (b) life expectancy, and (c) net immigration (the number of immigrants added to the population when those emigrating from the country are subtracted) (Day, 1993). One gauge of the impact of migration as a major component of this increase is the present migrant rate into the United States: In early 1998, one (net) international migrant was added to the population each 39 seconds (U.S. Bureau of the Census, 1998).

TABLE 1.3   Birth Rates per Female for Population Segments: 1993 and 2050

Group	1993	2050 Projection
Total population	2.07	2.15
White, non-Hispanic	1.84	1.84
American Indian	2.78	2.72
Asian	2.51	2.13
Black	2.47	2.45
Hispanic	2.90	2.47

SOURCE: Day (1993).

Several comments about each of these three factors will clarify why we will continue to see changes in the population mix. Regarding fertility rate, it is a simple statistical fact that the population of one group will grow faster than another if the women in that group have more children, on average, than the women in the other group. The fertility rate for Hispanic women ranks highest of all population segments, which means that Hispanics add more to the population through birth rates of residents than do other groups. In Table 1.3, the 1993 and projected 2050 birth rates demonstrate the effect of this factor in reducing the proportion of non-Hispanic whites in the population. Currently, Hispanics surpass non-Hispanic whites by over one child per female, with higher birth rates for Hispanics predicted to continue into the 21st century.

Life expectancies also contribute to the rate of growth for any population segment. The impact of lifestyle (including such things as diet and nutrition, activity level, and stress), patterns of illness and access to health care, economic circumstances, and crime are major factors in differential life expectancies. The life expectancy data for females and males displayed in Table 1.4 show the advantage of Asians over all other groups and the disadvantage of blacks. The most striking comparison is between black males and Asian males: On average, an Asian male in the United States is likely to live 14 to 15 years longer than a black male in the United States. The distribution of the population by age also contributes to differential projections over the longer term. Today's population shows non-Hispanic whites to be, on average, the oldest group, even though their life expectancies are not the longest. The median age for non-Hispanic whites in 1997 was 37.5 years, compared to Asians at 31.1 years, blacks at 30.0 years, American Indians/Eskimos/Aleuts at 27.8 years, and Hispanics at 26.5 years.

Net immigration is the third significant factor affecting population growth. In projecting the impact of net immigration, the Census Bureau considers

TABLE 1.4   Life Expectancy of Females and Males for Population Segments: 1993 and 2050 Projection

	1993		2050 Projection	
Group	Male	Female	Male	Female
White, non-Hispanic	74	80	81	86
American Indian	72	82	78	88
Asian	80	86	86	91
Black	66	74	71	79
Hispanic	75	83	84	87

SOURCE: Day (1993).

legal immigrants, refugees, undocumented workers, Puerto Ricans, and civilian citizens. The largest number of immigrants for the foreseeable future will be Hispanics, followed by Asians. For Hispanics, immigration combines with birth rate to account for projected population increases over the next half century. The Asian segment is the only population group for which immigration rather than births that occur within the United States accounts for the largest number of additions to the population (Day, 1993).

Of the three factors affecting rates of population growth, net immigration is the one most directly affected by policies of the U.S. government. All population projections by the Census Bureau are based on current numbers of immigrants, which by government policy are set at 880,000 per year. At the time of this writing, immigration policies are under review by the Senate and House of Representatives, with one likely result being the reduction in the number of annual immigrants. Yet, any reduction will only slow the projected demographic shifts but not dramatically alter the mix or change the trends already under way.

Languages Other Than English

Added to the mixture of race and ethnicity in the population are a significant number of immigrants and native born citizens for whom English is neither a first language nor the primary language of the home environment. The small Native American population alone includes speakers of about 200 different languages (Leap, 1981) although viability (defined by 100 speakers or more) exists for fewer than 100 of these.

According to 1990 census data, 31,845,000 people 5 years old or older speak a language other than English at home (Bruno, 1993). That number represents 13% of the population but does not include those younger than 5

TABLE 1.5   Speakers Age 5 Years and Older of Top 25 Languages Other Than English

Language	Number of Speakers
Spanish	17,339,172
French	1,702,176
German	1,547,099
Italian	1,308,648
Chinese	1,249,213
Tagalog	843,251
Polish	723,483
Korean	626,478
Vietnamese	507,069
Portuguese	429,860
Japanese	427,657
Greek	388,260
Arabic	355,150
Hindi (Urdu)	331,484
Russian	241,798
Yiddish	213,064
Thai (Laotian)	206,266
Persian	201,865
French Creole	187,658
Armenian	149,694
Navajo	148,530
Hungarian	147,902
Hebrew	144,292
Dutch	142,684
Mon-Khmer (Cambodian)	127,441

SOURCE: Bruno (1993).

who speak a language other than English at home nor those who are in the United States illegally. The census data also include self-assessments of facility with English. Those who say they "do not speak English very well" or not at all are considered LEP (a term we will return to later in the book).

Not surprisingly, after English, Spanish is the language most frequently spoken in the home setting. Over 17 million people age 5 and older use Spanish as the primary language at home. The next four most frequent languages have considerably fewer speakers—all in the 1+ million range: French at 1.7 million speakers, German at 1.5 million speakers, Italian at 1.3 million speakers, and Chinese at 1.2 million speakers (Bruno, 1993). A listing of the 25 languages with the greatest number of speakers is displayed in Table 1.5. A number of Asian and Pacific Island languages appear on this

TABLE 1.6 Percentage of Hispanic and Asian People Using Spanish and Asian Languages and Percentage of Spanish and Asian Language Users Who Are Limited English Proficient (LEP), by Age Group: 1990

	Age Group		
	5 to 17 Years	18 to 64 Years	65+ Years
Spanish	24	70	6
	39 LEP	50 LEP	62 LEP
Asian and Pacific Island languages	18	74	8
	44 LEP	55 LEP	72 LEP

SOURCE: U.S. Bureau of the Census (1993b).

list (Chinese, Tagalog, Korean, Vietnamese, Japanese, Hindi, Thai, Persian, and Mon-Khmer), but only one Native American language (Navajo) does.

To get some sense of both the degree to which languages other than English are prevalent and possess everyday vitality as well as the degree to which proficiency with English is at best limited, we can look to data on Spanish and on Asian and Pacific Island languages in aggregate. Table 1.6 includes information on both the percentage of people in the Hispanic and Asian categories who use a language other than English at home and the percentage of other language users who are LEP.

These data are reported in three age groupings: school age (5-17 years), young and middle adulthood (18-64 years), and older adulthood and elderly (65 years and older). Of the Hispanics who speak Spanish at home, 24% are age 5 to 17, 70% are 18 to 64, and 6% are 65 or older. For Asians who speak an Asian language, the age distribution is similar, with 18% in the school age group, 74% in the young and middle adult group, and 8% in the older adult and elderly group. For both Spanish and Asian language users, those who are younger are less likely to be LEP, which would be largely a function of education exclusively in English or bilingual education in English and the native language.

Native American Languages

Speakers of Native American languages in the United States represent a small proportion of those who have command of a language other than English, and many of these speakers have learned their "native" (tribal or clan) language not as a first language but as a second language. The situation of Native American languages deserves special comment, however, because the history clearly demonstrates linguistic genocide—a kind of genocide that continued long after the literal genocide of the native peoples of North America.

By policy, the U.S. government forced Native Americans to be educated in English. When Native Americans were isolated on reservations in 1850, English was established as the language of schooling. In 1880, when off-reservation schools were established, not only was English the language of education, but children who used their native languages received punishments including isolation, head shavings, and physical abuse (Hagan, 1961).

Not until 1970 did the U.S. government officially change its policy to emphasize "assimilation with preservation" of Native American languages and culture. Since that time, federal money has been designated to revitalize and save languages bound for extinction. In 1990, the Native American Language Act was passed, which funded preservation programs for native languages through a $1 million allocation—a small amount considering the enormous devastation wrought to native peoples and their languages.

Despite the evolution of policy over the past 30 years, native languages continue to die out. William Leap (1981), an anthropological linguist, estimates that there may have been 500 different Native American languages and many more dialects prior to European contact. The 1980 census documented 300 recognizable languages and dialects, but only slightly over 100 that had 100 speakers or more. More recent data point to a continuing threat to *ethnolinguistic vitality*, or the cultural and linguistic resources necessary to ensure continued use of particular languages.

The 1990 census suggests that about 175 Native American languages continue to have fluent speakers, but many of these languages are spoken by only one or a few elderly people and will become extinct with the death of those elders. Of the surviving languages, 81 have 100 or more speakers (U.S. Bureau of the Census, 1994b).

The fragility of Native American languages is starkly apparent simply through examining those languages with the *most* speakers. The Navaho language has the greatest number of speakers, giving it at least limited public audibility in the broader U.S. context. The 1990 census recorded 148,530 speakers of Navaho, and we can see from Table 1.5 that the Navaho language ranks 21st in number of speakers among languages other than English. The next most commonly spoken language is Dakota (which is a Sioux language), with 13,387 speakers—130,000 fewer than Navaho. Dakota is followed by Pima (11,449 speakers) and Cherokee (9,285 speakers). To put the ethnolinguistic vitality of Native American language in perspective, the largest number of speakers of any native language total no more than the population of a small U.S. city. Contrasted to the cases of language survival are the many Native languages with very few speakers: three speakers of Tillamook (a Wakashan language), who are adult males between 18 and 54 years of age; three speakers of Kansa, who are males at least 65 years old; six speakers of Miami (an Algonquian language), who are adult females between 18 and 54 years of age; and seven speakers of Han, all of whom are females age 65 or older (U.S. Department of Commerce, 1994). And when Red Thunder Cloud died in Massachusetts on January 15, 1996, the Catawba language died as well; no one is left possessing sufficient knowledge of the language to preserve it, which could be the fate of Kansa and Han.

The details presented here regarding Native American languages only scratch the surface but are intended to remind readers that language and cultural diversity in the United States extends beyond headline news about the growth of Spanish speakers and the influx of Asian with their many languages. The Native American language story also places into a new perspective the idea that languages other than English are "foreign." There are no languages less foreign to this land than those of native peoples but also no languages more threatened to the foundation of their existence.

Language Complexity Today

It does not take a trained ear to hear that today's voices in the United States present cultural multiplicity that can be traced to many different sources: indigenous peoples; slaves brought from Africa; Asian immigrants in pursuit of individual freedom, professional opportunity, or a better life and standard of living in the United States; migrants from Mexico who have sought employment; and the refugees from war-torn Vietnam, Laos, and Cambodia, to name only some of the major groupings. Although certain areas of the country continue to be sites where languages other than English are rarely heard and where complexions and cultural background vary little, these are increasingly the exception. Virtually every urban center teems with the sounds of different varieties of English and languages other than English, and every region of the country is home to Native American tribes, clans, and bands with rich linguistic histories. This diversity is the language situation of contemporary America and the context for even more diversity in the years to come.

Diversity in Language Use and Evaluation

The examples at the beginning of this chapter all reveal ways in which language use is evaluated. The judgments that people make about language stem from *linguistic perceptions and linguistic attitudes*, and a substantial body of literature exists that documents the impact of these attitudes (for examples, see Ryan & Giles, 1982; van Dijk, 1987). Linguistic attitudes may be positive, negative, or simply thematic in framing perceptions of groups of people. Hearing a person speak English with an accent identifiable as "Spanish" or "southern" often elicits negative attitudes about intelligence and motivation, whereas hearing a "Boston Brahman" dialect or the "speech from nowhere" typical of many newscasters elicits positive attributions about intelligence and motivation. An attitude is thematic when dispositions of speakers are projected based on the language variety they speak. For example, when Americans hear French, they may think of the speaker as romantic or artistic, whereas hearing German might elicit perceptions of rigidity and authoritarianism. Language is certainly not the only factor shaping these perceptions, but language functions powerfully to center impressions and judgments.

When a particular way of speaking triggers a stereotype that is then applied to the speaker, *linguistic stereotyping* results through a process whereby particular language characteristics evoke the stereotype, which is then applied full force to the speaker. One of the best illustrations of this was provided in an analysis by William Labov (1970), who demonstrated how middle-class verbosity often evokes the judgment of greater logical coherence when compared to the speech of children reared in the urban ghetto, where verbal patterns and relationships with adults are quite different. When the linguistic attitude is negative, especially when it is acted on in some way, the situation is one of *linguistic prejudice.* There is probably no country or culture where some degree of linguistic prejudice does not exist. Linguistic prejudice can intensify into *linguistic intolerance.* Such intolerance is one important factor underlying proposals to allow "English only" in the workplace or to try to eradicate special teaching methods for non-English speakers. At its extreme, linguistic intolerance in some parts of the world has led to the banning of certain languages; for example, when the Kurdish language was banned in 1990 from use in Iraq, Kurds who dared to speak Kurdish in public risked death. We may think that the United States is exempt from such extremism, but the history of official government intolerance of Native

American languages mirrors the kind of intolerance U.S. citizens usually assign only to others in the world.

The three examples given at the beginning of the chapter also demonstrate the veracity of the statement, "You are what you speak." Gloria Anzaldúa (1987), a Chicana, wonderfully captures this idea when she says, "ethnic identify is twin skin to linguistic identity—I am my language" (p. 59). Although ethnically grounded, her comment can be applied more broadly to the fusion of language and identity. We learn language and communication within particular contexts, and the impact of socialization and culture provide a linguistic background with the power to form and shape personal identities and to provide evidence for others of the social and cultural identities of communicators. Although conclusions are often drawn that are neither definitive nor empirically true, both speakers and hearers identify themselves and others according to how they speak. We convey our self-identity through the language style we embrace, and we attribute identity features to others based on their language. Most Navaho speakers could understand the Super Bowl as broadcast in English, but the power of hearing the broadcast in one's native language—especially when the language and its culture have survived against all odds—elevates the sense of cultural vitality. The Puerto Rican women who chose to speak Spanish could have opted instead to abandon the Spanish language or to reserve Spanish for use in the home, but speaking Spanish with a colleague at work gives a foundation for validating one's core personal and ethnic identity. The trustee who judged the young African American man made a judgment about his academic suitability for college based solely on speech patterns, yet disassociated such a judgment from himself.

It is commonplace to locate the identity of people by using their speech as our evidence. Just as commonplace, we expect the speech of people to sound a certain way based on their social identities. Often, laypeople will characterize what they hear as "accents" associated with regions of the country by remarking on "Southern speech," the "Boston accent," the "Texas drawl," the "midwestern twang," "hillbilly language," the "Jersey accent" and "Chicaga talk." These terms locate the regional origins of their speakers by generalizing across and glossing over differences within regions of the country. H. Ross Perot, the wealthy, politically independent Texan who ran for President of the United States in 1992 and 1996, is easily placed as to his regional background, but not all Texans speak like Ross Perot. Social class also voices itself in how a person speaks. In the 1993 mayoral race in Boston, the winner (Thomas Manino, who is the first Italian mayor of that city) was regularly characterized as carrying the liability of his less-than-proper, lower-middle-class, ethnic manner of speaking. Most of us think we can tell whether or not a person is well educated by how that person speaks, and we definitely have differing expectations for how women and men should speak. Judgments are also made about what many perceive as "foreign" languages that are spoken by those actually born in the United States: the NewYoricans (as those in New York City of Puerto Rican background are sometimes called); the children of Mexican immigrants who are the Chicanos and Chicanas; and second-generation Koreans, Vietnamese, Cambodians, and Thais are major examples. From these groups, we hear both accents of English and other languages, which often triggers the assumption by mono-lingual American English speakers that the speaker is and does not want to be American.

Those born and reared in other countries, with native tongues in English or other languages, bring distinctive accents to the speaking of English. Few would confuse a person speaking English whose native language is Spanish from one whose tongue reveals German or Chinese origins; once that judg-ment is made, other ideas about the person come quickly to mind. As already noted, the language we hear—accents and much more—carries information as well as stereotypes about its speakers. The auditor might imagine, for example, that the German would be more rigid and formal and the Venezuelan more passionate and spontaneous.

The result of all these variations in language use yields both an English language of substantial heterogeneity and a polylinguistic environment re-flective of ancestries and native languages quite "un-American" in the sense that their ancestries lie elsewhere. But when people rush to the judgment that this language mix or any particular language indicates something un-Ameri-can, they also show ignorance of American English at every stage of the nation's development. The varieties of English spoken by most monolinguals in the United States contain the legacy of many other languages in contact: the European languages of the early settlers, the immigrants of the 19th and early 20th centuries, and the African languages of slaves.

What has changed in recent years are the specific origins of new additions to the sound of America. The immigration boom over the past two decades accounts for many non-English speakers and English-as-a-second-language speakers whose origins are Hispanic or Asian. When in close quarters, this variety of new voices can lead to chorus or cacophony. At its best, this variety creates an opportunity for the United States to encourage bilingualism and cultural mindedness among all of its citizens. At its worst, this language variety, especially that accompanying the new wave of immigration and "foreign tongues," produces hostile reactions to anything other than English, which means some conception of "proper" English.

The many varieties of spoken language in contemporary U.S. society are remarkable not so much because this situation is new—it is not. Regional varieties of spoken English have been with us for a long time, as have other socially based variations in language use. Furthermore, there are few native English-speaking adults in this country who have to go back farther than their grandparents or great-grandparents to find family members with a native language other than English. What differs now is the greater presence of non-European languages being voiced alongside English and the greater resistance of both many non-English speakers and ethnically identified English speakers to forfeiting their native ways of speaking and their "home" language patterns to accommodate and assimilate into some homogenized ideal or melting pot. As a result, the public voice has become more hetero-geneous, and the explicit awareness of language diversity permeates every-day life experiences for more and more people.

The Myths and Reality of American English

Much of the furor over language diversity in the United States comes from the status of English (i.e., Standard English) as the national (although not official) language of the country. English monolingualism has dominated since World War I, and many Eurowhites (whites of European origin) simply take this status of English for granted without understanding the complicated history that led to such pervasive monolingualism. Moreover, laypeople and scholars alike have also labored under the false assumption that the English language we hear in the mainstream of society is solely a product of the influence of transport from Great Britain. The divergence between British and American English in the general sound system and in many terms of usage is in itself revealing of the shallowness of this assumption. Yet the theory hammered out until the 1960s through convoluted reasoning built the claim that the regional markers of language in the United States took their ancestry from British regional speech *and* that regional distinctions in English were more significant than, say, ethnic, race, or class distinctions. In writing about Black English in particular, J. L. Dillard (1972) comments more generally that "this lopsided interest in tracing American regional dialects to British regional dialects has damaged research on the speech of all American social groups" (p. 7). This "lopsided interest" likely accounts for lingering perceptions that American English owes its character entirely to British English either through continuity or resistance.

In a more general manner, the preoccupation with British-American comparisons and contrasts in the English language focuses centrally in U.S. history, where there were prerevolutionary concerns about the purity and control of the English language as used in America. H. L. Mencken (1980) documents various attempts to purify and regulate the American tongue. In 1724, mathematics professor Hugh Jones, from the College of William and Mary, "expressed the wish that a 'Publick Standard were fix'd' to 'direct Posterity, and prevent Irregularity, and confused Abuses and Corruptions in our Writings and Expressions' " (cited in Mencken, 1980, pp. 58-59). After independence, John Adams advocated in 1780 the establishment of an academy "for refining, improving, and ascertaining the English language," and under the leadership of Noah Webster, the Philological Society was formed in New York in 1788 (cited in Mencken, 1980, p. 11). Somewhat later, in 1806, Noah Webster's first dictionary appeared. Even though Webster believed that language change was a natural process that made orthodox rules and prohibitions fruitless, he used as his standard of usage "the pronunciations of educated New Englanders . . . based on current cultivated usage" (cited in Mencken, 1980, pp. 14-15).

As the dictionary tradition developed, many changes occurred in what was recorded about words and how that information garnered credibility. Most dictionaries claim to be recording rather than prescriptive devices, yet, even today, we can see the blatant ways in which dictionaries flatten and homogenize language through their methods of recording. In the 1995 edition of *Merriam-Webster's Collegiate Dictionary,* we find, for example, the following explanation for how pronunciation is described in the entries:

> The Merriam-Webster pronunciation editors have been collecting . . . citations from live speech and from radio, television, and shortwave broadcasts since the 1930s. . . . All of the pronunciations recorded in this book can be documented as falling within the range of generally acceptable variation, unless they are accompanied by a restricting usage note or symbol or a regional label. (p. 31a)

The phrase "generally acceptable" is critical here; reviewing specific dictionary entries reveals that it really means "standard." The entry for the word *police* (p. 900) places the stress on the second syllable (po-LICE) without even noting the common reversal in dialects such as African American Vernacular English, where "PO-lice" is more common. The variant in this case does not even get a "restricting usage note."

What we have inherited, then, are British-based attitudes about the English language whose origins are synchronous with the colonial and postindependence periods. Although those who championed the English language admitted the influence in vocabulary from groups such as the American Indians, the immigrant German, French, Spanish, and Dutch, and the African slave, these elements were not considered central to language usage in the United States. Their influence has, in fact, often been described as providing "loan words," as if to suggest that the words appeared (and then endured) only because the genuine article was temporarily unavailable. To describe something as "on loan" connotes both the lack of authenticity and a certain transient quality.

Although linguistic attitudes and prejudice are complicated matters, the nexus of viewpoints and passions does rest in the reality of English as the national language and Standard English as the variety that is taught and imposed as preferred language. Since the end of the 19th century, when the move to compulsory education occurred in the United States, the language of education has been almost exclusively English. The anti-Germany and more general antiforeign residues of World War I reinforced the exclusiveness of English as the national language and forced the closure of foreign language schools that had prospered (Malakoff & Hakuta, 1990). Later in the 20th century, the forces of assimilation, the ethos of a melting pot, and the lure of upward mobility led those who were new parents during World War II and the postwar era, who themselves often had access to languages other than English through their parents or grandparents, to rear children proficient in English only. As a child growing up in the 1950s, for instance, I heard German spoken between my mother and her mother and Swedish spoken between my father and his parents but never received any encouragement to learn either of these languages.

From its early experience as a nation made up of those from differing national identities and language facilities, the United States moved through a period of (seemingly) greater uniformity in language to the present public display of language variation—both within English and of multiple languages. Because of the growth in the population of non-English speakers through legal and illegal immigration, combined with the greater desire of many of those speakers to maintain their native language and cultural patterns, the United States more and more resembles a locale of language diversity much like what exists in most other parts of the world: Diversity reigns, and matters of language uniformity are problematic—indeed, they are often steeped in conflict.

Demography may not be destiny, but it is definitely directional. The language situation of the United States will continue to diversify as the population shifts away from its current ethnic distribution. Understanding the change now under way demands citizens who are better informed about both language and culture because the two are intertwined.

We move next to considering how language reveals cultural foundations and is organized differently by different groups of people. To grasp the vitality and diversity of language use, we must look to the circumstances for its use, to its users, and to the many symbolic meanings drawn from language. As our most significant cultural resource, we shall see that language can be understood and appreciated only when we look beneath its surface to the deeper levels of cultural meaning and pattern that give rise to what is spoken and what is heard and interpreted. Patterns of language use reveal much about the complexity in multicultural societies like the United States. In the next two chapters, we will consider perspectives on, first, language, and second, the cultural systems in which language arises and is used. These concepts will structure the analysis in subsequent chapters.

In writing about language and cultural diversity, I have tried to be sensitive to the language I use to describe that diversity. Some of the terms used to describe groups of people and particular aspects of language are themselves culturally sensitive, meaning that the terms convey nuances of cultural meanings through their symbolic tones.

Preferred terms for ethnic and racial groups change over time, moving in recent history, for instance, from *Negro* to *Black* to *African American,* from *Oriental* to *Asian,* and from *American Indian* to *Native American.* Yet even the most frequently used current terms pose problems when generalized. The term *black* may mean something quite different to a person descended from slaves in the United States and to a person from South Africa or England, Trinidad or Jamaica. Although for the focus of this book, I prefer the term *African American* over *black* because of its clearer cultural specificity, I have used both terms, with my choices made sometimes to convey different meanings, sometimes to create continuity between a point and the term used by an important source related to that point, and sometimes for technical reasons (U.S. census data on race include *Black* but not *African American* as a category).

The terms for certain features and patterns of language also carry both technical and cultural meanings. In this chapter, for example, I have written "Standard" English with quotation marks to call attention to the arbitrary nature of what it means to name a variety of language "standard." I do not continue with this quotation marking, but the reader will, I hope, interpret the meaning that marking suggests. Linguists commonly use Standard American English and its acronym SAE for a particular variety of English spoken and written in the United States, and there are places in the book, notably the last chapter, where I use the acronym because of its appropriateness to what I am emphasizing. Linguists frequently also use the term *Mainstream American English* and its acronym MAE. Although this term often simply replaces SAE, I use it to convey not just the formal, proper, educated way of speaking and writing but more broadly the ordinary language used by the majority, which serves as the comparison context for marginalized systems of expression. Consider the rise of *like* as a filler in American English ("I, like, asked him for some help") or the pervasive dropping of the final sound in *-ing* endings, even among otherwise polished speakers ("We are doin' everything possible to assist the tornado victims"). Neither feature would yet be considered SAE, but they absolutely characterize MAE. The term MAE rather than SAE is especially useful when commenting about the cultural and ideological dimensions of language; this is the case in Chapter 5, where so much of what characterizes African American English differs from the mainstream cultural discourses that dominate public life and social institutions.

Language as a dynamic, changing cultural resource challenges us to think about the words we use to help describe and understand the subject of language use. Linguistic tools, thus, contribute to speaking culturally.

2

The Language System in Its Communicative Contexts

Language-in-use represents the complexities of social and cultural meaning. Erving Goffman (1972) made this point with simplicity in his statement that "it hardly seems possible to name a social variable that doesn't show up and have its little systematic effect upon speech behavior: age, sex, class, caste, country of origin, generation, region, schooling; cultural cognitive assumptions; bilingualism, and so forth" (p. 61). The effects to which Goffman refers include those evidenced in the language code itself as well as those that more generally structure the choices made and interpretations given to communication events. The way we form sentences from words to make statements and ask questions is governed by regular rules. The meanings that we attach to words, sentences, and conversations in particular situations are culturally patterned. Grasping the impact of cultural diversity on language and communication processes requires that we consider many levels of the systematicity and pattern to language use. In this section, basic concepts central to understanding language-in-use are introduced.

Functions and Purposes of Language

Language-in-use serves many functions and accomplishes many purposes. Many of these functions and purposes are specific to the situation, such as seeking an account from a friend or family member about how his or her day was, conveying information about a product or service, voicing an opinion on a political candidate, phoning a store to determine its hours of operation, expressing anger because a fellow student failed to show up for a meeting at the scheduled time, explaining to a parent why you do not want to visit a relative, and so forth.

One important general function of language is to regulate boundaries between and among people. These *boundary functions*, explains Saville-Troike (1989), regulate interaction by "unifying its speakers as members of a single speech community, and excluding outsiders from intragroup communication" (p. 14). Boundaries for communication are often set, for example, between different professional and occupational groups by the use of technical vocabulary. Computer specialists, professors, bank tellers, insurance agents, auto mechanics, nurses and doctors, hair stylists, and lawyers all have their separate ways of speaking. Boundaries that are set by communication establish who is inside and who is outside particular social or cultural groupings, and they can also function to create barriers. Speaking in a language that is not understood by everyone present illustrates how language-in-use functions as a way of excluding some participants from the conversation. When doctors or lawyers use technical language, they often reduce their patients and clients to mere bystanders. Conversely, language use can draw others in, serving to create solidarity. This might happen when African Americans who are strangers exchange some form of greeting and recognition of one another through distinctive language symbols; the vehicle could be as simple as referring to an African American woman as a "sister" or as complex as engaging in conversation that is densely packed with black dialect and rhetorical forms (considered in Chapter 5).

Natural and Native Languages

Primary human language is oral. The spoken word is the raw material for writing, with written forms of language consisting of *re*-presentations of human language. Any written version reduces speech to graphic conventions. Linguists use the term *natural language* to refer to oral language as it is spoken in specific speech communities and acquired by children. Writing and reading—both of which are imposed language systems—must be taught and learned explicitly. In the process of writing down a language, conventions for its representation are developed, including alphabets or characters, spelling, punctuation, grammar, and so forth. When these conventions include rules that are not part of natural language, we say that the rules are *superposed* through the process of standardization. For now, suffice it to say that *standard language* is a variety that has been imposed on the many variations of a natural language through an intervention process. Although we usually think of standard language as a written variety, there are also standard oral forms that are deemed by some to be the "correct" and "proper" way to speak.

During the early years of life, the progression from infant to toddler to young child reveals the acquisition of a successively complex language and communication system, the evidence for which is in speech. The language learned by children in their home environment is called their *native language* or *first language*. In some cultural situations, children learn more than one language early. If one dominates, that language is considered the child's native language. For example, children who grow up in a Mandarin-speaking home with extended connections to Mandarin-speaking people but also speak some English with neighborhood children and some acquaintances outside the home would be considered native speakers of Mandarin.

In the United States, *monolingualism*, or the use and understanding of only one language, has prevailed for roughly the past 50 to 75 years, which is the span of time since children were born to the last large wave of immigrants (largely from European countries), which ebbed around World War I. Monolingualism is, however, not the norm throughout the world (Romaine, 1994). With the growth of speakers of languages other than English, we see in the United States today more and more evidence of greater similarity to language situations throughout the world. Public service information appears in many languages, some jobs call for bilingual abilities, and television channel surfing usually results in finding programming in languages other than English.

Speech Communities and Their Discourses

An African American woman in one of my graduate courses at a predominantly white university once remarked in class that carrying the "communication load" both in class and with white academic associates was exhausting. It felt good, she said, to "go back home" to her neighborhood—a place where she could talk freely "the way black folk talk." Given her eloquence and fluency in educated Standard English, the statement surprised many of her fellow (white) students. In making the statement, this woman captured the force with which a person's primary, native *speech community* can serve as an anchor and base for a range of communicative behaviors.

Using John Gumperz's (1972) seminal definition as a starting point, a *speech community* can be stipulated as "any human aggregate characterized by regular and frequent interaction by means of a shared body of verbal signs and set off from similar aggregates by significant differences in language use" (p. 219). A speech community, according to Gumperz, revolves around norms for language that relate to usage, origins, and the relationships between speech patterns and social action. The graduate student in the illustration above might, in Gumperz's scheme, be viewed as a member of both an African American speech community and an educated U.S. speech community. Dell Hymes (1972) adds that members of a speech community share "rules for the conduct and interpretation of speech and rules for the interpretation of at least one linguistic variety" (p. 54).

Many sociolinguistic studies are, in fact, studies of speech communities. For example, William Labov (1972b) studied the phonological features in the speech of New Yorkers from different social classes and, in another study, analyzed the relationship of diphthong changes in the sound patterns of native residents of Martha's Vineyard; Thomas Kochman (1981) provocatively reported on differences in speech strategies and their meanings used by black and white teenagers in Chicago; and Deborah Schiffrin (1984) demonstrated how argument defines a sociable form of communication in certain U.S. Jewish communities. Each of these studies is situated in a particular time and place, each describes discourse as it occurs in its natural setting, and each provides generalizations about the speech communities involved based on the discourse samples.

One difficulty with Gumperz's approach to speech communities is that it uses the community rather than the speaker as a point of reference. This approach tends to cast the speaker as a player in a particular speech community while giving insufficient attention to the speaker him- or herself, who will in most cases be a member of several or many different speech communities. Gumperz (1972), for example, defines *verbal repertoire* as the "totality of dialectal and superposed [standard] variants *employed within a community* [italics added]" (p. 230). Speech community seems here to represent a place or site for speaking in a particular manner. An alternative view, then, features the individual rather than the community as the starting point (Romaine, 1982). This view places the locus of verbal repertoires within the person, designating the degree to which that person sociolinguistically functions in one or more speech communities. Individuals can be full participants in a speech community, meaning that they demonstrate with regularity those aspects of speaking that distinguish the community and bind its members through some form of identity. They can also be marginal participants, or what Dorian (1982) calls "low-proficiency 'semi-speakers' " (p. 26). Furthermore, it is possible for a person to be proficient but to refrain from participation. An adequate account of language-in-use requires both the individual and the speech community vantage points. Speech communities precede the individual and provide the templates for meaningful language use, but individuals participate in (and often change) such communities.

At a national level, such as the United States, many different speech communities are interrelated through the ways in which their participants cross between them, thus providing links and facilitating mutual influences. Whereas some communities are closed and some individuals restricted to single communities (for example, older generation Korean immigrants who have not learned English and who function largely in Korean-speaking enclaves), this is not the usual situation.

Speech communities are made up of those whose participation brings them together as a social and communication network; there must be participation for there to be a community. The degree of participation is, however, quite another matter. Marginal participation can either anchor a person to a speech community or isolate her or him from it, as the following examples show. In the first example, a Korean American friend whose daily life does not bring her into regular contact with other Korean Americans maintains her ethnic connections through frequent visits to family members in another part of the country. The second example is taken from a well-known Mexican-American writer, Richard Rodriguez (1982), who poignantly expresses his estrangement from his Mexican-American, Spanish-speaking family and neighborhood after returning from a year of study in London:

> I rushed to "come home." Then quickly discovered that I could not. Could not cast off the culture I had assumed. Living with my parents for the summer, I remained an academic—a kind of anthropologist in the family kitchen, searching for evidence of our "cultural ties" as we ate dinner together. (pp. 160-161)

There are possibilities in a multicultural society for connection to speech communities other than those serving primary functions for the person. In some cases, only minimal facility with the patterns of a speech community is necessary to be accepted, as when very limited use of the Spanish language is enough to join a discussion among a group of bilingual Spanish-/ English-speaking parents focused on bilingual education. Knowledge about a speech community without participation in it can also serve an important function in a multicultural society because knowledge itself often increases empathy in ways that are important to achieving multicultural integration. Here, the ability to interpret the patterns of the speech community carries a premium. We can distinguish involvement in speech communities, then, on a continuum from full to marginal participation while also recognizing the role of knowledge about a speech community when that knowledge remains latent.

Rather than thinking of speech communities as large aggregates with substantial internal variation, it is useful to attach this concept to actual communication networks of people who develop particular patterns of discourse. One would not, therefore, identify Korean-speaking inhabitants of the United States as a monolithic speech community. Rather, Korean speakers differ in the degree to which they share speech patterns and interaction with one another *within* the Korean community as well as in what other speech communities they are entailed *outside* the Korean network. A married Korean graduate student couple might participate to some degree in traditional Korean cultural patterns for speech behavior while also participating in a younger generation Korean-speaking community where less formality and greater fluidity in gender roles are revealed through speech patterns. This same couple might also participate in various U.S. mainstream social networks in which differing patterns of communication are learned and used.

Levels of System in Language

M. A. K. Halliday (1978) proposed that language is a "social semiotic," or the centralizing process for establishing systematic social meanings. In Halliday's conception, language is both "a means of reflecting on things, and . . . a means of acting on things"; language is simultaneously expressive and a "metaphor for social processes" (pp. 2-3). The fields of sociolinguistics and the sociology of language both stress the patterned relationships of language use and attitudes about language to social factors such as socio-economic structure, class systems, race, and regional origins. Taken as a whole, this work represents a powerful documentation of the ways in which language systems reflect, shape, and sustain the social systems from which they arise. Speaking in a certain way can, for instance, be a kind of metaphor for working-class solidarity with others while simultaneously relegating the speaker to low prestige in the social system and excluding him or her from many possibilities and privileges.

My interest in elaborating a cultural linguistics (as stated in Chapter 1) arises in part from the limited range of social theories brought to bear on sociolinguistic analysis. Glyn Williams (1992) argues that much sociolin-guistic work is overly situated in traditional social theory that is steeped in functionalism. His main points are that such theory (a) places the individual in a relatively passive stance in relation to the social system, (b) relies on the notion that people consent to their positions in the social system, and (c) ignores ways in which people can resist the social system through language and communication. Although some of Williams's criticism is overstated, he does magnify the need to view language both as reflector and shaper of society and as a powerful human system for the seemingly contra-dictory processes of reaffirming *and* resisting the social order. In subsequent chapters, this type of complexity will be explored within a cultural frame-work.

From a linguistic point of view, all human languages are viable, legitimate, and adequate for purposes of communication because they are all systematic rather than haphazard. In this book, we will consider different ways in which language is patterned in U.S. cultural contexts. First, language variety will be defined, and then five language systems will be briefly explained: syntac-tic, phonological, lexical and morphological, semantic, and pragmatic.

Language Varieties

The term *language variety* is used by scholars of language to designate a particular way of using language. One of the most standard definitions of a language variety is "a set of linguistic items with similar social distribution" (Hudson, 1980, p. 24). We will use the term to designate any language or any version of a language the use of which includes some consistent features with close correspondence to social or cultural identity or to social or cultural activity. Language varieties are, however, relative rather than absolute.

Sometimes, the term *variety* refers to what are considered completely different languages (e.g., English, Hindi, Finnish, and Akan). In Canada, for example, it is meaningful to talk about the varieties of language designated English and French. Variety more commonly refers to distinctive ways of using "the same language," for example, as found in different regions of a country or different social classes and groups or different occupations. African American Vernacular English (AAVE), Cockney English, the Boston Brahman dialect, Ashanti (a dialect of Akan), gayspeak, rapping, and legalese are all considered language varieties, with some being distinguishable using formal linguistic criteria of phonology and syntax and others based more on stylistic, communicative criteria. Technically, language variety is a neutral term. Language varieties, however, often become the symbolic triggers for judging worth and associating social identity with privilege or prejudice.

Although the boundaries between varieties are not in every way absolute, it is useful to think of a variety as characterized by certain features that distinguish it from some varieties and liken it to others. When two varieties are distinguishable from one another on some particular feature (e.g., retaining vs. dropping the initial consonantal *h* sound in *humor* versus *'umor* or using first names versus honorific titles as in *Sarah* versus *Ms. Shea* and *Dr. Shea*), the distinctive feature is called an *isogloss*, which is from the Greek "*equal + tongue*"—to be equal in tongue or of the same tongue. A cluster of such distinctions between differing varieties is called an *isogloss bundle*. It is the bundling of isoglosses that forms the boundary, as in the set of phonological (sound) and lexical (vocabulary) features that provide meaningful contrasts between regional dialects (see Carver, 1989).

Syntactic Systems

The *syntactic system* of a language is made up of a finite set of rules governing the relationships of elements in the language. *Syntax* is the underlying structure of sentences, and is *descriptive rather than prescriptive* of the rules that generate sentences in the language. The syntax of a language accounts for what people actually say; it does not prescribe or set rules for how they should speak. Although there are similarities, syntax from the point of view of descriptive linguistics is not the same as the grammatical rules of a standard variety that are taught and enforced in the schooling process. The distinction is similar to the biomechanics of how a person naturally walks contrasted with how that same person might be taught to walk properly (and unnaturally) to be a model.

Early in the 1960s, Noam Chomsky (1965, 1966, 1968) launched what was to become a modern revolution in linguistics. He proposed that the cognitive knowledge of a system of finite rules for language explains our ability to create an infinite number of sentences. The finite rules of language, represented in the human cognitive system, are the deep knowledge that generates sentences and their interpretation; Chomsky termed this *linguistic competence*, distinguishing it from the manifestation of language in speech, which he termed *performance*. He posited an

> ideal speaker hearer, in a completely homogeneous speech-community, who knows its language perfectly and is unaffected by such grammatically irrelevant conditions as memory limitations, distractions, shifts of attention and interest, and errors . . . in applying his knowledge of the language in actual performance. (Chomsky, 1965, p. 3)

The presence of linguistic competence helps us understand why adult speakers accept sentences like "Cows eat grass" but reject "Cows grass eat" and find "Grass eat cows" amusing but not acceptable, or why a 4-year-old, who is still developing mastery of the rules for her native language, might ask "Is it going to be *many whiles*?" (meaning "Is it going to be a long time?" which occurs because the child treats the word *awhile* as "a while" and then pluralizes what she understands to be the singular noun *while*). Yet we know that "ideal speaker-hearers" do not exist and that language-in-use involves much more than the production of syntactically acceptable sentences. Yet, somehow, we manage as children growing up in speech communities to learn a particular language and to know what constitutes both meaningful and appropriate utterances in that language. We do not, however, learn the same language variety or participate in the same speech communities in common with everyone else.

Phonological Systems

Every natural language and every language variety has a pattern to its sounds. Sometimes, varieties are distinguishable by only a few features in the sound system, sometimes by systems totally different from one another. Part of what is involved in a child's language-acquisition process entails mastering the sounds used to produce that particular language. One reason why it is so difficult for monolingual adults to learn to converse in a foreign language is that they have long been habituated to a particular sound system and find it difficult physiologically to produce all the sounds in the new language. Several brief examples illustrate this. One attribute of the sounds in English is that they are either voiced or voiceless, meaning that they occur with or without vibration of the vocal chords as in the distinction between *vat* and *fat*. English does not use the click sounds characteristic of some African languages nor the ranges of meaningful tones in Mandarin Chinese, Yoruba, Thai, and Vietnamese. Learning the spoken forms of any of these languages is difficult for most native speakers of English, just as learning the *r* sounds in English is difficult for native Chinese speakers.

For any specific language variety, there is both a finite set of sounds (*phonemes*) and patterns in the way pitch, stress, and sound length occur (*suprasegmental features*). *Phonemes* are the smallest segments of meaningfully distinctive sound that can be distinguished from and contrasted with one another in the speech production of that language. The first sounds in the following series of words are distinctive phonemes in English because they cannot freely vary without changing meaning: /b/*at*, /c/*at*, /h/*at*, /f/*at*, /p/*at*, /m/*at*, /v/*at*. The study of the patterns of sounds within a language is called *phonology*. In American English, for example, the word *pattern* is usually pronounced with the *r* sound in the last syllable. But for some accents used on the East Coast, the sound of the word is much more like *patten*. Another example is the *th/d* distinction when pronouncing *these* and *those* versus *dese* and *dose*; the latter is typical of certain dialects within American English as well as in the pronunciation of English by some for whom it is not a native language. Interestingly, when the /d/ rather than the /th/ sound is used by a native U.S. English speaker, the judgment is often made that the person is uneducated, but when a foreigner uses this phonological feature, it may not even be perceived.

Any language's sound system also consists of *suprasegmental phonemes*, which include pitch, stress, and length of articulation. *PO-lice* versus *po-LICE*, for example, shows forward stress for the first pronunciation as is the case in AAVE and other English dialects. Pitch variation within an utterance is called *intonation*, which can be patterned differently in language varieties, as will be shown when Chicano English is described in Chapter 6.

Many of the differences among language varieties that people are consciously aware of are phonological in nature. Most people use the word *accent* to label these differences, as when the term *Southern drawl* is attached to a particular language variety. But many of the differences within varieties of American English can be heard with a tuned-up ear. Listen, for example, to an adult African American woman use the exclamation, GIRL to another woman—with heightened pitch, especially at the end of the word. Or listen to the mainstream sounding speech of a Connecticut Yankee—until you hear the quite un-mainstream *'umor* rather than *humor* and *'uman* rather than *human.*

Lexical and Morphological Systems

Lexicon and morphology pertain to the basic units of meaning that characterize a particular language variety. Like other aspects of language, these basic units can mark isoglosses between one variety and another.

Lexicon and lexemes. The *lexicon* of a particular language variety is the totality of words that make up the language. Each item is called a *lexeme* (from the Greek *lexis*, meaning word). Many elements within a lexicon are stable (making lexicon conservative), but the lexical system also constantly undergoes revision and change (making lexicon creative).

Many changes in lexicon come from what is called *vernacular speech.* A vernacular (there may be many vernaculars within a natural language) is an informal, oral form of speech that is characterized by considerable spontaneity in contrast to more planned discourses. "Vernacular discourse," according to Ono and Sloop (1995), "is speech that resonates within local communities" (p. 29). Youth in the 1980s, for example, sprinkled their oral language with the word *huge* as in "Television has a huge impact"—a feature now common in college and some journalistic writing.

New expressions in vernaculars can be short-lived, remain restricted, or cross over into general language use. The word *cool* originated in the jazz context of the Harlem Renaissance but was more commonly heard in the 1950s as part of the beat generation lexicon. Later, *cool* became part of youth vernacular more generally. The phrase "walk the walk and talk the talk" began in the urban African American [neighbor]hood but had crossed over sufficiently by 1996 to appear in presidential candidate Robert Dole's attack on his opponent, Bill Clinton: "He can talk the talk, but can he walk the walk?" asked Dole. Some view the incorporation of vernacular expressions as co-optation and a kind of linguistic theft, yet, this process keeps language from fossilizing.

Although we usually think of lexical influence as *within* a particular natural language, such as English or French, the situation is much more complex because of language contact, migration, telecommunications, and international trade. Whether the French like it or not, *le hot dog* is here to stay, just as the *croissant* overcame the *crescent roll.*

Morphemes. Related to lexicon but more closely wedded to language structure are the *morphemes* of language. A morpheme is the smallest unit of meaning in a language—often but not always a word. A *free morpheme* can stand by itself to convey meaning, as in the case of the following words: *talk, school, crude,* and *will.* Other morphemes are *bound,* which means that their meaning comes from being fixed to other morphemes. To the free morpheme *will,* many different bound morphemes can be added as suffixes to convey different meanings:

will-s, where the -s is a plural morpheme signifying more than one document regarding a person's possessions after death, or where -s is a singular verb marker corresponding to a singular subject, as in "He wills it to be done"

will-ed, meaning either that someone had the will to do something in the past or that someone bequeathed something in the past, called a past tense morpheme

will-ful, meaning to possess the characteristic of being filled with self-determination

Bound morphemes can also be affixed to the beginning of free morphemes as prefixes to change their meaning, as in *sub*basement, *un*pleasant, *pre*teen. The meanings of lexemes and morphemes do not fully convey the meaning component of language, but they do carry basic semantic content from which meaning is built.

Semantic Systems

The semantic component of a language variety designates the relationship between language and that to which it refers. Essentially, the semantic system is the referential system of language in which arbitrary verbal symbols attach to objects, properties, ideas, and so forth to create meaning. In semantics, the questions of importance pertain to *meaning as reference*—as contrasted to meaning in terms of impact or implication. Reference in this context should be understood broadly, rather than as a denotative, object-word relationship.

At the simplest level, semantics relates to morphemes and lexemes, implying much more than denotative or referential meanings. Words can vary in the degree to which they are concrete or abstract, clear-cut or context bound. "It was a *blue* pencil" specifies the color of the pencil, and not its psychological or mood state. "He's so *bad*" does not carry a negative meaning in African American vernacular but, to the contrary, indicates positive qualities.

At its more complex level, semantics deals with propositions that are expressed through language in a variety of ways and that we learn to distinguish in terms of relative degrees of truthfulness, essence, and accuracy within their linguistic and cultural context. I use the term *semantic notion* to refer to the ideational meaning of a lexeme as contrasted to referential meaning. *Freedom* is a semantic notion without concrete, referential meaning simply because there is nothing tangible that one can experience as freedom in the sense that one can experience an object by seeing it or touching it, as would be the case for the lexeme *key* when used to name an object whose function is to open locks. Even lexemes with referential meaning belie semantic notions when we delve more deeply. The object that we call a key can become a letter opener, a screwdriver, or a weapon, depending on the context. It can also become a metaphor for that which metaphorically opens something else: "The key to success in school is skill in reading" and "The key to salvation is faith." Semantic systems, like other systems of language, are, then, not universal.

Pragmatic Systems

To begin understanding language as a mode of communication, one must turn to the system of pragmatics, which pertains to ways in which language forms are related to their users. Pragmatics is roughly synonymous with the notion of "language in context" because it places prime importance on the specific situation in which utterances occur and the ways in which situations and participants affect both selection and interpretation of language forms. The pragmatic system for language use includes the rules and patterns that govern meaning and interpretation derived from context.

Levinson (1983) points out that pragmatics covers "both context-dependent aspects of language structure and principles of language usage and understanding that have nothing or little to do with linguistic structure" (p. 9). In subsequent chapters, emphasis will be given to the second type of pragmatics, which regulates the ways in which speakers use language to construct conversation. The system of turn-taking, for example, is governed by rules that are sensitive to context *and* to cultural definition. Sacks, Schegloff, and Jefferson (1974) proposed that turn-taking is an orderly process that for the most part stipulates that one person talks at a time. Yet, some cultural groups may be more or less likely than others to proceed as though it is appropriate to interrupt, which can lead to misunderstandings and conflicts. The most well-elaborated body of research on interruptions is in the area of gender and language; although variation in research results suggests caution in generalizing about how men and women view interruptions in conversation, there is ample research supporting the greater tendency for men to interrupt more than women and for women to be the recipients of interruption more often than men (see summary tables in James & Clarke, 1993). In a case such as interruption, the focus is on the ways in which context guides participants' utterances and interpretations within a communicative context. Pragmatic rules are learned in speech communities, which are embedded in culture.

Rhetorical Systems

Often overlooked in the pragmatics of language and communication are the rhetorical systems through which individuals appeal to one another and seek to persuade and influence. Political speeches, city and town politics, religious occasions, advertising, campaigns, and social movements are all examples of public rhetorical communication. Rhetorical communication occurs privately as well in the many contexts in which one person tries to persuade another regarding a belief, course of action, and so forth. As with other aspects of language and communication, rhetoric arises from cultural contexts rather than being universal, and rhetorical communication is perceived and evaluated through cultural frames.

In a diverse society of many different speech communities, misunderstandings often occur because the pragmatic systems differ among communities. One area posing special problems involves what are called *speech acts*, a term that refers to a speaker's intentions when using language and the impact on hearers of that speaker's language use (Austin, 1962; Searle, 1969). The propositional value of a speech act, called its *illocutionary force*, is what the speaker intends, such as to warn, to promise, to alert, to threaten, to make a request. The impact on the hearer is called *perlocutionary effect.* If both are the same, clear communication results.

Two examples illustrate how sociocultural identities can cause disparity in speech acts: (a) rising intonation at the end of a sentence and (b) verbal fighting.

Rising intonation (a final intonational rise at the end of a sentence whose illocutionary force is declarative) has been examined in two interesting groups: U.S. middle-class white women and Chicanos. Over two decades ago, Robin Lakoff (1975) described one characteristic of women's discourse as the use of rising intonation at the end of declarative sentences to indicate hesitancy and the desire for confirmation from the other. Consider the following, where /?/ indicates rising intonation and /./ indicates falling intonation:

A: Which route are you going to take.

B: Oh, I thought I would take Route 9?

Lakoff's interpretation would be that both A and B understand B's intended illocutionary force as requesting confirmation that Route 9 is an appropriate route. An alternative interpretation is that B might have intended the utterance to be an invitation to continue the conversation *or* an expression of personal decision that is open to comment but not to negotiation. In the analysis of Chicano English, the use of rising intonation has been discussed as a pattern occurring at the ends of emphatic statements (Penfield, 1984). Contrary to the cultural context for Lakoff's research, the Chicano context would lead its speakers and hearers to associate rising intonation at the end of declarative sentences to be a strong marker of emphasis, not a weakening of declarative force. Rising intonation then, is open to interpretation—some of it contextual and some cultural.

The example of verbal fights comes from Thomas Kochman's (1981) description of differences between urban black and white teens in what is understood to be verbal fighting versus argument. Whites, he says, consider fighting to have started when there is "a loud public dispute and the establishment of confrontation" (p. 45). For blacks, "fighting does not begin until someone actually makes a provocative *movement*" (p. 46). In this case, a white listener may interpret an utterance to convey greater threat than was intended. Obviously, attribution of meaning then frames subsequent verbal (and physical) action.

Analysis of pragmatics as a language system helps us understand many of the ways in which language-in-use leads to communication difficulties between individuals who are members of different speech communities.

Dialects and Registers for Language Use

Language situates identities, which can be understood in the metaphoric statement, "You are what you speak." What a person speaks generally reveals two important dimensions, that of identity and that of situated activity.

Dialects and Identities

The term *dialect* refers to the variety of language that is spoken based on a person's social identity, for example, social status, educational attainment, ethnicity, race, regional background, and native language. For a dialect to exist, the language patterns for a group of people must be distinctive in contrast to those patterns found in other groups. The boundaries between one dialect and another are made up of bundles of isoglosses—those features that mark the distinctiveness.

Dialects are linguistically patterned by phonology, syntax, and lexicon and morphology—alone or in combination. Taking regional dialects as an example, variations in the phonological systems typical of speakers from southern Texas and upper Maine are recognizable to most people, whereas lexical differences may be less well understood, as in the case of the word used to refer to a carbonated beverage, which is *soda* in the Northeast, *tonic* in some parts of eastern New England, and *pop* just about everyplace else. Phonological differences within the same native language can create communication problems or misinterpretations. The speech of most whose origins are in the Caribbean islands will systematically delete the *-g* from the *-ing* endings of words, producing *doin* and *wonderin* rather than *doing* and *wondering,* even in formal contexts. Although this pattern may be interpreted as casual by mainstream U.S. speakers, that interpretation would often be mismatched to the speaker's intent. In many instances, dialect differences pose no obstacle to interpersonal understanding even though they may evoke judgments and attitudes about the speaker. In some other cases, however, mediation or translation is necessary. The documentary filmmaker and journalist Paul Wilkes (1977), for example, provided subtitles for the dialogue among members of a large, poorly educated Appalachian family for his television documentary, *Six American Families.* He did so knowing that their speech would be difficult for mainstream viewers to understand, even though it was English. Differences in lexicon can cause confusion or absolute misunderstanding. "Keep your *pecker* up" and "Keep your *chin* up" carry similar meanings in British and American English, respectively, but an American would likely interpret *pecker* as a colloquialism for *penis.* If a person says that someone has a *tude,* some hearers might scratch their heads in confusion whereas others know both what having an *attitude* means and that *tude* is a shortened version of *attitude.*

Syntactic differences in dialects are less easily discerned by most people, often being mistaken for errors in grammar or lapses into formality. Many Minnesotans, for instance, delete the object *me* of the pronominal preposition *with,* producing utterances such as "Do you want to go with?" or "I'm going to take this with." To some ears, this sounds odd. A stable variant in what is called AAVE is the *be* form to indicate a habitual state, as in "He *be* workin" to mean that he is working all the time, rather than at this moment or temporarily. Most non-African Americans attribute this usage instead to sloppy and incorrect English. In the Minnesota example, the utterance would be easily comprehensible by outsiders, but in the African American example, comprehension by outsiders will likely be incorrect.

Dialects are neither static over time nor manifested in precisely the same way from speaker to speaker. Any aspect of language can be looked at *diachronically* (across a time span) to chart its changes or *synchronically* to describe usage at a particular time. Dialects exhibit *inherent variability,* which means that they differ from one another not in the absolute absence or presence of a particular linguistic feature or features but, rather, in the relative degree to which those features are used. In other words, dialects evidence different degrees of density for particular features; their use by speakers will also be more or less consistent depending on the other language varieties that become incorporated into them (Trudgill, 1974). The main point is that dialect features are rarely used with absolute consistency by their speakers. Speakers can often move in and out of dialects, changing their language variety according to the situation.

Registers for Situated Language Use

Whereas dialect relates to the speaker's social identity, *register* relates to the situation in which the speaker communicates. To communicate within a register implies that the speaker has selected—either consciously or through tacit understanding—among options available to her or him for how to use language appropriately in context. Halliday (1978) discusses register as determined by three aspects of the situation: (a) what is taking place, (b) who the participants are, and (c) the role of language in the situation. As an individual develops *communicative competence*, that individual's sensitivity to activity, places, and people evolves. The place and situation in which one speaks influence how one goes about the entire communication process. One does not speak in a courtroom in the same manner as one speaks while watching a basketball game, and what goes over well with friends may fall flat in the workplace. So, too, a person adjusts language choices depending on those with whom the interaction is taking place. One does not speak to a grandmother in the same manner as to a sibling, or to a teacher in the same manner as to a student. To complicate matters further, how one speaks to a grandmother, sibling, or teacher is guided by cultural rules as well—a fact increasingly evident in U.S. multicultural society.

Dialects and registers are not absolutely distinguishable in all cases. In some situations, a person's dialect may preclude command of a particular register; a speaker of AAVE, for example, may not be able to conform linguistically to the expectations for speaking in a school situation because the register of the schoolroom presumes Standard English. Moving in the other direction, a learner of English as a second language could develop perfect fluency from the perspective of native speakers who are in an educational setting with that person but have great difficulty when the situation shifts to the informal mode of a night club. Thus, dialect and register are comingled and interdependent.

It is also the case that registers both (a) are created by those who speak in the situations that they define and (b) precede the individuals who come into situations in which a particular register is expected. Most college students understand, for example, that there is a particular language register for formal, classroom education in a college or university setting in the United States. Foreign students often have difficulties adjusting their communication because in the home country, the classroom register is more formal, and students are expected to be more verbally passive. Looking from another perspective (this one historical), the classroom register typical of U.S. colleges and universities today differs quite dramatically compared to the 1960s. As part of the student movement of the 1960s and early 1970s, and the campus unrest that accompanied the Vietnam War, the role relationships between student and faculty member became more personalized and the classroom register less formal. The common language practice had been for students to be addressed by their professors as *Mr., Miss,* or *Mrs. (Ms.* was not then widely used) rather than by their first names. Students were also expected to be relatively more passive in the classroom than is the case nowadays. In all of these examples, we see, once again, the dual aspects of language (a) as symbolically conserving and reinforcing social and cultural patterns and (b) as constantly changing and creating the social and cultural fabric. Registers often hold isomorphic relationships with particular situations and settings, but they also undergo modification by those who participate in the very situations for which the communicative architecture seems complete.

Origins and Maintenance of Language Varieties

For both dialect and register, there is great variability even within the same person. Moreover, many people quite consciously reposition their identity through shifts in language use. At its extreme, shifts provide powerful symbolic resources for what is called "passing" (Bucholtz, 1995): ethnics passing for nonethnics, gays passing for straight, men passing for women. We also pass for different identities at different times in our lives. Individual, intrapersonal diversity in language use draws from preexisting dialect and register patterns in complex ways to create configurations of novelty and stereotype even in the same person.

Language varieties each have their origins, and one way to characterize the main factors involved is through the concepts of *barriers* and *distance.* Drawing from explanations for dialect differences, which often show their correspondence to geographic distance and geographic barriers such as mountains and rivers, Trudgill (1974) proposes that "social varieties can perhaps be explained in the same sort of way—in terms of *social* barriers and *social* distance" (p. 35). These concepts, with some refinement, are useful for talking about language varieties in general.

Some barriers are social in origin, as is the case for occupational groupings, but they can be cultural too, as in the case of neighborhood boundaries that coincide with ethnicity. *Sociocultural barrier* will be substituted for Trudgill's term *social barrier* to recognize the distinctive role of culture as well as the frequent intertwining of social and cultural factors. Some of the geographic factors are *natural*, whereas others are *created*, for example, in the ways in which urban transportation systems are laid out or housing

TABLE 2.1 A Typology of Barriers and Distance in Language Variation

	Barriers	*Distance*
Geographic	natural	natural
	created	created
Sociocultural	imposed	imposed
	assumed	assumed

developments located. Social factors are not naturally occurring, but they do differ depending on whether they are *imposed* or *assumed*. The segregation system in the South after slavery imposed legal barriers between whites and blacks lasting until civil rights legislation in the 1960s declared these barriers unconstitutional. The systematic exclusion of women from managerial jobs and certain professions resulted from imposed barriers that simply closed access to women. In contrast, the voluntary affiliation with culturally based religious organizations, such as Ukrainian Catholic or Hasidic Jewish, or the voluntary clustering in neighborhoods of like individuals (which often also produces de facto segregation for the outgroup with an imposed character to it) are all assumed barriers rather than imposed. One fascinating study has documented the ways in which high school students use the resources of discourse to differentiate themselves into groups designated as "jocks" and "burnouts" (Eckert & McConnell-Ginet, 1995). We can, then, locate the genesis and maintenance of distinct language varieties in one or more of several possible conditions, as shown in Table 2.1.

Barriers and distance, whether geographic or sociocultural, function to create different degrees of isolation and enclosure between and among people. The speech communities that result exhibit greater or lesser distinctiveness depending on the degree of isolation. What seems certain, however, is that the social, cultural, and geographic factors that create divides among people also create the diversity in language use that characterizes our multicultural society. Robin Lakoff (1990) sums it up by saying that, "the more two cultures are isolated from each other by time, space, or politics, the more different and exotic the rhetorical traditions of each may be to the other" (p. 216).

In the chapters that follow, these conditions will come into sharper focus as language varieties and speech communities are discussed in their cultural context. The different levels of language all operate in the dynamics of cultural definition, cultural assimilation, and cultural elaboration. Different aspects of the language system are more central to some speech community definitions than others, and different aspects of the language system can be magnified to create symbolic meanings corresponding to cultural demarcations. The cultural contexts in which people function provide a complex map of the conditions in which the communication process occurs.

3

Cultural Dimensions of Discourse

All communication bears cultural origins, conveys cultural meanings, and is interpreted through cultural frameworks. In this chapter, a perspective on culture used throughout the book is presented. I term this approach the *Language-Centered Perspective on Culture.* This approach features human language as the cornerstone of cultural meaning within an interrelated set of systems for elaborating cultural resources that includes ideational patterns (called *abstractions* in this perspective) and cultural products and events (called *artifacts* in this perspective). The focus on culture developed here provides the perspective for a richer analysis of patterned language use than is conventionally found in sociolinguistics.

The Language-Centered Perspective on Culture offers us a way of making sense holistically of the many systematic patterns of language use that occur everyday in the United States. It also takes us beneath the surface of terms such as *diversity* and *multiculturalism* to see just how important the contrasting worldviews making up the texture of the United States are to personal identities, interpersonal relationships, and basic ideas about the social and political world. This view of culture differs from some others, which will be described below. Using the theoretical approach described here as a foundation, subsequent chapters deal with the analysis of cultural groups and the language varieties characteristic in them and used by their members to create an understanding of the deeply complex cultural multiplicity that exists in the United States today.

Society and Culture Distinctions

Most communication research operates from a seemingly acultural perspective, meaning that culture does not figure centrally in defining or describing communication processes. When taken for granted, culture operates as a powerful normative force, creating the illusion that cultural identity is something that belongs only to minorities, immigrants, and other "special" groups. Cultural notions, however, always underlie communication even if they are not made explicit. Most textbooks about communication assume a particular cultural perspective, usually that of the dominant, Anglophile, Eurowhite populace. Regardless of the particular subject—intimate communication, communication between friends, conflict, family communication, managerial communication—a specific cultural foundation underlies most theories of communication and prescriptions for effective communication. For our purposes, let us call this kind of underlying cultural foundation *presumed culture* operating as *default cultural conceptions*; those who write and speak about communication *presume* a substantial degree of cultural commonality among all peoples in the United States. Culture thus becomes an exclusionary mental perspective, equivalent to the default option in a computer program, because it excludes other options unless they are explicitly specified. Increasingly, however, that presumption is invalid, which makes the cultural analysis of communication an imperative for our times.

Depending on the area of study, culture has been more or less emphasized in the analysis of language variation. Most anthropological studies of language either assume or explicitly view language as a cultural practice; this tradition of work embraces culture as the key to understanding how language systems come to be so distinctively different throughout the world and how these systems function to create and sustain different worldviews.

Culture has been less regularly featured in most sociolinguistic studies of language variation. In most sociolinguistic research, social structure predominates as the central organizing concept used to explain language variation. The substantial body of work on language and social class conducted in Great Britain, for example, rests on a model of society where the different social classes are defined as variables organized vertically within the larger social system: upper class, upper middle class, middle class, lower middle class, lower class. Other labels such as "working class" often substitute as contrasts with middle class to designate a quick reference for occupations requiring manual unskilled labor.

The study of social status and regional dialects in the United States has proceeded similarly by emphasizing those aspects of language use—especially phonological features—that vary depending on the particular class or regional origin of a speaker.

The social structure model looks to *variation within a system* that is organized into social groups with horizontal and vertical (hierarchical) relationships to one another. Social structure is generally associated with "the distribution of rights and duties across status positions in a society" (D'Andrade, 1984, p. 110). Although this model has much to offer by way of documenting systematic differences in language use, the social structure view presupposes that individuals are connected through a larger social system and are—at least theoretically—mobile in their language use just as they are in other aspects of their lives (which fits prevailing U.S. ideology about social mobility). There is, thus, a reifying impact in this tradition, such that differential patterns of language use come to represent the different social strata as functionally complementary categories. Social strata are reified not only on the basis of class and economic power but also according to race and ethnicity.

What is often lost in such analyses is the broader perspective on semantic and pragmatic systems that gives contextual meaning to language. Also missed is the vitality in divergent cultural systems, which accounts for the persistence of disfavored language variations against considerable odds, and the mechanisms through which mainstream institutions function to preserve preferred language varieties and the cultural systems they articulate. Of greatest consequence is the lost opportunity to understand the cultural processes at play when different varieties of language meet face-to-face and ear-to-ear. Sociolinguistics, then, often minimizes complex notions of how culture shapes language use in favor of more standard notions of societal groupings.

From the 1960s through the early 1980s, it was common in the United States to talk about complex societies as containing some set of *sub*cultures, which sometimes equated with minority groups. In the United States, groups such as blacks, Puerto Ricans, criminals, Mexican Americans, urban poor, and Appalachian hill dwellers came to be labeled as subcultures. This perspective positioned the study of "nonstandard" groups and their ways of speaking in a subcultural context to be contrasted with what was understood to be the main culture. Although the concept of culture made its way into the nomenclature of academic study, little emphasis was actually placed on the richness of cultural meanings within the reputed subcultures. Even more problematic, the subcultural orientation powerfully symbolized social worth. All of the meanings of *sub-* carry negative connotations: under, beneath, below, subordinate, secondary, inferior. These connotations tend to imply separate and unequal status for any language variety that happens to be associated with what is labeled a subculture. The only satisfactory way to deal with the problems created by both social structure and subcultural analysis is to reposition the analysis of language variation as a more complex analytical endeavor that begins with the assumption that multiple cultures coexist in complex societies. The move to cultural linguistics requires, then, a much clearer conception of how cultures are constructed, sustained, and changed.

Views of Culture

For all but the most isolated of social groups, culture conveys complexity arising from (a) the communication and intermingling of peoples with different origins, identities, and allegiances and (b) the interplay of the real and imagined past, the perceived present, and the projected future, whether probable or fantasized. Cultures, then, are not "pure" but, rather, are the product and creation of human contact between and across both groups and time. Simply stated, those who share in a culture also display a broad range of individual differences, and contrasting cultures in contact with one another also display the products of their mutual influence.

But what exactly is culture? In the many descriptions of culture, common threads can be found. First, cultures comprise symbolic systems that create webs of meaning. Much of what we know and believe to be real has no concrete manifestation at all but is made concrete only through its applications in everyday life: Justice, evil, beauty, ego are no more than arbitrary abstractions packed with symbolic meanings. Even material cultural products can only be understood based on abstract meanings: The clothes we wear, the food we eat, the pictures we look at in magazines all depend on abstract cultural meanings. Second, cultures—although constantly evolving and changing—endure over long periods of time. New cultures do emerge but the level of complexity within cultures is more than a brief blip of human interaction. Third, cultures are learned by humans through both explicit instruction and tacit acquisition that occurs in the everyday modeling and practice of meaningful action. We are not naturally of any particular culture, but we develop our skill to function in various cultures over our lifetimes. Once mastered, cultural learning becomes very much second nature.

In differing degrees, we all participate in multiple cultural systems ranging from our native culture of origin, to the local cultures in which we interact in daily life, to the global culture created through mobility, mass communication, and technology. Each influences the other. In discussing the transnational impact of one culture on another, Ulf Hannerz (1989) talks about how the centers and the peripheries in global affairs intermingle with the effect of "creolized and creolizing cultural forms which grow between center and periphery" (p. 213). Such is also the case nationally where the influences of one culture on another have a creolizing effect; for example, the greater numbers of people in the United States with Mexican origins resulted in changes in food preferences for Anglos but also for Mexican-Americans.

The philosophical foundations of the Language-Centered Perspective on Culture contrast with more traditional notions of culture articulated by Western scholars.

Enlightenment and Romantic Views

For purposes of distinguishing theories of culture from one another, Richard Shweder (1984) provides a useful review and synthesis of approaches to explaining culture by contrasting two major streams of thought: the Enlightenment view and the Romantic rebellion against it.

Briefly, Enlightenment theories assume that (a) humans are rational and (b) significant human practices across cultural settings are ultimately universal (or evolving toward the universal through successive advances of cultural development). The nomenclature of *primitive* and *modern/developed* cultures comes from the Enlightenment perspective. Goodenough (1981) points to the German word *kultur*, which refers to the process of becoming more civilized such that greater or higher *kultur* follows from greater or higher progress in civilization. Contemporary ideas about high culture as distinguished from popular or mass culture derive their meanings from the Enlightenment view.

In contrast, Romantic theories portray human beings as engaging in vastly different modes of rational behavior, sometimes called "nonrational" behavior simply because cultural practices are arbitrary and relative to their systems of meaning. In this view, each culture must be taken as unique, with patterns that represent no natural or universal order but, rather, are relative to one another. Shweder (1984) comments that "the most significant romantic development to emerge . . . is perhaps the definition of culture as arbitrary code" (p. 45).

The Role of Language in Culture

Elaborating on Shweder's analysis, we can compare and contrast culture theories for their perspective on language.

The role that language (and communication more broadly) occupies in culture varies considerably across culture theories. One perspective is that language is essentially a vehicle for transporting information and ideas. Like any vehicle, language in this view is a medium for getting from one place to another. And like any vehicle, language can be improved on, made more efficient and effective, and fueled with higher quality material. Language, thus, is seen primarily for its role in transmitting the culture, where the metaphor of transmission evokes the notion that getting something from one person to another, one place to another, or one time to another is purely a technical matter—much like engineering and electronics. In the second half of the 20th century, the transmission metaphor for language became especially powerful because it captured the U.S. fascination with science and emerging technology.

From a quite different perspective, the role of language in culture can be seen as formative because language is symbolic action that creates the very substance of culture. This view draws on the seminal ideas of George Herbert Mead, whose thinking early in the century provided the foundation for what was to become the symbolic interactionism perspective in social theory. Mead's theories about social life were developed in opposition to the early formulations of radical behaviorism in the United States. Mead's (1934) view was that the external world does not brutely impinge upon the individual. Rather, people use language to create situations and indicate those things that become regarded as important, significant, and in the realm of reality:

Language does not simply symbolize a situation or object that is already there in advance; it makes possible the existence or the appearance of that situation or object, for it is a part of the mechanism whereby the situation or object is created. (p. 78)

Carrying this idea into the realm of culture, language would be said to both symbolize and create culture.

The importance of language for a person's worldview is nowhere more central than in the writings of Benjamin Lee Whorf, whose work builds on that of Edward Sapir, both of whom studied Native American languages. Concerned primarily with natural languages taken as a whole, and not with the variations within particular languages, Whorf (1940/1956) advanced a "new principle of relativity" related to language and thought; this *linguistic relativity*, said Whorf, "holds that all observers are not led by the same physical evidence to the same picture of the universe, unless their linguistic backgrounds are similar, or can in some way be calibrated" (p. 214). His formulations about the relationship between culture and language, that is, how one influences the other, are aptly described by Emily Schultz (1990) as a *paradoxical unity* in which culture and language reciprocally influence one another.

The most frequently quoted Whorfian statement addresses how perceived "reality" is affected by the interplay of language and cognition within a culturally specific speech community context:

> We dissect nature along lines laid down by our native language. The categories and types that we isolate from the world of phenomena we do not find there because they stare every observer in the face; on the contrary, the world is presented in a kaleidoscopic flux of impressions which has to be organized by our minds—and this means *largely by the linguistic systems in our minds* [italics added]. We cut nature up, organize it into concepts, and ascribe significance as we do, *largely because we are parties to an agreement to organize it in this way* [italics added]—an agreement that holds throughout our speech community and is codified in the patterns of our language. The agreement is, of course, an implicit and unstated one, BUT ITS TERMS ARE ABSOLUTELY OBLIGA-TORY. (Whorf, 1940/1956, pp. 213-214, capitalization in the original)

Notice Whorf's use of the words *largely* and *an agreement* in the first part of the sentence and *absolutely obligatory* in the latter part. It is as though he is likening the relationship between language and thought to that of a contract: In a contract, we agree to certain things even though we may know that other possibilities exist, but once agreed to, the contract is binding. The explicit link to culture is that languages (in all their varieties) are culturally relevant and culturally relative. Cultural frameworks give rise to particular languages,

TABLE 3.1   Universal and Situated Culture

Universal	*Situated*
Reality is independent of specific cultures	Reality is relative to specific cultures
Humans operate through one system of rationality, which can be perfected to perceive the truth	Humans operate through many different systems of rationality, perceiving different truths
Culture resides in abstract knowledge systems found in people's heads	Culture resides in human action, manifested in human processes and products
Language is a vehicle	Language is symbolic action

which in turn shape mental processes and the organization of reality, which in turn create cultural frameworks. Cultural frameworks can be renewed, refreshed, reformulated through ever-changing processes involving language. Hence, thought is relative to language, which is relative to culture.

In current thinking about culture, the work of anthropologist Clifford Geertz (1973, 1983) is prominent for its emphasis on the role of symbols in cultural life. Geertz argues that the sharing of public symbols gives reality to cultural identity; it is the actual sharing through expression of values, mores, and orientations to the world that joins people together through symbolic action in a cultural context. Although Geertz concerns himself with more than language and communication, the relevance of his thinking lies in the claim that to understand a culture, one must be able to understand the "modes of expression" or "symbol systems" used by its participants (Geertz, 1983, p. 70). Rather than seeing culture as interior to the individual, Geertz sees culture as public because meaning is public (Geertz, 1973).

Using Shweder's (1984) basic ideas as a foundation, the perspective on culture and role of language in culture can, then, be contrasted. My analysis in this book features a situated viewpoint on culture (aligned with the Romantic view) in contrast with the universal viewpoint (aligned with the Enlightenment view. Table 3.1 shows the major distinctions in the two viewpoints.

The situated viewpoint shares assumptions with a new stream of social criticism that seeks to document cultural multiplicity. The African American philosopher Cornel West (1993a) boldly stakes out the territory of this criticism:

Distinctive features of the new cultural politics of difference are to trash the monolithic and homogeneous in the name of diversity, multiplicity, and heterogeneity; to reject the abstract, general, and universal in light of the concrete, specific, and particular; and to historicize, contextualize, and pluralize by highlighting the contingent, provisional, variable, tentative, shifting, and changing. (p. 3)

I turn next to the specific perspective that guides my analysis of culture throughout this book. Working from the premise that U.S. society consists of many cultures, the goal is to understand how meaning is created in these various cultures.

The Language-Centered Perspective on Culture

The Language-Centered Perspective on Culture emphasizes the special role of language in human interaction. Cultures, as complex systems, are made up of several different symbolic systems that generate meaning. Language, however, binds those systems together in a special way and serves as the major meaning system for contact among peoples.

Humans learn through the cultures in which they are reared, gaining competence as they mature and often possessing passionate loyalty to their cultural origins. Even when individuals break off with their cultural roots, linguistic enculturation from within native speech communities provides the foundation from which all other discourse options become elaborated. Speech communities function to center whole cultural systems through discourse. Most people today are entailed in multiple cultures, offering multiple bases for identity.

The locus of cultural identity is sometimes national, sometimes regional, sometimes racially or ethnicity based, always lodged in some dynamic of social class organization, and so forth. "American culture" can be understood, for example, in contrast to the dominant cultural patterns in countries such as England, Italy, Korea, and Iraq. Stewart and Bennett (1991) provide a useful discussion of American cultural patterns, citing dimensions such as individualism and emphasis on selfhood, belief in agency and causality, and separation of social and occupational roles. Other cultural identities arise from region in the sense that "southern culture" varies from "New England culture," and "down East Mainers" differ from Boston Irish. The locus of still other cultures is local and community based, such as a place labeled "Teamsterville" (Philipsen, 1975), which is a Chicago neighborhood with clear cultural boundaries and rules for speaking. Other loci for culture are

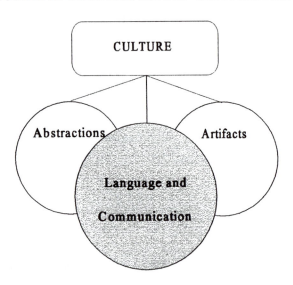

Figure 3.1. Model of Language-Centered Perspective on Culture

race (e.g., African Americans, teenage African American males living in urban settings, middle-class African American women); ethnicity (e.g., Italian, Polish, Swedish); or religious identity (e.g., Hasidic Jews, Sikh Indians, Jehovah's Witnesses). Cultural identity can also reside in lifestyle choices, such as participating in lesbian or gay culture, in pacifism as a way of life, or in gangs. A loosely structured neighborhood, a group that convenes briefly to accomplish some agenda, and a dyadic relationship are not, however, cultures in the sense that I use the term here because they have neither history nor collective identity that transcends their participants.

Adequate description of a culture necessitates a vision of the significant systems that account for action and meaning within that culture. Three such systems—all interrelated—are proposed here as constituting a useful view of cultures (see earlier version in Johnson, 1989):

> system of cultural abstractions
> system of cultural artifacts
> system of cultural language and communication

The three systems are interrelated, with the role of language and communication centrally placed, as seen in Figure 3.1.

System of Cultural Abstractions

The *system of cultural abstractions* influences and shapes cognitive possibilities and structures the range of choices that are most likely within a culture. Abstractions refer to a particular set of ideational concepts including values, morals, ethics, conceptions of right and wrong, conceptions of good and evil, the logical system, conceptions of justice and laws, rituals, spiritual and religious beliefs, and ideas that in themselves have no concrete or material reality (e.g., honesty, responsibility, kindness).

Several examples clarify the nature of abstractions. In U.S. mainstream culture, the integrity of the individual and the right to privacy are highly valued. This is not the case in Chinese culture, where the language does not even contain words to name and describe the concepts of individuality and privacy. In the realm of religion, predestination is not part of the Judeo-Christian belief system, whereas it plays a central role in Shintoism, the dominant religion in Japan. Those of the Jewish religion have no strong conception of life after death, whereas Christians do. Looking to legal concepts, democracy in the United States guarantees the right to vote to all citizens who have reached "legal" age (even though women did not win the right to vote until 1920, and even though it took the Voting Rights Act of 1965 to stop such impediments as poll taxes and literacy tests from disenfranchising southern blacks, the primacy of "one man [sic], one vote" to U.S. democracy has never been questioned). Until April 1994, this was not the case in South Africa, where the system of apartheid legally barred blacks, who make up 75% of the population, from voting. Nor does the legal right for all citizens to vote exist in Cuba or North Korea.

The system of abstractions serves as understructure for much of what is expressed through the system of language and communication. Fundamental abstractions lie beneath semantic notions such as *marriage* and *family*, *money* and *savings*, *beauty* and *appearance*, *law* and *justice*. Children must learn these fundamental abstractions and their applications to more specific concepts and notions. A friend told the story of her preschool-age daughter's first close inspection of a Barbie doll. On examining the doll, the child exclaimed, "What's wrong with her? She doesn't have a stomach!" Barbie's almost concave stomach looked quite different from the well-rounded middle sections of both her mother and father! The child's comments reflected her view on what is valued and what is judged normal in the human body. At least for that brief pre-school moment, this little girl was untouched by the American social value placed on thin-waisted female bodies.

When we engage in cultural communication within a cultural framework, the abstractions underlying language behavior are usually taken for granted. We become aware of cultural abstractions when circumstances bring together more than one cultural framework where the differences are conspicuous.

The 1994 case of Michael Fay, a 19-year-old from the United States, demonstrates how an alleged spray-painting spree in Singapore became an international incident because of different cultural conceptions of justice. Most U.S. citizens expressed outrage when Michael was sentenced in Singapore to punishment by caning, a painful and physically injurious beating with a specially prepared bamboo and leather cane, for an offense as minor as graffiti spray painting. Operating with the Western principles of jurisprudence that "the punishment should fit the crime" and that "cruel and unusual punishment" is not appropriate, the sentence of caning struck Americans as excessive and violent. Singapore defended its justice system by displaying its low crime statistics compared to the United States and many other nations. President Bill Clinton intervened with a strong appeal for leniency, and the boy's father vowed to pressure for an embargo and a review of most-favored-nation trade status for Singapore ("Singapore," 1994). The caning took place, but with a reduced number of lashings. This international incident put the clash of notions about justice on center stage.

Looking at another illustration, many misunderstandings occur within U.S. borders because definitions of family and familial responsibility differ across cultural groups. For example, *la familia* as the center of values for most Mexican-Americans is never separated from other spheres of activity (Gangotena, 1994). What might be perceived as honorable family responsibility in the Mexican-American cultural tradition would be judged as neurotic family attachment by many other cultural groups. Similarly, the concept of a "mama's boy" with its pejorative connotations in dominant U.S. culture would likely be meaningless within the Mexican-American cultural tradition.

Systems of abstraction, then, make up the ideational foundation for cultures. Abstractions guide behavior and symbolization in language. Discourse across cultures often makes little sense because of conflicting abstractions in the cultures.

System of Cultural Artifacts

The *system of cultural artifacts* includes products of the culture's participants, such as fine and plastic arts, crafts, photography, music, dance, clothing and jewelry, architecture and design, furnishings, material objects such as tools and computers, and so forth. Cultural artifacts express their particular cultural frameworks and sometimes rebel against them.

Artifacts have systematicity through the rules and patterns underlying their production, distribution, and placement. Within a cultural framework, jewelry, for instance, carries gender-related meanings. In Western cultures, women wear more jewelry for adornment than do men, and style varies by gender. African American men don more jewelry than do Anglo men, which likely expresses continuity with the importance of jewelry in many African cultures. The same is true of men from many Hispanic cultures. Teens and young adults—female and male alike—from various cultural groups now engage in significantly more body piercing than has previously been evident in the United States. It is not uncommon to see piercings all along the ear periphery and through the nose, eyebrow, navel, and tongue (extended occasionally to the nipples and genitalia). In a very different cultural tradition, married women among the Surma in southwest Ethiopia customarily make and wear lip plates, which are inserted into pierced holes in the lower lip, sometimes stretching to the size of a saucer. Color in clothing may also carry different symbolic meaning for different cultures. Black has been associated with mourning in the Christian and Judaic traditions, but white symbolizes mourning in China.

Artifacts may be enduring or ephemeral. Products like books, sculptures, tools, sound recordings, and buildings are relatively (although not absolutely) enduring, whereas musical performances, dance productions, poetry recitations and slams, or chalk drawings on sidewalks are ephemeral. Advances in photography, film, and video make it increasingly possible for some cultural groups to preserve artifacts whose inherent nature is ephemeral, thus extending the temporal dimension of their cultural meanings.

Artifacts channel cultural expression in many interesting ways. Artifacts of a more enduring nature often slow or thwart change simply because they exist. The changes in pedagogical style in U.S. schools had to account for the time and money it would take to remove rows of desks that were bolted to the floors of school rooms in neat rows facing the teacher's place at the front of the class. When "Men Only" clubs opened their membership to women, changes were required in such mundane matters as lavatory fixtures, entrances, and decor. In libraries, technology has gradually replaced the many drawers of wooden card catalogs with on-line computer catalogs, but the physical presence of the catalog drawers and the spaces they occupied slowed change, and explicit planning was required to help library users adapt to the new systems.

Even art or music that is judged heresy finds its basis in rebellion against particular rules and patterns that are culture based; the rebellion, hence, is culturally based. The Impressionist movement among French painters in the late 1800s, the rise of rock and roll music in England and the United States in the early 1960s, and the move to "street dress" among Catholic nuns all produced new artifact systems. The changes both departed from prevailing cultural practice and drew on those practices as context for the newer forms.

Cultural artifacts, then, are systematic expressions of arbitrary customs and symbolic meanings within a specific cultural framework. When cultural manifestations such as clothing, art objects, genres of literature, music, and furnishings are stable and well developed, they powerfully symbolize what is significant within a cultural framework. When they change, the change occurs as a kind of dialectic between conventional cultural meanings and oppositional or resistant meanings. Once anchored, the arbitrariness of artifact symbols seems anything but arbitrary to its users, who come to expect certain artifactual expressions just as they do certain conceptual notions and—as is my focus throughout this book—language practices.

System of Cultural Language and Communication

The system of *language and communication* is the central resource used by human beings to create, maintain, and change culture. Although the languages of the world number 4,000 to 4,500 (Kachru, 1981), it is not natural languages themselves that distinguish one culture from another. Languages encode cultures according to the ways in which they are structured through *rules for use*, which in turn incorporate the system of abstractions of particular cultures. Thus, cultures all have their particular discourse patterns, which convey differing worldviews.

James Gee's (1992) explanation of the term *discourses* shows the complexity of language in its cultural context:

> Each Discourse involves ways of talking, acting, interacting, valuing, and believing, as well as the spaces and material "props" the group uses to carry out its social practices. Discourses integrate words, acts, values, beliefs, attitudes, social identities, as well as gestures, glances, body positions, and clothes. . . . Discourses are always ways of displaying . . . *membership* in a particular social group or social network. (p. 107)

As *pragmatic* systems, discourses express cultural meaning systems.

Communicative competence. To use a language and to interact with others through a coherent discourse require the acquisition, development, and application of what has been termed *communicative competence*, which is the knowledge system underlying the appropriate use of language in context. The concept of communicative competence was originally developed by Dell Hymes (1971), who voiced concern about Noam Chomsky's notions of "language performance" as relatively uninteresting. Hymes argued that children must not only learn language rules but also the rules for *use* of language. Their utterances must, among other things, be culturally feasible and appropriate to the situation. Communicative competence is not a simple mastery of how-to rules for language use. Such competence "deals with how we *know* that a given situation requires a given speech variety and communicative approach" (Johnson, 1979, p. 14). In a similar way, Gee (1992) refers to *primary discourse*: that discourse "to which people are apprenticed early in life . . . as members of particular families within their sociocultural settings" (p. 108). As members of groups, people learn other ways to use language throughout their lives, making them users of multiple discourse. Gee calls these *secondary discourses.*

Culture, then, frames communication by directly influencing its form and content. Routine language use, for example, varies from culture to culture. In this regard, Forgas (1988) notes that *communicative episodes* (routine situations in which people interact) are both highly predictable and culturally specific: Culture provides an individual with shared cognitive schemas that shape language use and broader communicative conduct. The most straightforward example is the difference in greeting behaviors from culture to culture.

Communicative competence *within* a cultural system can vary widely from person to person. Some people use language more effectively because their knowledge system is more complex. An individual can also possess different levels of communicative competence *across* cultural systems, such that greater effectiveness and proficiency will be present when that person uses language in one cultural context compared to another.

Intercultural communicative competence. The importance of "cultural mindedness" for effective functioning in a society of cultural multiplicity has already been noted. Minimally, cultural mindedness implies cultural empathy. Ideally, it implies *intercultural communication competence* (ICC). Young Yun Kim (1991) defines such competence as the "overall *capacity* or *capability* to facilitate the communication process between people from differing cultural backgrounds and to contribute to successful interaction outcomes" (p. 263). Kim emphasizes that intercultural communication competence is not the same as having competence for communication within a specific culture but, rather, requires "metacompetence," or the ability to explicitly think about and adapt language use and communication to different cultural situations.

In sum, discourse patterns, as the heart of the pragmatics of language, play an especially important role when cultural backgrounds are taken into account. Cultural similarity enhances the prospect that language use will lead to communicative effectiveness. Cultural dissimilarity portends the opposite unless cultural mindedness or intercultural communication competence is developed.

Ideology and Cultural Complexes

In a multicultural society, there is plenty of room for communicative misunderstanding and conflict based on different language systems, which arise from different cultural systems and their accompanying discourses. Simultaneously with any cultural system that might be designated as mainstream or public, many other cultural systems operate. Such cultural multiplicity can be viewed as represented in Figure 3.2, which shows cultures co-existing up to any possible number *(n)* that may occur simultaneously in greater or lesser contact with one another.

Societies such as the United States contain many cultural groups and can be said to be *cultural complexes* made up of distinct but interrelated cultures. For reasons elaborated earlier, these different cultures will be designated as *co-cultures* rather than subcultures. In this example, C1 would be the dominant, mainstream culture. C2 through C7 all overlap with C1 and with each other to varying degrees: C3 has the most overlap with C1 and is the largest cultural group, with C7 close behind but overlapping less with C1; C3, C5, C6, and C9 form an overlapping cluster, but C5 and C9 remain distinct from one another; and so forth. C10 and C11 stand apart from the other cultures as isolates from the cultural complex—a rare situation but certainly possible for small groups.

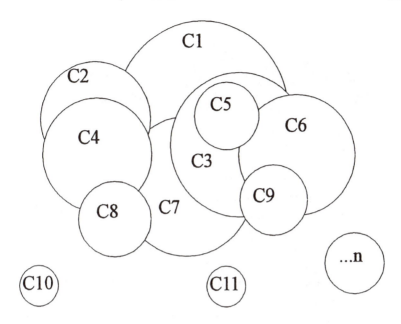

Figure 3.2. Model of Cultural Complex

Using the term *co-cultures* draws attention to the existence of different cultures within the same or contiguous spaces and to the importance of describing each of the coexisting cultures on its own terms. We can think of co-cultures visually as existing on a horizon—a metaphorical space in which cultures exist at the same level of complexity but with different degrees of closeness and separation from one another. Figure 3.3 represents the co-cultural horizon. Such a visual representation invites inspection of each culture from the same angle or the same rotation rather than seeing the array laid out with some cultures on a higher plane and others on a lower plane. Because the prefix *co-* means to exist together or along with each other, designating multiple cultures as co-cultures gives no particular advantage or status to any one culture in relation to the others in its company. This kind of attitudinal parity is critical to discovering the principles operating within cultures in a manner free of assumptions transported from the culturally biased gaze of someone in another culture. The co-culture perspective, then, affords the possibility for the unbiased examination of language varieties.

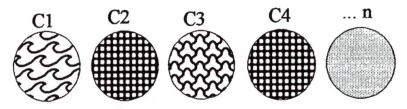

C1   C2   C3   C4   ... n

Figure 3.3. Horizon of Co-Cultures

We must keep in mind, however, that whereas cultures coexist in time and reflect complexity through their systems of abstractions, artifacts, and languages, their political relations involve patterns of subordination and privilege such as that represented in Figure 3.2. To the extent that something like "the American culture" exists, its mainstream manifestations displace, distort, and disregard many other cultural identities coexisting in time and space. As one manifestation, notions about Standard English, whether that means a variety of written English or some idea about accentless spoken English, are purely political in the sense that they exist only because those in privileged positions—teachers, editors of newspapers and magazines, television network executives, court judges—dictate their terms.

Where one culture's status positions it in a situation of control over the form and content of institutions and social processes, that culture imposes its authority in special ways. The term *dominant ideology* is used to characterize this situation. In multicultural societies, there is often one dominant culture, whose ideology shapes much of public life. Ideology, essentially, is the set of cultural practices and codes of meaning used in a culture. Dominant ideology guides conceptions of reality through repetition of preferred, privileged practices treated as though they were "natural." This control of meaning relegates other cultural systems to the margins by making their meaning systems seem wrong, deviant, unimportant, primitive, or even invisible.

In the U.S. multicultural context, we see cultural ideology at work in the way it constructs and maintains discourse practices in institutional contexts such as work, school, government, and law. Increasingly, ideology gains its force from the media of mass communication—television, advertising, popular music.

No person—mainstream or marginalized—can command all of the cultures and their corresponding language systems, but varying degrees of cultural mindedness and intercultural communication competence offer promise for bridging communication differences and difficulties that occur in moments of cultural complexity. These abilities are most likely to arise from a good grasp of the relationship between culture and communication and from an understanding of the way in which ideology privileges the discourses of certain cultural systems over others.

Axioms in the Language-Centered Perspective on Culture

The Language-Centered Perspective on Culture, which frames our consideration of language diversity in the United States, is grounded in six axioms. Together, these axioms form the context for understanding language as a cultural resource.

1. *Cultural inherency of communication: All communication, whether verbal or nonverbal, occurs within cultural frameworks.* Because communication arises within the cultural frameworks of participants, it is neither neutral nor objective but, rather, thickly cultured. Donal Carbaugh's (1990) distinctions between *cultural* and *intercultural* communication convey the two major ways in which cultural frameworks contextualize communication. Cultural communication occurs when culture is shared by the communicative participants. Intercultural communication occurs when the participants do not have full command of one another's cultural patterns or discourses and must somehow communicate across the divide.

2. *Tacit knowledge: Individuals possess tacit knowledge of the cultural systems through which they communicate.* Humans are rule-using and rule-following beings, and they learn their cultures by internalizing the sets of rules that underlie human conduct. The ability to organize behavior through elaborate rule systems allows for cultural communication to occur relatively spontaneously because the rules function out-of-awareness and exist as tacit, that is, unspoken, knowledge. Residing in the cultural mainstream, especially in a country where equality and equal opportunity are constitutional rights, tends to obscure the fact that human action is culturally founded and, thus, culturally variable. As Clifford Geertz (1983) incisively summarizes it: "Given the given, not everything else follows. Common sense is not what the mind cleared of cant spontaneously apprehends; it is what the mind filled with presuppositions . . . concludes" (p. 84). The presuppositions form tacit knowledge. A Norwegian or Swedish Lutheran in Minnesota does not need

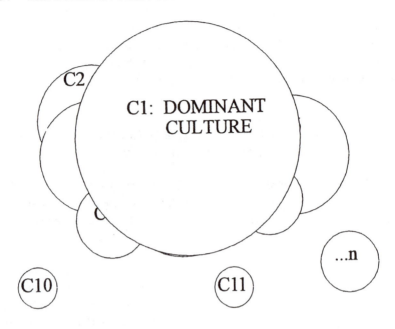

Figure 3.4. Effect of Cultural Ideology

to remind him- or herself that restraint and reserve are ways of life; demeanor and deportment of this ilk are simply "common sense." Common sense resides deeply in culture.

3. *Ideology and cultural marginalization: In multicultural societies, the ideology of dominant cultural groups produces patterns of cultural abstractions, cultural artifacts, and cultural language practices that displace, silence, or marginalize other cultural groups.* Ideology suppresses marginalized cultures through both tacit and explicit means. Because individuals possess complex tacit knowledge allowing them to function within their cultural communities, they can conduct their daily affairs without a sense that they live cultured lives. In this way, those enculturated into dominant groups take their ideas and interaction patterns for granted. Consider Figure 3.4, in which C1 as represented in Figure 3.2 has been imposed over the cultural groups that are clearly shown in the first of the two figures.

An everyday example will demonstrate the process shown in Figure 3.4. When a television script writer develops the story line for a soap opera or prime-time drama, she or he usually imports dominant ideology into the representation of family organization and gender relations. It may never occur to the script writer that other cultural practices are not only possible but viable within the viewing "public." Similarly, when a teacher defines a good student as one who actively participates in class discussion, she or he discounts the cultural practices of groups where such behavior is seen as disrespectful and inappropriate.

The power of dominant ideology explains why many of the discourse patterns discussed in this book are either unknown to or not well understood by white, non-Hispanic Americans. Those in dominant cultural groups rarely need to know much about the cultural practices of marginalized groups.

4. *Knowledge at the margins: Groups that have been dominated, subjugated, marginalized, made the object of prejudice and bigotry, discriminated against, or otherwise held in relatively powerless positions possess more explicit awareness of the components of their own and other cultural systems.* This axiom is a kind of corollary of the one just discussed. An example shows the implication of this axiom: A Latina with dark hair and complexion who speaks Spanish-accented English and works in a predominantly Anglo environment typically knows that she is different, not only in these ethnic markers, but also in manner of communication, preferences for food and clothing, family values, and so forth. At work, "common sense" must for her give way to common sense*s*, which may or may not lead the individual to deliberately and consciously *code-switch* among language varieties and discourses that differ in their cultural foundations. Although this type of code-switching is usually described as *situational* (Hudson, 1980), it is more appropriately an example of *cultural code-switching* and, thus, of intercultural communication where only one side has any genuine knowledge of the cultural differences involved. Cultural code-switching requires at least some degree of explicit knowledge about the cultures from which one is shifting and the cultures to which one is shifting.

This axiom about cultural knowledge at the margins is similar to the premise of what is termed *standpoint epistemologies* in feminism theory. A *standpoint* gives focus to what one knows depending on where one is situated in relation to dominant and subordinated groups. This idea, as expressed by philosopher Sandra Harding (1993), applies well to the United States:

In societies stratified by race, ethnicity, class, gender, sexuality, . . . the *activities* of those at the top both organize and set limits on what persons who perform such activities can understand about themselves and the world around them. . . .

In contrast, the activities of those at the bottom of such social hierarchies can provide starting points for thought . . . from which humans' relations with each other and the natural world can become visible. (p. 54)

The standpoint of the marginalized, in short, must be cognizant of the cultural practices of the ideologically dominant simply out of necessity.

5. *Historicity and innovation: Culture and its discourses are both passed from one generation to another (i.e., historically founded) and constantly revised and changed (i.e., innovative).* What makes cultures so resilient are their historical foundations. Yet, cultures are dynamic rather than static because people are constantly adapting to circumstances, new ideas, and innovations. The creative impulse in people also keeps culture on the move, vitiating static predictability.

Most often, the younger generations bring changes to the culture, which evolves with generational cohorts. Looking back on the recent history of almost any cultural grouping reveals generational contrasts, for example, in values, communication, and expressive forms. Several examples from mainstream U.S. culture demonstrate this cultural dynamic. Values have shifted as environmental exploitation has given way to greater environmental awareness and protection because of the impact of human action on nature. Terms such as *ecology* and *recycling* are now commonplace, even to the point of being used to express ideas metaphorically, as in the phrase, *recycling ideas*. Taking another example, sexual conduct has moved from extensive premarital prohibitions reinforced by all major religious groups, to much greater openness in sexual expression during the 1970s and 1980s because of both a relaxed youth culture and access to birth control, to the present concern about more restricted sexual practices because of the AIDS epidemic. Earlier terms such as *premarital sex* and *open marriage* still exist, but today's prominent semantic notions encode an age of concern about *safe sex* and *sexual preference*.

6. *Cultural interinfluences: In multicultural societies, cultures influence one another, which includes the interinfluence of discourse systems.* Although it is commonplace for people to notice the differences between cultures when they are in close contact with one another, it is also the case that sheer locale, proximity, and intermingling of peoples create a condition

of mutual influence among differing cultures. Cultural groups change in part because of their situatedness within larger cultural complexes. This process has been described above as cultural creolization. Cultural contact also influences the retention and conscious conservation of certain cultural practices, as might be the case when people refuse to give up their regional dialects and associated meanings even after living in another locale for a long time.

Immigrants provide a compelling case for the simultaneous permanence and change within cultural systems. Once in their new country, immigrant groups often develop *revised cultural patterns* based on the importation of the home culture as it is accommodated to the new environment and cultural situation. Parminder Bhachu's (1985) analysis of Sikhs who migrated from India first to East Africa and then to Britain provides a fascinating illustration of transportation and adaptation of marriage and dowry *(daaj)* patterns through migration. My own suburban locale west of Boston provides a timely example. A substantial number of Brazilians have settled in the area, and as their numbers have grown, so have their venues: banks, beauty and barber shops, auto mechanics, restaurants, each of which adapts to the surrounding culture.

One line of language research closely related to this axiom of cultural interinfluence deals with "language contact" and borrowings from one language into another (Haugen, 1950; Heath, 1984; McMahon, 1994). For example, Cuban Spanish has been influenced by American English; yet, Cubans living in the United States remain loyal to Spanish and what it symbolizes about cultural identity.

Implications

Together, these axioms point to elaborate and intricate cultural relations among many different groups in the United States. The Language-Centered Perspective on Culture leads us to think in complex ways about the discourses we hear and the cultural practices underlying these language variations. When discourses differ from one another, underlying codes of meaning differ too. As we consider some of the major cultural groupings in the United States, the discursive implications of cultural multiplicity will become evident.

In each of the chapters that follow, the workings of the cultural model presented here become evident. We will see the cultural integrity that provides the rationale for differing patterns of discourse and different interpretative systems for understanding discourse. The influence of dominant cultural ideology in silencing marginalized discourses compels us to look beneath the surface of our cultural diversity to discover the different realities and voices represented by that diversity.

PART

II

Locating Cultural Discourses

4

Gendered Discourses

At birth and even sooner, our biological distinctiveness as male or female
announces what is likely the first category of identity that will influence
our social identities for a lifetime. Intense interest surrounds the unknown
of whether the fetal being will be a boy or a girl. The relatively recent
possibility of knowing a baby's sex prior to birth through ultrasound techniques is welcomed by some parents, family, and friends because it helps
focus choices for names, clothing, and colors. Gender-specific names
quickly divide baby girls from boys, with the relatively small overlap of
names clearly an exception (names like Sean, Jessie, and Taylor for both boys
and girls); in fact, the usual practice when names are gender-equivalent is to
mark them in some way as nonequivalent, as in Eric and Erica or Alex(ander)
and Alexa(ndra). In the United States, the gender of a baby continues, no less
than in the past, to be symbolized by assigning pink to girls and blue to boys,
and reserving green and yellow as "safe" colors for those situations where
gender is not known. If ultrasound news is available, shoppers for baby
showers can simply gravitate to pinks and bows for girl babies or blues and
"little slugger" patches for boy babies. The centrality of gender also shows
up on birth announcements and balloons proclaiming "It's a boy!" or "It's a
girl!"—each appropriately accented in blue or pink. Imagine receiving a card

in the mail proclaiming "It's a baby!"—or an "It's a boy!" card with a pink ribbon laced through its borders.

Beyond the cultural naming practices and color coding for girls and boys, cultural constructions of gender convey language coding—coding in how boys and girls learn to speak, in how a gendered person is spoken to, and in elaborate constructions of the meaning of gender within its cultural context. Some linguistic markers of gender blatantly proclaim a world of contrasts: genderized pronouns in English *(he, she; her, his)* are taken for granted, yet such contrasts need not be marked in language; men curse more frequently and with a more elaborated sexual lexicon than do women, and no advances in "equality of the sexes" obliterate the differential consequences for women and men of being foul-mouthed. Other linguistic markers of gender are more subtle: In mixed-gender conversations, it is men and not women who talk more; although superficially parallel, the terms *boy* and *girl, lady* and *gentleman* engage nonparallel domains of meaning such that in American English, we would never hear "girls will be girls" as a gender equivalent to "boys will be boys"; or "bag gentleman" as a gender equivalent to "bag lady."

In this chapter, I address gender both as a meaning system made coherent within particular cultural contexts and as an organizing principle for grouping individuals in contrasting ways that produce over long periods of time what are at root genderized cultures. Gender groups differ from other cultural groups in one significant respect. Unlike ethnic, racial, and nationality groups—each with their histories embedded in geographic locales—gender is everywhere. U.S. citizens of Italian, African, Mexican, Cuban, Iranian, Japanese, and Korean descent, for example, possess distinctive ancestral genealogies as well as geographic and linguistic histories. These sometimes form the basis for neighborhood or regional clustering. Social class or status too has its own kind of history and geography. With very few exceptions, housing units for people of clearly different economic resources cannot be found in close proximity to one another. Distinctiveness in place and locale are reified through idioms for bad and good neighborhoods such as "the wrong side of the tracks" or having a "good address." There are, however, no analogous "gender neighborhoods" populated primarily by girls and women or boys and men. Gerda Lerner (1979), the preeminent historian of women, captured this fact a number of years ago in her observation that women "are distributed through every group and class in society . . . .[and] are more closely allied to men of their own group than they are to women of other classes and races" (p. 170). Gender then, is *embedded* in other sociocultural groupings and, as such, permeates social life. As a result, gender's powerful force in every aspect of living can easily be misunderstood, minimized, or missed completely.

Regardless of the reasons for downplaying discussions of gender, the historical pattern of male dominance over knowledge, institutions, and discourse; the division of males and females according to public and private spheres and same-sex socialization patterns, beginning in early childhood; and the commodification of sex and gender all manifest themselves in today's society. On close inspection, language use reveals much of the gender map that guides us every day.

I place this chapter on gender prior to other considerations of cultural diversity in language simply because gender is marked throughout all other language diversity. Even when the focus is on race or ethnicity, gender always marks and is marked through language. As Mary Bucholtz (1995) puts it, "any performance of ethnicity is also simultaneously a performance of gender" (p. 364).

In this chapter, gender differences in language use are explored by considering (a) the nature of gender cultures, (b) explanations and theories regarding gender differences in language use, (c) gendered discourse styles and strategies, (d) transgressions against gender, and (e) resistance to gendered discourse through social action. Although gender differences *within* different cultural groups are considered, that topic is also taken up in subsequent chapters (like most areas of study, however, scant literature is available on nonwhite populations in the United States). The gender patterns discussed here are typical of many males or females, but they are neither universal nor uniformly distributed. Many people fit the patterns, some do not, and others actively challenge them. The patterns also vary along dimensions of ethnic, race, age, social class, and regional identities.

Gender Cultures

Understanding that women and men are culturally differentiated is central to the logic of this chapter. Because the concept of culture has long been anchored in nationality, race, or ethnicity, an appreciation for gender as a fundamental organizing dynamic of culture requires a shift in thinking. The Language-Centered Perspective on Culture assists in understanding how culture can be said to be gendered. Even though men and women have lived, worked, and reared families together, their life experiences have differed markedly over time. Although life experiences are not differentiated in the same manner in different cultures, times, and places, we know of no national or ethnic culture where gender does not influence social relations and material conditions.

Consider two quite different gender systems operating in the United States. The first is the more publicly known: the dominant system of cultural practices found throughout middle-class Eurowhite society. The main factors polarizing men and women in this system are (a) the historic division of labor, which prescribed women's primary responsibility for hearth and home and men's for providing economic resources for the family; (b) women's positioning in the restricted, private orb of life (as in the case of "house-wives") and men's outside the home in work and other public activity; (c) the de facto segregation that placed men and women in different jobs, such that women continue to make up the bulk of secretaries, nurses, and elemen-tary/secondary schoolteachers, whereas men overwhelm the numerical counts of laborers, *master* trades*men* (the male terms marked in italics are revealing), politicians and government officials, and engineers.

The second gender system is one that exists for African Americans, with its characteristics deeply embedded in the historical circumstances of slav-ery. Writing about African American women, Patricia Hill Collins (1990) pinpointed three major forces from slavery that shaped the identity of African American women in ways that permeate their identities today: (a) exploita-tion as laborers, (b) denial to them of privileges accorded to white men and to "womanhood," and (c) channeling their images into narrow categories of "mammies," "Jezebels," and "breeder women." Postslavery, black women never shared in the white, middle-class gender system relegating women literally and symbolically to the domestic, private sphere; economic needs never allowed such a "luxury." The tradition of African American women, thus, includes labor outside the home to support their families. The degrada-tion of black men during slavery, the history of associating them with uncontrolled sexual instinct and the rape of white women, reducing them to brawn and "boy" rather than brain and "man," produced inaccessibility to Eurowhite models of maleness (dominance over women, breadwinner status, political participation, and so on). This continues today to shape the particu-larities of gender relations among African Americans. In short, many aspects of the gender system among African Americans sharply contrast with the dominant gender system in the United States.

Dominant gender ideology places different restrictions, controls, and possibilities on males and females, who in turn elaborate cultural practices both directly supportive of that ideology and sometimes contradictory to it. Looking at gender within the cultural model developed in Chapter 3 can help clarify how it is that gender is both embedded within particular cultural systems and constitutive of particular cultural systems. Take military systems as one concrete illustration of how this works. Military systems foster and enforce definitions of masculinity and femininity; they operate on a day-to-day level with gender as a meaning system that deeply influences the association of masculinity (and thus men) with the military and militarism such that women (and thus femininity) are excluded, marginalized, or accorded restricted roles. Cynthia Enloe (1989), a political scientist, offers an extensive analysis of how militarism works as a gendered process and how militarism and military practices create particular identities and roles for men and women—both within and outside the military. We hear commonly about policy debates "within" the military on whether or not women should be assigned to combat duty, but there are also gender roles that are created "outside" the military such as that of "military wife" or "sweetheart."

Thinking about gender and culture from a second perspective highlights what happens when gender meanings and practices become polarized. When long-standing (even if always changing) cultural systems continuously produce dualities between male and female, boy and girl, man and woman, then the resulting gender identities facilitate the elaboration of gender cultures such that when people take up the identity of man or woman, they also enter into cultural practices that are themselves gendered; the product is gender cultures. Like any cultural system in a cultural complex, gender cultures are porous, permeable, and fluid. Gendered discourses, as illustrated in the following sections of this chapter, are founded in gendered speech communities that develop within particular but larger cultural frameworks. Like participants in any speech community, gender-identified and -identifying individuals participate in varying ways and in varying degrees with those of similar identity.

Gender, thus, organizes meanings within particular groups, but gender also is the organizing principle that establishes and perpetuates gender cultures. In a particular time-place context, "the two sexes" participate together in meshed cultural practices but also in co-cultures literally and symbolically separated from one another by barriers (as identified in Chapter 2) that are more or less rigid. For example, even today, women's and men's lives continue to be differently balanced between the public and private spheres, with women's activities and associations, *even in the context of work outside the home*, focused heavily on home, family, and domestic details, and men's more focused on venues external to the home—whether experienced directly or vicariously (recent data reveal that, on average, women spend 35.1 hours per week compared to men's 17.4 dealing with domestic responsibility; Shapiro, 1997). In more postmodern terms, the domestic orb of women in the house occurs in conjunction with the sports-oriented orb of men. Flowing from these different spheres, women tend to orient to the more personal dimensions of living and to family maintenance, whereas men orient more to the external world of activities, spectatorship, and group contacts. Even when the activity involved is external to the home, we see mothers and fathers enacting different cultural roles: The "soccer mom" drives her kids to and from practices and games, makes sure the uniforms are clean and water bottles filled, and once at the soccer field tends to congregate with other moms to talk about the kids' school, meal preparation, and so forth. The term "soccer dad" does not really exist; the dads are either not there (especially for practices), are coaching, or otherwise engage in the business aspects of team organization.

Public conceptions about gender cultures have been framed more as mystery than as culture, with the sense of mystery leading men and women alike to wonder why members of the opposite sex behave as they do. The overwhelming public response to Deborah Tannen's (1990b) book, *You Just Don't Understand: Men and Women in Conversation,* tells us something about this quest. The book appeals to both women and men because of its tantalizing lure that between its covers lie insights into the divide between men and women and—we hope—a bridge joining the differences. For many of her readers, Tannen paints a validating picture of the frustrations of interacting with the opposite sex, which she sees as a challenge of "cross-cultural communication."

Gendered Cultural Abstractions

The contemporary women's movement, which began in the late 1960s, brought to light many aspects of women's lives that provide evidence for differences in the systems of abstraction used by males and females participating in mainstream cultural practices in the United States. Although the focus of the early period of modern feminism was on sex equity, what evolved was a claim not so much that beneath the history of sex discrimination, men and women are fundamentally the same but, rather, that the contributions of women in all walks of life are valuable in their own right. This analysis suggested that it is not just a matter of gross numerical imbalance of men over women in most domains of public life and employment but also a matter of different ways of understanding what men and women do and say and also a matter of the absence of qualitatively different contributions that might be expected from women. For example, women vote, but men both set political agendas stemming from their own political philosophies and hold most of the significant political and governmental positions; women read, but almost all works considered "great literature" bear male authorship and male thinking; women sustain religious life and spiritual direction in their families, but ministry remains largely a male profession and theology with few exceptions a male province; women enjoy art and music, but what has been deemed "great" art and music again bear the signature of male creators, critics, and theorists. In these domains and others, it is also significant that the male perspective (which in the United States is also Eurowhite) has been normative for judging the worth of something, establishing conventions, and providing intellectual and scholarly contributions.

Public culture—high and everyday—proclaims male definition because of the public roles that men have held in virtually all fields. Yet, from philosophy to painting (on canvas or on houses) to plumbing to politics and across music, medicine, and ministry, the public conception of culture largely erases this male control by culturally constructing it as gender neutrality—a neutrality in which these endeavors are not seen as engendered. Putting gender into a cultural perspective helps us grasp how a person's gendered position typically fosters somewhat differing systems of abstractions for most males and females. It also helps us see how the hegemony of a dominant culture can keep a subordinate culture invisible and inaudible—even when that subordinate culture is not in the numerical minority.

Recall that a cultural system of abstractions, as described in Chapter 2, includes values, morals, ethics, conceptions of right and wrong and of good and evil, notions about logic, conceptions of justice and laws, rituals, and the spiritual and religious beliefs of the culture's participants. Although it would be impossible (and dangerous) to posit a simple dualism between gender cultures polarized into male and female, no social location exists where gender does not function to partition social relations. Evidence of male and female differences in the system of abstractions spans a broad range of human activity from literature to politics to moral reasoning. In recent years, a number of provocative analyses have explored a range of philosophical issues pertaining to how it is that women reason, think, and know (Falmagne,

1997; Harding, 1991; Nye, 1988). These analyses arise from intellectual deficiencies in the prevailing ideas about these subjects—all of which claim to address humans but are limited by their implicit male gender specificity.

As the contributions of women writers, musicians, and artists have been recovered to create a history of women, so too have narratives and voices differing from the official published histories that have been written and taught for decades. The history of men is filled with great heroes and major figures in conflict with one another, often referred to as the history of great men and important events. Conveying quite a different story, women's history features much more of everyday life, family, and interpersonal relationships (Cott, 1977; Smith-Rosenberg, 1985). These two sides of history reflect corresponding domains of contrasting values, morals, and percepts: winning and losing versus cooperation, individual achievement versus interpersonal good, segregated roles versus holistic functioning. These contrasts reappear in recent research that documents gendered ways of thinking. Much of this scholarship engages a particular Western discourse to address the experiences of Eurowhite men and women, which is its main limitation. Yet this work also helps us think through the genderized cultural practices occurring every day in ethnic and national cultural contexts markedly distinctive from one another. The work covered here, then, is included not to make a universal claim about women's or men's worldviews and ways of thinking but to give a particularized set of examples from the dominant U.S. cultural frame.

Of particular interest for understanding the abstraction systems of males and females is work on various levels of mental functioning. Here, I briefly consider selected work on moral development and reasoning, epistemology, and consciousness.

Psychologist Carol Gilligan (1982) became known in the early 1980s for her pathbreaking studies on moral reasoning in girls. Working with Lawrence Kohlberg, one of the most prominent figures in moral development research, led Gilligan to challenge stage theories in psychology that depict moral reasoning as moving through a certain and regular succession of steps culminating in formal and abstract thought and revolving around a morality of rights and rules. Her insight challenged prevailing conclusions in this research domain that girls often fall short of the culminating stages in moral thinking. Because boys and men were the subjects of moral development research, Gilligan argued that the theory was not of human development but, rather, of male development. Gilligan's examination of girls and women revealed a different view of morality revolving around care, conflicting responsibilities, context, and narrative thought. Gilligan found female morality to turn on understanding relationships and responsibilities, contrasted with male morality, which turns on understanding rights and rules at an abstract level. These differences are often displayed in discourse, which then symbolically creates the sociocultural identities of male and female. Men speak in metaphors of hierarchy, Gilligan concluded, stressing individuation and autonomy, whereas women speak in metaphors of web, stressing complex attachments and interconnections among people and events. Gilligan's book title, *In a Different Voice*, carries the kernel idea of her work: that women speak in a voice different from men.

In sum, Gilligan's (1982) thinking and research established a basis for understanding the ways in which men and women reason differently about moral problems and dilemmas. She demonstrated that gendered life fosters diverging visions of moral situations and different worldviews of thinking about morality. Men hold a *justice perspective* compared to the *care perspective* of women, which Virginia Held (1993) summarizes as follows:

> The justice perspective emphasizes universal principles and individual conscience. The care perspective pays more attention to people's needs and to the relations between actual people; it considers how these relations can be kept in good condition or repaired if damaged. (p. 66)

The problem with Gilligan's (1982) work lies, expectedly, in the relative homogeneity of those participating in her research and from whose experience she built theory. Looking back, that limitation is understandable based on the academic paradigm that she challenged. Kohlberg's influential work focused on white boys but generalized to all adolescents; Gilligan's corrective faulted such generalization by showing its fallacy when applied to girls.

In later work, others have joined Gilligan in broadening the project on girlhood (Taylor, Gilligan, & Sullivan, 1995) by focusing on issues of voice and silence among girls identified as African American, Caribbean, Latina, Portuguese, Irish American, and Italian American who are "at risk." One of the conclusions of this more recent study is that although the girls who were interviewed over a 3-year period demonstrated the same kind of vibrancy as girls in earlier research, they also faced a kind of double bind wrought by the risks of speaking their experience. They felt isolated and were at risk not only because of their particular social position but because of issues facing girls more generally, especially the risk of not being heard, here magnified because of these girls' marginalized, social positions:

Girls in the study live in a territory between voice and silence: If they continue to speak from their experience they may find that their voice is out of relationship, too loud, off key. If they remain silent they are in immediate danger of disappearing. (Taylor et al., 1995, p. 202)

Different theories have been proposed for why it is that girls and women develop different guiding principles, priorities, and values—in short, different systems of cultural abstraction in comparison to their boy/men counterparts. Some maintain that the different moral perspective of women is sited in their role as mothers, which facilitates "maternal thinking" (Ruddick, 1989). Ruddick suggests that what is culturally labeled "maternal instinct" (reflecting a sense of biological origins of maternal naturalness) is, in fact, socially developed through the location of women in domestic caregiving roles. Others address the bonds of female friendship, which are formed through caring, intimacy, and self-disclosure outside the maternal and familial context (Johnson, 1996; Johnson & Aries, 1983b; Raymond, 1986). Although maternity may in some sense be the first or original condition of greater caring and intimacy on the part of many women, a broad range of culturally focused female activities, including friendship and familial life, likely underlies the proclivity for caring and intimacy.

One explanation for the culturally focused gender pattern in thinking that has gained broad public attention comes from Tannen (1990b), whose work was previously noted. In discussing why women and men often understand things differently, she emphasizes women's greater enmeshment in the world of *connection,* which is linked with *intimacy,* contrasted to men's enmeshment in the world of *status,* which is linked with *independence.* In the world of women, "individuals negotiate complex networks of friendship, minimize differences, try to reach consensus, and avoid the appearance of superiority, *which would highlight differences* [italics added}"; in the world of men, "a primary means of establishing status is to tell others what to do, and taking orders is a marker of low status" (p. 26). This idea resembles the early work of Gilligan as well.

Another line of work relevant to the systems of abstraction in women and men focuses on epistemology. Epistemology deals with the theory of knowledge, engaging questions such as what counts as knowledge and on what basis can a claim of knowledge be made. Traditional philosophical approaches to knowledge have been based on many of the same premises as the universalist perspective on culture, which was described in Chapter 3. In this approach, the imagined, ideal, disembodied knower is exalted—a view not unlike that of the "ideal speaker-hearer" in Chomsky's linguistic theory. Traditional, mainstream Western epistemology has embraced the assumption that knowledge claims should be devoid of particular people, circumstances, or locations by centralizing the ideals of rationality and objectivity. It is against that tradition that views of gender and epistemology have been developed.

Through the work of—largely—feminist philosophers but also those in other fields, the study of knowledge has been opened in recent years to address the exclusion of perspectives on knowledge other than those lodged in formal objectivist philosophy. Specifically, the project of feminist epistemology stresses *variability* rather than *universality* in what is regarded as knowledge and its justification. Subjectivity, understood as the person's location and circumstances (not as the biased, emotional viewpoint so often denigrated in the social sciences) has been considered (Code, 1993), with the most prominent perspective being standpoint epistemology. Sandra Harding (1993), a major figure in the standpoint perspective, articulates four characteristics of the subjects (knowers) of knowledge in this perspective: (a) knowers are "embodied and visible"; (b) objects, just like knowers, are socially constructed; (c) "communities and not primarily individuals produce knowledge"; and (d) knowers are "multiple, heterogeneous, and contradictory" (pp. 63-65). Although standpoint epistemology has been critiqued as leading to an overly relativistic account of knowledge, this problem can be overcome through positing the kind of community-based knowledge stipulated by Harding rather than an "anything goes" perspective.

One example of research on women's epistemology can be found in the work of Mary Field Belenky and associates (Belenky, Clinchy, Goldberger, & Tarule, 1986), who reported on interviews with 135 rural and urban U.S. women across the age, social class, educational, and ethnic spectrum. From their interviews, they extracted five epistemological perspectives, also called "ways of knowing." The most frequent emphasized *subjective knowledge*—a finding in clear contrast to notions of detachment and objectivity. Their classification system along with the percentage of women in each category is shown in Table 4.1.

Of particular interest across the groups was the investigators' discovery that women expressed growth as "gaining a voice" and their epistemological premises in "metaphors suggesting speaking and listening" (p. 18). The latter they contrasted to the tendency of men to use metaphors such as light and vision.

TABLE 4.1 Categories for "Women's Ways of Knowing": Belenky and Associates

	Knowledge Type	Percentage of Women
Silence	Viewing the self as without voice; passive, reactive; others as powerful	few
Received	Discounting self-experience and listening to others to receive knowledge	9
Subjective	Listening for the authority of the "inner voice"; seeing truth as subjective rather than universal	46
Procedural	Stressing reason and skills acquisition for achieving knowledge	24
Constructed	Integrating different voices to construct knowledge through a process in which the knower participates	18

SOURCE: Belenky et al. (1986).

These several lines of inquiry suggest that the abstraction systems for women's cultures and men's cultures show distinctive orientations. In the examples cited, women tend to think, judge, and reason with a greater orientation to situational complexity, personal concern, contingencies, and distributed good. Men orient more to detachment, formal knowledge and percepts, status, self-worth, and sharply delineated roles. Although not absolute nor the same in its realization across differing ethnic and racial cultures, gendered thought must be reckoned with if we are to understand the foundations for women's and men's discourse systems and the construction of gender through discourse systems.

Gendered Cultural Artifacts

The cultural products associated with men and women in the United States convey gender attributes as part of their message. Gendered artifacts exist in two categories: those imposed on women and men and those created by women and men. In the age of mass-marketed images, some cultural products are designed to appeal to one sex or the other (such as gender-segmented magazines like *GQ* and *Vogue*, fishing paraphernalia for men, and makeup for women). In this sense, they are imposed artifacts. Little girls do not create Barbie dolls nor little boys Ninja warriors, and few men (even fewer women) create the gender-segmented products that define commodity culture—clothing, jewelry, cologne, shaving instruments, and even some cars (Nissan, for instance, manufactured two versions of the Maxima: the women's version, equipped with automatic transmission and sedan styling, compared to the men's version, equipped with 5-speed standard transmission, rear spoiler, and sport design features). Such products serve to construct gender and to create and reinforce the need to cultivate certain gender identities.

Artifacts that are expressive of one gender or the other's experience and meaning systems reveal complex dimensions of cultural meaning far beyond what appears in the images of mass culture. Operating within a gendered society, men and women often express their gendered perspectives by creating markedly different artifacts or styles within the same artifact classification. Although separating imposed and created artifacts is somewhat artificial simply because they reciprocally influence each other, focusing on women's and men's creations helps us learn how different gendered experiences lead to different forms of expression. Visual art and literature illustrate how this works.

Taken broadly, visual art includes media such as painting, printmaking, ceramics, sculpture, and photography, but it also includes needlework, quilting, weaving, and basket making—all of which mainstream U.S. culture relegates to the lesser status of "craft." Regardless of the value placed on certain cultural productions (*fine* versus *applied*, *high* versus *low*; *highbrow* versus *popular*), all such productions demonstrate the movement of symbolic meaning into cultural practice.

If we look at the broad division between art and craft, we notice that crafts such as needlepoint, weaving, collage, and ceramic painting are practiced mainly by women, or by minority cultures, such as the Native American tribes that produce pottery, jewelry, and woven materials. The fine arts singled out for praise are largely of male expression, although this is gradually changing.

Judy Chicago provides a fascinating case of the woman committed to producing women's art that represents women's experience in an artistic world of men and male ideas. She became well known in 1979 for the massive, collectively produced ceramic work called *The Dinner Party*, which includes 39 place settings arranged on a triangular table, each representing a woman from history. The plates are placed in temporal order around the table, progressing in their boldness of color, design, and three-dimensionality (see Chicago, 1979). Chicago's next project, completed in 1984, involved 150 needleworkers who produced "The Birth Project," which includes 80 birth images.

Judy Chicago came to this form of collective artistic expression featuring women's media and themes after struggling with male art forms and finally deciding "I could no longer pretend in my art that being a woman had no meaning in my life; my entire experience was being shaped by it" (quoted in Foss & Foss, 1991, p. 231). She was, in short, bringing women's artistic sensibility to the public eye.

Literature, although a form of language expression, is a cultural production as well and, thus, an artifact form once its products exist. Like other artifact forms, literature carries gender code. More women than men write about themes of relationship, interior life, personal struggle, and intimate and romantic relationships, whereas more men than women create scenarios situated in war, business, politics, nature, and space.

As women writers gain more stature in public culture, the mark of gender on fiction becomes increasingly evident. In the genre of the novel, women often write from the "inside out" by exploring minutiae of daily life, inter-action and conversation, and the nature of personal identity. Consider two prominent women writers. Pulitzer prizewinner Ann Tyler's novels (*Breathing Lessons, The Accidental Tourist*, and others) are close-up narratives of everyday family and friendship issues, of individual people and their inter-actions with one another. The settings are inside houses, cars, and restaurants. The "action" centers in conversation and the events of daily living. Amy Tan's writing gives voice to women in the context of their ethnicity. *The Joy Luck Club*, which is autobiographical, focuses on Chinese American women and their relationships to one another: mothers and daughters, female relatives, and friends. Tan's lens puts women's lives in the center where other perspec-tives would marginalize them. These are stories of everyday life, the meaning of interpersonal relationships, and the vicissitudes of identity. These authors differ markedly from American male writers, such as Norman Mailer and John Grisham, who have achieved broad recognition.

Gendered Language

Within the context of gendered abstractions and cultural artifacts, lan-guage and communication systematically create the symbolic spheres of women and men, establish gender identities in both explicit and subtle ways, and construct the foundation for relationships with those of the same and opposite sex. Language-in-use also re-creates gender, both by maintaining its past patterns and by changing or challenging discourse patterns perpetu-ally taken for granted.

In the past 25 years, a vast amount of theory and research has emerged that explores and explains how men and women use or relate to language differently. Does sex role socialization still foster different language norms for boys and girls? Do women and men use language differently? What happens when women and men interact with one another? I do not deal exhaustively with all these questions in this chapter but do consider representative examples of scholarly inquiry. Before turning to the specific overview of work on the ways in which gender organizes discourse, I consider several lines of theoretical thinking about gender and discourse. The theoretical approaches should be useful in interpreting the more specific research studies on gender and language that are discussed.

Theorizing Gender and Discourse

Cheris Kramarae (1989) aptly characterizes the study of gender (along with race and class) as concerned with hierarchies and with "difference as a result of inequalities" (p. 319). This does not imply, however, that the cultural systems of groups defined by inequalities are completely defined by those inequalities or that the cultural systems of such groups are themselves deficient or inferior.

In recent decades, many theories have been developed to explain gender and its effects. Among these, several significant lines of theorizing are important to the present project. Four topics are addressed: (a) comparison of two different approaches to positioning gender as a cultural organizer, (b) male construction of natural language, (c) the power of discourse in creating "sex" and "gender," and (d) resistance to gendered discourse.

Relativistic and Ideological Cultural Models

As with any analysis of culture, the approach to gender cultures can be developed as a neutral endeavor in which no or few judgments of political consequence are made or as an ideological critique in which the implications for power and the distribution of status are central elements.

Relativistic accounts of gender cultures propose that males and females are socialized differently into separate gender worlds. As a result, men and women view the world differently, think differently, enter and have different expectations for relationships, and speak differently. Tannen's (1990b) approach is the best-known relativistic account of gender cultures. She describes gender styles, uses the concept of culture and its extension to cross-cultural communication to anchor these styles, and encourages better understanding between the sexes through knowledge of their differences. She engages in no political or ideological analysis and offers no interpretations about the function of male conversational dominance and control. She concludes her book by reassuring her readers that "understanding genderlect improves relationships. Once people realize that their partners have different conversational styles, they are inclined to accept differences without blaming themselves, their partners, or their relationships" (p. 297). Tannen's apolitical perspective and others like it mask the role of dominant ideology in constructing codes of meaning for gender (see Tröemel-Plöetz, 1991). Uchida (1992), who characterizes the Tannen-type perspective as the "difference/cultural approach" (I prefer the term "relativistic cultural model"), sees its appeal resting exactly in its apolitical stance; that is, "it is culturally sensitive to both sexes, less susceptible to being interpreted as claiming female deficiency or to being accused of engaging in male bashing activities" (p. 553). This appeal is precisely the problem in the approach: ignoring the ideological dimension of cultural complexity.

Ideologically sensitive models of gender retain the notion of gender cultures but add the analysis of power and dominance. Psychologist Sandra Lipsitz Bem (1993) develops her approach to the construction of gender identity using the idea that children are enculturated into gender identities through the gender-polarizing schemes that are "embedded in cultural discourse and social practice," which then lead children, once knowledgeable of these schemes, to reproduce gender polarities in their developing identities (p. 139). But the child does not simply act out the gender polarities; because the dominant culture is what Bem (and others) call *androcentric* (male-centered), children's enculturation replicates the androcentrism built into the polarities. The individual, says Bem, "is a deeply implicated—if unwitting—collaborator in the social reproduction of male power" (p. 139).

The ideological model of gender cultures uncovers, then, the ways in which the elaboration of gender cultures as part of larger cultural organization systematically predisposes and constructs certain meanings and discourses for boys and girls, men and women. Individuals can resist and oppose particular versions of polarization and androcentrism, but they do so against a social world replete with conventional, ideologically saturated gender practices. This point is addressed more fully in the section on Resistance to Gendered Discourse. For now, one can say that engaging in gender resistance demands at least some recognition of the politics of gender, a recognition not explicit in the relativistic cultural model devoid of ideological interpretation.

Gendered Codes in Language

Another perspective on theorizing gender in discourse examines not the style of gendered language users but the language code itself. Posing the question, is English a male language, suggests there is something lurking in the history of English (and other languages) that bears gender coding.

Dale Spender (1980), in her book *Man Made Language*, develops the thesis that English is the creation of men, which means that women do not have a natural, native language because the linguistic systems they must master are male creations. Her thesis rests in cultural analysis:

> Historically, women have been excluded from the production of cultural forms, and language is, after all, a cultural form. . . . In fairly crude terms this means that the language has been made by men and that they have used it for their own purposes. (p. 52)

Although this position is overly deterministic in that all users of language are creative, it does unmask realities about the language code that might otherwise go unnoticed. American English, like other languages (especially those with written forms), *from a linguistic perspective* was standardized by men. Although standardization is always arbitrary, the standardizers who codified our languages were and largely continue to be men. Noah Webster, in first writing down the spellings and pronunciations of words in 1806, did not consult women about matters such as what words should be included and how they should be distinguished in pronunciation from British English. And it was certainly not women who decided that by convention *he* would be understood to mean both male and female (Bodine, 1975) or who elaborated an everyday language filled with sports metaphors.

Julia Penelope (1990) extends this analysis of the male control of language in her discussion of what she labels the Patriarchal Universe of Discourse (PUD). A universe of discourse, says Penelope, "provides descriptions of what the culture believes to be important categorizations of those objects, events, ideas, and beings which give them their 'place' in the world, and assigns certain values to behaviors" (pp. 36-37). She goes on to explain that the PUD selects what is talked about through male bias and that it also conveys meanings through specific syntactic structures that themselves carry meaning. The heavy use of passive voice in American English, for example, is a way of distancing the actor from his or her actions, as in "She was abused as a child by her uncle" versus "Her uncle abused her when she was a child." The elimination of agency works similarly, as in "She was abused as a child [by her uncle]," where the sentence is structurally acceptable without including reference to the perpetrator of the abuse. The cliché "Research shows that . . . " demonstrates another way in which agency is removed from language: Whose research? What kind of research? Done for what reason?

Metaphoric orientation is another way in which English can be said to be men's creation into which women must fit their experience. George Lakoff and Mark Johnson (1980) make a compelling case that American English is dramatically skewed in meaning through the use of certain metaphors: War and sports are the major ones. Both war and sport encode male experiences and domains, and both metaphor clusters involve competition.

> We *fight* for things that are important.
> We *take aim* at cavities.
> We try to *get to first base* with a person.
> A politician *scores a knockout* if he *wins* the debate.
> We *attack* the ideas of others.
> We like to be on the *offensive* rather than the *defensive*.

Expressions such as these arose from male experience. Although females use them, they repetitively encode ideas compatible with men's cultural experiences and incompatible with women's.

The position on gender-marked language can be seen as either *deterministic* or *formative*. The deterministic stance sees women as victims robbed of natural language and authentic speech. This stance seems too extreme and rigid. The formative stance recognizes the far-ranging influence that men in power across different social institutions wield over the syntactic, semiotic, and pragmatic patterns within language.

Discursive Constructions and "Sex" and "Gender"

The most common way of thinking about the distinction between sex and gender is to stipulate sex as biological and gender as cultural. One major challenge to this line of reasoning has been developed by Judith Butler (1990,

1993) who sees the category of sex as no less a cultural construction than that of gender. (Using quotation marks around "sex" and "gender" highlights Butler's assertion that these are products of discourse.) The concept of gender, in fact, allows the concept of sex to be understood as *natural* as opposed to cultural:

> Gender is not to culture as sex is to nature; gender is also the discursive/cultural means by which "sexed nature" or "a natural sex" is produced and established as "prediscursive," prior to culture, a politically neutral surface *on which* culture acts. (Butler, 1990, p. 7)

Her point implicates the idea of gender (as a cultural construction) in a kind of vicious cycle through which biological sex can be positioned as dichotomously natural in ways that are said to exist prior to language, that is, prediscursively. For Butler, then, both sex and gender exist in the social world as processes, not nouns. These processes privilege white male power by sustaining sex and gender as primary categories used to organize the world. She identifies the result of such categorization as "regulatory fictions that consolidate and naturalize the convergent power regimes of masculine and heterosexist oppression" (p. 33).

Key to understanding Butler's (1990) theory is the idea that gender exists through successive performances of what gender is understood to be. Gender is "performatively produced and compelled by the regulatory practices of gender coherence" (p. 24). By *performativity*, Butler means that the discourse can produce what it names, that is, the discourse can produce in a cultural context the "reality" of sex and gender. The production of sex and gender "happens through a certain kind of repetition and recitation" (Osborne & Segal, 1994, p. 33). It is more appropriate, then, to say that we *do* gender—over and over repetitively—than that we *are* gender identities. Sex (both the concept and the word) is both perceptual and discursive. Sex is culturally constructed through discourse, which in turn shapes the perception of sex as a unitary, largely natural, and uncomplicated concept. Butler does not deny the existence of the body, but she does insist that what we understand to be sex is only meaningful because it has been discursively created.

Because Butler's (1990) perspective features discourse as a cultural construction through which the status quo is supported—particularly the status quo of compulsory heterosexuality and the dualities of male/female, masculine/feminine necessary to sustain heterosexuality—she is especially interested in resistance to the discursive construction of sex and gender. One site that she writes about is drag, which explicitly plays with the doing of sex and gender by undoing what is compulsory in the cultural codes for sex and gender. Butler (1990) sees parody as a critical form of social resistance; drag uses parody to show how to break the compulsory dictates for sex and gender: "The parodic repetition of gender exposes as well the illusion of gender identity as an intractable depth and inner substance" (p. 146). Drag is an obvious example, but other forms of gender resistance exist—some of them less consciously calculated than others: enactments culturally labeled as *tomboy* and *sissy* (where the girl and boy, respectively, are perceived as inappropriately outside compulsory sex and gender practices); *butch* and *fem* in lesbian enactments where the goals might be to (further) elaborate on the arbitrary cultural constructions of feminine and masculine; but also more subtly resistive strategies, such as refusal by men to brag about sexual conquests over women or the refusal by "weaker women" (as in the "weaker sex") to seek help or solicitousness from "stronger men." In the latter case, the option for help seeking might be situationally appropriate, but the rejection is entered into mainly to transgress the expected gender repetition.

What Judith Butler offers, then, is a radical view on sex and gender as constructed through cultural practices lodged in discourse. One reading of her work is that she sees everything as discourse, everything as arbitrary and nothing as fixed: in short, a kind of relativism in any articulation of gender that undermines any construction of the self apart from cultural enactments and defies political action (in the Butlerian perspective, a protest, for example, about sexual harassment or gender equality in the workplace reconstructs sexual dualisms simultaneously with protesting the effects of those dualisms). Butler (1993) has attempted to address the relation between discourse and material aspects of gender by showing their interconnection; sex, she says, is "a cultural norm which governs the materialization of bodies" (p. 3) such that "language and materiality are fully embedded in each other . . . but never fully collapsed into one another, i.e., reduced to one another" (p. 69). What is done materially to construct gender (clothing, wages, spaces, cultural artifacts) grows from the larger discursive constructions of sex and gender— a process understandable within the perspective on culture developed in Chapter 3.

Thinking about how sex and gender are discursively constructed through repetitive enactments helps us understand gender as cultural practice and the evolution of gender-based cultures, but questions about selfhood, authentic identity, and the nature of the person remain. The problem of locating the self in Butler's theory is posed clearly by Seyla Benhabib (1995) whose questions are raised within the metaphor of cultural performance:

> If we are no more than the sum total of the gendered expressions we perform, is there ever any chance to stop the performance for a while, to pull the curtain down, and let it rise only if one can have a say in the production of the play itself? Isn't this what the struggle over gender is all about? (p. 21)

Thinking through issues of identity, self, and gender enactments relates directly to considerations of social and cultural change, the evolution of gender practices in relation to political action, and what can be done in the realm of everyday language-in-use to create gender differently or to un-create gender by challenging its legitimacy as an organizing construct in specific situations.

In the next section, I look at various ways in which gendered discourse evolves, functions in day-to-day life, and, thus, reveals cultural organization.

Discourse Patterns of Males and Females

As cultural beings, women and men discursively display their gender identities across the life span. From birth onward, how men and women speak, how they are spoken about and to, and their more general relation to discourse are profoundly fashioned through social experience. In this section, I first consider the concept of gendered folk linguistics and then evidence documenting the impact of gender on children's and adult language-in-use.

Folk linguistics. I begin with the notion that, as cultural beings, all of us learn and carry in our heads certain ideas about men's and women's speech. These ideas about speech (whether verifiable or not) comprise *folk linguistics*, or the ideas about speech held by those who are not specialists in the analysis of language. I frequently ask students in my class on language diversity to characterize the language and communication style of males and females by using words and phrases that come to mind quickly. Over more than a decade, women and men alike consistently characterize men in comparison to women as more direct, harsher, less willing to reveal emotions, more impersonal, more likely to use slang and swear words, more assertive, more likely to promote their own ideas, more sports-oriented, and so forth. When it comes to characterizing women's communication, they say that women tend to be less forceful, softer in voice, more personal, likely to talk a lot, oriented to trivia and gossip, more polite, more grammatically correct, less inclined to promote the self, and so forth. These consistencies convey a commonality in the folk linguistics of gendered language use for mass U.S. culture. What my students said in the late 1990s and what they said in the 1980s also mirror the results of studies accessing the perceptions and stereotypes of men's and women's speech done back in the mid-1970s (Kramer, 1977 [later citations to the same person are under the name of Kramarae]; Siegler & Siegler, 1976).

Although certainly a mixture of fact and fiction, folk linguistics guide individuals in framing perceptions, social expectations, and personal evaluations. For example, a folk linguistic perception might hold that soft voices are nonassertive or that gossip is trivial. Moreover, folk linguistics guide the training of girls and boys in the "ought-ness" of their language use: Girls "ought" to speak politely; boys "ought" to speak confidently.

The Language of Boys and Girls

As preschoolers, my two sons took great delight in an enactment that I call "We're girls." They presented themselves with dishtowels on their heads to signify long hair and gleefully exclaimed in unnaturally high-pitched, whiney voices, "We're girls! We're girls!" Naming many girls (and women) who had neither long hair nor high voices failed to dampen the boys' enactment; it was repeated many times, revealing their own folk linguistics of gendered (in this case girls') speech. Where had they gotten this representation of girls? Was it from friends? If so, from boys or girls? From teachers? From stories that had been read to them? From watching cartoons? Although we smugly exonerated the nuclear family as a teacher in this case, cultural learning about gender enactments spoke powerfully in their play behavior. The precise locale of learning is impossible to pinpoint simply because gender models abound. Our boys were already gender-saturated.

The tacit knowledge possessed by children about gendered language has been the focus of intriguing academic research. Elaine Andersen (1986) looked at children's folk linguistics when she studied the discourse produced in puppet situations where the children played the role of father, mother, or child in family, school, or medical situations. She found that 5-year-old girls and boys clearly distinguish the language of mothers and fathers in their enactments. Mothers' speech was portrayed as softer; more talkative, polite, and qualified; and filled with more endearments and baby talk; compared with fathers' speech, which was louder; more straightforward, forceful, and unqualified; and pitched more deeply. This research corresponds with what one hears from young children when they are play-acting: They force their voices into lower-pitched ranges when playing dads and men and into higher-pitched ranges when playing moms and women.

But how does gender manifest itself in the more mundane day-to-day discourse of young children? The picture appears to be one of early enculturation into gendered language patterns for topics spoken about, styles in same-sex interactions, and sex role-linked language in situations where girls and boys interact with one another.

Same-sex interaction. A number of studies compare the language patterns of preschool and early school-age boys and girls when interacting among themselves. In one study (Austin, Salehi, & Leffler, 1987), the interactions in preschool of 3- to 5-year-old children from middle- and working-class backgrounds revealed different speech characteristics for girls and boys. Girls' speech exhibited more devices that served to facilitate interaction and to reinforce what others said, both of which provide continuity for the interaction. Boys' speech was replete with devices to get attention and to initiate a line of activity. Similarly, Cook, Fritz, McCornack, and Visperas (1985), found preschool-age boys to be more assertive than girls in their spontaneous language use while playing together with non-sex-typed toys, such as puzzles. Topics also emerge in this age group in sex-typical fashion. Boys as young as 4 years have been found to talk more about sports and particular locations and places for things compared to girls, who talk more about identity, wishes, needs, and preschool activity itself (Haas, 1979). The studies of young children also show the greater proclivity of females for talking as an activity in itself and of males for concrete activities and physical action. Deborah Tannen (1990a) observed that second-grade girls easily talked together and shared personal stories; boys were uncomfortable being placed in a situation with nothing to do but talk. In a study of African American youth, Marjorie Harness Goodwin (1990) documented that girls from preschool onward spent more time talking than in any kind of play activity, which was not the case for boys.

An interesting set of analyses of "conflict talk" has been undertaken by Amy Sheldon (1990, 1992, 1993, 1996), who studied the discourse of 3- to 5-year-olds in day care centers. Although she found girls as well as boys to engage in conflict, their verbal strategies sounded quite different. The boys she observed handled conflict in a more heavy-handed fashion, expressing more self-assertive statements and dominance, whereas the girls used more collaborative discourse and negotiation as strategies to mitigate conflict (Sheldon, 1990, 1993).

Boys and girls together. There is less research that directly assesses the language behavior of boys and girls when they are together in interaction, but what does exist points to sex-role patterns that are strikingly conventional. Anita Esposito (1979) looked at mechanisms of dominance in the language of 3- and 4-year-olds playing together in a day care center. She found that boys interrupted girls twice as often as girls interrupted boys—a finding that will be of interest when adult language use is discussed. Haas (1979) found in studying 4-, 8-, and 12-year-olds that girls laughed more when interacting with boys than with each other. Almost 10 years later, Jacqueline Sachs (1987) reported that preschool girls soften their statements with an accompaniment of smiles.

It appears, then, that little girls and little boys demonstrate gender-linked language behaviors at an early age. They tend to gravitate toward same-sex play, and their verbal displays in that context reveal different patterns for what it means to engage in interpersonal discourse. Many toys and activities are sex-specific: Consider the proliferation of Barbie and other dolls for girls and road construction vehicles and combative action figures for boys. And clothing seems to be an escalating field for gender marking: Baby girls wear ribbons in their hair and little socks rimmed in lace, and although girls do wear pants, dresses and tights are currently *de rigueur*); boys' jeans come in styles with names like "Tough Skins," and pink, even if occasionally worn in combination with other colors during infancy, disappears in boys' clothing as they reach school age. Kids are often verbally enjoined by grown-ups—especially their parents—to behave in gender appropriate ways: Boys are told to "toughen up" and to "stand up for yourself" and "don't be a sissy"; girls are told to "act like a lady," "sit up properly," and "keep your dress down where it belongs." One incident I observed starkly exemplifies the parental role in verbally shaping gendered behavior. A mother, whose 3-year-old daughter was jumping down some steps in a public place with a 3-year-old boy, told her little girl several times to stop. Having no effect, she finally shouted, "Emily, stop that! Girls don't jump like that!"

Clearly, kids learn the implications of these many-gendered things early in life, as the cultural gendered worlds of men and women begin to take shape in guiding their thought, action, and language. In a provocative and widely cited essay, Daniel Maltz and Ruth Borker (1982) discuss the ways in which girls and boys learn to express friendliness differently—ways that implicate different cultural assumptions and not simply lack of precision in communication. They summarize the discursive world of girls as centered in friendships that are formed through talk, expressive of criticism without being overly aggressive, and reliant on deciphering cues about the motives of others. They characterize the discursive world of boys as centered in establishing the self as dominant, maintaining the attention of others, and asserting the self when others are the focus of attention. These patterns form the foundation for gender cultures that mature over time.

One fascinating aspect of children's enculturation into gendered identities and discourses is the persistence of gender dualisms alongside the greater fluidity of some cultural practices across boys and girls. Little boys, for instance, play with child-size cooking utensils and engage in pretend meal preparation; and little girls are on the soccer and T-ball fields as early as boys. Yet, *at the same time*, the clothing, the array of activities, and the verbal strategies all replicate the gender status quo, re-creating dualities, polarities, and the dominant ideology of gender relations. Along with changes (sometimes called "advances" in gender equality or gender freedom), it seems that "everything old is new again."

I turn now to several vantage points on gendered language use in adult society.

Gendered Language Patterns in Adulthood

The considerable amount of scholarship now available on gender and language points to distinctive ways of speaking among women and men and to a range of explanations for the role of gender in shaping discourse (see Cameron, 1992; Coates, 1998). Questions about gendered language can be grouped into two categories. First are questions of fact about women's and men's communication: Do men and women talk about different topics? Do they participate differently in conversations with members of the same sex contrasted to the opposite sex? Do they differ in their styles of speaking?

Does one sex or the other tend to talk more? Interrupt more? Second are questions focused on interpreting those facts in the context of various theories about gender differences in language use: Why do women and men use language differently? Do they communicate interculturally from the perspective of co-equal cultures, or are men culturally dominant and therefore dominant in their discourse?

Topics in discourse. Topicality, or the subject matter of conversation, is a good starting point in our consideration of women's and men's language-in-use because most of us can easily recognize at least the surface content of speech. Yet, although we can usually summarize the topics covered in a conversation (e.g., what movie to see, what you did last night, why you forgot your lover's birthday, your fight with your partner about who should be doing the laundry, a decision about buying a car, and dealing with parents about financial responsibilities), we are less able to characterize topic patterns in our discourses with others.

In the area of gender and topics, an early study by Elizabeth Aries (1976) continues to be cited as a foundation piece. Her content analysis of group discussions among same-sex and mixed-sex college students who were brought together to get to know one another revealed several patterns. First, all-male groups focused on themes of superiority and aggression through sarcastic teasing and talking about movies, books, current events, politics, sports, and travel. Second, all-female groups shared information about themselves, their feelings, their homes, and their relationships with others. Third, when femaleand males talked together, women talked less about home and family and males talked more about themselves and their feelings; in other words, each sex modified its topicality in the presence of the other sex. In a subsequent study, Aries (1982) reported that in mixed-sex college groups assembled to discuss a case study involving an ethical dilemma, females engaged in more socioemotional talk and men in more task-oriented talk.

In another study, Pamela Kipers (1987) studied 470 conversations that occurred in the faculty room of a middle school in New Jersey. Kipers's findings also confirmed a gender pattern in topics. In order of frequency, the primary conversation topics among women were focused on (a) home and family, (b) social issues, and (c) personal and family finances. For men, the most frequent topics were (a) work-related topics about specific educational programs, summer jobs, and pay and (b) recreation. The findings for the women are particularly interesting because the setting is the workplace,

TABLE 4.2 Most Frequent Topics for All-Women, All-Men, and Mixed-Sex Conversations From the Kipers Study of Informal Teachers' Conversations

All-Women Groups	*All-Men Groups*	*Mixed-Sex Groups*
Home and family, 28%		Home and family, 22%
Social issues, 21%		
Personal and family finances, 12%		
	Work related, 39%	Work related, 25%
	Recreation, 21%	

where one might expect more work-related talk. Yet, women seemed to reflect on their dual responsibilities for home and work by talking about their children, child care arrangements, and cooking. Men simply did not discuss these topics with one another. A number of the social issues discussed by women also related to children—drug abuse, child abuse, the effects of television violence on children, juvenile suicide—none of which were featured in the men's conversations. When men and women conversed together, the top two topics were (a) work related and (b) home and family. In sum, the most frequent topic for each sex was drawn into the mixed-sex conversations, suggesting cross-gender topical accommodations. These results, including the percentages for topics, are displayed in Table 4.2.

Gender divisions in topicality also emerged in research conducted by Monica Hiller and myself (Hiller & Johnson, 1996), which focused on conversations in two coffee shops (one frequented by young adults and the other by middle-aged and older customers). An analysis of topics showed that whereas both men and women talked about work and social issues, women talked about personal issues, unlike the older men, who virtually never discussed personal issues.

This sampling of studies suggests a broad distinction in what women and men are likely to focus on in conversation, especially when those conversations are with members of the same sex. Women favor more personal and domestic topics. Men stick more to external subject matter and sociable discourse.

What men and women talk about in the more informal context of close friendship also shows gendered patterns for topics of conversation. Johnson and Aries (1983a) asked college students to indicate what they talked about with their closest same-sex friends. Young women reported that they talked more frequently about themselves, their problems, and their close relationships than did young men, although they too reported conversations on these topics. As we might expect, young men talked much more about sports than did young women. A companion study of adults in their 40s and 50s (Aries & Johnson, 1983) found that women, compared to men, reported more frequent talk about their doubts and fears, personal and family problems, and intimate relationships; only for the topic of sports did men report significantly more frequent conversations than women.

These topic patterns, in addition to the proclivity of women to define talk itself as an essential agenda in their personal relationships with other women (Johnson, 1996; Johnson & Aries, 1983b), point to different subject matter domains for language use that may well emerge from different levels of cultural abstractions pertaining to what is salient and of value. These subject matter domains interrelate with experience to create different ways in which women and men come to "voice" their existence and relatedness to others. And although women and men frequently talk to one another, their cross-gender talk differs in topic focus from that of either man-to-man or woman-to-woman talk.

Talkativeness. The folk linguistic "theories" of Eurowhites in the United States are replete with references to the greater talkativeness of women in comparison to men. Culturally symbolic phrases such as "yackety-yack," "jibber-jabber," "cackling hens," "blabber-mouth," "chit-chat," and "idle chatter" all convey a distinctly female image of the talker. These phrases capture not only a belief that women talk more than men but that the substance of their talk is generally unimportant. Within mainstream U.S. culture, the "chatty woman" and the "gossip" contrast to the "taciturn man" and "man of few words" in representing two orders of discourse—one characterized by excess and one by restraint. But is the folk linguistic knowledge fact or fiction?

One way in which women typically differ from men is in their greater valuing of conversation as a legitimate activity in itself—especially talk with one another. When Elizabeth Aries and I (Johnson & Aries, 1983b) interviewed a broad range of women about their close friendships, we found uniformity in their reports that talk is the most important aspect of these relationships. In contrast, men tend to view activity as a more central focus of friendship. In some cultural groups, such as the white, urban, working-class Chicago neighborhood studied by Philipsen (1975), extensive talk among men is even frowned on. In other groups, such as urban African Americans, verbal performance such as rapping or doing the dozens may be a significant part of male identity (Folb, 1980; Kochman, 1972), but such performances focus on creativity rather than conversation.

Many studies have assessed the sheer amount of talk (usually measured in clock time) by men and women in various circumstances. A comprehensive review by Deborah James and Janice Drakich (1993) of 63 studies conducted between 1951 and 1991 concludes that "the bulk of research findings indicate that men talk more than women" (p. 281).

This pattern in the research of more talk by men than by women in cross-gender conversations is anecdotally evident across a range of situations. Especially in work settings, women report that in discussions with men they are often the ones who have difficulty getting a word in edgewise. I have observed a number of community meetings about policy or problem issues where women's attendance is high but their proportion of talk low. In my own teaching over a number of years, I have observed that male students usually emerge as the main talkers in class, even when the women outnumber the men. More women seem to be speaking up in class, but the pattern remains one of asymmetry. In the classroom context, this and other patterns of discouragement for women students have been termed the "chilly climate"—a climate that is cool toward women and that tends to discourage participation (Hall & Sandler, 1982).

Patterns of control in male-female discourse. Most people have at some time or another felt totally overwhelmed by the talk of others. Sometimes, we cannot get a word in edgewise; sometimes, we simply want the other person to shut up; sometimes, we sense that a conversation with another person or in a group situation unfolds in an unbalanced way. Although the greater quantity of talk by men compared to women in cross-gender situations implicitly points to discourse control, other research deals more directly with the question of how discourse patterns systematically establish control. Two areas of scholarship on conversation are considered: (a) topic control and (b) turn-taking. Even though the research in this domain raises as many questions as it answers, it also suggests ways in which women and men participate differently in conversation.

Topic dominance, achieved by introducing topics and controlling the flow of topics within a conversation, sets the agenda for what people in a conversation will discuss. Topic control functions to regulate the content of dis-

Male Pattern	Female Pattern
T^1_____	T^1_____
x	x
T^2_____	x
T^3_____	x
x	x
x	x
T^4_____	T^2_____
x	x
T^5_____	x
x	x

Figure 4.1. Illustration of Male and Female Topic Patterns
NOTE: T = a topic; x = a comment made on that topic.

course. Sometimes, the right to control the topic of conversation exists through social convention, as when a boss controls talk about an employee's job performance or an attorney controls the topic when examining a witness. Often, however, topic control is an open issue to be subtly negotiated by the participants. But is it open when it comes to gender? Unfortunately, little research exists to address this question, but what there is suggests possible patterns.

The studies by Aries (1976, 1982) pinpoint patterns in topic control among college student groups. First, when women talked with one another, topics were much more distributed among participants than was the case with men. Women also talked in greater depth on the topics they initiated than did men, which is consistent with what men and women report about their conversations with same-sex friends (Aries & Johnson, 1983; Johnson & Aries, 1983a). The comparison can be visualized as shown in Figure 4.1.

In this illustration, the male conversation has five different topics, three with one follow-up comment, one with two follow-up comments, and one with none. The female conversation has only two topics, but each gets developed more extensively: one with five follow-up comments and the other with three. One possible explanation for this pattern is that the males are asserting content control by continuously changing topics whereas the females facilitate the development of a topic in a balanced way prior to initiating new subject matter. In my discussions with students and groups with whom I have consulted, these patterns always ring true to what both women and men think they experience in conversation. Women typically say "that's exactly what happens when I get together with my girlfriends," and men note something such as "guys really don't do much discussing but they like to joke and one-up each other."

In Aries's (1982) second study, the women talked more than the men in mixed-sex groups, but the functionality of their utterances differed: Males gave opinions, suggestions, and information in a proactive fashion, whereas females more often responded to what the males said by agreeing, disagreeing, or asking questions.

West and García (1988) looked at topic control by analyzing how topic shifts occur in conversation. They found that all instances of unilateral topic shifts were initiated by men. Their research is limited because of its restriction to a small sample of college students, but, again, the findings suggest a possible pattern of gender-skewed topic control.

One of the most provocative approaches to examining discourse control in conversations was undertaken by Carol Edelsky (1981/1993), who studied what she calls the conversational *floor* or "the acknowledged what's-going-on within a psychological time/space" (p. 209). Edelsky distinguished *collaborative floors* in which participants jointly develop and sustain the topic from *singly developed floors* in which one person holds forth, thereby controlling the topic, or manages to keep the topic focused even if others comment on it. Floor is a more complex notion than topic in the sense that one might introduce a topic and even develop it without "having the floor." Imagine a conversation among five people focused on mortgage rates, during which two individuals briefly comment on the possibility of buying vacation homes; this topic is heard by the others but never becomes the focus of the group's discourse. Or think about a situation I observed in which a group of parents were discussing their children's use of the Internet; one parent talked at length about why his kids are not allowed to use the home computer, only to have his remarks politely ignored as the group quickly returned to Internet use.

Edelsky's (1981/1993) analysis of conversations among a faculty committee revealed that men and women participate essentially as equals in collaborative floor segments of conversation but that men and not women control singly developed floors. In fact, she found no singly developed floor segments where a woman spoke.

The second topic pertinent to discourse control is *turn-taking*. Consider conversation to be the give-and-take of utterances that are jointly developed by the participants. That give-and-take, however, can occur through the full range of egalitarian to lopsided distribution of the conversational speaking turns.

Neatly ordered turn-taking occurs when one participant completes an utterance before the next person beings speaking. Such discourse might be described as polite, civil, formal, considerate, or stilted depending on the context of the conversation and the cultural background of the participants. Another form of turn-taking moves the turn more abruptly from speaker to speaker by (a) overlapping one utterance onto the end of another person's utterance or (b) interrupting the progress of another's utterance, which is like a conversational tackle tactic. Overlaps are less intrusive but still can cut off another speaker. Interruptions, if successful, take control of talk, as shown in the example below; here, B cuts off A mid-sentence (// marks the point of interruption):

A: I really don't care what we do so let's//
B: //I guess I really don't want to go to a movie again tonight.

Although a prevailing view in U.S. linguistics has been that the normal state of affairs is for one person to speak at a time (Sacks et al., 1974), that view is culturally biased and does not reflect the normal state of affairs in many ethnic discourses, where interruption and overlap are common. Schiffrin (1984), for example, shows instances of interruption as part of sociable Jewish argument. Whether normative or not, interrupting and overlapping function to assert control over discourse. The key question is whether men compared to women are more likely to exercise this kind of control.

The early studies of interruptions and overlaps were conducted by Candace West and Don Zimmerman (West & Zimmerman, 1983; Zimmerman & West, 1975), who investigated these devices in mixed-sex interactions. In their first study, they found that 96% of all interruptions were initiated by men who interrupted women; in the second study, 75% were male initiated. These data suggest that males are overwhelmingly more likely to interrupt females than vice versa, but subsequent studies show varied results.

Based on reviewing 33 studies conducted between 1965 and 1991, James and Clarke (1993) concluded that no pattern exists between gender and interruptions. Their analysis resulted in the following breakdown:

17 studies with no gender differences
11 studies with significantly more male interruptions
5 studies with significantly more female interruptions

James and Clarke's conclusion of no gender effect is, however, misleading. Even though half of the studies show no gender differences, the other half are weighted 2:1 toward the males; that is, males are found to interrupt more often than are females in twice the number of studies where there are gender differences—certainly not a trivial pattern.

James and Clarke (1993) did raise important questions about the function served by interruptions, noting that some are disruptive whereas others serve a supportive function; Kennedy and Camden (1983) refer to these two types of interruptions as *confirming* and *disconfirming*. Several studies point to the greater use of confirming interruptions by women, but the data are sparse. Furthermore, as with any body of research, methods and situation vary greatly, which makes it more difficult to determine whether any trends exist.

In addition to what we know about interruptions from research studies, self-report of perceptions provides another vantage point. Over the years, I have asked numerous students, colleagues, and individuals in training sessions whether they believe there is a gender pattern to interruption behavior. Although many men report that there "probably is," women more emphatically assert that they frequently experience being interrupted by males. What is not clear is whether these reports arise from frequency alone, from a greater sensitivity among women to interruptions when they occur (which might be part of the pragmatic rule system for women but not men), or to folklinguistic perceptions. Some women also report that they "fight back" by interrupting men or refusing to let men interrupt them. This might explain why Kennedy and Camden (1983) found female graduate student teaching assistants to out-interrupt their male peers. Yet, the women in this study were interrupted more than the men, even by women.

Gendered Discourse Styles

The Language-Centered Perspective on Culture suggests that discourse style is significant in giving meaning to a culture. Discourse manifests culture by bringing its abstractions to articulation. When women and men talk together, they bring elements of both shared and separate cultures. Depending on the domain and context, the discourse styles that prevail may be more female-marked, more male-marked, or hybrid. To speak as an American woman and as an American man, a Chicano and a Chicana, a Greek American woman and a Greek American man are not the same.

Linguistic precision. The clearest line of evidence for distinctive gender styles points to greater precision in language use by women compared to men. Such precision has been noted in research on phonological features such as the presence or absence of the final sound in /-ing/ versus /-in'/ (*going* vs. *goin'*), which distinguishes careful speech from casual speech. Landmark studies usually cited include William Labov's (1966/1972b) study of Lower East Side, New York speech and Walt Wolfram's (1969) study of African American speech in Detroit. Other types of supporting research point to care in communicating detail and content clarity. Susan Philips and Anne Reynolds (1987), for example, conducted a study on the discourse of prospective jurors who were being interviewed by judges. They found that women were more linguistically redundant in their discourse than men, which suggests that women speakers, compared to men, place greater emphasis on their ability to be clear as speakers rather than relying on hearers to interpret their intent.

Why is it that women tend to be less casual and more precise in their speech than men? First, women are often said to be the "guardians of the language" because, as mothers and teachers of young children, they bear greater responsibility than men for modeling and teaching language behavior to young children. Second, women are also said to be more careful in their speech because doing so reflects on their social status as "ladies." Robin Lakoff (1975) asserts that women are socialized to speak like ladies, which means to speak politely because "politeness involves an absence of a strong statement, and women's speech is devised to prevent the expression of strong statements" (p. 19). (Again, this line of reasoning fails to account for certain cultural differences.)

Obscenity. Over many decades, scholars have been interested in the degree to which males and females use obscenities and the consequences for using "unsavory" and taboo language (Johnson & Fine, 1985). The strictures on women's use of obscenity have eased some in recent years (Risch, 1987), but a linguistic double standard still exists. Undoubtedly, it takes less "off-color" language to be labeled a "foul mouthed" woman than would be the case for men. Likewise, the idiomatic expression "pardon my French" is most often addressed to women or in the presence of women to announce or justify an obscene expression. The strictures on women's use of obscenity emanate from complex attitudes that have to do with speaking like a lady as well as avoiding sexually explicit talk. Women who view obscenity as powerful language may choose to appropriate it for their own use (Sutton, 1995), and women who see it as a derogatory male creation negatively directed at women may choose not to perpetuate its use. Men who see such language as demeaning may choose to avoid its use, just as men who want to sound tough and cool or to express sexual, masculine power may cultivate its usage.

Whatever the basis for obscenity, with rare exception, women's version is toned down compared to men's. Because obscenity is taboo in certain settings (one does not swear in school, in a church or temple, or in an elegant restaurant) its power potential intensifies when used as part of the vernacular variety. Men's repertoire of obscene expressions far surpasses women's (Johnson & Fine, 1985), especially in reference to the opposite sex and sexual behavior. And particular forms of discourse that are associated with obscene expressions, such as signifyin' or rappin' (as verbal game and musical form) in African American culture, are typically genderized such that female compared to male usage relies less on repetitive obscenity (Houston Stanback, 1985; Rose, 1994).

Doing discourse. From a cultural perspective, language in its most mundane, everyday articulation produces what we know as gender. Evidence from varied research traditions points to patterns in how women and men do discourse differently.

One form of evidence for gender styles in discourse comes from the domain of surgically reconstructed sex. As part of the long preparation for transsexual surgery, which involves therapy and training to cross over into the opposite sex by mastering a cultural gender code, the soon-to-become woman (man) receives speech therapy training in how to speak as the appropriate gender (Gunzburger, 1996). The personal account and advice from a male-to-constructed-female named Melanie Ann Phillips (1994) stresses developing a "female voice" as the most important key to becoming and being the opposite sex without seeming to pretend at being the opposite sex. Believing her success so complete, Phillips has produced not only written advice but also a video on the "seven steps to achieve a fully feminine voice": pitch, resonance, dynamic range, enunciation, vocabulary, grammar, and body English. Based on dualistic notions of how women and men "do" discourse, Phillips's advice, *because it is based on passing rather than camp performance,* cuts deeply to the cultural foundations of appropriate gender enactments.

Every person—not just the transsexual—engages day-to-day in the process of "passing": passing for the gender (among other things) we claim to be. It is only because gender often feels "second nature" (notice that the term is not "first nature") that we usually forget about the cultural challenge of passing. Sometimes, however, we remember, which prompts us to plan our gender performance and to make choices that we feel will reflect on our womanhood or manhood. The substantial academic research now available allows us a fuller understanding of what is produced to do gender, that is, what constitutes genderized discourse styles and their complexities.

Robin Lakoff's (1975) early work focuses on how gender is accomplished, and the ideas in this work continue to be influential. Her position was that women are discriminated against in their language socialization, which produces a female way of speaking that is less forceful, assertive, and direct; more timid, qualified, and hesitant; and ultimately less effective than the male way of speaking. Subsequently, she has characterized the gender differences in language use that appear in every culture by saying that "language represents behavior supposedly typical of women across the majority of cultures: alleged illogic, submissiveness, sexual utility to men, secondary status" (Lakoff, 1990, pp. 202-203).

Lakoff's position has been controversial because she placed negative connotations on women's language and communication patterns and because she seemed to be focused only on white, middle-class women, which from today's standpoint looks like universalizing. Houston Stanback (1985), for example, states emphatically that African American women do not demonstrate the language style that Lakoff describes. Despite the controversy, Lakoff is recognized for confronting sexism as a contributing factor to differences in women's and men's language (Hall & Bucholtz, 1995).

One interesting illustration of how male power is established in the doing of discourse can be found in a research report by Elinor Oaks and Carolyn Taylor (1995), who describe a particular conversational routine using the title of a classic family television series: the *Father Knows Best* dynamic. They studied transcripts of dinner conversations in seven Eurowhite, middle-class, two-parent families, showing how both parents participated in establishing the husband/father's status. Summarizing their analysis, these authors write,

> First, mothers introduce narratives (about themselves and their children) that set up fathers as primary recipients and implicitly sanction them as evaluators of others' action, conditions, thoughts, and feelings. Second, fathers turn such opportunities into forums for problematizing, with mothers . . . as their chief targets, often on grounds of incompetence. And third, mothers respond in defense of themselves and their children via the counterproblematizing of fathers' evaluative, judgmental comments. (p. 116)

Based on research (most of it focused on Eurowhites), the discourse features most typical of women's style and values for communication cluster around several functions: (a) integrating participants; (b) facilitating cooperation; (c) positioning meanings as contingent rather than absolute or clear-cut; (d) encouraging the participation of others; (e) mingling experiences rather than separating them into domains such as work, home, recreation, and so forth; and (f) personalizing meanings and acknowledging subjectivity. Men's discourse features tend toward the reverse of this and cluster around the functions of (a) differentiating self from others, (b) accentuating competition, (c) conveying certainty in meanings, (d) taking responsibility for the participation of self but not others, (e) particularizing meanings to specific domains, and (f) emphasizing the locus of meaning as external to the self.

The emphasis on gender as action rather than as static identity recognizes the everyday processes through which gender happens. "Gender is not," says Mary Crawford (1995), "an attribute of individuals but a way of making sense of transactions" (p. 12).

Transgressing Gender

Lesbian and Gay Discourse

In recent years, many aspects of gay and lesbian life have permeated public awareness (although with varying degrees of acceptance)—lifestyle issues, employment issues and benefits, health concerns, entertainment. Along with this greater public recognition has come increased scholarly attention to the lives of U.S. lesbians and gays, including research and writing about lesbian and gay discourse. Not surprisingly, then, the prior situation of scholarly paucity has now been replaced by a growing literature addressing gay and lesbian discourse and broader themes addressing rebellions against conventional sex and gender identities.

It is instructive to think about the evidence used by people from all walks of life to draw conclusions about sexual preference. That evidence often draws upon folk linguistic notions of typical genderized discourse, with language and appearance forming the basis for speculations, conclusions, and surprises ("Why, he certainly didn't act gay!"). Against this folk linguistic theorizing, gays and lesbians, like any cultural group, exhibit great variation. Generalizations about "gay speak" that might once have been comfortably made now stand out as glaring, invalid essentializing. In fact, those who write about lesbian and gay language today emphasize the variability and heterogeneity of lesbian and gay speech communities and discourse (Jacobs, 1996; Leap, 1995). Yet, like other groups that have been marginalized by dominant ideologies, gays and lesbians have used language as an important resource in both forming group cohesion and identity and in protecting themselves in what is often a hostile social environment. The discourse dimensions associated with the kind of gender transgression entered into by gays and lesbians offer insight not only into the gender dynamics in these cultural groups but also into the larger complexity of gendered discourse and gender cultures.

Although I focus in this section on the terms and identities associated with *gay* and *lesbian,* the implications of what we can learn about marginalized gender groups based on same-sex affiliation aid in our understanding of different types of sex and gender transgression. *Bisexual, transsexual,* and *transvestite* all challenge gender ideology through enactments of counterdiscourse to dominant gender ideology, that is, counter to what Butler explains as "compulsory heterosexuality" and the cultural system sustaining the "naturalness" of two sexes, from which the meaning systems of two genders arise.

To show how language bears on transgressive gender enactments and identities, three topics are considered: lexicon, aspects of voice and vocal production, and discourse pragmatics.

In the past, much of the scholarship on gay and lesbian discourse was limited to examinations of lexicon, especially specialized vocabulary, code words, and in-group references. Early work, such as Bruce Rodgers's (1972) *The Queens' Vernacular,* covered entries of current usage and their historical derivations. The value of lexicons is their role in documenting how language-in-use becomes adapted both to the need for cohesion within speech communities (the function of day-to-day vernacular) and the need for boundary maintenance and protection from hostile forces external to the community (the function of protective code). Words that claim identity and celebrate group strength powerfully legitimize lived experience, and words that either keep nonmembers out or that shield those within a speech community from others provide the linguistic protection necessary for comfortable (and even safe) conduct in heterosexual society. Lexicon, however, shows only one facet of discourse as enacted by lesbians and gays.

Another type of research emphasizes voice and vocal qualities—especially of gay males. Does vocal production define gayness? If so, what dimensions of pitch, stress, intonation, stress patterns, and so forth are involved? One relatively recent study offers a complex answer. In his comparison of the voice pitch properties of gay and straight men, Rudolf Gaudio (1994) found that listeners could definitely identify gay speakers based on the voice they heard. Analysis of various aspects of pitch and vocal quality did not, however, reveal any uniformity in the features that signify gay identity.

Increasingly, the study of lesbian and gay discourse concentrates on the pragmatics of language use. William Leap (1995), an anthropological linguist, characterizes scholarship in this vein as "at the site" because it delves into understanding the development of lesbian and gay language-in-use as a contextual process. In introducing the collection he edited, Leap says this about site and locale:

> *Discovering locale* becomes a recurring theme in lesbian/gay socialization. . . . *What we discover* in that regard figures prominently in the content of our day-to-day public conversations and influences the more specialized texts which we create during private, personal communication. *How we discover* is closely tied to the ways we organize discourse in heterosexually controlled and lesbian/gay-positive spaces, and the knowledge of language on which that discourse depends. (p. ix)

This notion of discovery appears very similar to the "knowledge at the margins" axiom in the Language-Centered Perspective on Culture and standpoint theory.

Looking into discourse at the site, Leap himself (1996) has examined what he calls "the language of gay city" to determine how gay men describe their urban scene in Washington, D.C. He has studied the use of narrative strategies by Euro-American, African American, and Hispanic gay men to create gay space from urban space and to interpret everyday life. One feature he finds across the different men's descriptions of gay city is the absence of explicit references to race, ethnicity, and class and, consequently, "the appearance of whiteness" (p. 412). It seems that the explicit locus of narrative features gay space, which leaves matters of diversity tacit—Leap thinks "erased."

Another example of the examination of "at the site" narrative is Ruth Morgan and Kathleen Wood's (1995) study of lesbian "recreational [social] conversations." They anchor the analysis with a comment about speech communities:

> We engage in recreational conversations with each other to connect as lesbians—to create a conversational space that is uniquely lesbian. We do this with an unspoken collusion which enables us to work together in our conversation building to mark our conversational space as lesbian. (p. 235)

In the discourse analysis they present, one feature highlighted is two kinds of lesbian topics: L-esbian and l-esbian, where the first entails specific reference to lesbian experience and identity and the second deals more with establishing the lesbian group (speech community) cohesion by talking about things past and present that are "common" to "us." Morgan and Wood make an interesting point in stating, "When lesbians converse, all topics are lesbian topics" (p. 240).

The research described above is only a sampling, but the studies together provide insights into both the ways in which speech communities function to connect their members and the vitality of resistance to dominant discourses carrying gender ideology.

Resistance to Gendered Discourse

Resistance can be enacted in many ways, and women (and increasingly girls) have taken the lead in several types of pragmatic action intended to subvert gender-disciplined discourses. In the area of language patterns that are "man made," women of varying political persuasions (joined by some men in many cases) have chosen to change their usage to make it more comparable with and less hostile to women's experience (Kramarae & Jenkins, 1987; Penelope, 1990). Women have been the leaders in changing male generic references to gender inclusive references such as *he/she* and *him/her*. Women, because of their standpoint in the ideological gender structure, are also likely to recognize the ill fit of "unisex sizing" when war and sports metaphors are used to clothe a broad range of experience.

Resistance can also take the form of doing an activity or engaging in a cultural practice in a manner differing from the (gendered) norm. The "same" activity can be performed differently, whether that activity is performed on the job (e.g., the manner in which a female or male supervisor communicates with subordinates), in the family (e.g., the way mom-dad parents model gender through decision making), or in a social setting (e.g., the topics discussed by men or women at a barbecue). When women (white, black, Latina, Korean American, Filipina, and so forth) are engineers, custodians, soccer coaches, or elected officials, they need not function in these roles as though they are men in women's bodies. When women bring their cultural patterns to these activities, resistance can be enacted and gender cultures challenged.

But beyond these situations in which women are seen as crossing over into the traditional male domains, there can be influences of gender cultures simply through gender affiliations. Ample evidence from job situations shows that women do, in fact, often seek out other women for talk and see personal affiliation as a way of knowing about themselves and their environment. At a more formal level, many professional groups for women serve precisely this function—women's caucuses within professional and political organizations, women's affairs task forces in businesses, and so forth.

Men, too, are part of this equation through which gender cultures are defined. Most men are not preoccupied with the privileges they may enjoy because of gender inequalities. Yet men's culture continuously evolves, and with that evolution come changes in discourse patterns. Some men may consciously resist any behavior—language or otherwise—that relinquishes male privilege, and others may cultivate changes in gender cultures by consciously monitoring the ways in which men's discourse patterns and activities dominate women. Resistance among men can, then, serve very different goals: the goal of preserving gender dualisms on the one hand or rejecting such dualisms and working to elaborate new cultural practices on the other.

In the state where I live, a recent episode occurred in the political arena that shows the different sides of gender resistance. A woman running for lieutenant governor announced her pregnancy, with the timing such that she would give birth about 2 months after the election. The range of views reported by the mass media included (a) speculation that the pregnancy would help her candidacy because verbal attacks and nasty politics would be less likely directed toward a pregnant women, (b) calls for her to step aside because motherhood of an infant would compromise her effectiveness, and (c) protest that her pregnancy was irrelevant to her political candidacy. Both (a) and (b) reflected conventionally dominant ideologies about gender: the first because of its implication of the "delicate condition" of pregnancy, and the second because no analogous call to step aside would be made if a male candidate was about to become a father. The sentiment expressed in (c) illustrates a pragmatically resistive definition of gender and its impact. All of these views and the news focus on them, however, created a "gender issue" and set the public's agenda for thinking about and discussing women in a particular way.

Implications

Amid rapid changes both in gender relations and in the racial and ethnic complexity of the United States, we continue to interact through genderized systems with deep cultural implications. Even though the particulars constantly change, the fact of gender cultures will likely persist long into the future—perhaps forever—although in newly elaborated ways.

Gender permeates, indeed saturates, discourse in ways that we do not often monitor in our everyday experiences. Although much of the focus in the past has been on documenting, understanding, challenging, and changing women's cultural practices to achieve greater parity with men and greater public visibility, more recent attention focuses on gender as an elaborate cultural system affecting men as well as women. Various analyses of the pressures toward masculinity and the tests of manhood evident in all cultures (Gilmore, 1990) demonstrate how constricted the latitude for culturally appropriate maleness can be. Even though dual definitions of gender and compulsory heterosexuality privilege males, they also strongly sanction lapses of "in gender" behavior and language. One interpretation of the heavy demands regarding masculinity in most cultures proposes that masculinity, along with accompanying compulsory heterosexuality, becomes culturally elaborated as a way of rejecting cultural definitions of woman and femininity. In this line of reasoning, the most important, ongoing challenge for maleness involves proving that one is not feminine or homosexual (Kimmel, 1994). We are beginning to hear and read more about gender cultures from the male perspective, and these probings will likely advance our understanding of the intricacy of gender ideology.

In this chapter, I considered different ways in which language reflects gender cultures and also constructs gender as an ideological meaning system. Thinking about the foundation of both sex and gender in discourse should give us pause in drawing conclusions about the naturalness or inevitability of even the simplest male-female dualism. Biology is, indeed, not destiny, but when cultural discourses build on the biological dualities of male and female to infuse social life with gendered meanings, biology is made to look like part of destiny. Even in most resistance to the ideological dimensions of gender, gender itself (and sex too) remains firmly fixed as a center for meaning. In subsequent chapters, I discuss how cultural organizers, especially race and ethnicity, elaborate gendered discourses differently. Genderless speech and genderless speech communities must for now remain subjects for our imagination and some engaging science fiction.

5

African American Discourse in Cultural and Historical Context

Black Talk crosses boundaries—of sex, age, region, religion, social class—because the language comes from the same source: the African American Experience and the Oral Tradition embedded in that Experience. On one level, there is great diversity among African Americans today, but on a deeper level, race continues to be the defining core of the Black Experience.

—Geneva Smitherman (1994, p. 2)

Geneva Smitherman, long regarded for her scholarship on black language and communication and for her use of an African American voice to convey her knowledge, begins her dictionary of black usage, *Black Talk: Words and Phrases From the Hood to the Amen Corner* (Smitherman, 1994), by anchoring the talk she describes to a unifying experience underlying the diversity of African Americans. Although not every African American speaks the same "black talk" or has the same views about the role and value of particular patterns of language use that are marked by common racial-historical heritage in the United States, the history-language-culture connections for African Americans continue to delineate distinctive discourses and speech communities. Later in her introductory comments on *Black Talk,* Smitherman notes of everyday life that

> Regardless of job or social position, most African Americans experience some degree of participation in the life of the COMMUNITY—they get their hair done in African American BEAUTY SHOPS, they worship in Black churches, they attend African American social events, and they generally PAR-TAY with Blacks. (p. 25; capitals in the original to indicate words that are defined in the book)

The discourse of African Americans maps the social circumstances of a people. From the slave trade through legal segregation in the South and de facto segregation in the North, through housing and employment discrimination that continues today, African Americans have lived separated, both literally and symbolically, from the majority Eurowhite population of the United States. The circumstances of separation account for the prototypical barrier conditions that encourage distinctive language varieties and discourse patterns. The language and discourse patterns heard today carry with them many historical influences: West and Central African languages and cultures native to slaves; the functional necessity for slaves to communicate in code so their masters would not understand what they meant; segregation in all its forms—education, housing, employment, entertainment, and recreation; and the legacy of racial prejudice. These same language patterns also reflect the dynamic circumstances of living every day in a world where, to use a book title from Cornell West (1993b), *Race Matters.* If anyone doubted West's phrase, which was coined after the Rodney King case but before the O. J. Simpson trial, the Simpson trial left unequivocal the divide between blacks and whites in America. Yet, despite the historical legacy of slavery, segregation, and residential separation, all American people—regardless of color—have been culturally influenced by the presence of African Americans through contact and, more recently, mass-mediated communication.

The discourse patterns of African Americans present an amazing case study of language and cultural vitality despite a long history of overwhelming devaluation and stigma. The perspectives on African American language detailed in this chapter offer evidence for rich, enduring systems of communication. African American communication with all its variations exists in a society where the negativity toward it has been repeatedly articulated, most recently in the media frenzy over the Ebonics policy of the Oakland, California, school committee (covered in Chapter 9). Labels attached to black dialect during this century—such as *deviant, incorrect, sloppy,* and *handicapped*—bear witness to ingrained negative attitudes about the language used by many African Americans and about African Americans as a people. Yet, language vitality prevails.

In this chapter, the discourse patterns characteristic of African Americans are addressed within a broad cultural perspective. The chapter includes four main topics: (a) an overview of the historical circumstances of African Americans, (b) a demographic profile of African Americans, (c) a discussion of African American cultural patterns, and (d) a review and analysis of linguistic features and communication forms representative of African Americans.

African Americans in Historical Context

African Americans are the only ancestral group in the United States whose presence originated involuntarily. The legacy of slavery in contemporary patterns of contact between blacks and whites, in race relations, and in racism so infuses daily life that many of its manifestations go unnoticed by whites. Discrimination against African Americans in housing, employment, and mortgage lending still makes headline news. African American models used in advertising continue to be disproportionately light-skinned. Few whites know that African American women carry small purses into stores so that they will not be unduly scrutinized for shoplifting, or that African American men *regardless of social class* are more likely to be stopped and questioned by police officers, especially if they venture into white communities at night. And the language spoken by many African Americans remains stigmatized. These and other features of everyday life translate the legacy of slavery into what Stokley Carmichael and Charles Hamilton (1967) over three decades ago labeled *institutional racism.*

From the late 1600s through the early 1800s, the slave trade brought about 600,000 slaves to what would become the United States (Kolchin, 1993). The slaves were drawn primarily from two major African ethnic groups: the Mande of West Africa and the Bantu of Central Africa (Holloway & Vass, 1993).

Several features of slave origins are significant for understanding the influence of Africa on cultural practices, including language use, in the United States. Joseph Holloway (1990) extrapolates the following from historical documents and prior research:

1. Different regions of the country favored certain slave groups, with the upper colonies drawing more from West Africa and the lower colonies from Central Africa.

2. Domestic servants and slave artisans were mainly West Africans from groups within the Mande civilization, including Senegal, Guinea, Sierra Leone, Liberia, Mali, Ghana, Volta, and the Ivory Coast.

3. The Wolofs (a Mande group often selected as house servants and artisans) were likely the first African group to have aspects of their language and culture retained in the developing American culture. Many words in use today can be traced to the Wolofs: among them, *bogus, bug, jazz, jam, phoney,* and *rap.*

4. Field workers tended to be Central Africans and represented a relatively homogeneous cultural group unified by the Bantu language family.

5. Because field slaves (Bantu) were the numerical majority of slaves, it was among them that African American culture and language patterns developed.

Holloway and Vass (1993) conclude that "the Mande displayed the greatest influence on white American culture, the Bantu on black American culture" (p. xxiv). Most Bantus were kept in relative isolation from whites and did not experience the pressures to assimilate white cultural practices that were more common among the Mandes: "Their Africanisms, shared and adopted by various African ethnic groups of the field-slave community, gradually developed into African American cooking (soul food), music (jazz, blues, spirituals, gospels), dance, language, religion, philosophy, customs, and arts" (Holloway, 1990, p. 17). In contrast, the West African culture was likely suppressed much more by slave owners. Yet, the West African influence survived in cultural practices and ideas related to agricultural production; animal husbandry; folk tales such as Brer Rabbit, Brer Fox, Brer Wolf, and the Uncle Remus stories told to children by their slave mammies; and language cross-overs that continue today to be part of the American idiom (Holloway, 1990; Holloway & Vass, 1993). More will be said about specific linguistic influences in the section on discourse patterns that follows.

Following slavery, which officially ended with the Emancipation Proclamation in 1863 and passage of the Thirteenth Amendment to the Constitution in 1865, African Americans faced legal segregation in the South and de facto segregation elsewhere. Segregation forced the existence of two societies and two cultural systems, one white and one black, fostering a complex system of white privilege. Evelyn Brooks Higginbotham (1992) explains how segregation forced a merger of race and class:

> The most effective tool in the discursive welding of race and class proved to be segregation. . . . Jim Crow railroad cars, for instance, became strategic sites of contestation over the conflated meaning of class and race: blacks who could afford "first class" accommodations vehemently protested the racial basis for being denied access to them. (p. 259)

Higginbotham continues the analysis by pointing out that the "ladies car" in trains not only literally excluded blacks but symbolically excluded black women from the definition of ladies.

The force of segregation to propel the development of two cultures divided by race was strengthened through the famous "separate but equal" doctrine resulting from the *Plessy v. Ferguson* case of 1896. This case made segregated institutions (schools) legal so long as they were equal to white facilities. It was not until the civil rights era that the inequality of segregated schools was addressed. In *Brown v. Board of Education,* the landmark case of 1954, the U.S. Supreme Court declared that segregated schools were unconstitutional because they were unequal. Ironically, many cities today look little different from the "separate and *un*equal" conditions that led to school desegregation (see Kozol, 1991).

Ghettos, the concentration of African Americans in low-paying jobs, poll taxes and literacy tests for voting in the South, and blatant discrimination all fueled the Civil Rights Movement of the late 1950s and 1960s, which culminated in the Civil Rights Act of 1964 and the affirmative action programs that followed.

During the historical sweep of slavery, segregation, and separation of blacks and whites in America, the conditions sufficient for cultural distinctiveness were and continue to be more than ample. Blacks and whites have shared elements of a common culture, but they have been more separated literally, spiritually, and symbolically than they have been joined.

Demographic Profile of African Americans

The present-day population of non-Hispanic blacks in the United States is about 32.5 million, or about 12% of the entire population (U.S. Bureau of the Census, 1999). (The Census Bureau defines *blacks* as people with African

TABLE 5.1   Black (Non-Hispanic) Population in States With Greatest and
Fewest Black Residents (1996 estimates)

Five Highest States	Five Lowest States
New York = 3,198,201	Montana = 3,216
California = 2,371,293	Vermont = 3,500
Texas = 2,336,165	Wyoming = 4,082
Georgia = 2,074,548	North Dakota = 4,111
Michigan = 1,368,805	South Dakota = 4,542

SOURCE: U.S. Bureau of the Census (1996c).

origins.) This number includes those who are typically called African Americans, some Caribbeans individuals, and African immigrants. The 1990 census reported 364,000 individuals in the population who were born in Africa
(U.S. Bureau of the Census, 1993b). To avoid misrepresentation of the
demographic data, the term *black* is used in this section.

The Black Population and Its Geography

As of 1996, over 11 million blacks in the United States (one third) lived
in five states: New York, California, Texas, Georgia, and Michigan (U.S.
Bureau of the Census, 1996f). In contrast, the black population in several
states numbered fewer than 5,000: Montana, Vermont, Wyoming, North
Dakota, and South Dakota. These data are shown in Table 5.1.

Detailed information on city populations for 1992 indicates heavy clustering of African Americans in a selected group of cities where they initially
settled or migrated to seek employment. The 15 cities with the largest number
of blacks in the population as of 1992 are shown in Table 5.2 (U.S. Bureau
of the Census, 1996f).

In a number of these cities, blacks constitute the majority of the population: Detroit (76%), Atlanta (67%), Washington, D.C. (66%), New Orleans
(62%), Baltimore (59%), and Memphis (55%). Blacks make up one quarter
or more of the population in all of the 15 cities except Los Angeles. In other
large cities, the black population is small: 1.3% in Honolulu, Hawaii; 1.9%
in Mesa, Arizona; 2.5% in Anaheim, California; 3% in Albuquerque, New
Mexico; 3.4% in El Paso, Texas; 4.3% in Tucson, Arizona; and 4.7% in San
Jose, California.

There is, then, a particular geography to black residence. The overall
profile of inner-city economics in the United States is grim, housing is often

TABLE 5.2 Cities With Largest Black Population: 1992

Rank	City	Black Population	Percentage of Population
1	New York, NY	2,102,512	28.7
2	Chicago, IL	1,087,711	39.1
3	Detroit, MI	777,916	75.7
4	Philadelphia, PA	631,936	39.9
5	Los Angeles, CA	487,674	14.0
6	Houston, TX	457,990	28.1
7	Baltimore, MD	435,768	59.2
8	Washington, D.C.	399,604	65.8
9	Memphis, TN	334,737	54.8
10	New Orleans, LA	307,728	61.9
11	Dallas, TX	296,994	29.5
12	Atlanta, GA	264,262	67.1
13	Cleveland, OH	235,405	46.6
14	Milwaukee, WI	191,255	30.5
15	St. Louis, MO	188,408	47.5

SOURCE: U.S. Bureau of the Census (1996f).

marginal or substandard, and the quality of schools is poor. Blacks dispro-portionally live in these inner-city environments. I turn next to the major indicators of income associated with the black population.

Standard of Living

In a capitalist society such as the United States, a person's standard of living consists of many characteristics that emanate from income. Higher income brings greater discretion in choosing where to live, what car to drive, where to shop, what to buy and eat, where one's children will be educated (and if they will participate in activities such as soccer, gymnastics, dance, and camp), and what constitutes leisure and recreation activity. Low income correlates with substandard housing, insufficient medical attention, health problems, and nutritional deficiencies.

In aggregate, blacks are at the bottom of the U.S. income ladder. The poverty rate for black families in 1996 was 29% (well over one of every four families), compared to 8% for white families (1 of every 12 families), with a median income level of households at $23,482 compared to $37,161 for whites—a difference of close to $14,000 (U.S. Bureau of the Census, 1996a, 1996e). It is also the case that the poorest blacks are poorer than whites, with the income of close to half of all black families below $25,000, compared to

TABLE 5.3 Income Comparisons of Blacks and Whites: 1996

Indicator	Blacks	Non-Hispanic Whites
Poverty rate for families	29.3%	8.5%
Per capita income	$11,899	$19,181
Median household income	$23,482	$37,161
Families below $25,000 annually	48.6%	22.6%
Families $50,000 and above annually	21.0%	44.0%

SOURCE: U.S. Bureau of the Census (1996a).

slightly over one fifth of white families; at the higher levels, black families fall substantially behind white families: 21% of black families compared to 44% of white families had incomes of $50,000 or higher (U.S. Bureau of the Census, 1996a). Comparisons between blacks and non-Hispanic whites on various indicators of standard of living appear in Table 5.3.

The demographics of geographic locale and income levels do, in fact, demonstrate the degree to which blacks remain separated through barriers, both geographic and economic, from "white America." Advances have been made, and one can flip through the pages of *Ebony Magazine* any month and see examples of blacks who are judged to be successful in terms of position and income; yet, these portraits show only a sliver of reality. Overall, barrier conditions facilitate the continued cultural elaboration among Africans Americans. We look next to what defines African American culture in the United States.

African American Cultural Themes

Little public discussion of African American culture was evident in the United States until the Civil Rights Movement sparked a submovement for black pride. Demands for equality of opportunity rallied diverse blacks to racial unity and engaged the conscience of liberal whites. Calls for "Black Power" as well as the "black is beautiful" ideology rose to challenge prevailing European standards. Linguistically, interest turned to legitimizing and cultivating what some scholars called *Ebonics*—a variety of English spoken by the majority of Black Americans (Seymour & Seymour, 1979).

In the decades following the Civil Rights Movement, a philosophy termed *Afrocentrism* gained shape and public recognition to the degree that *Newsweek* devoted a cover story to it (Asante, 1991). Jesse Jackson cam-

paigned for president in 1984 and 1988. African Americans became important to the burgeoning commodity culture. Jazz became the music of choice
for many Eurowhites, and rap music went public.

African Americans are not, of course, culturally monolithic, nor do all
African Americans embrace and cultivate an African American cultural
identity. Many African Americans do, however, spend considerable time in
contact with one another, especially in social and neighborhood contexts.
And most African Americans, regardless of occupation or economic status,
identify with race as galvanizing an identity based on the meaning of race in
the United States.

African American culture is also American culture, and not just in the
sense that it is part of the cultural multiplicity within a nation. It is American
culture because of the many cross-overs resulting from cultures in contact.
The most obvious and long-standing cross-over is jazz, but there are certainly
others. Contemporary American literature has been dominated by African
American writers, especially women such as Toni Morrison (a Pulitzer prizewinner), Gloria Naylor, and Alice Walker; their literary voices and the genres
they create convey a distinctively African American experience and sensibility, but the literature is not just for and about blacks. As cultural artifacts, the
novels created by these authors become part of the cultural experience of
non-African Americans. Lexicon is one of the major areas for cross-over
(some would characterize it as co-optation) from African American communities to white communities: Common words such as *ballyhoo, jiffy, poke* (as
in "a pig in a poke"), and *yackety-yak* can be traced to Bantu origins through
African Americans (Vass, 1979); vernacular words such as current usage *phat*
to mean good (previously expressed as *cool* and then *bad*) have recently
crossed over from African American speech communities to more mainstream teenage vernacular English. The more that cross-over occurs, the
more every person who is not African American becomes increasingly
African American; this is the course of cultures in contact.

The ideas presented here about African American culture exist in a situation of dynamism. They are themes, not universals. They guide but do not
dictate the identities of millions of people, some of whom are not African
American. Adherence to the past coexists with new ideas and forms of
expression. As such, African American culture draws at any point in time
from its African roots, from its American roots, and from the evolving
circumstances of daily life in a culturally complex country. To be African
American is, then, to be both of Africa and of America; to be of African
ancestry and American enculturation. W. E. B. Du Bois (1903/1961) wrote

early in his career of this duality in the now-famous formulation of "double-consciousness":

> The Negro is . . . born with a veil, and gifted with second-sight in this American world—a world which yields him no true self-consciousness, but only lets him see himself through the revelation of the other world. It is a peculiar sensation, this double-consciousness, this sense of always looking at one's self through the eyes of others. . . . One ever feels his twoness—an American, a Negro: two souls, two unreconciled strivings; two warring ideals in one dark body. (pp. 16-17)

We may today reject Du Bois's notion that blacks in America have no true self-consciousness, but the kernel idea that two radically different worlds exist for African Americans and that they must always be contextualized in (at least) two different ways bears the test of time as a way of thinking about the cultural situatedness of those whose ancestors were African slaves. Again, not every African American will think of or experience the dualities of culture similarly, but race in the United States rarely recedes from personal and social interpretation.

The focus here is on a set of cultural abstractions loosely tied to African origins but developed in the American context and on various cultural artifacts spanning a range of African American communities. These broader cultural themes provide the foundation for understanding African American language and communication as a set of systems of cultural expression.

Connections to African Heritage

Two constructs have guided much of the research and thinking about the connections of African American culture to Africa through historical links and symbolic identity: *Africanisms,* which designate particular beliefs and practices with lineage to Africa, and *Afrocentrism,* which designates a set of ideas about the cultural coherence of African American life.

Africanisms. The concept of Africanisms is central to interpreting much of what has come to be identified as African American culture. Melville Herskovits's 1941 book, *The Myth of the Negro Past,* is most often cited as the primary source for this perspective. An anthropologist, Herskovits studied African survivals among blacks in the Caribbean and Brazil. He extended his findings to demonstrate that these survivals influenced populations in contact with those of African descent.

One appraisal (Meier & Rudwick, 1966) specifies the domains of African-isms evident in the United States to include folklore, magic, medicine, music, dance, and language. In the linguistic domain, the most significant work on Africanisms appeared in 1949 when Herskovits's student, Lorenzo Turner, published *Africanisms in the Gullah Dialect,* in which he demonstrated direct influence on American English from African languages (Turner, 1949/1968). This line of analysis reappeared in the late 1960s and 1970s (for example, Dillard, 1972; Vass, 1979) to challenge prevailing linguistic explanations attributing the influences on African American English primarily to British dialects.

Over the past two decades, scholarship adding evidence for Africanisms (usually called *retentions* and *survivals*) in the United States has flourished. Holloway (1990) has compiled an excellent series of papers on various domains of African retention.

Afrocentrism. The second important construct for understanding African American culture is Afrocentrism. The term is relatively recent, dating only to the 1980s. Developed primarily by Molefi Asante (1980, 1987, 1990), the ideas lodged in this term are extensions of the Africanisms construct drawn into a larger philosophical frame. Afrocentrism means interpreting memory and experience from an African American perspective. Asante (1987) aims to create a complex African cultural center for African American life: "*Afrocentricity* is the most complete philosophical totalization of the African being-at-the-center of his or her existence" (p. 125). The perspective takes issue with prevailing historical accounts of the development of civilization, which exclude Africans (Asante, 1987); seeks the African heritage at the root of current practice; and looks to African traditions as a guide to current practice. "It is a commitment to a historical project that places the African person back on center" (Asante, 1987, p. 125).

There are skeptics, of course, about the viability of an Afrocentric philosophy, some on the grounds of historical inaccuracies (Lefkowitz, 1997) and some for essentialistic thinking (Gilroy, 1995). Yet the concept informs both an understanding of themes in African American culture and a way of thinking about the experience and discourse of African Americans. In this sense, it becomes a cultural resource for centering identity.

Cultural Abstractions

Over several decades, scholars have written about the influence of traditional worldviews of African peoples on African American culture. In the mid-1970s, Jack Daniel and Geneva Smitherman (Daniel & Smitherman, 1976; Smitherman, 1977) described five basic themes that run through different African tribes and cultures to form a Traditional African Worldview: (a) unity between material and spiritual life, (b) centrality of religion as a pervasive force, (c) harmony of people and nature in the universe, (d) social patterning according to the natural rhythms of the universe, and (e) defining time as participation in experienced events rather than as an abstract notion. In all aspects of this worldview, community and community participation are central. These authors comment that "basic underlying thought patterns do exist amid the unending diversity of African people" (p. 28).

These propositions about an African worldview are used by Smitherman (1977; Daniel & Smitherman-Donaldson, 1990) and others (Kochman, 1972; Stuckey, 1987) as the interpretive mechanism for the meaning of African American communication forms, and they also emerge as central in the philosophy of Afrocentrism.

What this means is that individuals who strongly identify with African American culture and participate or have histories of participation with others within this cultural frame will tend to function with a set of ideas, values, and beliefs differing from most European-based cultural systems. The language patterns and communication forms expressive of these cultural abstractions may, thus, be poorly understood by those outside the cultural frame.

I turn next to a brief overview of frequently noted cultural abstractions in African American communities: (a) community, harmony, and connection; (b) individual uniqueness; (c) expressive spiritual meaning; (d) time as participation and experience; (e) improvisation and inventiveness; and (f) primacy of the Word. These notions function in coordination with related cultural artifacts and communicative forms.

Community, harmony, and connection. First and perhaps the most dominant of the cultural abstractions among many African Americans is adherence to the belief in community, harmony, and connection. The experience of blacks in slavery powerfully explains the emphasis on community and linkages among people for survival. Postslavery, the impact of segregation, racially motivated lynchings, racism, and discrimination all layered the priority for community identification as a way of mobilizing connection and support among African Americans. Smitherman (1977) links this value to the African theme of interdependent rhythms of the universe: "Balance in the community, as in the universe," she says, "consists of maintaining these interdependent relationships" (p. 75).

Several examples illustrate how community functions. The first is from my personal experience with a child who attended preschool with my son. This African American girl's mother had a history of drug abuse, which eventually led her to a drug treatment program. Rather than being allowed to enter foster care, the child was cared for by a woman friend (single and with no children) of the mother as her "aunt" for close to a year until the child moved to her grandmother's. A second example, which involved voter redistricting, was reported on National Public Radio on July 5, 1996. Representative Cynthia McKinney, an African American Democrat from Georgia, faced a tough reelection bid in a state with a history of voting on racial lines. Her district changed from 60% to 40% black, and high black voter turnout in the primary was judged essential for retaining her House seat. The story focused on a largely African American delegation from Pennsylvania who traveled to Georgia to assist with door-to-door campaigning. McKinney prevailed in her reelection bid in November 1996. Finally, a sense of connection figured powerfully in black viewpoints about the murder trial of O. J. Simpson. In this case, community encompassed large numbers of African Americans around the country who were joined by their bonds of experience to support the view that Simpson *as a black man* was the victim of racism rather than a murderer.

Individual uniqueness. Individual uniqueness complements the emphasis on community. This aspect of African American culture places the individual within a community where it is expected and accepted that personal distinctiveness should define the individual. It is this characteristic that influences the modes of discourse associated with African Americans. Individual uniqueness, moreover, anchors the belief in the integrity of personal experience as a way of knowing about the world. "Uniqueness is inculcated in childhood, where children are taught to do their best and not compare themselves to others" and "to 'be real' and express their true self through actions and style" (Hecht, Collier, & Ribeau, 1993, pp. 101-102).

Expressive spiritual meaning. Expressive spiritual meaning in the U.S. context is founded in religious participation as a means of hope and a hub for larger community life. Religious and spiritual beliefs form "the core foundation of the African world" (Holloway, 1990), and the emergence of spiritual life as an anchor for African Americans during slavery was a logical outgrowth of African belief systems. African American spiritual and religious life exhibits a mixture of cultural continuity and discontinuity. The continuity is in the anchor to deities, and discontinuity is in the displacement of most specific African religious beliefs by Christianity. As the black church developed from slave practices, the blend of the African and American worlds continued.

Time as participation and experience. African Americans have long referred to their sense of time as "Colored People's Time"—being *in* time, not *on* time. Much lies behind that phrase. One explanation is that not being on time is a position within African Americans' subjective reality that may symbolize defiance of a system of time and the dictates of time historically thrust on blacks (Hecht et al., 1993). A more complex perspective is suggested by Dorothy Pennington (1979), who explains that the idea of "in time" means what occurs in a particular time period and also a sense of grasping and understanding the right time for things. Beliefs about being in time would explain, for example, taking as much time as necessary to discuss a problem rather than taking only a preallotted and scheduled amount of time. Differences in beliefs about time that produce contrasting "on time" and "in time" perspectives can create misunderstandings between blacks and whites. Blacks may feel alienated when whites do not—in their view—spend enough time with them to indicate sincere commitment to an issue, and whites may feel alienated when they think that blacks are demanding too much time from them.

Improvisation and inventiveness. In slavery, the need for improvisation and inventiveness arose from inability to determine one's own course because of insufficient material goods, prohibitions against communication with other slaves, different languages in contact, and the need to communicate with fellow slaves without whites knowing what was being said. Improvisation and inventiveness continue to be hallmarks of African American creativity and linguistic expression.

The Word. The final cultural abstraction to be described here points to the primacy of the Word, to a value placed on language itself that is quite different from what one finds in most of white America. The oral tradition among African Americans carries forward the oral cultures of Africa. The

African word *nommo,* which symbolizes the power and magic of words to give life, underlies the stress on orality and the significance of what is said by individuals (Asante, 1987; Smitherman, 1977). The primacy of the Word underlies songs, stories, and folk sayings as well as the emphasis on lively, verbal interchange and expressiveness between people.

Significant Institutions

The institutions of religion and the family contrast sharply in African America and Euro-America. These institutions lodge complex meanings and powerfully shape lived experiences among many African Americans today.

The church. The African American church evolved as a separate religious institution in the United States, with beginnings in the Second Great Awakening, a Christian revival movement between 1780 and 1830 celebrated through camp meetings (Lincoln & Mamiya, 1990). Today, the black church remains a center for African American culture. Even middle-class black suburban families drive considerable distances to attend black churches.

Daniel and Smitherman (1976) describe the black church (meaning Christian and Protestant) as defined by the "cognitive content" of Judeo-Christian tradition and the "affective process" of Africa. Capturing the special role of the black church in the late 20th century, these scholars see it as

> our ages-old landmark . . . still a place where weary souls are fortified, where a sense of secular and sacred community is affirmed, where joyful ceremonies take place, and where the cultural life-blood of the Black community is purified and enriched by the Spirit. It is still a place where call/response is the communicative well-spring of collective catharsis, and where visions of Black survival and advancement are seen in the mind's eye. (p. 42)

The black church also is unique in its historic and contemporary role as the center of community. In modern times, we associate it first with the Civil Rights Movement and more recently with afterschool programs for children, with drug education, and with support programs for teens and single parents in distress.

Based on the National Survey of Black Americans (NSBA), 52% of African Americans are Baptist and 10% Methodist (Taylor & Chatters, 1991). Small but growing in numbers, the religious movements associated with the Black Muslims and Nation of Islam carry a core spiritual meaning resonant with the history of African Americans. Combined with a philosophy stressing knowledge and purification, Islam offers special appeal to those who associate Christianity with slavery and racism. Within the Nation of Islam, Elijah Muhammad, Malcolm X, and Louis Farrakhan have galvanized support by using religious beliefs as a means for purification and racial unity.

The family. The African American family in its various iterations has been the product of economic forces as well as cultural patterns. The race-based cultural circumstances creating the African American family institution produced entities quite different from what was common *and* idealized in white America. Three characteristics are significant.

First, whereas the nuclear family is the standard among Eurowhites, extended family defines the norm among blacks (Hatchett, Cochran, & Jackson, 1991; Martin & Martin, 1978). Extended family may include several households as well as individuals treated as family and called by family names but not related through birth or marriage.

Second, as discussed in the preceding chapter, African American women never had the luxury of restricted family life. Houston Stanback (1985) reminds white readers that "the black woman's heritage from slavery—and its aftermath of poverty and racism—is a *tradition* of work outside the home" (p. 181) and a "second shift" of primary domestic responsibility in the home.

Third, against the historical pattern of low wage earnings for African American males, African American families increasingly are female-headed across the age range. The most recent data found that 47% of black households were headed by women, with no male present, compared to 13% for non-Hispanic whites (U.S. Bureau of the Census, 1996a). Female-headed families reflect both the absence of husbands through separation or divorce and the increasing trend for children to be born to mothers who are not married to the birth fathers of their children.

Cultural Artifacts

Many cultural artifacts expressive of African American peoples are well known throughout the United States, at least at a superficial level. The African Americanness of blues, jazz, hip hop, and rap, of *Native Son, The Color Purple,* and *Beloved,* is not news to non-African Americans. The meanings of these artifacts, however, vary significantly when interpreted in the context of African American experience contrasted to non-African American experience.

I briefly consider two artifact groupings: music and literature. Each relates to the abstractions discussed above and to the language and communication patterns discussed below. Like most cultural practices, clear lines cannot be drawn between the systems of cultural expression involved. A novel, for example, is a material artifact with an artistic form and a particular role and function; its text draws from imagination in cultural context, and the author's expression represents different styles of language, some intended to represent naturalistic discourse.

Music. The musical forms attributed to blacks are blues, jazz, rhythm and blues, spirituals, gospel, and rap. Each arose in sites of black experience that influenced the form that evolved, and each is rightly characterized as Afrocentric even though the forms draw from the American context and have evolved beyond black musicians. To illustrate, I focus on jazz, rap music, and spirituals.

Jazz, defined broadly, has become so mainstream in the 1990s that it is difficult for many young adults to imagine that it was once a restricted form of music played almost exclusively by and for African Americans, suspect and even feared among whites for its "immoral" expression and influence. Robert Ferris Thompson (1990) identifies the centuries old west-central African Kongo culture (essentially the Bakongo and Bantu cultures) as a direct influence on North American jazz, Brazilian samba, and Cuban rumba. Kongo slaves were numerous in New Orleans, the birthplace of jazz, and elements of Kongo musical and dance forms made their way into early jazz forms, especially rhythms and drumming. The word itself has Bantu origins, taken from *jaja,* which means "cause to dance, make dance" (Vass, 1979).

Many of the cultural abstractions associated with African Americans are manifest in jazz. Improvisation prevails. Creativity within particular forms reigns as the signature of talented jazz musicians. When a jazz group jams, connection among its members is paramount, but individual uniqueness takes center stage as focus shifts among saxophonist, pianist, drummer, and bassist, each of whom improvises. These formal properties contrast sharply with most Western music.

The deaths of Cab Calloway and Ella Fitzgerald in 1996 provided a moment for commentary on one vocal jazz element called *scatting,* which is an improvisational melodic "doo-waa-ah-do-ee-doobee-doo-waa" type of nonverbal singing. Fitzgerald and Louis Armstrong were famous for scatting, but Calloway invented it. In an interview with him replayed on National Public Radio after his death, he was asked how he came up with scat. He answered that it happened one night when he forgot the words to the song he was singing, so he had to do something. The something was singing without words, and everyone loved it: thus, the birth of scat and a perfect example of improvisation.

The rise of *rap music* during the mid-1970s and early 1980s evolved from the oral form of rappin (discussed in the section on modes of discourse). Tricia Rose (1994), in her engaging analysis of rap music and black culture, locates the origin of rap music in the South Bronx of New York City and the context of hip hop culture. Rap music and controversy go hand in hand, with many of the male performers who dominate the genre receiving both praise for their authentic, bold, cultural expression and criticism for their depictions of life in the ghetto and the sexual degradation of women. Michael Eric Dyson (1993), for example, emphasizes that rap must be understood on its own terms but "that doesn't absolve us from the responsibility to say that the use of parody, when expressing misogynistic, woman-bashing sentiments, needs to be criticized" (p. 18). Noteworthy is the emergence of black women rappers, who express both strong anti-sexist messages and the integrity of the female voice (see Rose's, 1994, chapter "Bad Sistas").

The form of rap is unmistakably African American. Rap music, explains Rose (1994), is a form of rhymed storytelling in a highly rhythmic musical mode; rappers "speak with the voice of personal experience" (p. 2) usually through the first-person voice, and their stories "articulate the shifting terms of black marginality in contemporary American culture" (p. 3).

Spirituals, as the third example of African American music, can be viewed as a synthesis of African forms and diasporic circumstances. C. Eric Lincoln and Lawrence Mamiya (1990) discuss music in the black church as a retention of the African holism of music, religion, and life. Early spirituals used a call-response form and "were constantly recomposed and rearranged, so that a single spiritual might eventually have numerous musical and textual variations" (Lincoln & Mamiya, 1990, p. 349). In content, spirituals sound otherworldly, but they also carried tacit meanings and code tied to earthly struggle; getting to heaven might have meant not only life after death but life in the North after escape.

Literature. African American literature began flourishing in the wake of the civil rights era. Blacks and white alike read the works of Ralph Ellison, James

Baldwin, Richard Wright, Alice Walker, Toni Morrison, Gloria Naylor—all authors who write of the experiences of being African American in the U.S. diaspora. Beyond their readership, African American authors have become cultural symbols for the African American voice.

The significance of African American literature, taken as a whole, stems from its narrative voice of experiences in living African American identities. The stories provide cultural narrative—some of it historical, some contemporary, some a mixture of time periods used to weave the connections and community of African American people and the complicated relationships of blacks with whites. In many cases, the authors also write down a representation of the oral styles of their characters, which is a way of amplifying and legitimizing discourse styles and voices whose existence resides in speech and memory but not in written form.

African Americans Today

We live in a society vastly more integrated than was the case at mid-century, and we enter the millennium with far greater consciousness of the profound impact of race on culture and cultural practice than existed even two decades ago. Yet most white Americas remain ignorant of the complexities of African American culture, largely because most whites have limited experience with African Americans in contexts other than those defined by white cultural practices. Few white Americans eat, worship, or socialize with blacks in predominantly black settings. These experiential divides result in cultural awareness restricted to certain public artifacts such as African American music or dress or sport, to overhearing rather than participating in black discourse, and to information about African Americans that is heavily influenced and filtered through the media of mass communication, which offer limited representations of the range of African American lifestyles and cultural practices. Restricted knowledge such as this fuels stereotyping as well as inferences about one culture that are the product of interpretations through another culture's abstractions. An example from the 1996 Summer Olympics in Atlanta makes this point clearly. Muhammud Ali, former heavyweight champion, handsome, once known as a man of words but now devoid of facial expression and the victim of both Parkinson's disease and the physical beating of his sport, was selected to carry the torch to its pinnacle. Over and over, broadcast journalists proclaimed Ali to be "the most famous man on earth." Even the president of the United States reported on his brief conversation with Ali. This man may be famous, but the symbolism of an ex-fighter as cultural icon does nothing to broaden the image of Africans Americans in the eyes of the world.

The interinfluence of blacks and whites continues, just as the separation according to race continues. Of the range of manifest cultural practices, white Americans have been especially resistant to African American discourse, both misunderstanding it and diminishing its purpose, value, and linguistic complexity. Yet African Americans offer the only long-standing example in the United States of the primacy of oral culture and continuity of oral tradition. I examine next a variety of patterns for language-in-use that are found in African American speech communities.

Discourse Patterns

African American discourse comprises a complex array of linguistic and communicative characteristics, some carrying forward African retentions and others produced by contemporary cultural conditions. Lexicon, phonology, and syntax all mark varieties of African American discourse, as do distinctive registers and broader pragmatic systems for language use.

In this section, I examine a number of discourse features. The discussion is organized around five different domains: (a) distinctive lexicon that has been created within African American speech communities, (b) historical influences of African languages on English lexicon, (c) the pidgin-creolization-decreolization process, (d) the phonological and syntactic markers of what is termed African American Vernacular English (AAVE) (previously known as Black English Vernacular [BEV]), and (e) various modes of discourse that exemplify the web of history-culture-language connections. From lexicon to discursive mode, the African American cultural value for nommo/the Word infuses language with the importance of expressiveness and the connections that create continuity and community across time and place.

Lexicon

Lexicon unique to or originating in African American speech communities ranges from the ephemeral vernacular words that come and go to the more enduring elements both uniquely a part of the African American idiom and evident in cross-over usage found in Mainstream American English (MAE) speech. A major source of information about the African American lexicon is contained in the various dictionaries that have been compiled over the years.

The early dictionaries of note recorded black lexicon and black meaning from the black perspective, which added important information to mainstream dictionaries of MAE. Zora Neale Hurston (1934/1995), an anthropologist, documented the lexicon of the 1920s Harlem Renaissance and traced the origins of terminology. Cab Calloway's (1938) *Cat-alogue: A Hepster's Dictionary* recorded terms common in the world of jazz and night clubs.

The more recent dictionaries and other analyses of lexicon provide rich sources of information about both usage and origin. J. L. Dillard (1976) examined both Africanisms in African American naming practices and the mix of diachronic African language retentions and synchronic influences on African American vernacular usage (Dillard, 1977). Based on many prior works, Bruce Kellner (1989) compiled a glossary of over 300 Harlem Renaissance slang words and expressions. He included entries such as *August ham* (watermelon), *buckra* (a white person), *eel* (a pretty girl), *funk* (body odor), *hot* (wonderful), *Mister Charlie* and *Miss Ann* (white male and white female, usually derogatory), *Niggerati* (a black literary critic), *solid* (perfect), *thing* (penis), and *woofing* (casual gossip). Many terms in this dictionary that refer to black people are noted as carrying a negative connotation if used by whites: *boggy, crow, darkey, dinge, smoke, suede, zigaboo,* and a number of others.

Some lexical markers die, some endure within black speech communities but do not cross over, and others become common parlance but often with distinctive meanings in different speech communities. The word *cool* is one such example. In African American contexts, the word carries long connections to a certain type of demeanor and ability to adapt to all kinds of situations. Coolness is a cultural practice and not just a personal attribute. Marcyliena Morgan (1998) describes *cool* as "the ability to act on symbolic incidents and subtle varieties of cultural practice with eloquence, skill, wit, patience, and precise timing" (p. 253). As a crossover term into MAE, cool can serve as equivalent to *savvy, neat, very fashionable, even tempered,* and so forth—all without the connotations central to the African American meaning. Clarence Major commented in the introduction to his 1970 *Dictionary of Afro-American Slang,* that "the language of the black musician has had the greatest total effect on the informal language Americans speak" (pp. 12-13). In his more recent book, *Juba to Jive,* Major (1994) makes the point as follows: "African American speech and slang form is . . . one of the primary cutting edges against which American speech—formal and informal—generally keeps itself alive" (p. xxxiv).

Contemporary lexicon in historical context is the subject of a book by Geneva Smitherman (1994). Subtitled *From the Hood to the Amen Corner,* Smitherman presents 200 pages of entries inclusive of current usage in the urban (neighbor)hood, enduring usage in the places of black people such as the "traditional black church" (TBC), and terms traceable to African languages. In a style that has become Smitherman's signature, she writes in the vernacular and the oral style of African Americans, rendering the terms orthographically as they would be pronounced (*thang* for thing; *check yosef* for check yourself). The entries range from the sacred to the profane, and many are annotated with critical or historical notes. Smitherman also glosses terms that have crossed over into MAE. The definitions of some terms reveal meanings quite different from more mainstream English varieties: *ballin* means "playing basketball superbly" and not a man having sex with a woman; *cakes* means either "the vagina" or "cocaine, crack, or heroin" and not a sweet confection; *heads* means "one's children" or African Americans in general and not the leaders of groups or organizations; *testify* means "to give affirmation to the power and truth of something" in the church or elsewhere and not to give evidence in court. *Phat,* Smitherman conjectures, comes from *em*-phat-*ically* and also is a play on *fat* as a positive term used as a reversal of conventional meaning, just as *bad* some time ago came to indicate that something is good.

The creation of novel words and novel meanings for already existing words is a specialty of African Americans dating back to slavery. Restricted language and verbal strategies for indirection (or what we sometimes call *in-group language*) serves important protective functions for groups dominated and brutalized by others—functions critical in slave times but important today as well. Language use creates special bonds among African Americans and can also exclude non-African Americans from the speech community. In sum, boundary maintenance and the establishing of shared identities may well be the most significant motivations for the continuous elaboration of lexicon. If a person either does not understand or cannot produce the lexicon, she or he is marginalized or at least made to feel "out of it." Consider this example from a conversation between two professors, one African American (Professor A) and the other white (Professor W): Professor W has just discovered in the conversation that Professor A knows a black professor at another university whom she too knows:

W: The only person I know on the faculty there is Charles [last name deleted here].

A: Oh, you know Charles? Why he's my brother!

W: Really. He's your brother?

A: [silence] Well, not my *real* brother. He's my really good friend. You know what I mean.

W: Oh sure. He's a great guy.

When novel meanings and reversals cross over, the influence and power of a minority group becomes evident in the language used in more mainstream contexts. Whites often appropriate vernacular words and expressions from black speech communities in an attempt to show that they are current, "in," and "hip." When Robert Dole, Republican candidate for president in 1996, attacked the incumbent President Bill Clinton by saying "He can talk the talk, but can he walk the walk?" black people in this country were much more likely than white people to know that the phrases bear African American origins.

Africanisms in American English Lexicon

An especially interesting area of scholarship in historical linguistics looks at the African origins for words used in the United States—words used in some cases exclusively by black communities and used in other cases as a part of MAE.

One of the most significant linguistic sites for historical analysis has been the Gullah variety. Gullah (also known as *Geechee*) is a creole language variety that evolved from African languages in contact with English. Today, Gullah is spoken in its most distinctive form by African Americans living on the Sea Islands off the Georgia and South Carolina coasts (Hilton Head being the best known). For those who have never heard what Gullah sounds like, a sample is included in a documentary television program titled *Black on White* (Cran, 1986). Because of the island geography associated with Gullah, barrier conditions account for the high degree of African language survivals among Gullah speakers. Modern mobility has weakened the enclosure of the Gullah speech communities in recent years, but Gullah survives, with one explanation positing the economic class barrier between Gullah speakers and newcomers to their locales (Mufwene, 1997).

The landmark study of Gullah usage was conducted by Lorenzo Turner (1949/1968). As part of his 15 years of fieldwork, Turner collected lexical items from Gullah speakers and then analyzed their West African origins, largely to the Wolof, Malinke, Mandinka, Bambara, Fula, Mende, Vai, Twi, Fante, Ga, Ewe, Fon, Yoruba, Bini, Hausa, Ibo, Ibibio, Efik, Kongo, Umbundu, and Kimbundu languages. He reported on 3,938 words showing evidence of African retentions. The largest number of lexical items were traceable to Bantu origins (1,891), followed by Kwa/Sudanese (1,668), and Mandinka (1,254), which Turner classified as Bantu but which is now understood to be from the Niger-Congo language group. His lists included entries giving the Gullah word and its African connection. A few illustrations demonstrate words that are unusual to MAE and those whose relation to MAE is clear: *ban!* (from Vai) for "It is done!"; *fut* (from Wolof) for "to be nude or to have sexual intercourse" (note resemblance to *fuck*); *guba* (from the Angolan languages Kimbundu, Umbundu, and Kongo) for peanut (close to *guber*); *na* (from Mende) for "that"; *nanse* (from Twi) for "spider"; and *tanda* (from Kongo) for "to grow."

With considerably more resources available to analyze how these Gullah vocabulary items compare to current usage in what was once the Congo and is now Zaire, Winifred Vass (1979; Holloway & Vass, 1993) concluded that 35% of the words collected by Turner are traceable to Bantu usage by Luba-Kasai speakers. She also offered fascinating evidence for the direct influence of Bantu languages on Black English and on American English more generally (Vass, 1979). Examples from Vass's compilation are listed in Table 5.4; the examples recognizable as crossovers into MAE are marked with a superscript.

In the first chapter, the tendency of historical linguists to discount the influence of slave varieties on other varieties of English was noted. One indication of this tendency is the current dictionary notation given for the origins of the crossover words listed in Table 5.4. *Merriam-Webster's Collegiate Dictionary* (10th edition, 1995) attributes a Bantu origin to only one of the seven words noted with an asterisk in Table 5.4: *goober.* Yam is noted as likely of African origin ("earlier *iname*, fr. Pg [Portuguese] *inhame* and Sp [Spanish] *name*, of African origin"). *Tote* is likened to a Gullah word but not to its Bantu origins ("perh. [perhaps] fr. [from] an English-based creole; akin to Gullah & Krio *tot* to carry"). The origins for three of the words (*ballyhoo, jazz,* and *jiffy*) are listed as unknown. *Boo-boo,* which appears straightforward from Gullah with Bantu origins, is given a peculiar, overly modern origin: "probably baby-talk alter. [alternative] of boohoo, imitation of the

TABLE 5.4 Samples of Bantu Language Origins in Black English

Bantu Word and Meaning	Black English Word and Meaning
balapu [read about it]	*ballyhoo*[a] [publicity, blatant advertising]
diuba, juba [pat, beat the time]	*juba* [black dance; clap hands in time]
jaja [cause to dance]	*jazz*[a] [music originating in New Orleans]
kala [rice]	*cala* [creole rice cakes]
lulamatu [uprightness, loyalty, faithfulness]	*luluh* [a respected woman, nurse; understanding; faithful wife]
mbubu [stupid; blundering way of acting]	*boo-boo*[a] [blunder, error]
mpampa [I have mastery; charge over]	*pompasset* [ostentatious person]
nguba [peanut]	*goober*[a] [peanut]
ndufu [it is death]	*duppy* [apparition, ghost]
nkuda [turtle]	*cooter* [turtle]
nyambi [sweet potato]	*yam*[a] [red sweet potato]
nyidi [I am learning]	*yeddy* [to hear]
tota [lift a burden down from one's head; carry, pick up]	*tote*[a] [carry, pick up]
tshipi [in a short time; just a moment]	*jiffy*[a] [in a moment, short time]

SOURCE: Vass (1979) in Holloway & Vass (1993). Used by permission.
a. Crossover term into Mainstream American English, sometimes regional.

sound of weeping." Also included is the ludicrous attribution that the earliest recorded use of this word in English was 1953! Perhaps that is when it fully crossed over, but its use among African Americans long predates the 1950s.

These dictionary entries show how political the study of language can be: Fifteen years after Vass's publication (and with Turner's work in the background), compilers of the major dictionary used by college students have virtually silenced the Africanisms in American English lexicon.

The Pidgin-Creolization-Decreolization Explanation

Over the past several decades, an impressive range of evidence has been amassed to tie aspects of present-day African American English to dialect forms dating from slavery. Called the *creole hypothesis,* the reasoning links past and present in a three-part chronology: pidgin, creolization, decreolization. John Rickford (1998) provides a clear summary of this work.

A *pidgin* is a simple language variety that does not exhibit the regular grammatical form of natural languages and has no native speakers. Pidgins arise in circumstances where people who speak different languages come together in the same place and need to communicate. Pidgins draw on vocabulary from the various languages involved, with usage varying from person to person. Pidgins, notably Pidgin Portuguese and Pidgin English, spread widely with the maritime expansion of Western Europe. Pidgin English as a product of sea navigation dates to the 17th century (Dillard, 1972), first moving east to China and Australia and then west to the Americas.

The pattern associated with slavery was for enslaved Africans to develop English-based pidgin either prior to arrival in America or early in the period of relocation as slaves. Unlike house slaves, who were forced to learn English quickly, field slaves had far less contact with plantation masters and far less encouragement to learn fluent English—factors that prolonged the pidgin state. Pidgin English facilitated necessary communication between slave and plantation boss and among slaves who did not share the same African language.

The research that has been done on language varieties of slaves presents evidence that these early pidgins moved next to *creole* varieties. As a pidgin moves to creole form, the variety expands in complexity and becomes the native language of a second generation of speakers, in this case second-generation slaves. Like pidgins, creole varieties lack a written form.

The widely accepted linguistic argument is that the most common creole form pre-Civil War was *plantation creole* (Dillard, 1972; Stewart, 1970). This creole variety, says Dillard, was geographically dispersed, which accounts for its influence on southern varieties of English more generally.

Historical research on slave language draws from a variety of sources typically including notices of slaves for sale or for the capture and return of runaway slaves and attributions of slave English found in stories and narrative accounts (see Dillard, 1972; Holloway & Vass, 1993). When the English used by a slave was described as "good," it was likely either plantation creole or a more mainstream variety. "Bad" English likely meant pidgin.

The best-known English-based creole in existence today in the United States is Gullah. Several examples from Turner's (1949/1968) study of Gullah creole serve to illustrate the heritage of creole in the 20th century. These occur in a story told by a woman about "Hard Times on Edisto" Island of South Carolina.

You pick a basket of bean for five and one cent. Two basket—what it come to? I wouldn't go there today; not me!

I satisfied [with] what God done for me.

Ain't it? Ain't slavery coming back? All who never saw it—ain't it coming back? . . . Nobody ain't worry where Diana is, because my time done come through.

The first example shows the nonredundant plural, that is, marking the plural only once: "basket of bean[s]" and "five and one cent[s]." The second indicates deletion of the verb auxiliary, *am,* which is discussed below in the section on AAVE. The third shows classic multiple negation. The use of *ain't* carries the meanings of *am not, isn't, hasn't, haven't,* and *didn't,* depending on the context.

Patricia Nichols's (1983) field research during 1974 and 1975 in an area of Georgetown County, South Carolina, demonstrated that Gullah retentions reflect both gender and occupation. From language samples that she gathered, she was able to analyze the presence or absence of three Gullah features:

1. *ee* and *um* used as third-person singular pronouns

   ee [it] was foggy.

   He took *ee* [his] mother 'long with *um* [him].

2. *fuh* as an infinitive marker or complementizer

   I come *fuh* get my coat.

3. *to* used as a locative preposition equivalent to *at*

   Can we stay *to* the table?

Older men and women used more creole forms than the younger generations, and occupation also correlated with usage. Women found employment opportunities in sales, nursing, and teaching—all of which required more standard language forms and, thus, yielded more "standard" speech. Men found employment opportunities mainly in construction; these jobs, although paying substantially more than the jobs available for women, did not demand fluency in standard speech which thus encouraged the retention of creole forms.

The process of *decreolization* occurs when a creolized variety moves closer to the dominant variety/varieties of the superordinate language variety (in this case, it would be standard Southern English) but still retains features of its creolized precursors. AAVE, which is discussed in the next section, is considered by many linguists to be a decreolized variety (see Fasold, 1990, for a summary of this line of reasoning).

Although the creole hypothesis continues to be strongly supported by many prominent linguists, there are notable dissenters, the best known of whom is William Labov. Labov (1987, 1998; Labov & Harris, 1986) proposes that a stronger argument can be made that current patterns in African American English show linguistic divergence from other varieties rather than historical retentions. Yet it is not clear why one position or the other must be chosen. Rickford (1998) and others (see Spears, 1992) make clear that today's African American English has elements in common with other varieties and elements distinctive from other varieties—with some of those being linked to earlier language forms traceable to the pidgin-creolization-decreolization process. Even John Myhill (1995), whose examination of recently discovered oral recordings of ex-slaves born between 1844 and 1861 revealed few linguistic features present in modern AAVE, concludes that such evidence does not rule out the possibility of retentions; the speakers, he speculates, may have been using an interview style of language that would suppress such vernacular features.

African American Vernacular English

Since the early 1960s, the vernacular style of (especially) urban African Americans has been recognized by linguists as a sophisticated, fully functional language variety rather than a flawed version of Standard English. Even though a wealth of scholarship has been focused on what is termed African American Vernacular English (AAVE), and a common core of linguistic features appear solidly documented through a range of research studies, several limitations and provisos are in order regarding the speech communities from which the research draws. First, the research overwhelmingly describes the language of African American males, especially teens and young adults from urban areas. Houston Stanback (1985) called attention to this as a trend in research that has contributed to the silencing of African

American women's voices. Second, like all other varieties of American English, AAVE exists in a context of cultural and linguistic contact. This means that features of AAVE can be found in the speech of other groups, especially those in close contact with African Americans, for example white women on plantations during slavery or contemporary Puerto Ricans in New York City neighborhoods populated by both groups. Third, AAVE in its most complex forms is class based. Relatively enclosed, densely populated urban African American communities with constrained economic possibilities foster the most elaborated form of the dialect. Yet, it is also true that African Americans across classes and geographic locales customarily use at least some AAVE features in at least some situations. Estimates of those African Americans who use at least some recognizable set of features range from 60% (Spears, 1987) to 80% (Dillard, 1972). Finally, every discussion of AAVE must begin with the reminder that the dialect demonstrates linguistic integrity and communicative utility. Negative attitudes continue to fuel beliefs that AAVE is "bad English," "incorrect English," "deficient command of language," and an indicator of intellectual and communicative limitation. Where these beliefs occur out of ignorance, there is room for attitude change. Where they exist despite information to the contrary, the problem is more deeply one of racism.

Many of the AAVE features described here bear intimate connection to African American cultural abstractions or to the historical ancestry of African American language-in-use. More detailed information on these and other features can be found in a wide range of books and articles (see, e.g., Baugh, 1983; Jordan, 1985; Labov, 1972a; Mufwene, Rickford, Bailey, & Baugh, 1998; Smitherman, 1977, 1994; Wolfram, 1969).

Phonology. Of the various phonological features that have been identified, I have selected several that are commonly heard and that contrast with MAE. In some cases, the phonological variant implies the likelihood that non-AAVE speakers will interpret the meaning of what they hear differently than it is intended by the AAVE speaker; in other cases, interpretation across American English varieties is not problematic for content, although it may be for speaker stigmatization (Johnson & Buttny, 1982).

1. *l-lessness.* The sound /l/ is a "liquid sound," which means that it resembles vowels in using freer air flow in the vocal tract than do most consonants (saying the words *liquid* and *plastic* out loud is useful for feeling the difference in sound production). In contexts where /l/ follows a vowel,

AAVE assimilates the /l/ sound to the preceding vowel: *help* becomes *hep*, *felt* becomes *fet*, *toll* and *told* can become *toe*, and so forth.

2. *r-lessness.* Like the liquid /l/, the /r/ sound assimilates in AAVE to its preceding vowel: *fort* becomes *fot*; *car* and *card* become *cah*; *storm* becomes *stahm.* In the middle of words, (*medial* position), manifestations such as *intahresting* and *sahface* will replace *interesting* and *surface.*

3. *Weakening of final consonants.* A regular feature of AAVE phonology is the weakening of final consonants at word endings. The effect reduces the distinctiveness of the consonantal sound in these contexts: Thus *cold* will be produced as *coal*, *rest* as *res*, *seed* as *see*, *fac* for *fact*, and so forth.

4. *Substitution of voiceless /th/ sounds.* When a sound is voiced, the vocal chords vibrate during articulation. The /th/ sound has two manifestations in MAE, one voiced as in the words *then* and *there* and one voiceless as in the words *thick* and *thin.* Voiceless /th/ does not, in fact, exist in most of the world's languages, and one will easily notice that many non-native speakers of English produce *dah* rather than *the*, *dese* rather than *these*, and so on. In AAVE, the /d/ sound will be used in words such as *then* and *there*, yielding *den* and *dere.* In final position, a phoneme distinction also occurs: Thus *mouth* is *mawf* and *birth* is *birf.*

5. *-ang/-ing substitution.* In certain contexts, the *-ing* ending on words is phonologically realized as *-ang.* Smitherman (1977) lists three words where this substitution commonly occurs in AAVE: *thing = thang, ring = rang,* and *sing = sang.* In the first example, the distinctive sound does not influence meaning across dialects although it can mark speaker identity. *Thang* occurs in the speech of many African Americans, but it is also common among speakers from the southern United States who use regionally marked dialects. Male rappers too use *thang* but to mean *penis.* In the second and third examples above, the phonological variable corresponds to how the past tense would be heard in MAE and other dialects of American English. In such cases, contextual cues are necessary to distinguish whether sentences like "They *sing* it" and "He *ring* the bell" refer to present or past action.

6. *Construction of "going to."* In AAVE, *going to* is phonologically contracted to form *gon.* This phonological pattern yields oral sentences such as "She was *gon* go home," meaning "She was *going to* go home. A person not

familiar with AAVE might interpret that sentence to mean "She was gone and she went home."

7. *Suprasegmental forward stress.* Recall that a suprasegmental phoneme is a feature of patterned sound in language marking pitch, stress, duration, tone, or intonation. One suprasegmental characteristic of AAVE is the forwarding of stress in multisyllable words: *po-lice* is stressed *PO-lice, pe-can* is stressed *PE-can,* and *De-troit* is stressed *DE-troit.* For hundreds of years, there has been a trend in English to forward stress, especially in words borrowed from French, but AAVE appears to magnify this trend in certain cases.

8. *azxe.* One of the most distinctive phonological markers in AAVE is the use of *axe,* and sometimes *ass,* for the word *ask,* as in "I'll *axe* her if she knows." The phonological principle involved in this case is simplification of consonant clusters, as described in Item 3 above. When *ass* is realized for *ask,* the /k/ sound has been simplified. *Axe* likely occurs because of the simplification of the /s/ yielding *aks,* which sounds like *axe* (see Moulton, 1976, p. 158). Although no data are available on the incidence of *axe,* it is one of the features of AAVE that seems to be increasing in frequency. The "*axe* trend" may be in part a conscious choice among some African Americans to "sound black."

Syntax and morphology. Most linguists agree that the syntactic and morphological properties in AAVE provide the most significant evidence for the perseverance of a distinctive language variety. Some of these features show historical retention of forms traceable to plantation creole, whereas others seem more a product of the cultural identities produced by the boundaries of African American speech communities. Various features of the verb system provide especially compelling evidence for the continuities and distinctiveness in the linguistic expression of culture. Eleven syntactic and morphological features are described here, most of them related to the AAVE verb system either directly or indirectly (see Mufwene et al., 1998, for a more complete overview).

Turner's (1949/1968) characterization of tense in Gullah creole provides a helpful context for understanding the lineage of verb characteristics in AAVE. He noted that West African languages handle aspects of time in ways similar to Gullah:

In Gullah, little importance is attached to the actual time when an event takes place. *Accordingly, the form of the verb used to refer to present time is frequently the same as that used in reference to the past, and often there is no change in form when the future is intended* [italics added]. (p. 225)

Although his work on this aspect of Africanisms in Gullah receives less attention than do the word retentions, the significance is important to the argument regarding historical continuity of African languages into the American English context.

1. *Habitual aspect "be/bees."* Aspect is a syntactic property indicating the type or character of action. One aspect, called *habitual,* marks action that occurred in the past but continues, is ongoing, or reoccurs: "Robins sing" and "Cream rises to the top" are examples. This contrasts with *terminate* aspects, which marks completed action, as in "He caught the ball" or "She thought about it before deciding to go" (both examples indicate that something was completed and is no longer continuing).

In comparison to most other varieties of English, habitual aspect *be/bees* stands out as a unique feature in AAVE. Comparable forms are, however, present in Gullah, West Indian creoles, and West African languages (Lourie, 1978). Habitual *be* indicates that an action or condition is ongoing or repetitive rather than temporary or time-bound. "He *be* sick" means that he is sick all the time, but "He is sick" or "He sick" means that he is sick now or sick today or has a temporary illness. Several illustrations reveal the complexities of this form.

When they get caught stealin—they *be* talkin bout how innocent everybody is. (Baugh, 1983, p. 70)

Darryl *be* tellin me and Darryl *be* tellin Henry the same thing, that he *be* comin around here to see you. (Myhill, 1988, p. 311)

In the first example, the use of *be* indicates that protestations of innocence are the usual, typical response when they get caught stealing something. In the second statement, *be* refers back to what Darryl has been saying. *Be* functions as a proposition that what he has been *tellin* is not true: Either he has not been *comin around* at all, or he has been *comin around* for some other reason.

Bees is more likely to be selected to indicate habitual aspect than *be* under two conditions (Bernstein, 1988): (a) with a third-person singular reference ("It *bees* dry") or (but less often) with a third-person plural reference ("It *bees* red [berries]"), and (b) where a vowel sound follows the construction, as in "You *bees* icy cold" versus "You *be* cold." Smitherman (1994) adds that *be/bees* can also be used as "an existential reference to the human condition" (p. 56). In her novel *The Color Purple,* for example, Alice Walker (1982) has Celie use *bees* in this latter sense, as when she writes to God about her father, who has offered her as a wife to Mr. _____ (A man whose name Walker omits to symbolize that he has no personal connection to Celie): Celie writes, "Mr. _____ still don't say nothing. I take out the picture of Shug Avery. I look into her eyes. Her eyes say Yeah, it *bees* that way sometime" (p. 18).

Overall, the uses of AAVE provide evidence that the aspect system for AAVE is more complex than is the aspect system for MAE, meaning that MAE speakers are likely to be unfamiliar with the meaning contrasts involved. Some linguists (see Bailey & Maynor, 1987) interpret recent data to support the conclusion that this linguistic variable is actually increasing in complexity among African Americans.

2. *Remote time "been."* Remote time *been* is used to indicate that something started a long time ago, that it is not news, or that it occurred in the past. In this sense, the syntactic pattern follows the meanings associated with habitual *be.* The sentence "He *been* go" (Dillard, 1972) means "He went a really long time ago." "I *been* knowing that" (Fasold, 1990) means "I learned that a really long time ago, why would you think it's news to me?" And "I *been* had it there for years" (Baugh, 1983) means "I have kept it there for years." "The woman *been* married" (Martin & Wolfram, 1998) means, "The woman was married but no longer is."

3. *Absence of "be" copula and auxiliary "be".* In AAVE, *be* is absent in a variety of syntactic environments, two of which are the *be* verb copula and the auxiliary *be* (Labov, 1972a). A verb copula joins two parts of a sentence, as shown by the use of *is* in the MAE sentence "He *is* a fast-talking politician." AAVE would show absence of the copula *(zero copula)* by realizing the same sentence as "He a fast-talking politician." Another context for *be* absence occurs where MAE would use *be* as an auxiliary verb, producing syntactic constructions such as "She *is* getting sick" and "The music *is* sounding better." In this context, the AAVE syntactic rule would delete the auxiliary *is* to yield "She getting sick" and "The music sounding better."

4. *"Done" constructions.* Two different syntactic constructions involving *done* characterize AAVE. In the first, *done* is used to signal completion of something (i.e., *completive* done): "You *done* aced the test"; "He *done* axed for it." The second construction uses *be done* to indicate completed action in the future. The sentence, "We *be done* washed all the cars by the time JoJo gets back with the cigarettes" (Baugh, 1983) points to action that will be completed in the future. The MAE contrast in this case would be to use "will have washed all the cars" or "will have finished washing all the cars."

5. *Semi-auxiliary "come."* When *come* precedes a verb + *ing* construction, its role is like that of an auxiliary verb. The meaning implied by this construction expresses indignation, as in the sentence, "Just because I'm black, the police *come* questioning me." Spears (1982) offers this interesting example, where *come* is juxtaposed to *go*: "She *come* going in my room— didn't knock or nothing" ("She had the nerve to go into my room without knocking").

6. *Unmarked plurality in noun phrases.* In MAE, the regular syntactic rule marks plurality with the bound morpheme *-s/-es*: *shoe* becomes *shoes, cow* becomes *cows, dish* becomes *dishes,* and so on. In AAVE, certain types of nouns are not marked for plurality in this way. Nouns of measure are the most common example: where MAE would stipulate "two gallon*s* of milk," the unmarked AAVE form would be "two gallon of milk." Other AAVE examples are "I drive six mile," "The box was 40 pound," and "Dan grew seven inch this year." Notice that the rule in MAE for *adj + noun* constructions of measure likewise does not mark plurality at the noun: "A 10 inch [not '10 inches'] board" and "a 2 pound [not 2 'pounds'] weight." Various scholars (Labov, Cohen, Robins, & Lewis, 1968; Mufwene, 1998; Schneider, 1989) point out, however, that unmarked plurality in AAVE occurs infrequently relative to the contexts in which it could occur. Yet, its occurrence is conspicuous.

7. *Unmarked past tense.* The occurrence of the unmarked past tense in AAVE is difficult to interpret because either syntactic of phonological rules could account for it. If the explanation is phonological, the pattern follows the tendency to weaken final consonants. The realization in speech of the past-tense sentences, "He *pass* the salt" and "I *look* for him" could occur because the */-d/* phoneme is weakened. If the explanation is syntactic, the rule stipulates that for regular verbs (those that in MAE use the *-ed* bound

morpheme to indicate the past), AAVE relies on context rather than the past-tense morpheme to indicate the past. Comments by African American scholars provide support for the syntactic explanation based on their experience as AAVE speakers. Smitherman (1994) says simply that context and not "-ed" conveys time (past or present). Jordan (1985) lists "minimal inflection of verbs" (p. 131) as one guideline for Black English. Her subsequent guideline to "listen for, or invent, special Black English forms of the past tense, such as: 'He losted it' " further emphasizes the speaker consciousness of the past-tense verb patterns in AAVE.

8. *Zero third-person singular verb.* In MAE, the present-tense verb associated with the third-person singular follows a pattern that marks the verb with an -*s*: "I take" but "she take*s*"; "we ride" but "he ride*s*; and so forth. In AAVE, the third-person singular is unmarked in the verb (*zero /-s/*): "she take the bus"; "he eat the apple." The prevailing interpretation is that the variant is syntactic without implying a difference in meaning when contrasted to MAE. Labov and others (Labov & Harris, 1986) have advanced the proposition based on evidence in Philadelphia that this variant has diverged from MAE in meaning as well. Specifically, they suggest that /-s/ has become a marker of the "narrative past"—when a speaker is telling a story about the past using the present tense. An utterance showing this feature might sound as follows: "I was runnin and he *run* [runs] faster so you see I take the back way and he just *fly* [flies] pas[t]."

9. *Multiple negation.* Marking negation at more than one place in sentences is part of many vernaculars of English and is heard in constructions such as, "I *ain't* got *no* money" and "I *didn't* do *nothing.*" AAVE users often go beyond double negation, evidencing multiple negation. This feature is sometimes termed *negative concord,* referring to the grammatical agreement achieved by marking every element negative that can be so marked. Lourie's (1978) prototype quadruple negative sentence "Nobody won't never bring nothing" would translate into MAE as "No one will ever bring anything," which does not have quite the same meaning because it lacks the emphasis on the negation. Prior to the 18th century, when grammarians imposed the rule that negatives should be marked only once, multiple negation was common practice in speech (Labov, 1972a). The grammarians' "logic" was that double negatives cancel one another out to create a positive, just as the adding of two negative numbers equals a positive number. AAVE speakers may well have retained the historical form as a matter of group cohesion and

for its effect in marking meaning more emphatically, which is consonant with the priority for *nommo*.

10. *Dummy "it."* In linguistics, a "dummy" subject is used in sentences where the noun phrase has no prior reference (also called *existential sentences*), such as the use of *this* and *there* in the sentences, "*This* is my point" or "*There* is no gas left." The use of dummy *it* (Labov, 1972a) corresponds to particular meanings in AAVE. Roughly equivalent to MAE *there, it* can be found in contexts such as the following: "*It* wasn't nothing to do" and "*It's* a new car," which compare to MAE "There wasn't nothing to do" and "There's a new car." This dummy *it* usage exists in Gullah as well and is likely a direct retention from plantation creole.

11. *Zero passive voice.* Passive voice constructions, in which the agent or agency of an action or situation is absent in the surface structure of the sentence, have become commonplace in MAE (see Penelope, 1990). Whereas a deep structure of a sentence might be "James hit Janice," the passive form on the surface would appear as "Janice was hit." Jordan (1985) asserts that "there is no passive voice construction possible in Black English" (p. 129) because the cultural importance of asserting human presence, survival, and truth are paramount among African Americans. For example, Jordan says that the statement "Black English is being eliminated" is not an AAVE sentence because it names no agent or agency. The AAVE form would be active voice—for example, "White people [are] eliminating Black English" or "The schools [are] eliminating Black English." In this case, cultural values directly affect linguistic structure to produce certain sentences noteworthy for their zero passive voice.

As a whole, AAVE represents a range of variety densities for its speakers. For some, it is the primary variety spoken, whereas for others, its use is situational and focused on certain features. In all cases, AAVE exists as a linguistic variety among other linguistic varieties in the United States and *not* as a deficient or ill-formed version of Standard English.

Modes of Discourse

Various modes of discourse ranging from rhetorical forms to everyday conversational practices mark the communication of African Americans. Most of these forms are long-standing and demonstrate many of the cultural abstractions embedded in African American life. With the exception of the black sermonic form which scholars have been interested in for many years, African American modes of discourse received serious attention beginning only in the mid-1960s and early 1970s (Abrahams, 1963; Kochman, 1972; Liebow, 1967; Smitherman, 1977). The early studies focused almost exclusively on males but were followed by the work of Edith Folb (1980) and Thomas Kochman (1981), both of whom studied the language of black female and male teenagers.

The descriptions of African American discourse found in the literature attest to the power of the Word, to *nommo*. More than most speakers of English, African Americans demand and also respect the artistic elements of language-in-use and the power of "on your feet" language-in-use to infuse language with meaning.

In this section, I consider seven communicative forms that provide a perspective on the distinctive discourses arising from African American speech communities: (a) the African American sermonic form and the call-response mode embedded in it, (b) tonal semantics, (c) narrative sequencing, (d) signifying and the dozens, (e) rapping, (f) emphatic language routines, and (g) discourse devices associated with black women's language.

For those who have little contact with African Americans, most of these discourse forms remain unknown and little understood. Radio and television provide limited exposure of these modes to the popular domain, but often what is represented is stereotypic at best and inaccurate at worst. Typically, local newscasts in urban areas (which are broadcast to surrounding regional towns) contain the voices of very few African Americans: urban blacks at crime scenes, who often do use features of AAVE; a few black mayors, most of whom are proficient code-switchers; the voices of substantially accomplished African Americans with public visibility, such as retired General Colin Powell, former Surgeon General Jocelyn Elders, Vernon Jordan, and Professor Anita Hill—none of whom use many if any of the language features to be discussed in the contexts in which they are recorded for television. Situation comedies such as *Family Matters, Blossom,* and *Fresh Prince of Bel Air,* which portray African Americans a bit more realistically than earlier programming, follow scripts with few African American language features beyond intonation patterns and some phonological markers. As in earlier programs, the language features portrayed are not always accurate representations and often serve to boost laugh lines (Anderson, Fine, & Johnson, 1983). Even coverage of Jessie Jackson and Louis Farrakhan provide only glimpses, often crescendos, of their complex African American rhetorical forms. Talk shows offer more extensive views and voices, but their subject matter is often so ludicrous that the effect is one of negatively associating the language used with the lunacy of the topics and, by association, the lunacy and deviance of the black (and white) talk show guests.

The black sermon, call-response, and secular continuities. The black sermon occupies a central role in African American discourse, and many Americans recognize its basic features because of familiarity with the oratory of the Rev. Dr. Martin Luther King, Jr. The black sermon is both locus of the call-response mode (unique to African Americans) and foundation for a distinctive rhetorical style in secular as well as sacred discourse.

The black sermonic form shows continuity with West African panegyric poetry, the role of the griot, and the folk-preaching style that developed in the U.S. diaspora (Jackson, 1981). The lineage is from the panegyric praise poems, to the folk-preaching style among black preachers, to more formalized preaching styles, and finally to public discourse. As summarized by Walter Pitts (1989), panegyric poetry, which is chanted by the griot, uses rhythmic breathing accompanied by drums and string instruments to praise the courageous acts of hunters. These praise poems contain three distinct states, which build to full song in the conclusion (Jackson, 1981).

The folk sermon, which is performed in a chant style by preachers who are not seminary trained, follows the praise-poem tradition in its structure. John Gumperz (1982a) describes the prototypical sermon as moving through three states: (a) "an invocation or introductory phase which takes the form of dialogue-like interchanges," (b) a second stage in which the rhythm increases in intensity and audience responses become frequent, and (c) a climax delivered with "heavy breathing, staccato delivery, hyperventilation" (p. 190). Pitts (1989), who provides a detailed analysis of one such sermon that occurred in Tuskegee, Alabama, in 1985, notes that in the third state "the preacher can excite his hearers by running down the aisle, jumping vigorously behind the pulpit, waving his white handkerchief while pounding the lectern" (p. 143).

The audience responses during the sermon to the preacher's utterances are what constitute the call-response mode. Common responses like "Amen" and "Oh yeah" give only a surface sense of this complex system; the responses can encourage or discourage particular messages from the preacher or can be addressed to other audience members as well as to the preacher.

The folk sermonic style lays the structure for more formal sermons in the black church. King's many sermons drew from this style, even if missing the preacher's physical animation in the third stage.

The African American sermonic form occurs in a range of public contexts where African Americans control the discourse. This form has long been the signature of the Rev. Jesse Jackson. I analyzed the speech that Jackson gave at Louis Farrakhan's "Million Man March" in Washington, D.C., on October 16, 1995, and the pattern emerged clearly. Jackson builds from a measured introduction to a middle section in which he begins to invite audience responses through the pacing and tempo of his speaking. He concludes with a powerful, shouting chant-repetition to draw a response from his audience. When LaSalle LaFalle, chief of surgery at Howard University Medical School, gave the commencement address at my university several years ago, his dynamic, no-notes speech was punctuated with responses from black students. Call-response is also a customary discourse feature of more informal events, ranging from community meetings to card games. Smitherman (1977) posits that call-response is "a basic organizing principle of Black American culture generally, for it enables traditional black folk to achieve the unified state of balance or harmony which is fundamental to the traditional African world view" (p. 104).

Tonal semantics. Many African Americans find the speech of whites to be bland and monotone, and many Eurowhites find the speech of African Americans to be overly emotional and loud. The contrast pivots partly on the element of *tonal semantics,* which is "the use of voice rhythm and vocal inflection to convey meaning" (Smitherman, 1977, p. 134). Tonal semantics occur through variations in suprasegmental phonemes largely absent in other versions of American English. Pitch, stress, intonation, volume, cadence, and rate all carry particular meanings (thus the use of the word *semantics*) in African American discourse. The tonal qualities involved create a kind of artistry, akin to the acoustics of poetry and song.

The importance of tone in African American language may possibly show a retention from African languages. Many African languages are *tonal languages,* meaning that totally different meanings are conveyed through suprasegmental phonemes such as stress and contrasting pitch. Turner, for example, pointed out that Bantu words that are spelled alike carry different meaning depending on pronunciation "with high or low, long or short, rising or falling glides" (cited in Holloway & Vass, 1993, p. 1).

Narrative story style. Several years ago, a prominent African American professor came to my campus to interview for a position as head of a department. Reactions from the white faculty who met him were mixed, in fact polarized. Some found him engaging, rich in experience, and well qualified to lead the department. Others thought he evaded questions, did not offer clear answers to specific questions, and told too many stories rather than projecting what he could do in our institution. The cause of this difference in response, I thought, was his use of narrative story style (sometimes called narrative sequencing or narrative form) throughout the interview; my conclusion was uniformly confirmed by the few African Americans who met him. Our guest answered many questions with stories from which one could draw conclusions and lessons. These stories created scenarios alive with characters, drama, narrative development, and physical animation. This style stems from the oral tradition characteristic of African Americans over the years—an oral tradition likely drawn from African heritage.

Smitherman (1977) describes various narrative forms common among African Americans, including ghost stories, human interest stories, stories designed to explain something (e.g., why mosquitoes buzz in people's ears), stories about the triumphs of the underdog (the exemplar being the famous *Brer Rabbit* stories), and proverbs:

> The story element is so strong in black communicative dynamics that it pervades general everyday conversation. An ordinary inquiry is likely to elicit an extended narrative response where the abstract point or general message will be couched in concrete story form. (p. 161)

The narrative story form also structured the earliest slave narratives. In his discussion of slave autobiography, William Andrews (1986) claims that whites typically wanted objective accounts and passive voice narration, which forced black authors to assert their first-person narrative story style.

Narrative story style *as an everyday mode of language use* is not the style dictated by Eurowhite dominant ideology for how to speak in classrooms, employment interviews, and other settings of consequence. Narrative story style sharply contrasts with the standard question-answer format that guides so much of daily routine in mainstream American cultural contexts.

Signification and the dozens. These two related discourse forms feature the art of verbal "put down" (Smitherman, 1977). In *signification* (also called *signifyin* and *siggin*), the focus is the addressee. Houston Stanback (1985) provides the following example from a conversation between two black men and two black women, where Jean and Marv are siggin on Ted:

> Jean: So what is the ideal woman, Ted?
> Marv: Testify, Ted; tell-the-truth-tell-the-truth-tell-the-truth!
> Jean: Knee deep! Lift your pocketbook, Rose, [it's gettin'] knee deep.

In the *dozens* (which is sometimes known as *capping, sounding,* or "yo mamma" routines), the object of the put-down is the mother or other relative (usually female) of the addressee. "Doing the dozens" is aggressive verbal action and is called the "dirty dozens" when the content is obscene or sexually explicit. The form of the dozens at its best is the rhyming couplet, as in "Yo sista's so dumb, she can't count her thumb" or "Yo mama so ugly and fat, yo old man gotta cover his eyes with his hat." It also occurs in unrhymed form, as in "Yo sista kiss so much that her tongue just hang on the ground" or "Yo mama stinks so bad, even winos run and hide." Males, especially adolescents and young adults, engage much more in the dirty dozens than do females, but females are not excluded from participation. Smitherman (1977) notes that the name likely came from "the fact that the original verses involved twelve sex acts, each stated in such a way as to rhyme with the numbers 1 to 12" (p. 132).

The content of the dozens, however, need not be sexually oriented and anti-female. Consider this example from a professional African American woman to a professional white woman: "Yo mama was soooo white she must-a invented Wonder Bread." Unfortunately, little attention has been given to the ways in which girls and women use this discourse mode.

As verbal art, both signification and the dozens evidence the importance in African American speech communities of mastering elaborate oral forms. These forms offer a humorous, even if biting, strategy for dealing with conflict (Garner, 1983). Non-African Americans often feel uncomfortable when they hear siggin and the dozens because for them, such language is too direct, too aggressive, too blatant. Conversely, their tendency to beat around the bush and be less direct bothers many African Americans.

Rap. In Major's 1970 dictionary, rap was defined as "to hold conversation; a long, impressive monologue" (p. 96). Thomas Kochman gave particular attention to this mode in his 1972 book, *Rappin' and Stylin' Out: Communication in Urban Black America.* Somewhere in the burgeoning of consciousness about black forms of discourse in the 1970s, *rap* as a term crossed over into white American vernacular speech. Rap is yet another case of discourse that is not quite the same in a black speech community context and a white speech community context. For whites, "to rap" means "to talk freely and frankly" (*Merriam-Webster's Collegiate Dictionary,* 1995, p. 967). For African Americans, rap is a much more nuanced word. Rap is inventive, fast-paced, and highly connotative, and it demands conversational exchange, even amid what can be long personal statements.

Rap originally referred to romantic conversation in which a black man tries to win a woman's affections and sexual consent—a meaning largely lost in the process of crossover (Smitherman, 1994). Garner (1994) describes rap more generally as a "personally stylized, lively, and fluent way of talking" (p. 86).

The most current mass culture meaning for rap resides in rap music, which drew upon rap language as a resource. Rap in the oral tradition and rap music alike incorporate many of the modes of discourse that are quintessentially black, with the premium being on rhyming and other poetic devices. Yet Rose (1994) is careful to point out that rap music is not simply oral discourse set to music: Rap music uses rap discourse but is "a complex fusion of orality and postmodern technology" (p. 85). Like all modes of discourse deeply embedded in an ongoing cultural context, rap and its performance, "to rap," require intricate enculturation into the rules of a speech community.

Emphatic language routines. In the many accounts of African American modes of discourse, several discourse devices used to achieve emphasis typically appear. Some of these are *boasting* and *bragging, dissing, reading,* and *talking trash.*

Kochman (1981) describes *boasting* as a humorous inflation and exaggeration of self-accomplishment or abilities; boasting shows inventiveness and need not correspond to the truth. A black female, for example, says, "I can look through muddy water and spy dry land. I can look through any bush and spy my man" (Kochman, 1981, p. 64). Idle boasting sometimes goes by the name *woofin,* which is from the black idiomatic expression "selling woof [wolf] tickets" (Smitherman, 1977, p. 83), which likely originated from the notion of exaggeration captured in the idiom of "crying wolf." *Bragging* contrasts to boasting because it is a serious form of self-elevation that requires foundation. According to Kochman, bragging about one's abilities is acceptable (even desirable as a way of reflecting positively on blacks in general), although bragging about one's possessions and social status is not.

Dissing or *to diss* someone is a more current mode of discourse referring to verbal put-down. Smitherman (1994) notes that this verbal action can be either a sincere expression of disrespect or less serious if it is part of verbal play. Morgan (1998) discusses "the diss" as a form of what she terms *reading,* which functions to directly denigrate another person. In its primary form, reading is face-to-face and usually in front of witnesses, although rappers bring it into mass culture music. As Morgan explains, "When a target gets read, he or she is verbally attacked for inappropriate or offensive statements or for . . . false representation of his or her beliefs, personal values, etc." (p. 263).

Talkin trash is another way of referring to the verbal action of dissing. This term may have originated in the context of competitive games in which one player could distract the other by articulating insults and put-downs, but its general meaning is "the art of using strong, rhythmic, clever talk . . . to entertain, to promote one's ego, to establish leadership . . . or to project an image of BADness" (Smitherman, 1994, p. 221). Like other oral modes, talkin trash draws on the oral tradition in African American culture in which artistry and sentiment conjoin.

Women's discourse devices. In the past decade, we have begun to learn more about the voices of African American women. Houston Stanback's (1985) study of code switching by middle-class black women broke ground for subsequent study. Based on her discourse analyses, she concluded that black women used language in ways different from either black men or white women. She coined the term *smart talk* to refer to "black woman's most outspoken communicative style" (p. 183), which combines various modes of speech to express strong negative feelings in a humorous manner. She stresses that smart talk functions by juxtaposing outspokenness and indirectness. As such, it both positions black women rhetorically within African American culture and distinguishes them from other women, especially Eurowhites. Houston Stanback stresses that black women, unlike white women, function in a situation of greater communicative parity with men. Not surprisingly, the black women Houston Stanback studied used smart talk more often with blacks (both women and men) than with whites.

The type of code-switching that Houston Stanback observed has also been documented in the speech of girls. Signithia Fordham (1993) notes that when black girls want to succeed they learn to keep quiet and to suppress their African American communication style when around whites.

Recent work documenting the stylistic factors associated with black women's discourse follows the lead of Houston Stanback. In her research with black women college students, Karla Scott (1995a, 1995b) probed the stories told by these women about their communication with other black women. She isolated the function of the words *girl* and *look* as markers of code switching between cultural discourses; the black women consistently used these words to mark a shift in style when they were talking about aspects of race and language use or establishing commonality as black women. In the example, "Gi::rl let me tell you what he said to me . . . ," the introductory *girl* frames a report about something that happened or was said (the :: marks indicate prolongation of the sound).

From a somewhat different perspective, Patricia Hill Collins (1990) discusses the importance for African American women of finding and expressing their voice. Using the concept of *safe spaces*, she offers the observation that black women define their resistance to both racism and sexism in a "realm of relatively safe discourse": extended families, churches, and African American community organizations. In these safe spaces, black women can use discourse to express their standpoint in relation to others.

Collins includes in her analysis the historical significance of the space for early classic blues singing, which was dominated by female singers who expressed black women's experience:

> The songs . . . were originally sung in small communities, where boundaries distinguishing singer from audience, call from response, and thought from action were fluid and permeable. . . . The songs can be seen as poetry, as expressions of ordinary Black women rearticulated through the Afrocentric oral tradition. (p. 100)

The point here is that African American women among themselves have participated and continue to do so in modes of discourse contextualized both by their experience as members of African American speech communities in the larger society and their experiences as women in these communities and the larger society.

Implications

In this chapter, I have examined the linguistic features and discourse modes of African Americans. The context for this examination draws on broad cultural continuities that adapt and change as a function of both greater contact between African Americans and whites and continuing separation of "the races" both literally and in symbolic ways that ensure the maintenance of African American speech communities.

From a linguistic perspective, many of the features characteristic of African American speakers show evidence of African retentions or of long-standing retentions in a variety of English that evolved in the African diaspora. In Dillard's (1985) social history of American English, he singles out the dialect of blacks in the United States as "strikingly the most distinctive among American English speakers, especially when one considers that it has a very wide geographic distribution and that its history does not show any special localization at any time in the past" (p. 95). As such, African American English provides an important example of linguistic and communicative vitality in a larger context of considerable negative valuation by the majority white cultures surrounding it. For many (although certainly not all) African Americans, to be African American means to speak (at least some of the time) the present-day linguistic variety that makes claim to both the memory and present vitality of African American people in a national context where race matters. Even for the seemingly fully integrated professional African American, use of particular phonological or syntactic forms can speak volumes about his or her own sense of identity and the larger connections to communities not literally present in many of that person's daily experience. I am continuously struck, for example, by how many African American speakers present their academic talks in some version of MAE but then clearly move to a variety recognizable as African American English during some portion of the question-answer period.

From the perspective of modes of discourse too, the historical continuities are heard through the retention and creative modification in the voices of African Americans. Cultural abstraction—the stuff of how people think about the world—elaborated into cultural institutions and systems of expressiveness in artifacts all interrelate and mutually support the discourse patterns considered in this chapter. For many African Americans, these modes of discourse are the primary discourses of daily life. For others, they are discursive spaces and places where identity can be enacted outside the cultural force of mainstream institutions and practices—spaces and places to challenge dominant ideology.

In the context of mainstream, especially white, devaluation of African American linguistic and discourse forms, it is not surprising that African Americans themselves possess complex and often contradictory feelings and attitudes about their own language. Many African Americans value their culturally marked language practices but know that success demands standard language and communicative practice (Hoover, 1978; Speicher & McMahon, 1992). The cultural, economic, and political subordination of African Americans in the United States remains pervasive enough to completely exclude African Americans and the presence of African American voices from many situations; many schools and workplaces, for example, continue to be exclusively white, with the ownership, management, and administration of many more being exclusively white. White ignorance of African American culture and language continues too because of the conditions of African American subordination and marginality, on the one hand, and the perpetuation and recycling of racism, on the other. Take as an example my recent conversation with a young, liberal, Eurowhite women with a new M.A. degree in English, who is teaching college writing for the first time. Knowing that I have some expertise in what she designates as "black speech," she asked for advice about how to help her African American students "correct" their English grammar. She lamented that "they just don't get what's wrong with it." The problem was that she just didn't get it. We talked about linguistic and communicative legitimacy in African American language, the need for her to learn about both AAVE and many of the discourse forms mentioned in this chapter, and pedagogical practices with students such as hers that have been around for two decades. What's positive about the exchange is that this young teacher headed off to the library, eager to know more about African American language. What's disturbing is that the exchange happened recently, and she voiced an attitude about African American language still all too prevalent in our society. The irony is the deeper failure to even recognize the inherent racism of posing the question as one of "correct" rather than "Standard" English.

The United States educational system needs vastly better methods for teaching about language diversity before Eurowhites and even some African Americans move away from reducing African American language-in-use to "jive," "incorrect English," "slang," "hollering and stomping," and "lingo." And for African Americans, the burdens of code-switching between varieties marked and unmarked for their cultural identity, and the consequences of embracing language forms deemed inferior by others, will not be eased unless better understanding is achieved about the historical and cultural foundations of their discourse patterns. The American public continues to direct many prejudicial practices to African Americans, such as discrimination in employment and bank lending, even in the context of reasonably good public information about these practices. As the Ebonics controversy demonstrates, there has been nothing constituting effective education let alone public information about African American language. That being the case, the misunderstanding, disregard, and inherently racist attitudes about this vital voice in the United States should surprise no one. An important challenge in our multicultural and multilingual society is to better understand the longest-standing minority voice in the country and to make constructive use of that understanding.

6

∽

Hispanic Peoples and
Their Language Patterns

∾

Our understanding of the evasive concept of borderland—a never-never land near the rim and ragged edge we call frontier, an uncertain, indeterminate, adjacent area that everybody can recognize and that, more than ever before, many call our home—has been adapted, reformulated, and reconsidered. Hyphenated identities become natural in a multiethnic society.

—Ilan Stavans (1995, p. 17)

The Jewish-Mexican-American writer Ilan Stavans (1995), in his book *The Hispanic Condition: Reflections on Culture and Identity in America,* evokes the concepts of both *borderland* and *hyphenated identities* to describe the experience of Hispanic peoples in the United States. Stavans uses the phrase "life in the hyphen" to symbolize through a linguistic metaphor the state of continuous translation between cultures. Although a controversial metaphor, Stavans's hyphen suggests the sense of reciprocal influence between two identities—not quite a third identity to be named differently but yet neither the whole of either side of the hyphen. Gustavo Pérez Firmat

(1994) draws on the same linguistic metaphor to symbolize the Cuban experience in the United States, but he changes the preposition, making the phrase "life *on* the hyphen." So whether immersed *in* the juncture of two cultures or balancing *on* two cultural borders, the energizing cultural forces draw from two broad cultural experiences. From a grammatical perspective, too, the hyphen establishes a certain connection between two nouns, two distinctive cultural systems, in this case one *American* (meaning U.S.) and the other either broadly *Hispanic* or specifically an ancestry such as *Mexican* or *Puerto Rican* that has merged with other ancestries. Without the hyphen, the grammatical relations of two cultural/national words next to each other might symbolize the noun adjunct: two things. The two words might also symbolize the adjective: a modifier lessening and subordinating identities such as *Mexican* to *American*. Hyphen or not, the presumption of American primacy lies in the word order; we never see *American-Mexican* or *American Hispanic*. The complexities, thus, engage questions about being Hispanic in an American cultural milieu shaped by dominant U.S. ideology.

Unlike African Americans for whom the United States is a diaspora, the vast majority of Hispanics in the United States experience life as more immediately connected to an ancestral culture whose proximate borders invite continuous cultural interplay. Even for Cubans who have come to the United States as refugees, the "homeland" is proximate, and some newcomers arrive each year.

The Hispanic experience mixes and draws from differing cultural systems, which Gloria Anzaldúa (1987) describes as producing "the *mestizo* worldview" of mixed Spanish and Indian blood that embraces ambiguity. The word *mestizo* carries Latin origins meaning "to mix." Linguistically, mestizo draws on Spanish of at least four major varieties, including Mexican, Puerto Rican, Cuban, and European, while it also draws on the many varieties within these ancestry groups, as well as the many varieties of American English.

The term *Hispanic* generalizes across a broad diversity of cultural meanings and practices. Unfortunately, many Anglophiles (usually referred to as *Anglos,* which is the word used in this chapter to mark the contrast with Hispanic peoples, many of whom are white) assume that all Hispanics are foreign-born immigrants who speak Spanish and lack motivation to learn English or participate in "American society."

Because *Hispanic* is such a broad term, more culturally meaningful labels often name the identity of particular peoples: Sometimes, these labels refer to countries or regions, as in *Caribbean* or *Brazilian; Latino* and *Latina* describe those who identify themselves with Latin American culture; *Chicano* and *Chicana* frequently replace both *Hispanic* and *Mexican-American* as the preferred cultural term. Hispanic peoples also vary in skin color, largely as a result of the mixed progeny representing the Americas, Africa, and Europe. Thus, the Census Bureau defines Hispanic as an ethnicity whose specific members can be of any race, but even these definitions represent symbolic approximations because of their complex cultural meanings. Those who we call *Hispanic* comprise, then, a rich variety of peoples, complexions, and traditions tied together in greater or lesser degrees depending on a myriad of factors. The dynamics related to skin color—metaphorically designated as *black, brown,* and *white*—complicate any definition because these "appearance symbols" carry cultural and political meanings stemming from the privilege of whiteness. Consider the 1997 news reports about Luz Dina Villoslada, one of the members of the Peruvian Tupac Araru Revolutionary Movement, which held hostages in the Japanese embassy in Peru. A press profile of her included this: As a baby her parents nicknamed her "La Gringa" because at birth "blond hair billowed from her head 'like cotton,' her mother recalled" (Fainaru, 1997, p. A1). In the context of the United States, the ties that bind Hispanics may depend just as much on differences from the Anglo population as on similarities among Hispanic peoples.

In this chapter, I consider (a) an overview of the composition of Hispanic peoples in the United States, (b) the cultural characteristics and themes of the major ancestry groups making up the Hispanic population in the United States, and (c) the language patterns and issues of Hispanic peoples, who make up a growing part of the cultural multiplicity of the United States. The three largest Hispanic ancestry groups will be considered in some detail: Mexican-Americans, Puerto Ricans, and Cubans. Each of these groups represents a different type of cultural contact with mainstream America, and each, although present in various locales, is concentrated in a different region of the country (Mexican-Americans in the Southwest and California, Puerto Ricans in New York, and Cubans in Florida).

Just as caution must be exercised in attributing cultural and language characteristics to all African Americans, so must we proceed with caution when characterizing Hispanic culture and language. Hispanic peoples represent different "ancestry" groups, and even within a national origin group, say, Puerto Ricans, differences exist depending on factors such as place of birth (Puerto Rico or the United States mainland) and socioeconomic status. Yet even accounting for intra-Hispanic diversity, broad cultural patterns reveal meaningful contrasts between Hispanic- and Anglophile-identified

TABLE 6.1 Distribution of Hispanic Peoples by Ancestry Origin: 1993

Ancestry	Percentage of Total Hispanic Population
Mexican	64
Puerto Rican	11
Cuban	5
Central and South American	13
Other	7

SOURCE: U.S. Bureau of the Census (1995a).

peoples. These contrasts contribute to the cultural complexity in language and communication that is evident in so many parts of the country.

Hispanic Peoples in the United States

Census data on the approximately 30 million Hispanics in the United States show the substantial presence of Mexican-Americans, who make up well over half of the entire Hispanic population—64% (see Table 6.1). Puerto Ricans account for 11% of the Hispanic ethnic category, Cubans for 5%, and all Central and South Americans combined for 13%. The remainder identified themselves as Spanish or simply Hispanic or Latino.

Geographic Distribution

By sheer numbers alone, Hispanic peoples are concentrated in California, the Southwest, Florida, and certain parts of the northeastern United States. Over one third live in California and over one fifth in Texas—both states bordering on Mexico. Those states with the largest and smallest numbers of Hispanics as of 1996 are listed in Table 6.2. The density of the Hispanic population in specific geographic centers is made clear by considering that close to three quarters of all Hispanic peoples reside in three states: California, Texas, and New York.

Like other "minority" groups, Hispanics live primarily in a small set of urban areas. The cities with the largest Hispanic populations are shown in Table 6.3. Note too that Hispanic peoples make up over 50% of the population in some of these cities: San Antonio, El Paso, Miami, Santa Ana, and Corpus Christi (Mexican-Americans accounting for most of the population in all but Miami, where Cuban-Americans dominate).

TABLE 6.2   Hispanic Population in States With Greatest and Fewest Hispanic
Residents (1996 estimates)

Five Highest States	Five Lowest States
California = 9,630,188	Vermont = 5,704
Texas = 5,503,372	North Dakota = 6,359
New York = 2,537,597	South Dakota = 7,266
Florida = 2,022,110	Maine = 8,446
Illinois = 1,136,282	West Virginia = 9,892

SOURCE: U.S. Bureau of the Census (1996c).

TABLE 6.3   Cities With Largest Hispanic Population: 1992

Rank	City	Hispanic Population	Percentage of Population
1	New York, NY	1,783,511	24.4
2	Los Angeles, CA	1,391,411	39.9
3	Chicago, IL	545,852	19.6
4	San Antonio, TX	520,282	55.6
5	Houston, TX	450,483	27.6
6	El Paso, TX	355,669	69.0
7	San Diego, CA	229,519	20.7
8	Miami, FL	223,964	62.5
9	Dallas, TX	210,240	20.9
10	San Jose, CA	208,388	26.6
11	Phoenix, AZ	197,103	20.0
12	Santa Ana, CA	191,383	65.2
13	Albuquerque, NM	132,706	34.5
14	Corpus Christi, TX	129,708	50.4
15	Tucson, AZ	118,595	29.3

SOURCE: U.S. Bureau of the Census (1996f).

In 1994 alone, the Hispanic population increased by 3.5% compared to the white, non-Hispanic population, which increased only .4%. In absolute numbers, 1994 marked the first time that the United States gained more Hispanics than non-Hispanic whites: 897,000 compared to 813,000 (U.S. Bureau of the Census, 1995b). Annual growth such as this dramatically illustrates why the nation's demographic mix is shifting.

Standard of Living

Like blacks, Hispanics fare poorly in terms of standard of living, although variability exists among the different Hispanic groups. Hispanic unemploy-

TABLE 6.4   Income Comparisons of Hispanics With Non-Hispanic Whites: 1996

Indicator	Hispanics	Non-Hispanic Whites
Poverty rate for families	30.3%	8.5%
Per capita income	$10,048	$19,181
Median household income	$24,906	$37,161
Families below $25,000 annually	50.8%	22.6%
Families $50,000 and above annually	19.3%	44.0%

SOURCE: U.S. Bureau of the Census (1996a, 1996d, 1997b).

ment rates consistently surpass national averages, and Hispanics compared to non-Hispanic whites are underrepresented in "managerial and professional specialties": In 1996, 12% of Hispanic men and 17% of Hispanic women, compared to 30% of non-Hispanic white men and 33% of non-Hispanic white women, were in this category. The contrasting pattern is for Hispanics to be overrepresented as "operators, fabricators, and laborers" (29% of Hispanic men and 14% of women, compared to 18% of non-Hispanic white men and 6% of women [U.S. Bureau of the Census, 1996h]).

On the major income indicators reflective of overall standard of living, the Hispanic situation is substantially inferior to national norms. Their family poverty rates are more than three times higher than those among non-Hispanic whites, with close to one third of Hispanic families living in poverty as recently as 1996. Per capita income for 1996 lagged behind that of whites by $9,000, and the gap in median household income was over $12,000. As is the case with blacks, among Hispanics, the poor are poorer than non-Hispanic whites, and those in the financial middle class are less numerous compared to whites. Income data for 1996 show slightly over half of all Hispanic families below $25,000 annually compared to just over one fifth of non-Hispanic white families; at the higher levels, about one fifth of Hispanic families have annual incomes of $50,000 or more, compared to 44% of non-Hispanic white families (U.S. Bureau of the Census, 1996e). Comparative data for these indices appear in Table 6.4.

Language Profile

Based on 1990 census data, about 17.3 million people in the United States age 5 years and older speak Spanish, and another 430,000 speak Portuguese (Bruno, 1993). The number of Spanish speakers increased by about 10.8

TABLE 6.5   Distribution of LEP Spanish Speakers by Age

Age Group	Number of LEP Speakers	LEP Speakers as Percentage of Group
5 to 17 years	1.6 million	39
18 to 64 years	6.0 million	50
65+ years	660,000	62

SOURCE: Derived from U.S. Bureau of the Census, *Statistical Abstract of the United States* (1994).
NOTE: LEP = limited English proficiency.

million from 1980 to 1990—a dramatic 166% gain. Based on a sample of Spanish-speaking people in the United States, the Census Bureau estimates that close to half (48%, or 8.3 million) speak English less than "very well" (U.S. Bureau of the Census, *Statistical Abstract,* 1994c). The distribution of those with limited English proficiency (LEP) by age group shows the increasing tilt away from Spanish dominance toward Spanish-English bilingualism or English dominance in the group composed of school-age children and adolescents (see Table 6.5). This would be expected, because their schooling is either bilingual (if they entered public school as LEP students) or exclusively in English.

Although the majority of Hispanic people in the United States speak Spanish, a sizeable minority do not speak Spanish in the home. Some are monolingual American English speakers or have limited proficiency in Spanish, and some speak Portuguese.

Because Hispanic peoples cluster much more heavily in certain regions of the United States than in others, some Anglo citizens live in areas where Spanish is commonly heard, whereas others rarely if ever hear Spanish spoken in their sociolinguistic environment. The complexities of Hispanic language use and the perceptions associated with Spanish speakers often reveal geographic overtones; it is easy for Anglos who feel overwhelmed by Spanish in their immediate environment to overestimate the presence of Spanish in the United States, just as it is easy for Anglos who rarely hear Spanish to underestimate its presence or vitality.

Hispanic Cultural Themes

The cultural context for understanding both the discourse patterns and important language issues of Hispanic peoples can be approached from a view toward both broad Hispanic cultural themes and more specific cultural characteristics embedded in particular ancestry groups. I first take a broad look at Hispanic cultural characteristics and then examine distinctive features associated with the history and cultural background of Mexican-Americans, Puerto Ricans, and Cubans residing in the United States.

Four distinctive themes run through Hispanic cultural systems. These involve (a) strong national, ancestral, and Spanish-language ties, (b) the centrality of religion, (c) family bonds and loyalties, and (d) belief in the unifying spirit of race, or *La Raza*. In addition, the vast majority of Hispanics (Cubans excepted) are in the lowest economic strata of the United States, which fosters a liberal attitude toward government involvement in social welfare programs. To say that Hispanics are liberal, however, inappropriately generalizes certain political persuasions to other attitudinal perspectives.

National, Ancestral, and Language Ties

Hispanic peoples tend to hold strong allegiance to their specific kinship origins and to particular places that have national, nationlike, or place-situated identity. Several factors underlie this allegiance. First, Hispanics remain a numerical minority in the United States, and the majority of them are in the economic underclass. Second, many Hispanic peoples in the United States share the cultural commonality of the Spanish language, which about 70% speak at home. Third, Hispanics are proximate rather than distal in both time and place to geographic locations of personal or family birth. Mexican-Americans often travel back and forth between the United States and Mexico, with extended family members doing the same. Puerto Ricans even if born in New York make contact with newcomers, interact with Puerto Rico-born family, neighbors, and friends, and travel back and forth to Puerto Rico. The same is true for Dominicans. Cubans in the state of diaspora retain family ties across the Cuban embargo and, in recent years, have had opportunities to see televised images of Cuban life.

The concept of *Latino/a culture* (I will consistently use the masculine and feminine forms together to avoid androcentric interpretation of the term) evolved to transcend the specific national and ancestral lineages of Hispanic Americans. The very terms *Latino* and *Latina* embrace the cultural connections of heritage. To be Latino/a is to rotate the angle of identity from the intersection of American with Puerto Rican or Mexican or Dominican culture to the broader themes of connection between and among these particular cultural groups with their particular histories and memories.

The Spanish language also functions to create and cement cultural unity. Bilingual education was created, for example, in Miami during the early

1960s because Cuban refugees wanted their children to be educated in both Spanish and English.

Among Hispanics, passion and commitment to one's native language are deeply emotional sentiments and not just superficial linguistic loyalties. Stavans (1995) remarks that the differences in the Spanish and English languages construct different worldviews. He gives as an example the fact that the past tense can be constructed in Spanish in many ways, contrasted to the future tense, which is seldom used; English syntax is the converse. To this observation about language he links the idea that "Hispanics, unable to recover from history, are obsessed with memory" (p. 127). The process of moving to English (whether a single person's development of bilingual fluency or the generational changes from Spanish to English dominance) involves either struggling to use a language (in this case, English) creatively to convey a cultural sensibility not natural to its expression or departing from the very cultural identities that the Spanish language has evolved to articulate. But, as Stavans so eloquently explains, new languages and new cultural situations can also energize identities not otherwise possible. Yet the Spanish spoken by Latinos/as is not the same everywhere because varieties differ. Stavans offers the humorous example (p. 131) of a lexical choice gone awry when advertisers in the early 1980s created a Spanish version of an ad for an insecticide that would kill *bichos*; this Spanish word means *bug* in Mexico but *penis* in Puerto Rico!

Taken together, national ties, ancestry, and the Spanish language provide a unifying cultural context where the specific identities of ethnic peoples become points of common identification. Here, my reference is to general notions of cultural abstractions that are interconnected to cultural artifacts such as clothing, rituals, and modes of language and communication.

Centrality of Religion

The majority of Anglo-Americans who profess adherence to some religion do not integrate religion into most aspects of daily life. Work, school, civic activities, and recreation usually remain secular. In contrast, religion occupies a more central role in the lives of Hispanics.

Hispanics are noteworthy for their religious adherence on two counts. First, they are largely Roman Catholic, with about 75% of their numbers claiming this religious orientation (Kanellos, 1993). For the U.S. population overall, slightly more than one fifth (21%) is Catholic. The Catholic religion, thus, provides a point of unity across different ancestral groups.

Second, Hispanics place much more importance on religion and practice it quite differently than do Anglos. "Hispanics," says Nicolas Kanellos (1993), "are an eminently religious people" (p. 367). The local parish typically functions as a cultural center, whose reach extends far beyond Sunday services and Sunday school. Many Spanish-language churches have sprung up in Hispanic-dense communities, with these parishes contributing to the sustenance of ethnic culture. I remember, for example, the day in 1990 when a new sign went up at St. Peter's Catholic Church across the street from the urban university where I teach. The new sign emblazoned in gold letters the evolution to a Spanish-speaking congregation by posting the church's name as *San Pedro Iglesia Catolica.*

In Hispanic Catholicism, the Virgin Mary receives special veneration: Our Lady of Guadalupe and Our Lady of San Juan de los Lagos for Mexicans, Our Lady of Providencia for Puerto Ricans, and La Caridad del Cobre for Cubans. Other cultural markers of religion's importance include an expansive number of holy days, religious significance for events such as a girl's 15th birthday, exhortations to the Virgin Mary and God during many daily activities and events (notice how often Hispanic athletes cross themselves, for example), and the continuing practice of pilgrimage to various religious shrines. Like African American women, women in Hispanic culture are very much the center of religion, and they are looked to for spiritual anchoring.

Family Bonds and Loyalties

Several years ago, I met a Mexican-American professor from California who was in Massachusetts visiting his niece. The niece had come from Texas to begin college at a prestigious women's school and was having adjustment problems. The uncle felt it was his responsibility to assist her and then to reassure family members back in Texas that he would look out for her well-being. Although the Anglo reaction to his "intervention" was that it was highly unusual, especially for a man, the professor said it was a natural thing to do. His actions point to the importance of family as a unit that cannot be broken, which implies less potential for voluntary separation from one's place in the extended family system. Loyalty to family, in fact, anchors much of Hispanic culture. Of note, the rhetoric of *la familia* generalizes to relationships in the community and neighborhood, or the *barrio*. This energizes community solidarity rather than encouraging mobility and the weakening of family ties. Propensity toward group orientation generalizes to work and professional situations as well, making family a more meaningful metaphor for Hispanics in the workplace than would be the case for Anglos (Condon, 1985).

La Raza

For many of Hispanic background, unity resides in the spiritual notion of *La Raza,* literally meaning *the race* but culturally meaning *the people. La Raza* provides a unity for the webs of connection through culture in a hyphenated land. Although it is primarily associated with a Mexican-American interpretation drawing on concepts of Mexican descent, *La Raza* captures the essence of a connected cultural and ethnic community.

As a cultural notion, *La Raza* celebrates commonalities in history and survival. It has to do with resilience against the forces of domination, both in ancestral history and in the context of Hispanic marginalization and otherness in the United States. And it has to do with faith in and loyalty to others who live in a hyphenated cultural identity and who value a language other than English. In an early essay on Chicano culture, Juan Gómez-Quiñones (1979) comments that the most persistent form of resistance to domination is the enactment of culture—either through " 'tradition' for its own sake, or a synthesis of tradition and creation" (p. 57). *La Raza* as a cultural abstraction is this kind of synthesis. As a spiritual force, the abstraction operates like the notion that African Americans are brothers and sisters to one another, no matter how removed in time, place, or familiarity, or that Jewish people everywhere are one people.

These cultural themes—national, ancestral, and language ties, the centrality of religion and spiritual life, *la familia,* and *La Raza*—create a common sense of cultural identity for a range of specific groups who are situated in the circumstances of U.S. residence and the social, economic, and ethnic marginality implied in that residence. From a range of experiences including substantial heterogeneity and ancestral between-group strife comes the sense and commitment to commonality of those who are Latino/a in the United States. To be Latino/a is fundamentally to be in the hyphenated space of U.S. cultures, and that cultural space creates its own meaning. Anglos often misunderstand Hispanic cultural themes either because of limited access to Hispanic daily life or because of resistence to their difference from dominant ideology. Lack of access means lack of understanding, which gives rise to many communication problems between Hispanic and non-Hispanic peoples. Yet Hispanic cultural systems in the United States, although distinctive, continuously evolve through contacts with a broad range of other cultural systems that are present in everyday life: the workplace, the mass media, schools, government, and so forth. Like those of others in the United States, Hispanic cultural identities, then, are both plural and multicultural.

Hispanic Group Profiles

Having commented on Hispanic themes, I turn now to a brief discussion of the heterogeneity of Hispanic peoples in the United States. Although the focus in this section is on the three largest groups—Mexican-Americans, Puerto Ricans, and Cubans—the whole of this heterogeneity includes Dominicans, Chileans, Peruvians, Argentineans, Salvadorans, Columbians, and many more. It is from these heterogeneous groups situated in a U.S. context that a Hispanic culture has grown and continues to emerge. Every Hispanic group, with the exception of Puerto Ricans, includes those who have immigrated to the United States and those who were born in the United States. Because Puerto Ricans are U.S. citizens whether living on the island or the mainland, they are not foreigners—a fact that many Anglos fail to recognize. Data for 1994 indicate the following percentages of foreign-borns in each Hispanic group in the U.S. population: 38% of Mexican-Americans, 70% of Cuban-Americans, and 69% of those with ancestry to Central and South American countries (U.S. Bureau of the Census, 1995a).

Mexican-Americans

Officially, over 17 million Mexican-Americans reside in the United States, over a third of these individuals were born in Mexico. The border status of the United States and Mexico both historically and today provides a unique situation for continuous articulation of two worlds to one another. Guadalupe Valdés (1988) defines Mexican-Americans as including "all persons of Spanish origin whose ancestors settled in what had been Mexican-owned territories before the signing of the Treaty of Guadalupe-Hidalgo in 1848" (p. 111). That definition encompasses families who have lived in the United States for a number of generations—some of whom speak Spanish, but some of whom do not—as well as newcomers to the United States, those who cross back and forth as seasonal workers, and legal or illegal immigrants.

The legal immigration of Mexicans to the United States has been largely patterned according to U.S. needs for cheap labor, especially in agriculture.

About half of all Mexican-Americans work in farm labor (*Worldmark*, 1998). During the 100 years from 1820 to 1920, a total of somewhat over 9 million Mexicans immigrated to the United States. The 1920s brought about 11 million additional Mexicans—more than had come in the prior 100 years, and with the exception of the 1930s and 1940s, each successive decade has swelled the number of new immigrants (McKay & Wong, 1988).

The economic status of Mexicans in the United States and Mexican-Americans is low, largely because of the combined impact of educational and job factors associated with this group. Education completion for Mexican-Americans ranks low in the context of overall U.S. statistics. Data for 1995 indicate that in this group only 47% of adults 25 years of age or older completed high school, compared to 86% of non-Hispanic whites, and that 53% of Mexican-American families had income levels less that $25,000, compared to 22% of non-Hispanic whites (U.S. Bureau of the Census, 1996b). This educational and economic profile depresses the standard of living and creates the conditions for marginalization and stereotyping.

Although Mexican-Americans are present in almost every part of the country, their concentration naturally lies proximate to the Mexican border in Southern California, Texas, Arizona, and New Mexico. The border town is a special phenomenon of cultural geography. Large cities such as El Paso, Texas (population about 550,000), are well known, although few Anglos not from that region are familiar with the Mexican border city Cuidad Juarez. There are many small towns, too. One of my students grew up in Eagle Pass, Texas, for example, a border town of about 21,000 people, many of whom move back and forth between it and its "twin" Mexican city, Piedras Negras. During the 1997-1998 school year, 80% of the children in Eagle Pass schools (that's 4 out of 5) were involved in some kind of bilingual education. In locales such as this, the concept of minority is a numerical misnomer, although the larger context of cultural practices in which the community is embedded may marginalize the Mexican-American economically and in terms of status.

Puerto Ricans on the Mainland United States

In 1990, the Puerto Rican population on the mainland United States numbered about 2.7 million—a dramatic number in the context of the population of Puerto Rico itself, which was about 3.5 million at the time.

Historically, Puerto Rico became an occupied U.S. territory at the conclusion of the Spanish-American War in 1898. In 1917, residents of Puerto Rico were granted U.S. citizenship, but commonwealth status was not achieved until 1952. Puerto Rican citizens hold all rights except the right to vote in national elections.

With the official possession of Puerto Rico, the U.S. government mandated that education be conducted in English. Ann Celia Zentella (1985), in her description of the history of language policy in Puerto Rico, notes that the U.S. attitude toward the variety of Spanish common in Puerto Rico was negative, judging it to be an inferior form of the Spanish common to Spain. In 1952, the United States allowed the reinstatement of Spanish as the primary language of instruction but mandated English as a compulsory subject. Theoretically, then, all Puerto Ricans are bilingual in Spanish and English, but in reality, many develop only limited facility with English.

The status of English on the island continues to be controversial. In 1993, Governor Pedro Rossello signed a bill adding English as the second "official language" of Puerto Rico (Ross, 1993). He viewed this action as part of the movement toward statehood, whereas opponents characterized it as "cultural treason" and "the destruction of the Puerto Rican nationality." Of interest in connection with this issue, the citizens of Puerto Rico voted against statehood in both 1994 and 1998.

Today, the population of Puerto Rico is about 3.8 million (*Worldmark,* 1998). In 1990, per capita income on the island was a startlingly low $7,020 (U.S. Bureau of the Census, 1993b). Not surprisingly, the lure of a better life has brought many Puerto Ricans to the mainland, especially New York City, where close to 60% of all mainland Puerto Ricans live.

Geographically, Puerto Ricans now residing in the continental United States are heavily concentrated in New York City (first in "Spanish"/East Harlem but now in other sections as well), complemented by large groupings in other northeastern states, especially New Jersey. The 1990 census figures showed a clear geographic clustering, with Puerto Ricans accounting for 34% (762,429) of the Hispanic population of New York and numbering well over 200,000 in New Jersey (*Worldmark,* 1998). Over 100,000 also lived in Illinois, Florida, and California. Economically, Puerto Ricans fare poorly. Estimates for 1995 put 55% of Puerto Rican families below the $25,000 annual income level (U.S. Bureau of the Census, 1996d). With a family poverty rate of 36%, Puerto Ricans fare the worst of the Hispanic groups. The overall economic picture, then, is bleak.

The Cuban Population in the United States

Of the Hispanic groups in the United States, Cubans are unique in many ways. Their sizable minority presence owes to refugee status, which makes the concept of homeland distinctive for Cubans. Their economic condition compares favorably to other Hispanic groups in the United States. Their political orientations encompass a greater span of the spectrum, with a notable political and economic conservatism among the older population. There were relatively few Cubans residing in the United States prior to 1959, when Fidel Castro and his revolutionary forces overthrew the government of Fulgencio Batista, replacing a totalitarian dictatorship with communism. The demographic history of Cuban-Americans is temporally compact. About 794,000 migrated to the United States between 1959 and 1980 (Boswell & Curtis, 1983), in a post-Castro era where the flow of immigrants was controlled on the U.S. side by immigration and refugee reception policies and on the Cuban side by Castro's policies about who could leave the country under what conditions. Those in the first group to leave Cuba between 1959 and 1962 are often referred to as "Golden Exiles" because a sizable number (about 40%) were economic and cultural elites. These emigrés assumed their stay would be short. The next major period of immigration spans 1965 to 1973—the period of "airlifts." Cubans in this period were motivated to seek economic opportunities and political freedom in the United States because of the growing economic strains in Cuba brought about primarily by the U.S.-led trade embargo, which began in 1962.

The Refugee Act of 1980 severely limited the number of Cubans permitted to enter the United States because Cubans were no longer considered refugees. Nonetheless, a third major spurt of immigration occurred from April to September 1980, its drama portrayed on U.S. television. The period, known as the Mariel Boatlift, brought 125,000 people to U.S. shores, consisting of a different demographic mix of Cubans than had come previously: more blacks, unskilled workers, single men (homosexuals), and certainly some of what the press labeled "undesirables" (criminals mainly)—although not in the numbers first feared. Immigration figures for the two decades during which most Cubans came to the United States are shown in Table 6.6.

Geographically, Cuban-Americans reside primarily in Florida (Dade County), New York City, New Jersey, and Connecticut. In 1990, Florida was home to about 1.6 million Cubans—4% of the state's population (*Worldmark*, 1998). Miami has become a kind of "spiritual center" whose essence is "Cubanía" (Pérez Firmat, 1994, p. 12).

TABLE 6.6   Cuban Immigration Into the United States: 1959-1980

Years	Group	Number of Migrants
1959-1962	"Golden Exiles"	215,300
1963-1965	Restricted period	58,500
1965-1973	Family reunification "Freedom Flights"	302,000
1973-1980	Restricted period	50,500
1980	Mariel boatlift	125,000

SOURCE: Compiled from Boswell and Curtis (1983) and Garcia and Otheguy (1988).

Economically, Cuban Americans are between other minority groups in the United States and non-Hispanic whites. Contrasted to other Hispanic groups, the percentage of Cuban-American families with annual income below $25,000 in 1995 compares favorably: 38% compared to 53% for Mexican-Americans and 55% for Puerto Ricans (U.S. Bureau of the Census, 1996d). Yet this low-income bracket accounts for more families than the comparable level for non-Hispanic whites (22%). On the other side of the economic divide, we see the same pattern, with 30% of Cuban-American families commanding annual incomes of $50,000 and above, 14% fewer than non-Hispanic whites, but more than both Mexican-Americans and Puerto Ricans (17% and 21%, respectively).

Because of the circumstances for their presence in the United States and the geographic concentrations of Cubans, some argue that many of the cultural traditions typically Cuban are more pronounced and better preserved than in Cuba (Boswell & Curtis, 1983). A kind of "refugee mentality" that continues to imagine a return to the island explains some of this propensity for cultural retention, but for the younger generations, the tradition interlaces with regional and mass American culture. Thus, what marks Cuban culture in the United States at late 20th century draws from the pre-Castro Cubanía, from the adaptation of that sense of Cubanness to the reality of life in the United States, and to the elaboration of new cultural forms, especially among the younger generations. The vitality of Cuban cultural life is clearly evident to anyone who visits Miami Beach, where life is Cuban (or more accurately, Cuban-American). Food, music, decor, dress, and the presence of cross-pollinated Cuban Spanish and Cuban English (see Fernandez, 1983) create a cultural place of intense significance.

Crossover elements from Cuba to mainstream America have always been most evident in music. Long before Castro's Cuba, millions of Americans heard the conga music and accented English of Desi Arnaz. Arnaz first performed in Miami in 1937 but later became famous as Ricky Ricardo, the "crazy Cuban" husband to the "crazy redhead" (Lucille Ball) in the long-running *I Love Lucy* show. Although the "airhead" portrayal of Lucy as a statement about women's role in the 1950s has often been mentioned by media critics, the many occasions in which Ricky's "broken" English was the butt of jokes is less often cited but was equally negative in its stereotyping. The most famous contemporary crossover star and entrepreneur is Gloria Estefan, who also owns a well-known restaurant in Miami Beach (Estefan's).

Hispanic Culture Today

The reality of Hispanic life in the United States is, then, laced with both threads of unity and distinctive ancestral and cultural identities. As we (either Hispanic or Anglo) think about the presence of Hispanic peoples and cultures in the United States, the turn of the century offers a marker of significance for a nation rapidly becoming Hispanicized. Just in the period from 1990 to 1997, the Hispanic population segment increased by 32%, which is a gain of over 7 million people (U.S. Bureau of the Census, 1999). The projected population transformation, which may have seemed remote or even unbelievable to some back in the 1980s, now shows in the demographics that bring us into the 21st century. Language issues in our Hispanicized culture are deeply embedded in the population transformation that is occurring with momentum and certainty.

Language Complexities of Hispanic Peoples

The language situation for Hispanic peoples in the United States is a mixture of factors related to the Spanish and English languages, factors embedded in the larger cultural patterns of Hispanic and Anglo peoples, and factors central to the impact of Spanish-English contact in the U.S. cultural setting. One source of complexity lies in bilingualism (for example, changes in language dominance and bilingual balance in successive generations), another in the cultural distinctiveness of each ancestral group (for example, different varieties of both Spanish and English not only in different ancestral groups but also in the different locales and social classes within these groups), yet another in the situations of language contact (for example, the phonological distinctiveness of English spoken by monolinguals in contact with Mexican-Americans), and another in multicultural experience (for example, the contact of Puerto Ricans and African Americans in New York City). Speech communities for Hispanic people are more complex in many cases than they are for others in the United States because their members interact in the context of complex social factors salient for identity and language use. Otto Santa Ana (1993) uses the term *Hispanic language setting* to characterize the language mix among Hispanics: monolingual speakers of both Spanish and English, bilingual speakers, and some individuals who are not by ancestry Hispanic but who nonetheless participate in Hispanic discourses. In this section, I focus on four dimensions of Hispanic language: (a) the ways in which Spanish, both in contact with English and contextually influenced by multiple cultures, exhibits distinctive varieties; (b) attitudes toward and levels of bilingualism among Hispanic peoples; (c) code-switching between languages; and (d) Chicano English.

Spanish in the United States

As noted earlier, the 1990 census recorded 17.3 million people age 5 years and older who use Spanish as their primary language in the home. Assuming a stable proportion of Spanish language users within the Hispanic population, that number would have risen by 1996 to about 23 million, with more than that today. This estimate excludes those who are fluent in Spanish but do not use it as the primary home language, children under 5 years of age who are learning Spanish as their first language or in the context of Spanish-English bilingualism, and those not counted in the census data (some citizens and legal immigrants who did not participate plus illegal aliens).

For the majority of Hispanics, the Spanish language runs deeply into cultural and personal identities. Anzaldúa's (1987) eloquent phrasing of this principle captures the language-identity fusion: "Ethnic identity is twin skin to linguistic identity—I am my language" (p. 59). To relinquish Spanish either literally or symbolically (which many monolingual citizens of the United States seem to think is appropriate for integration into the country) is to relinquish a significant and powerful dimension of personal and social identity. As John Attinasi (1979) discovered in his interview study with New York Puerto Ricans two decades ago, proficiency in English does not replace the importance of Spanish because "Spanish [even limited usage] is the assumed basis of community interaction" (p. 435) and serves to bind Puerto Rican culture.

Spanish vitality. There are many reasons why Spanish language use flourishes in the United States. Taken together, five main reasons suggest that turning back the trend for Spanish to be the second national language of the country is unlikely.

First, geographic proximity to an ancestral homeland fosters native language use just as it fosters cultural maintenance. New entrants to the United States through both legal and illegal channels travel across the U.S.-Mexican border and to Central and South America, and Puerto Ricans retain their island-mainland fluidity. Despite what may evolve to disassemble bilingual education (see Chapter 9), Spanish maintenance has been encouraged through years of bilingual education. Economic interests, too, encourage Spanish fluency so that job vacancies related to trade with Spanish-speaking countries need not be filled by bringing Spanish speakers into the United States explicitly for these employment needs.

Second, for native speakers of Spanish in the United States, loyalty to and love for Spanish partly explains the continuing vitality of the language in the cultural context of English dominance. Stavans (1995) declares that "unlike other ethnic groups, we Latinos are amazingly loyal to our mother tongue" (p. 123). Joyce Penfield and Jacob Ornstein-Galicia (1985), who have studied Chicano language in Texas, argue that Spanish has resisted destruction and creolization by English because of deep cultural factors, such as lifestyle and socioeconomic situation. Investigating a different locale, Ofelia García, Isabel Evangelista, Mabel Martínez, Carmen Disla, and Bonifacio Paulino (1988) found loyalty to Spanish to be uniformly strong. Their study compared residents of two New York communities populated by Hispanics: Washington Heights (in Manhattan), which is poor and home to a large number of Dominicans, and Elmhurst-Corona (in Queens), which is middle class and includes a broad range of Hispanic peoples. Described by the researchers as "fiercely" loyal to their countries or locales of origin and to their native language, these diverse Hispanics also claimed deep loyalty to the United States.

Third, the commitment of many Hispanics to extended family ties provides motivation to cultivate at least some level of Spanish language proficiency in the context of English dominance in the public sector, education, and employment. Whether to communicate with older members of a family or to make contacts with relatives elsewhere, *la familia* exerts its own language influence.

A fourth reason for Spanish language vitality pertains to the local circumstances of many Hispanics. Many Hispanics live in de facto segregated, enclosed communities within the United States. Fernando Peñalosa (1985), who was one of the early scholars of Chicano language, pinpoints the role of enclosure in these remarks:

> As Chicanos have remained concentrated in low-paying, marginal occupations, residential and educational segregation remain at a high level. The resulting isolation from the Anglo community helps promote the maintenance of Spanish and [in this case] the inadequate mastery of English. (p. 15)

Finally, as the Spanish-speaking population has grown, so have resources and entertainment via Spanish. Public schools offer bilingual-bicultural education more often to Spanish speakers than to any other language group because of sheer numbers. Most of the courtroom translation services are in Spanish. Spanish signs, ballots, product labeling and instructions, public service announcements, and so forth reinforce the status of Spanish as a major U.S. language. The expansion of mass media in Spanish likewise provides daily access to a host of resources including Spanish language and "Spanglish" magazines (such as *Latina*), television programming, and news. In short, there are many places in the United States where most of what goes on in daily life can now be conducted and consumed in Spanish.

Because Spanish in the United States is continuously in contact with many varieties of English, varieties of Spanish are influenced both by ancestral varieties and American English varieties. In Puerto Rican Spanish, for example, the final -*s* is often dropped in words like *gracias,* producing either *gracia* or the added light aspiration to produce *graciah.* There are "pecking orders" among Spanish varieties, just as there are among varieties of American English. Puerto Rican and other Caribbean Spanish varieties, for example, are often stigmatized as inferior to Central and South American Spanishes, just as these varieties are often judged unfavorably—especially by Anglos—in comparison to Castillian Spanish.

Many American English monolinguals mistake the value placed on Spanish language vitality by Hispanics for rejection and devaluation of English. This is simply not the case. At issue here are differing values associated with bilingualism. The issue cuts to the core of cultural identity and cultural practice and, ultimately, to notions about nationalism itself. When English is equated with patriotism and nationalism, cultural distinctiveness becomes threatening—especially when articulated within a language other than English, which is not only used but passionately loved by its users. When articulated or even suspected, such sentiments about patriotism and language loyalty can evoke even greater loyalty to languages other than English. As the debate over bilingual education continues, the context surrounding Spanish language vitality will change too (see Chapter 9).

Bilingual Patterns

Hispanic peoples who have ties to Spanish offer the best prospect for facilitating a move away from the peculiar monolingualism that evolved in the United States—peculiar in the sense that monolingualism is not the norm in the world, and monolingualism diminishes the appreciation people can have for others. The sheer number of native Spanish speakers in the United States, coupled with the growing importance of learning Spanish as a second language for native English speakers, opens possibilities for bilingual practice in the 21st century.

As we consider the realities and possibilities for bilingualism, we need to bear in mind that the term is used in many different ways, sometimes meaning fluent bilingualism in the spoken and written forms, sometimes a lesser degree of proficiency, and sometimes oral proficiency only. Literacy is crucial, however, to the kind of bilingualism that serves both its speakers and the larger community because literacy links to reading, writing, and employment opportunities.

Not surprisingly, the distribution of bilingual and monolingual speakers among Hispanics in the United States varies by region. Santa Ana (1993) notes that Texas has the lowest proportion of English-speaking Hispanic monolinguals, California has the highest proportion of Spanish-speaking monolinguals, and New Mexico the largest proportion of retained bilingualism in higher income earners.

Ample evidence points to the value placed on bilingualism by Hispanics in the United States. The study of residents in Washington Heights (Manhattan) and Elmhurst/Corona (Queens), already mentioned above (García et al., 1988), provides an interesting case study related to bilingual values. About half of those interviewed who lived in Washington Heights were bilingual compared with two thirds in Elmhurst/Corona. Yet, *all* who participated in the study thought it very important to learn English and for their children to be bilingual and biliterate. This group of Hispanics also voiced concern about what sociolinguists call the distinction between *elite bilingualism* and *folk bilingualism*: To be bilingual where they came from was a mark of status, but to be bilingual in the United States, when English is not the first language, is stigmatized. Finally, the researchers concluded by saying, "It is clear to us that the Hispanics we interviewed feel that their major obstacle in the United States is the lack of majority support for their community's bilingual use of Spanish and English" (p. 509). This peculiar reversal of prestige afforded bilingualism has been confirmed many times over by my own students; students from countries other than the United States who are native speakers of languages such as French, Norwegian, or German report that U.S. monolingual students admire their bilingualism but seem to be unimpressed by the Spanish-English bilingualism of a growing number of U.S. citizens.

This case study and the more general lack of priority for a bilingual citizenry in the United States point to the need for better understanding of the complex nature of multicultural society. Many monolingual Americans live in an immediate situation where that complexity of language and culture does not show its face or express its voice. Others simply do not accept or appreciate what it takes to live a bicultural, bilingual life. Attitudes revealed in statements such as "If you don't want to speak English, go back to where you came from" are unfortunately familiar to most people. An equally common response is to assume that Spanish (or any other language) should and can easily be compartmentalized for home life only. The attitude extols "live and let live" as long as living is confined to family; if you want to be a citizen and earn a living, you need to check your Spanish and your Hispanic culture at the door. Such a division whereby different languages are used for different situations is called *diglossia*. In the Hispanic situation, diglossia often means devaluation of Spanish.

Ironically, one of the best-known statements of the diglossic principle as applied to Spanish and English in the United States comes from a Mexican-American critic of bilingual education. In his 1982 autobiography, Richard Rodriguez (he does not mark the acute accent over the *i*) proposes that Hispanics in the United States should accept Spanish as a *private language* and English as a *public language*. The split distinguishes family and intimacy from education and individuality. Public individuality, he says, requires English (p. 26). Rodriguez favors a "sink or swim" approach to learning English in school, believing there is no place for bilingual education in the U.S. educational system. His position is problematic because he never considers the possibility that bilingualism and biliteracy are themselves of great value and because he fails to represent the complexity of the language setting for Hispanics. His personal circumstances were in many ways the worst possible: a Catholic school demanding English at the expense of

	Parents		Children	
	Spanish	*English*	*Spanish*	*English*
I	to each other	none	to parents	to each other
	to children	none	to each other	
II	to each other	one speaks some to children	usually to parents	usually to each other
III	one speaks some to children	to each other	understand	to parents
	to children	to children		to each other
IV	to each other	to each other	[just learning to speak]	
	to children	to children		

Figure 6.1. Spanish-English Models for Family Communication
SOURCE: Zentella (1985).

Spanish, parents with limited proficiency in English, and teachers who discouraged the parents from speaking Spanish with their children—thus yielding a restricted language environment for the children at home.

In Table 6.5, the data displayed show the age trend associated with Spanish-English bilingualism. Native Spanish speakers with limited English proficiency would be on the borders of bilingualism. Those in the older age groups are unlikely in their lifetime to develop greater bilingual fluency, but it is very likely that the younger cohort will develop in that direction. There are also differing patterns in the mix of mono- and bilingualism.

Ana Celia Zentella's (1985) model for Puerto Rican language and communication patterns in the family provides a useful vantage point on the bilingual configurations and shifts that tend to exist for Hispanics in the United States. She describes four patterns of communication that were evident in her study of 19 families on a particular block in *el Barrio* of East Harlem, New York City; these are summarized in Figure 6.1. Although limited to immediate family, the four patterns show different balances of bilingualism. Because English is the target language of education, we would expect the Hispanic children (i.e., younger generations) of families with Spanish as exclusively or occasionally a home language to develop English language proficiency of varying degrees. Pattern I shows the relationship of monolingual Spanish-speaking parents to bilingual children. Pattern II shows the influence of some English in the parental language mix, whereas Pattern III is the converse, where Spanish has less dominance and English greater dominance for the parents. Pattern IV shows a situation where first language acquisition is bilingual, which is the context for the children's primary discourse.

The word *dynamic* most accurately characterizes the balance of bilingualism for many individuals who have at least limited proficiency with the nondominant language. In a summary of studies conducted in the southwestern United States (Floyd, 1985), younger people were found to shift away from Spanish to preference for English. Pedro Pedraza's (1985) study of a Puerto Rican neighborhood in East Harlem revealed the same age pattern, wherein younger generations shifted to preference for English, but he also found Spanish to be significant for all dwellers in the neighborhood in some situations where "even fluent English speakers of the community . . . accommodate by using at least some Spanish" (p. 60). A few years later, Lourdes Torres's (1989) research on Puerto Ricans in New York showed position in the life cycle to have yet another effect. Second-generation New York Puerto Ricans (in their 20s and all self-identified as English dominant) were reactivating their use of Spanish in their *barrio* community as they become older, which the author suggests may also occur in other communities.

The vitality of Spanish-English bilingualism in all of its configurations will in the coming years likely endure. Along with the role of language in cultural retention, job opportunities for Spanish-English bilinguals keep growing: translators certainly, but also jobs in sales, retail, marketing and advertising, broadcast media, and financial services.

Code-Switching and Other Language Influences

Sociolinguists have long studied the influence that languages in contact have on one another. These influences can encompass any of the multiple aspects of the linguistic system from the simplest lexical borrowing from one language to another, to the more complex semantic and syntactic changes that occur in one language because of the contact of its speakers with speakers of another language.

Several distinct types of interlanguage influence characterize English and Spanish in contact. We focus here on two discourse practices: *code-switching,* which entails the shifting back and forth between languages; and *calquing,* which evidences a particular kind of semantic influence that is manifest in the language that undergoes change as a result of contact. A note on "Spanglish" concludes the section.

The influence of English on Hispanic varieties of Spanish is of considerable interest to speculations about the longer-term status of Spanish as a major second language in the United States. Does English undermine Spanish and weaken its vitality? Apart from situations where Spanish is not understood, why do Spanish-English bilinguals use both languages? Do varieties of Spanish spoken in the United States evidence change because of their contact with varieties of English? Research on both code-switching and calques offers some insights about these questions.

Code-Switching

In the study of language contact, code-switching is the term used to describe the switching from one language to another within an utterance or a particular situation (the same idea underlies switches between varieties of the same language, such as from African American Vernacular English [AAVE] to Mainstream American English [MAE]). Code-switching occurs, for example, when two speakers who are conversing in Spanish in a cafe or while walking to class occasionally use English words, expressions, and even full sentences. The switching might also occur during a conversation predominantly in English.

The most common misunderstanding about code-switching is that it allows the bilingual to seek refuge in her or his native language when there are fluency problems or memory lapses in the second language. In Zentella's (1985) study of a Puerto Rican community in East Harlem, switches functioning as language crutches accounted, in fact, for only a small portion (10%) of the entire sample of switches. What, then, is the character of switching?

For Spanish-English bilinguals, code-switching appears to be a language variety and style in and of itself (Penfield & Ornstein-Galicia, 1985; Romaine, 1994). Like other varieties, it functions to announce specific identities, create certain meanings, and facilitate particular interpersonal role relationships. It can serve as "a badge of community membership" (Zentella, 1985), which symbolizes authentic identity in two cultures and their languages. Silva-Corvalán's (1994) example of the statement, "*Y no le crei,* you know" ("I didn't believe him, you know") reveals precisely this multicultural enmeshment in language by making the statement in Spanish and adding the vernacular American English filler *you know* precisely as a native speaker would do in casual speech.

Zentella's (1985) research on code-switching among Puerto Ricans in East Harlem provides interesting insights about how code-switching functions. First, she found code-switching to be more prevalent in the most informal styles of speaking, which suggests that switches are relatively spontaneous, unedited, and "natural"; furthermore, switches often were used to mark changes from casual to formal style or the reverse. Second, she found switches in contexts where control was intended, especially between parent and child; for example, "*Callate* [shut up]. Shut up." A third finding was that code switching often achieves "footing," which aligns the speaker in some particular manner to the topic or other participants in the discourse event. The switch could imply footings such as, "I'm speaking English now, so take me seriously"; "I'm changing the topic by changing from English to Spanish"; or "I'm now positioning my identity as Hispanic." (Recall from Chapter 5 that Scott, 1995a, found the same pattern in the code switching of African American women.)

Yet another function of code-switching was observed in the study of Dominicans, Puerto Ricans, and Cubans in New York City previously cited (García et al., 1988). Those with limited proficiency in English or no bilingual facility did occasionally code-switch, which appeared to be a way of demonstrating that they knew at least some English.

Yet another function, that of facilitating communication, is emphasized in research by Maria Dolores Gonzales Velásquez (1995). She undertook an intensive ethnographic investigation of code-switching and other language practices among women in Cordova, New Mexico, which is a small Hispanic community with stable bilingualism. She was able to differentiate the women in terms of their participation in three types of speech community: Spanish dominant, English dominant, and code-switching. She found that the women with the highest rates of code-switching were the ones with the most balanced frequency of contact in the three types of speech community.

Code-switching at the lexical level often brings words and phrases into one language that are not available in the other or that have linguistic currency in a particular cultural context in which they are uttered. Where code-switching is from Spanish to English, the English words or phrases are usually referred to as *loan words* or *borrowings*. Embedded in Spanish discourse, we might, for example, hear phonologically clear American English words such as *potato chips, soda, computer, e-mail, Internet, answering machine,* and *talk show.* Many instances where the change is from English to Spanish correspond to claims for individual or group identity. One illustration is Mary Romero's (1988) analysis of the discourse of Chicano/a teachers of Spanish in northern Colorado, who were discussing their attitudes about the class they were teaching. She demonstrated that Spanish words are usually used within English sentences to "claim group membership" (p. 123).

The syntactic placement of switches provides a particularly significant entrée to interpreting what code-switching implies about linguistic and communicative competence. Switches between languages with structural similarly usually occur at points of syntactic equivalence. Romaine (1994) gives the example of Spanish and English, where switches easily occur between a subject noun phrase and a verb phrase or between a verb and its object; conversely, switches produce ungrammatical constructions between adjectives and nouns because English places the adjective before the noun and Spanish does the reverse ("his favorite spot"/*su lugar favorito* cannot structurally yield "his favorite *lugar*"/"*su* spot *favorito*"). Following the work of Shana Poplack (1981), and based on her Puerto Rican sample, Zentella (1985) comes to the following conclusion about language proficiency and code-switching:

> The overwhelming majority of switches link constituents that are grammatical in one language with constituents that are grammatical in the other. . . . Prolific code switching is also a mark of proficiency in each of the bilingual's languages. In fact, our data showed that *the most prolific intrasentential code switchers were also the best speakers of English and Spanish* [italics added]. (p. 55)

Zentella's research reveals that code-switching is not a cover for fluency problems. Code-switching manifests linguistic and communicative sophistication by employing language varieties to mark aspects of the discourse situation and the speaker's identity. Shana Poplack (1982), in reporting on a study of Puerto Rican code switching in *El Barrio* (East Harlem), offers corroborating evidence for the fluency argument. She found that the most complex code-switches came from fluent bilinguals and indicated syntactic mastery of both languages.

A sophisticated linguistic study of the Spanish of Mexican-American bilinguals in East Los Angeles by Carmen Silva-Corvalán (1994) approaches questions about interlanguage influence somewhat differently. Language data were obtained from older speakers born in Mexico and from U.S.-born younger speakers with parents who were U.S.-born or came to the United States as young children. Her main interest was in uncovering what strategies speakers use to maintain Spanish, especially for individuals born in or with permanent residency in the United States. She confirmed the hypothesis that "in language contact situations bilinguals develop strategies aimed at lightening the cognitive load of having to remember and use two different linguistic systems" (p. 207). She confirms that the structural integrity of Spanish is preserved through the ways in which the language is used, but that the influence of English does not impose changes in the structure of Spanish even for those who are less proficient Spanish speakers. Those less proficient in Spanish tend never to use certain verb forms (e.g., verbs in the preterit tense).

Code-switching is, then, a style of language use with both functional and linguistic dimensions. For many native Spanish speakers in the United States, it is a legitimate and sometimes highly valued form of language use.

Calquing

The word *calques* (taken from the French word meaning to trace) is used to represent a strategy for accommodating language influence at the semantic level without actually code-switching to the other language or borrowing words directly. Calques incorporate *both* the meaning and form from the model language without violating the syntax of the host language. A word or phrase is borrowed from the model language and translated as literally as possible. Two examples from Silva-Corvalán (1994) illustrate calques:

1. the word *weekdays* incorporated into Spanish as *dias de semana* (where *semana* means *a week*) to replace the Spanish construction *dias de trabajo* (where *trabajo* means *work* or *job*)

2. the term *answering machine* incorporated into Spanish as *maquina de contestar* (machine to answer) to replace the construction *contestador automatico* (answer automatically).

The implications of calquing are several. In one sense, word calques evidence a strategy of giving primacy to the host language (in this case, Spanish) over the model language (in this case, English) in a situation of language and cultural contact. The calque can also bring a new meaning or connotation into a language (often a language of lesser status) without actually adopting the vocabulary of the model or dominant language. From another perspective, calquing gives in to the domination of another language. Otheguy, García, and Fernández (1989), who studied two generations of

Cuban-Americans, suggest this when they conclude that "most calque-words . . . are superfluous, since there exist in traditional Cuban Spanish other serviceable formulations of the message types for which the calque-words are used" (p. 51). Yet they also demonstrate that calque words coming into Cuban Spanish from English are compatible with the Spanish formula-tions they modify. Calquing, compared to code-switching, is a mixture of both resistance and adaptation to other languages, and it certainly represents a natural result of languages and cultures in contact.

Spanglish

Spanglish has become a key term for defining the mixing of Spanish and English, where Spanish language and Hispanic culture dominates the mix. Spanglish, as a form of code-switching or calquing, occurs as a cultural practice of increasing importance to Hispanic Americans. Writing about this language variety in the *New York Times,* Lizette Alvarez (1997) describes its reach as encompassing glossy magazines, Hispanic rappers, and serious poets and novelists. Alvarez calls it "an effortless dance between English and Spanish" and quotes Zentella as saying "It's a sign of linguistic dexterity" (p. B4).

Although Spanglish is frowned on by language purists—as any evolving vernacular variety usually is—listening to young Hispanics talk about its vitality conveys that it is more than ephemeral, vernacular usage. A cursory look at magazines new to the scene such as *Moderna* and *Latina* demonstrates how easily this variety can move into the media of popular culture: Some phrases and sentences reveal code-switching, some calquing; some articles are English dominant and others Spanish dominant; some ads use Spanish text, some English, and some Spanglish. What makes the magazines distinc-tive and interesting is the mixing of all these modes—definitely an example of what the hyphen as energizing influence can create.

Chicano English

The one Hispanic group whose varieties of English have been the focus of considerable study is, not surprisingly, Mexican-Americans. The variety of English used by Mexican-Americans is usually designated *Chicano English*

(ChE). Within that variety, different features occur depending on particular speech community participation.

Numerous studies of ChE exist, many of them based on naturalistic discourse samples. I first consider basic definitional issues embedded in the research on ChE and then move to examples of the linguistic features common to the ChE variety.

Defining ChE

One sign of the relative maturity of ChE as a subject of study is the presence of alternative viewpoints in the literature about the varieties of English spoken by Mexican-Americans. As early as 1970, Philip Darraugh Ortego concluded from his research that phonological aspects best distinguish ChE from other varieties of American English, sometimes leading to communication difficulties. Not until the early 1980s, however, did scholarship about ChE and its relationship to communication in a multicultural society gain visibility. In 1981, scholars gathered for the first conference on *Form and Function in Chicano English,* held at the University of Texas-El Paso; edited papers from that conference are among the contents of a book published in 1984 (Ornstein-Galicia, 1984/1988). The early 1980s brought attention to ChE in ways similar to what happened with African American English or AAVE in the late 1960s and early 1970s. One main difference in early studies of ChE and AAVE was that Hispanics conducted most of the scholarship on ChE, whereas early work on African American English was dominated by white linguists.

In 1980, Fernando Peñalosa characterized Chicanos as speaking at least two types of English—a view that emerges in the literature over and over as scholarship matures:

> One kind [of English spoken by Chicanos] is that spoken typically by immigrants from Mexico who have learned English as a second language and show marked interference from Spanish. The other is the fluent kind spoken by many Chicanos as their first language. It undoubtedly originated in the first variety, but has become nativized and serves as the only means of communication in Chicano communities where Spanish is no longer spoken. (p. 118)

The first variety pointed to by Peñalosa, which is essentially under the direct influence of Spanish, Santa Ana (1993) terms *Mexican interlanguage English,* defined as a version "of the target language that is learned" (p. 6). In contrast, he defines ChE as "an ethnic dialect that children *acquire* as they acquire English in the barrio or other ethnic social situation during their language acquisition period" (p. 15). Like AAVE, Vernacular Chicano English (VCE) is "the spoken dialect of Chicano speakers of English who have minimum contact with non-Chicanos in their daily communicative life" (Santa Ana, 1993, p. 25). Like AAVE, whose features can be heard outside densely populated centers of African Americans, we would expect that aspects of VCE generalize to speakers beyond the homogeneous communities that foster vernacular speech. Likewise, we would expect regional variations; indeed, Santa Ana confirms such varieties in examples such as the phonological realization of *shoes* as *chose* in Texas but not in California.

Joyce Penfield and Jacob Ornstein-Galicia (1985), who have studied ChE in Texas, identify this variety differently than Santa Ana. They describe ChE as a *contact dialect* spoken mainly by bilingual Chicanos, and they attribute its vitality to both regular border contact and some degree of isolation of Chicanos from Anglos. Consistent with Santa Ana (1993), they say that ChE is passed on to children as the primary discourse of American English spoken in the family.

Penfield and Ornstein-Galicia's (1985) perspective on the range of language varieties spoken by Hispanics and, thus, influencing each other provides a useful starting point for considering ChE as a contact variety. Their taxonomy is reproduced with minor modification in Figure 6.2.

In this taxonomy, certain varieties have specified definitions: (a) Standard Mexican Spanish corresponds to the variety spoken in northern Mexico; (b) Southwestern Spanish includes similar varieties from northern New Mexico and southern Colorado—both archaic varieties traceable to the 16th- and 17th-century Spanish conquistadores; (c) *Pachuco Caló* is a vernacular variety originally associated with Spanish gypsies, which became associated after World War II with the speech of gangs and delinquents but later more generally with adolescents and lower socioeconomic classes (the terms *Caló* and *Cholo* are most often used, meaning mixed blood or *mestizo*); and (d) code-switching (consistent with its definition above) functions as a distinct variety in and of itself. This taxonomy does not show the dimensions of context that may be expected to encourage or discourage certain varieties. Minimally, it would be important to consider the ways in which ChE (and other varieties) is (are) situated and influenced through major institutional

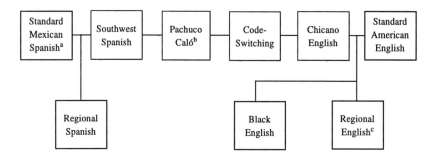

Figure 6.2. Hispanic-English Language Contact in the Southwest
SOURCE: Penfield and Ornstein-Galicia (1985). Used by permission.
a. Corresponds to the northern dialect of Mexico.
b. A vernacular variety that originated with gypsies but is now generally associated with the lower socioeconomic class and is understood more broadly than it is spoken.
c. The term *non-standard* is used in the original along with *regional* but is not reproduced here.

and cultural modalities of communication: the family, education (bilingual as well as monolingual English), peer culture, religion, and mass media (especially television).

Scholars emphasize that Spanish language influence alone does not predict the particular features that occur in ChE. Manuel Godinez, Jr. (1984/1988), for example, demonstrates through a corpus of language collected in East Los Angeles that certain phonological features of ChE differ from both Spanish and what he calls General California English.

From those different perspectives on defining ChE, several conclusions are warranted. First, the variety of ChE spoken by Chicano English monolinguals in the United States will certainly provide the best evidence for those features of the variety that are the most stable in the context of multicultural and multilingual contact. Second, ChE can be spoken by fluent bilinguals (or those whose fluency is better in English than in Spanish) who embrace Chicano cultural identity. Third, ChE might be best understood as a contact variety in the context of a number of English and Spanish varieties. Both English and Spanish varieties influence ChE, but ChE features also show distinctiveness from both the English and Spanish used in the particular language situation.

Features of Chicano English

In this section, a selection of language features that distinguish ChE are presented. The features presented are neither exhaustive nor universal across speakers of ChE but, rather, representative of what scholars have studied. The features outlined here are of three types: (a) phonological, (b) syntactic, and (c) prosodic (see Penfield & Ornstein-Galicia, 1985, and references cited therein).

ChE phonology. Among the commonly cited phonological features are the following seven, which together give a sense of the sounds of ChE.

1. *alternation of /ch/ and /sh/: Chews* for *shoes* and *sheck* for *check.* These two phonological features freely alternate, that is, they are not consistently used even in the context of the same utterance by many speakers. Although more common in bilingual Spanish-ChE speakers, monolinguals use this alteration as well.

2. *devoicing of /z/ in all environments: hase* for *haze, gayse* for *guys.* A common feature of ChE, this devoicing variant also shows regional markings such that the particular patterns of devoicing *z* differ from region to region.

3. *Devoicing of /v/ in word-final environments: laf* for *love* and *half* for *have.*

4. */dh/ and /d/ for /th-/ and /t-/: dare* for *there, dis* for *this,* and *dah* for *the.* This feature, which is called "defricativization," is common to dialects of English other than ChE—most notably AAVE—and also to the English spoken by native speakers of languages other than Spanish (common even in the educated speech of those speaking Englishes learned in places such as Germany, Iran, and India). One possibility is that the feature is associated with social class generally, but there is sufficient counterevidence for that line of thinking both in Hispanic language and in the varieties of English used by native speakers of languages other than Spanish. It is likely that both AAVE and Spanish contribute to this pattern of defricativization.

5. */a/ for /ah/ and /awh/ in stressed syllables: dak* for *dock* and *Mandey* for *Monday.*

6. *reduction of consonant clusters in word final position: frens* for *friends, star* for *start,* and *is* for *it's.* Whereas regular past-tense endings are deleted, possessives, plurals, and third-person, present-tense singular phonemic realizations are reduced. This feature occurs in AAVE as well.

7. *laxing of Standard English vowels /e/, /ooh/, and /eh/: spik* for *speak, skul* for *school,* and *mel* for *mail.*

ChE Syntax

Syntax is less distinctive a marker of ChE as a variety of American English. Several syntactic markers have, however, been identified. Two examples follow.

1. *Double negative constructions:* "I don['t] want no dinner" in contrast to "I don't want dinner" or "I don't want any dinner." This marker is the same as in AAVE.

2. *Different use of comparative case, especially* more: "She uses more English" rather than "She uses English more often." In this case, ChE uses *more* to mark frequency in contrast to an implied comparison without linking it to *often,* thus an adjective/adverb contrast.

ChE Prosody

Prosody has to do with the sound contours of language including aspects such as intonation, volume, stress, pitch, and rate. Joyce Penfield's work (1984/1988) is the most often cited in this area of analysis. She observes that Anglos often describe Chicanos' use of English as sounding "sing-song," a description that results from prosodic features.

Penfield (1984/1988) examines stress and intonation patterns drawn from a sample of spontaneous conversations between Chicanos from El Paso, Texas, in several settings. Several of the major prosodic features detailed by Penfield are summarized here.

Intonation Features

1. *Rising glides for emphasis*: ChE contrasts to MAE in its high incidence of rising glides, which are used to mark emphasis within an utterance. Penfield notes that the mid-sentence glide illustrated below is not typical of MAE.

Are there any r/u l e s |for a| fair fight?

2. *Rising glides at the end of declarative sentences:* This is a special case of the more general tendency for rising glides in ChE. Penfield's point is that such rising glides accompany sentences whose meaning is clearly emphatic rather than tentative or intended to draw in the listener. She uses an example of a woman declaring her resolve to be awake during the birth of her baby; in this example, the woman's intention is not associated with tentativeness or the seeking of agreement from the listener.

I want to be a w a k e.

3. *Rise-fall glides at the ends of sentences:* Penfield associates this pro-sodic feature with what Anglos characterize as the typical Chicano accent. Here, the rise-fall glides actually occur within one-syllable words. In the example below, Penfield shows the intonational contour for a sentence that begins below the person's normal pitch level and rises to the normal level twice in the sentence, both times accompanied by a falling glide.

To me /that| sounds good.

Stress Features

Several consistent patterns in the way in which stress occurs in ChE compared to more mainstream varieties of American English have been noted.

1. *Backward stress on noun compounds: week-END* rather than *WEEK-end* and *black-BOARD* rather than *BLACK-board.* This pattern contrasts with the general pattern in English over a long period of time to forward stress or to even the stress across the syllables in compound words.

2. *Forward stress on verb compounds: SIT-down* rather than *sit-DOWN* and *SHOW-respect* rather than *show-RESPECT.* Here, heavier stress is placed on the main verb rather than the particle. This ChE stress pattern can impede communication with non-ChE speakers because the changes in stress accompany changes in meaning. For example, the distinction in "show respect" would be to *demonstrate* respect through various actions that are visible in the case of forward stress, but *to be respectful* in the sense of indi-cating respect rather than some other state in the case of backward stress. "He can't SIT up" would likely have the contrastive meaning in MAE that "He can't sit up but he can stand up."

Conclusions

As we would expect, the English spoken by Chicanos often evidences patterned features distinguishing this language variety from others in the United States. Although there is no universal Chicano English, patterns associated with different ages and regions have been identified as marking the boundaries of an ethnic speech community. Phonology and prosody are particularly prominent identifiers of ChE. Prosody, especially, has implications in some contexts for communication clarity. Rising intonations at the ends of sentences may lead Anglos to wait for a sentence to be finished when the speaker has, in fact, come to closure (Penfield, 1984/1988), or such sentences may be interpreted as tentative statements when they are, in fact, emphatic. We do not, however, know much about the ways in which social class, educational level, and gender map onto the ChE variety or how dialect and register interrelate. We could expect ChE to be used in less density by most middle-class Chicanos/as, but, again, this would also depend on the situations for use. Gender may also influence the particular form of ChE.

Implications

In this chapter, I have approached Hispanic language issues by looking at the emerging reality of Hispanic cultural identity in the United States as the context for language use and attitudes. Themes underlying Hispanic culture as well as the distinctive ancestral heritage of the major Hispanic groups in the United States have been examined. My focus on language has provided viewpoints on the vitality of Spanish use in the United States, on bilingualism, on Spanish-English code-switching, and on the manifestations of Hispanic identity in English as exemplified by ChE. In this way, language is once again shown to be the realization of complex and dynamic cultural phenomena and a major symbolic system in day-to-day cultural life.

The Hispanic confluence of cultures and languages presents an interesting case study for the United States as a multicultural nation. In the Hispanic peoples of the United States, we see the evolution of a Hispanic culture from separate but interrelated ancestral groups, each with its distinct history and character but all with some commonality in the context of the cultural fabric of the United States. Language issues definitely play a central role in that cultural evolution because of the place of Spanish in the history and ongoing patterns of daily life for the several groups comprising the U.S. Hispanic population.

The Hispanic population likely will change the language landscape of the United States for the foreseeable future. Several factors account for this likelihood: (a) the continuing growth of the Hispanic population; (b) the cultural, demographic, and geographic factors that encourage Spanish language vitality; and (c) the value placed on bilingualism by many Hispanics. Economic and labor conditions place many Hispanics in the worst of situations in terms of standard of living, but they also ensure greater ties to both native language and culture than might otherwise be the case. Yet, even those Hispanics in greater contact with and participation in mainstream American culture and employment usually possess the strength of ethnic identity needed to foster vital bilingualism and ethnically marked varieties of English in certain situations.

The 21st century in the United States will manifest the rise of Hispanic peoples and their cultures, altering what we call "American culture," even for those citizens relatively isolated from the Hispanic population. Recognition of this by Anglos and Hispanics alike is necessary for informed thinking about multicultural communication in a society of increasing multiethnicity. Language will, indeed, increase in salience across educational, civic, political, and employment contexts.

7

Language and Cultural Complexity in Asian American Identities

In a scene from Gish Jen's novel (1996), *Mona in the Promised Land,* Mona Chang (the teenage daughter of Chinese immigrants) argues with her mother over the right of a teenage girl to privacy. Mona wants her own phone line, rationalizing this to her mother by saying, "So you won't eavesdrop." Her mother Helen's reply symbolizes the stresses of incompatible cultural meanings:

> "If I like to know what my daughter is up to, I don't see what's wrong about it." It has to do with the Chinese way versus everyone else's way, as Mona sees it, but Helen doesn't even agree with her on that. "I think I'm very Westernized. I brought you children up without you even speak Chinese." (p. 48)

The tension in Jen's novel is not only between the "Chinese way" and the "American way" but also between conceptions of what being American means to China-born Helen and her American born daughter. The novel, thus, confronts simplistic notions of Asian and Asian American identity through portrayals of genuinely multicultural life.

As we approach the topic of Asian American language and culture in the United States, we must first recognize that the ancestral and national histories of U.S. residents with Asian roots are many, and the experiences of specific Asian groups within the United States are varied. Recent immigrants, immigrants of longer residence, and U.S. natives all make up the category of Asian American. Different languages too are represented in the population labeled Asian American.

A number of Asian Americans have written about the tendency among U.S. whites to universalize Asian American identity. Thomas Nakayama (1997) calls this "the specter of the Orient" (p. 13)—a perceptual representation that identifies those who visually appear to be Asian as "foreign" and "oriental." In a broader context, Edward Said (1979) wrote with eloquence about the legacy of colonialism and imperialism for present-day European-based imagination and identity constructions of "orientalism." He argues that this legacy objectifies (and thus reifies) the Orient and its peoples, and that this continues in the present just as it did during periods of colonial and imperialist expansion.

To the extent that Eurowhites are aware of complexities among those who are Asian by ancestry or geographic homeland, that awareness usually encompasses only a limited range of stereotypic variation. Japanese are associated with World War II, the attack on Pearl Harbor, and subsequent internment of Japanese Americans in camps, and more recently with technology and finance. The contemporary notion of the Japanese is closely linked with the production of automobiles, advanced engineering, and technology: cars, cameras, and computers. Koreans are associated with the Korean War (1950-1953), in which the United States fought with the south against the north in a battle over democracy, and more recently with ethnic conflict in Los Angeles. Vietnamese people are identified as refugees of another ill-fated war (once again over democracy) that intensely divided the population of the United States for well over a decade (1957-1975) and became the defining cultural experience for many post-World War II baby boomers. For many, a sense of the Chinese is completely contemporary, with its fixedness on the opening of China during the 1970s and 1980s followed by the crackdown on student dissidents at Tiananmen Square in April 1989.

Less often thought of as part of the Asian American complexity are peoples with ancestry in India, Pakistan, or Middle East countries. The prevailing ideology of race, which divides the world into three symbolic groups of white (Caucasian), black (Negroid), and yellow (Mongoloid) does not easily accommodate these Asian groups.

What Eurowhites typically think of as Asian American also depends on regional location. Filipinos, for example, are the second-largest Asian American population, but non-Asians who do not live in the west or Hawaii may not readily think of this group as part of the Asian American presence in the United States. Many of my own students (a large number of whom are from eastern states), for example, identify Asian Americans as consisting of three groups: Chinese, Japanese, and either Korean or Vietnamese, depending on their experience.

Three semantic notions commonly skew perceptions of Asian Americans by identifying them as (a) foreigners, (b) the model minority, and (c) sexual exotics. The association with foreignness implies "foreign until proven otherwise."

This underlying aura of foreignness has led a number of Asian American scholars to write about the problematic nature of hyphenated identities (Chen, 1997; Nakayama, 1997; Somekawa, 1995). In contrast to the treatments of hyphenated Hispanic identity as source of energy for new cultural definitions that were discussed in Chapter 6, these Asian American writers stress the difficulties associated with never being perceived as fully American. Victoria Chen (1997) describes the symbolic impact of an identity label that qualifies the authenticity of Americanness: "The hyphen is a metaphor which highlights the boundary between minority Americans and white Americans. *The hyphen often provides the locus for homelessness while marginalizing the social position of Asian Americans* [italics added]" (p. 10). Dominant ideology, thus, displaces Asian Americans into the margin based on minority and authenticity criteria. (Consistent with this construction of the hyphen for Asian groups, I do not use it in the term *Asian American* although I do use it for Hispanic groups.)

The second perceptual orientation typically places Asians as model minorities. Asian Americans, *unlike other minorities,* are seen as models who work hard, achieve success, integrate themselves effectively into work and community, and do not cause trouble. A number of Asian American authors in recent years have tried to counter the essentializing identification of Asians as model minorities with analyses pointing to both the great economic variability among Asians in the United States and the structural barriers that result in Asian Americans being underpaid in comparison to non-Hispanic whites when education level and qualifications are similar (see Min, 1995).

The third significant biasing factor in the ways in which Asian Americans are perceived rests in sexual identity. In the case of Asian Americans, sexuality takes on an exotic quality in the minds of many Americans, who are led by long-standing ideological notions to see Asian women as sexually submissive and available and Asian men as effeminate or asexual. I use the term *exotic* here to engage the meanings of that stereotype in constructing meanings for Asians as "mysteriously different."

For women, histories in other countries as concubines, as "comfort women" to sexually service American military and business men, and as submissive war brides all feed into their sexual construction as unlike more typically American women. The continuing booming business in mail-order brides reinforces this history. Asian American women as exotic others evoke these long-standing meanings. In a fascinating discussion of Asian American women, Kandice Chuh (1995) connects ideological notions about Asian women to rape:

> Cultural expectations and stereotypes work together to construct the "normal" Asian American woman as a submissive being, whose very nature describes her as sexually and otherwise oriented toward the purpose of serving men. Literary and other mediated images of the Asian American women describe and define women only in relation to men . . . in the (sexual) service of men. (p. 240)

Chuh draws the conclusion, consistent with analysis of others, that Asian American women *because of this dominant cultural construction* are "un-rape-able." Even if one does not draw that conclusion, the notion of Asian American women as sexually exploitable is pervasive in U.S. society.

Asian American men's sexual identity as constructed through dominant American ideology draws from several significant sources to render then asexual, sexless, or effeminate (Said, 1979). First, the historical patterns of immigration of Asian peoples first brought men who left their wives and families behind. One effect of their living in "bachelor societies" was to remove them from the normal realm of male sexuality related to family life. Second, much of the work that Asian American men performed in serving whites reduced them to something other than "true men" because they did women's work—"house boys," food service, laundry, dry cleaning. Third, the ideology of appearance has marginalized or made Asian men totally invisible as masculine symbols and sexual beings because their physical appearance does not measure up to American conceptions of masculinity.

Against this context of Asian American essentializing, providing insight into the cultural situatedness of Asian peoples in the United States is hampered by the scant research available. This chapter covers four topics: (a) an overview of Asian American demographics, (b) profiles of the most populous Asian American groups, (c) a discussion of Asian American cultural themes, and (d) an overview of relevant language issues for Asian Americans.

Asian Peoples in the United States

Estimates of the population for 1997 place the number of Asian Americans and Pacific Islanders at 10.1 million, or 3.8% of the total population (U.S. Bureau of the Census, 1999). This number represents an increase of 2.6 million since the 1990 census. Immigration has been the key driver of Asian growth in the United States: From 1990 to 1994, immigration accounted for about 85% of the 1.5 million new Asians (U.S. Bureau of the Census, 1995b), and it is immigration that will push the Asian sector of the population to triple over the next half-century.

The Asian population is dominated by two groups, which together account for about 40% of the Asian population. Using 1994 data as an illustration, the largest group is Chinese (22%), with most of ancestry to mainland China but some from Taiwan (also known as the Republic of China) as well. Close behind by official Census Bureau count are those whose ancestry is to the Philippine Islands; these individuals make up about 19% of the Asian population, and some scholars believe the number is close to 2 million (Agbayani-Siewert & Revilla, 1995). Three other ancestral groups account for at least 10% each: Japanese at 11.5%, Koreans at 10.5%, and Asian Indians at 10.4%. The distribution of Asian people by their ancestry is displayed in Table 7.1.

Foreign- and U.S.-Born Asians

The mixture of foreign-born and U.S.-born Asians underlies one of the dimensions most critical to understanding the language and cultural complexity of Asian Americans. The majority of Asians are not U.S.-born. For the groups with the largest populations, the pattern generally is for two thirds to four fifths to be foreign-born (see Table 7.2). In 1990, the proportions of foreign-born for each nation group were as follows: 69% Chinese, 64% Filipino, 73% Korean, 75% Asian Indian, and 80% Vietnamese (U.S. Bureau of the Census, 1994a).

TABLE 7.1 Distribution of Asian Americans by Ancestry Origin: 1990 Census
Data (1990 adjusted to 1994 projections) for Groups With 5% or
More of Asian Population

Place of Ancestry	Percentage of Asian Population (N)
China and Taiwan	21.8 (1,649,000)
China = 20.8%	
Taiwan = 1.0%	
Philippine Islands	18.8 (1,420,000)
Japan	11.5 (866,000)
Korea	10.5 (797,000)
India	10.4 (787,000)
Vietnam	7.8 (593,000)
Pacific Islands	4.6 (351,000)

SOURCES: Day (1993) and U.S. Bureau of the Census (1994a).

The marked exceptions are for Japanese Americans and Pacific Islanders,
the latter of whom are concentrated in Hawaii.

The Japanese have a stable generational lineage in the United States
because of (a) the history of the Japanese people in the United States
(discussed in the section on Asian group profiles) and (b) a high standard of
living in Japan in recent years that has discouraged immigration. The successive generations of Japanese Americans are referred to as *issei* for first
generation (born in Japan), *nisei* for second generation (born of parents who
immigrated from Japan), *sansei* for third generation (born of U.S. natives),
yonsei for fourth generation—and so on.

Past U.S. immigration policies and conditions in the Asian countries
yielded patterns of entry shown in Table 7.3. Major revisions to immigration
policy enacted in 1965, which ended racial discrimination and gave priority
to family reunification, changed these patterns more than any other factor.

Geographic Distribution

Like other groups outside the cultural mainstream and demographic majority, Asians and Pacific Islanders in the United States are clustered by
geographic locale. States with the greatest and fewest Asians are listed in
Table 7.4.

Not surprisingly, Hawaii is densely populated with Asians and Pacific
Islanders. The largest number of Asians resides in California. The East Coast
states of New York and neighboring New Jersey, plus Texas (with Illinois not

TABLE 7.2 Percentages of U.S.-Born and Foreign-Born Asian Americans in the United States, by Ancestral Origin

Ancestry Group	Percentage U.S.-Born	Percentage Foreign-Born
Chinese	31	69
Filipino	36	64
Japanese	68	32
Korean	27	73
Asian Indian	25	75
Vietnamese	20	80
Pacific Islanders	87	13

SOURCE: U.S. Bureau of the Census (1994a).

TABLE 7.3 Recent History of Asian Immigration Into the United States, by Country of Birth: 1965-1995

	China Taiwan[a]	Philippines	Japan	Korea	India	Vietnam[b]
1965	4,100	3,100	3,200	2,200	600	—
1970	14,100	31,200	4,500	9,300	10,100	1,400
1975	18,500	31,800	4,300	28,400	15,700	3,000
1980	27,700	42,300	4,200	32,300	22,600	43,500
1985	24,800	48,000	4,100	35,300	26,000	31,900
1990	31,800	63,800	5,700	32,300	30,700	48,800
1992	38,900	61,000	11,000	19,400	36,800	77,700
1993	65,600 14,300	63,500	6,900	18,000	40,100	59,600
1994	54,000 10,000	53,500	6,100	16,000	34,900	41,300
1995	35,500 9,400	51,000	4,800	16,000	34,700	41,800

SOURCE: Immigration and Naturalization Service as reported in *Statistical Abstracts of the United States*, various years.
a. China and Taiwan were combined until 1991. Beginning in 1992, the Immigration and Naturalization Service reported immigration data separately.
b. The largest number of refugee entrants from Vietnam (88,543) came in 1978.

far behind), are the other most populous Asian states. Certain cities (most of them in California) have also attracted people of Asian background. In Table 7.5, the top 10 cities are ordered, including each city's percentage and rank order of Asians (for example, New York City has the most Asians but, at 7% Asian, ranks 16th in percentage of the population that is Asian).

TABLE 7.4 States With Greatest and Fewest Asian and Pacific Island
Residents (1996 estimates)

Five Highest States	*Five Lowest States*
California = 3,711,786	Wyoming = 3,731
New York = 921,811	South Dakota = 4,485
Hawaii = 745,725	Montana = 5,139
Texas = 498,275	North Dakota = 5,192
New Jersey = 395,214	Vermont = 5,356

SOURCE: U.S. Bureau of the Census (1996c).

TABLE 7.5 U.S. Cities With Largest Asian American and Pacific Islander
Population: 1992

Rank	City	Asian/Pacific Islander Population	Percentage of City Population	Rank Order for Percentage Asian
1	New York	512,719	7.0	16
2	Los Angeles	341,807	9.8	12
3	Honolulu	257,552	70.5	1
4	San Francisco	210,876	29.1	2
5	San Jose	152,815	19.5	4
6	San Diego	130,945	11.8	9
7	Chicago	104,118	3.7	26
8	Houston	67,113	4.1	23
9	Seattle	60,819	11.8	9
10	Long Beach, CA	58,266	13.6	7

SOURCE: U.S. Bureau of the Census (1996f).

Socioeconomic Condition

Asian Americans fare less well in socioeconomic terms than the model
minority stereotype suggests. The data all point to a pattern where higher
educational attainment relative to other groups does not correspond to
commensurate higher income. A second significant pattern reveals a bipolar
"two worlds" distribution of work and income not captured in the model
minority image. Pyong Gap Min (1995) succinctly makes this point in saying
that:

Occupationally, larger proportions of Asian Americans than white Americans
occupy both the highest and the lowest tiers of the occupational hierarchy.
Economically, a much larger proportion of Asian Americans than white Ameri-

TABLE 7.6 Educational Attainment for Persons 25 Years of Age and Older, by Race and Ethnicity: 1996

Group	Less Than 9th Grade	High School Degree or More	Bachelor's Degree or More
Asian American and Pacific Islander	12.6%	81.9%	36.1%
Black	1.9%	84.5%	13.7%
Hispanic	30.3%	53.1%	9.3%
Non-Hispanic Whites	1.2%	92.0%	30.6%

SOURCE: U.S. Bureau of the Census (1996a, 1996b, 1997a).

TABLE 7.7 Attainment of Bachelor's Degree or Higher for Asian American Groups, by Gender: 1990

Group	Percentage Female	Percentage Male
U.S. TOTAL	17.6	23.3
Asian Indian	48.7	65.7
Chinese	35.0	46.7
Filipino	41.6	36.2
Japanese	28.2	42.6
Korean	25.9	46.9
Vietnamese	12.2	22.3

SOURCE: U.S. Bureau of the Census (1994a).

cans is at the poverty level, although proportionally more of them belong to the high-income brackets. (p. 43)

In aggregate, a higher proportion of Asian Americans compared to non-Hispanic whites have less than a ninth-grade education. Yet, at the top of educational attainment, Asians surpass whites with a greater percentage earning bachelor's degrees or more (see Table 7.6 on educational attainment for 1996).

The Asian American aggregated educational data conceals, however, marked differences in the groups making up the category. As shown in Table 7.7, the disparities between national groups and between women and men tell more than the aggregate data convey. Asian American Indians surpass all others in educational attainment, with Vietnamese at the bottom. Women tend to be disfavored regardless of ancestry (women from the Philippines are an exception), but the Korean and Indian differences show even less gender parity than obtains elsewhere.

TABLE 7.8 Income Comparisons of Asian Americans and Pacific Islanders
With Whites: 1996

Indicator	Asians and Pacific Islanders	Non-Hispanic Whites
Poverty rate for families	14.6%	8.5%
Per capita income	$17,921	$19,181
Median household income	$43,276	$37,161
Families below $25,000 annually	25.6%	22.6%
Families $50,000 and above annually	46.0%	44.0%

SOURCE: U.S. Bureau of the Census (1996e, 1997a).

In contrast to the educational data, economic indicators show Asians in the
United States lagging behind their non-Hispanic white counterparts. Median
household incomes for Asian Americans and Pacific Islanders are higher than
for non-Hispanic whites, but per capita income is lower. The explanation lies
in patterns of family living: more extended and fewer nuclear families (see
Table 7.8 for comparative information).

The bipolar distribution of Asians pointing to an economic underclass
alongside more visible Asian American prosperity shows clearly in the
statistics on poverty rate. In 1996, for example, close to 15% of Asian
American families lived in poverty, compared to 8.5% of non-Hispanic white
families. Looking at the economic situation for specific Asian American
groups shows even more clearly why the model minority myth is truly out
of kilter with reality. Information for eight different Asian groups, detailing
per capita income and families living in poverty, appears in Table 7.9.
Japanese Americans fare the best overall and southeast Asian refugees the
worst. For the other groups, the situation is more mixed.

Asian Americans in professional positions face substantial challenges in
rising to the ranks of leadership and management. This situation has led
Asian Americans to use the "glass ceiling" metaphor (which originated in
analyses of women in the workplace) to describe "the difficulty . . . in reach-
ing the top of the occupational ladder" (Min, 1995, p. 43).

In the next section, profiles of a subset of Asian groups in the United States
highlight the complexity of language use in the Asian American context.

Asian American Group Profiles in Historical Context

The profiles presented here function to highlight factors most relevant to
cultural themes and to language and communication in everyday use (more

TABLE 7.9 Per Capita Income and Family Poverty Level for Selected
Asian American Groups: 1990

Group	Per Capita Income	Percentage of Families Below Poverty Level
U.S. AVERAGE	14,420	10.0
Japanese	19,373	3.4
Asian Indian	16,214	7.2
Taiwanese	16,079	11.2
Chinese	14,821	11.1
Filipino	13,616	5.2
Korean	11,178	14.7
Vietnamese	9,033	23.8
Cambodian	5,121	42.1

SOURCE: U.S. Bureau of the Census (1994a).

information on each group appears in sources such as McKay & Wong, 1988; Min, 1995; Takaki, 1993). The groups covered are Chinese, Filipino, Japanese, Korean, Asian Indian, and Vietnamese.

The Asian American population in the United States today carries the legacy and memory of racially based official government policies, discriminatory treatment, and toxic negative attitudes. The early history of Asian Americans was shaped by three U.S. government policies:

1. 1882 Chinese Exclusion Act

2. 1907 Gentlemen's Agreement, which restricted Japanese immigration

3. 1924 Quota Immigration Act, also known as the Oriental Exclusion Act

In brief, after a period of time in the mid-1800s (beginning with the Gold Rush of the 1850s) during which a controlled number of Chinese men came to the United States as laborers in mines, agriculture, woolen mills, and on railroads, the United States passed the Chinese Exclusion Act of 1882, which barred further immigration and denied naturalization rights to those already in the United States. The act was not repealed until 1943. The 1907 Gentlemen's Agreement halted what was a limited flow of Japanese laborers but did allow entry of wives and children of Japanese men already in the United States (Espiritu, 1997). In 1924, the Quota Immigration Act barred all Asian peoples from immigration as part of a larger immigration reform that set quotas for countries of origin; with only a few exceptions, that exclusion remained policy until 1952. Because Asian countries were targeted in this new policy, it became known as the Oriental Exclusion Act (Nishi, 1995). Simply stated, racism toward Asians molded immigration policy.

Chinese Americans

The presence of Chinese in the United States dates to 1848, when mainly uneducated men came in search of opportunity through mining and agriculture. Lured by the Gold Rush, Chinese made up a portion of the California's Forty-Niners. They contributed as well to the development of agriculture in California. Their motivations for coming to the United States included the search for sanctuary from the Opium Wars, escape from peasant rebellions, and the search for better economic conditions (Takaki, 1993). "By 1870, there were 63,000 Chinese in the United States. . . . Seventy-seven percent were living in California, . . . [and] about half of them stayed and made the United States their permanent home" (Takaki, 1993, pp. 194-195).

When the economy slowed, white laborers resented the Chinese for their willingness to work for low wages. Resulting conflict pushed the Chinese into self-employment in stores, restaurants, and laundries. Takaki (1993) explains that the male-operated Chinese laundry, doing what had been considered women's work, grew as an option to paid laboring jobs because of the small capital investment required and the minimal amount of English and math required. The Chinese also worked on southern plantations after slavery.

Women were virtually invisible from the early Chinese presence in the United States. In 1900, only 5% of the Chinese in the United States were women, and they were expected to be subservient (Takaki, 1993). Many more remained in China, hoping to receive money from their husbands sojourning in the United States (Espiritu, 1997). Other Chinese women were sold into prostitution, some of whom eventually made their way into jobs such as housekeeping. On the more positive side, Chinese women eligible for marriage benefited from their status as a scarce commodity. In families that opened small businesses, "the woman performed much of the manual labor in back, such as ironing and folding customers' laundry, preparing food and washing dishes in restaurant kitchens, or stocking merchandise in stores" (Espiritu, 1997, pp. 37-38).

Significant in this history was the growing rhetoric of racism against the "yellow" Chinese, which led to their exclusion from the United States in 1882. The Chinese came to be seen as undesirable, an inferior race, and a threat to racial purity. These factors led to high enclosure of the Chinese and vitality for Chinese language and culture; businesses serviced those within the community, and Chinatowns emerged.

Following World War II, the experience of Chinese in the United States changed. No longer barred from immigration, the population gradually grew. U.S. policy admitted only 105 immigrants per year up until 1965, but others entered as refugees following communist takeover after 1949. The War Brides Act of 1945 also allowed women to enter as wives of U.S. veterans. Overall, the male-female ratio came into greater balance, allowing the development of a family system in the United States. With the removal of small quotas and the institution of a family reunification priority, the 1965 Immigration and Naturalization Amendments led to growth among Chinese Americans—especially those from Taiwan and Hong Kong (included in British immigration quotas). In 1979, normalized relations with the People's Republic of (or mainland) China began the process of immigrant flow to the United States. The student crackdown in China of the late 1980s, culminating in the Tiananmen Square attack, resulted in a more permanent status for many Chinese students studying in the United States: They were allowed to extend their stays under provisions of the Chinese Student Protection Act.

As it is among other Asian groups, education is important to Chinese Americans (see Table 7.7). They are twice as likely as the U.S. population in general to earn at least the bachelor's degree, and they rank third among Asian American groups for educational attainment.

The socioeconomic standing of Chinese Americans is reasonably strong. Their presence in white-collar occupations and professions proportionally exceeds that of whites, with the advantage on the side of those born in the United States (Wong, 1995), who are aided by greater proficiency in English. Official reports of per capita income and percentage of families who live in poverty place the Chinese very close to the U.S. average (see Table 7.9).

Culturally, the Chinese American family structure tends to be traditional, with family size larger and divorce rates lower than among non-Hispanic whites. Following from Confucian principles (discussed in a subsequent section), status belongs to men over women and accrues with age (for both women and men).

Filipino Americans

Subsequent to the immigration reforms of 1965, Filipinos have been one of the largest groups of immigrants into the United States. Entrants between 1990 and 1995 totaled 228,998—far more than any other Asian country of origin. Filipinos are also the most "westernized" of the Asian peoples and in many respects the least like other Asians in cultural orientations (a point to which I return in the section on cultural themes).

The demographic, cultural, and linguistic situation of present-day Filipinos arises from several significant historical facts. First, the Philippine Islands were the colonial territory of Spain from 1521 until the United States prevailed in the Spanish American War in 1899. The Spanish influence continues today, including retention of Hispanic surnames. Second, the Philippine American War of 1899-1902 resulted in establishment of a U.S. colony complete with U.S.-imposed style of government and an education system that required English in school. The Philippines gained semi-independence in 1935 and formal independence in 1946, even though the United States maintained military operations there until 1992. Third, because of colonial status, Asian immigration restrictions were not applied to Filipinos.

Although Filipino presence in the United States dates to late 18th-century fishermen and shrimpers in Louisiana, two waves of immigration after the Philippine American War established this group's footing in the United States (Agbayani-Siewert & Revilla, 1995). The Pensionado Act of 1903 brought Filipino men to the United States to attend college. The second wave, between 1903 and 1934, resulted from the Chinese Exclusion Act and the Gentlemen's Agreement, which eliminated cheap Asian-based labor. Many Filipino men traveled to Hawaii during this period to work on sugar plantations and in mills "on the lowest rungs of the ethnic ladder" (Agbayani-Siewert & Revilla, 1995, p. 138). Yet, at 30% of the plantation labor force, their presence affected the economy (Takaki, 1993). Beginning in the 1920s, Filipino women were encouraged to immigrate to Hawaii so that families could be established. During this same period, Filipinos worked in California agriculture and Alaskan canneries. In all locations, they emerged as labor and union leaders.

When the Philippine Islands were granted commonwealth status in 1934, they became subject to immigration quotas. Yet Filipinos quickly became a large segment of emigrés, owing largely to their relatively high Americanization, their role as part of the U.S. forces in World War II, and the abundance of Filipino women who married U.S. servicemen.

Today, Filipinos evidence two education and occupational profiles corresponding to the distinction between U.S.- and foreign-borns. Their overall college education rate is 42% for women and 36% for men (see Table 7.7), making them the only group where women surpass men educationally. Unlike other Asian American groups, Filipinos born in the United States are less likely to be college educated; in 1990, 43% of the foreign-born Filipinos attained at least 4 years of college, compared to 22% of the U.S.-borns (Agbayani-Siewert & Revilla, 1995).

In aggregate, Filipinos enjoy a standard of living at least equivalent to the U.S population as a whole. The percentage of families living in poverty is relatively low, as shown in Table 7.9. Yet important variation exists. More foreign-borns are in professional occupations (U.S. Bureau of the Census, 1994a). Larger average family size also influences the data: More wage earners per family yields higher income, but per capita income falls below that of whites (Agbayani-Siewert & Revilla, 1995).

The Philippine culture is remarkable for its emphasis on gender equality rather than patriarchal authority (Espiritu, 1997). Of particular interest are the large number of Filipino women immigrants in health-related professions, especially nursing. Despite this greater gender equality, marriage is deemed almost obligatory for Filipino women. "Filipino society," says Nena Cervantes (quoted in Yang, 1996), "regards spinsterhood as pathetic" (p. 4). This may partially account for the fact that the Philippine Islands provide a major source of mail-order brides.

In capsule form, the Filipino peoples in the United States appear to be doing reasonably well relative to other minority groups. From their unique history among the Asian groups has evolved a style of living that is likely more Americanized and certainly more linguistically anchored in English. Yet major differences characterize today's U.S.-born and foreign-born Filipinos.

Japanese Americans

Sizeable numbers of Japanese people traveled to Hawaii beginning in 1884—just 2 years after the Chinese Exclusion Act—to work as plantation workers. The sugar plantation owners needed labor, and the Japanese were drawn by the lure of prosperity at a time when Japan was struggling to maintain its autonomy against Western colonization (Takaki, 1993). Unlike the earlier Chinese immigrants, the Japanese included a sizable number of women. Takaki attributes this to the tradition of women working as laborers in Japan and the desire of the Japanese government to create a family environment in Hawaii. Between 1894 and 1908, when the Gentlemen's Agreement barred immigration of Japanese laborers, some 142,000 Japanese came to Hawaii (Nishi, 1995). Subsequent to the Gentlemen's Agreement, smaller numbers emigrated, with women coming as "picture brides" in arranged marriages. By 1924, about 200,000 Japanese had emigrated to Hawaii and 180,000 to the mainland (Takaki, 1993).

Those who emigrated to the mainland worked as laborers and in farming. Families grew and a second generation (the *nisei*) assured Japanese continuity in America despite the 1924 exclusion of Asians from immigration. In plantation camps and on the mainland, aspects of Japanese culture were preserved, and emphasis was placed on education as a path to a better life for the second generation. The *nisei* embraced both the Japanese culture of their parents and the American culture of their own maturing lives.

With this gradual stabilization as context, the dramatic disjuncture in Japanese American life following Pearl Harbor shows just how tenuous the Asian presence in the United States could be. The Japanese bombing of Pearl Harbor on December 7, 1941 led to the internment of about 112,000 (90%) mainland Japanese. Declared "enemy aliens" by President Franklin Delano Roosevelt and stripped of their citizenship rights, these Japanese Americans were dispersed into 10 camps and treated as prisoners of war. Ironically, the Japanese in Hawaii were largely spared internment because of their involvement in the economy and defense of the island. Once the war concluded, the Japanese were "resettled" in 1945, but they had lost their property and savings.

The resettled Japanese Americans were augmented by a steady immigration flow subsequent to the war. From 1952 through 1960, some 2,500 to 6,500 Japanese immigrated annually. Because of the relatively low pressures to emigrate from Japan, the 1965 U.S. immigration reforms influenced these numbers very little (see Table 7.3).

After the war, the Japanese became much less distinctive in occupational clustering than in prewar days. By 1990, very few were in agriculture, fishing, and personal services, whereas many were entering finance, insurance, real estate, and the professions (Nishi, 1995). The war legacy, however, created a dual pattern for U.S.- and foreign-borns. By 1990, only 36% of the U.S.-born Japanese men had completed 4 or more years of college, compared to 60% of the Japanese-born men; the ratios for females were 22% and 32%, respectively (Nishi, 1995). Yet even the U.S.-born Japanese achieved higher rates of college education than the U.S. population in general.

The situation for Japanese Americans in the United States today compares favorably both with other Asian groups and with their history in the country. Of the ethnic groups, their poverty rates are lowest and per capita income highest (see Table 7.9). Japanese Americans remain, however, seen through the lens of American ideology as "other" and "foreign orientals" rather than "true Americans." Nishi (1995) observes that the recent phenomenon of "Japan bashing" stems from the global context: "Japan is viewed as the primary competitor, and the rise and fall of trade tensions have their barometric indicators of violence against Japanese Americans" (p. 108).

Korean Americans

Images of Korean Americans in the 1990s picture them in conflict with blacks at Korean-owned grocery stores. In 1990, national media focused on the African American boycott of two produce stores in Brooklyn. Then, in 1992, when the Los Angeles police officers on trial for the beating of Rodney King were acquitted, the whole world watched media coverage of Korean merchants being attacked and their stores looted in the heat of racial rioting. There is, of course, more to their portrait in the United States than shows in these pictures.

Not surprisingly, the Korean presence in the United States is entailed in the history of Asians in general, but that presence also stems from U.S. political interests in Korea (or more accurately the Korea*s*). Korea and Koreans became much more salient to U.S. interests during the Korean War nearly 50 years ago, and Korean Americans carry that war legacy with them.

Pyong Gap Min (1995) identifies three periods of immigration: (a) the early, restricted period from 1903 to 1949, (b) the post-Korean War period from 1950 to 1965, and (c) the period following the 1965 immigration policy reforms.

The early period is dominated by the movement of about 7,200 Koreans to Hawaii between 1903 and 1905 to work as contract laborers on the sugar plantations. Capitalizing on the antagonism that Koreans felt toward Japanese aggressors, the plantation owners used the Koreans to break the labor organization of Japanese workers (Takaki, 1993). About 85% of these early immigrants were men, with the remainder divided between women and children (Kim, 1988). A disproportionate number were Christian (about 40%), a trend that continues today (Min, 1995). Between 1910 and 1924, about 1,100 Korean women immigrated as "picture brides" for new husbands, who surpassed them in age by 18 years on average (Yim, 1989). Although making up only 20% of the Korean immigrant population by 1924, women played a substantial role in developing the Korean American sector. Sun Bin Yim (1989), who interviewed a number of elderly women among the early immigrants, assesses their impact not only on family formation:

"Their work in and outside of their homes was an important element in the economic survival of this population" (p. 50).

The second period of immigration occurred from the conclusion of the Korean War through the 1965 U.S. immigration reforms. About 14,000 Koreans immigrated during this period (Kim, 1988), and women continued to be an important component, many of whom entered as "war brides" of U.S. soldiers. Many war orphans also entered, marking the beginning of Christian-sponsored Korean adoption programs.

Like other Asian groups, Koreans took advantage of the immigration reforms of 1965. From 1970 to 1992, 676,118 Koreans came to the United States (Min, 1995). The mid-1980s were the high points, with over 35,000 annually. Koreans live in many areas of the United States but cluster in two areas: In 1990, 32% lived in California and 17% in New York and New Jersey combined (U.S. Bureau of the Census, as reported in Min, 1995).

Compared to other immigrant groups, Korean Americans are described as having the highest degree of "ethnic attachment" and cultural retention and the lowest degree of assimilation into the mainstream U.S. culture (Kim, 1988; Min, 1995). Three factors are commonly cited for this high degree of cultural enclosure: greater cultural and linguistic homogeneity compared to other Asian groups, concentration of Korean Americans in small ethnic businesses, and participation of Korean Americans in ethnic churches and other organizations.

Compared to other groups, immigrant Korean Americans have the greatest likelihood of maintaining strong patriarchal patterns of family organization (Espiritu, 1997; Min, 1995; Yim, 1989). Despite their work outside the home, Korean American women carry virtually all of the domestic responsibility. The impact of patriarchal retention also shows up in the professional sphere. Immigrant Korean American women physicians, for example, specialize in peripheral areas of medicine (research by E. Shin & K.-S. Chang, reported in Espiritu, 1997).

Korean Americans today carry forward the traditional value placed on education. In 1990, 47% of Korean American men and 26% or Korean women had received a bachelor's degree or higher (see Table 7.7).

Economic indicators for Korean Americans are positive. Min (1995) stresses that the official statistics (see Table 7.9 for example) underestimate earnings because a high proportion of Korean Americans run small businesses and may tend to underreport their income.

As the fourth largest Asian American group, Koreans stand out for their emphasis on cultural retentions. The high percentage of immigrants in the

Korean American population will continue into the future, making cultural and language retention likely as well. Children, of course, are more subject to the influences of other cultures, including mainstream mass culture, and they are educated in English.

Asian Indian Americans

Although a small number of Punjabi Indians came to the United States as early as the mid-1800s, it was not until the 1965 immigration reforms that the Asian Indian population began to grow toward its present size of over a quarter of a million people. Unlike other Asians, those from India were first classified by stereotypic religious association as "Hindoos," were judged at one point not to be "mongoloid," and were until 1980 grouped with whites by the U.S. Bureau of the Census. This history explains why many in the United States fail to think of Asian Indians as *Asian*.

The first period of immigration spanned a 20-year period from 1904 to 1924. By 1924, 13,000 Asian Indians had entered the United States. Early immigrants were largely farmers and laborers who worked on railroads and in lumber mills and who represented a diversity of religions—Sikh, Muslim, and Hindu (Sheth, 1995). As in other Asian immigrant groups, men made up most of this group, with many leaving wives in India (Leonard, 1982). Smaller numbers from the middle class entered, some of whom married white women and stayed in the United States. Some students came, too, who were part of the movement for India's independence from British rule.

Asian Indians were again allowed to enter the United States in 1946, when the Luce-Celler Bill set an annual quota of 100 per year and provided naturalization rights for those already in the country (Espiritu, 1997). Although symbolically important, the bill yielded little numerical impact. The small quota, India's independence in 1947, and the absence of U.S. military connections to India kept the number of immigrants low. The 1965 immigration reforms dramatically changed that situation.

Just over 500 Asian Indian immigrants came to the United States in 1965, but the annual numbers exceeded 20,000 by 1980 and rose as high as 40,000 in 1993 (see Table 7.3). Manju Sheth (1995) characterizes the post-1965 immigrants as consisting "mainly of college-educated, urban, middle-class professional young men and women of religious, regional, and linguistic diversity" (p. 169).

The diversity of Asian Indian Americans accounts for their tendency to identify most strongly with their own particular ethnic group rather than with

216   LOCATING CULTURAL DISCOURSE

the Indian group as a whole. Indian ethnic identity concentrates around "religions, languages, families, and specific Indian values such as nonviolence" (Sheth, 1995, p. 184). The vast majority of Asian Indian Americans, regardless of subgrouping, compares favorably with the U.S. population as a whole on a variety of socioeconomic indicators. First, Asian American Indians tend to hold strong family values yielding (a) low divorce rates because divorce is a stigma, (b) few female heads of household, and (c) the highest fertility rate among Asian Americans (Sheth, 1995). Second, religion serves as a cultural binder and location for the enhancement of Asian Indian ethnic identity. Finally, interest in "home" languages is high; although Asian Indian immigrants are, according to Sheth, "rapidly losing touch with their linguistic roots" (p. 185), language schools are flourishing.

Indicators all point to a relatively high standard of living for Asian Indian Americans. Their education levels are higher than those of any other group (see Table 7.7), per capita income is robust (see Table 7.9), and poverty rates are low. As of 1990, 30% of the Asian Indian Americans, compared to 14% of the total U.S. population, held professional positions, many of which cluster in the medical specialties and allied health fields (Sheth, 1995). Other common professions are consulting businesses and ownership of hotels, motels, newsstands, and gas stations. Income analyses by occupation and education nonetheless show that Asian Indians have low incomes relative to their qualifications (Barringer & Kassebaum, 1989). Laborers are also present in organized groupings. Marcelle Williams (1989), for example, studies Punjabi women who immigrated in the early 1970s and work in canneries in California, where they form gender communities and remain somewhat insulated from mainstream forces because of their real and feigned limitations with the English language.

Gender roles in the Asian Indian American population tend to follow prescribed patterns of male patriarchal control and female domestic responsibility, even when the women are well educated and employed in professions or white-collar jobs. Other cases evidence complexities of gender and work. Amarpal Dhaliwal (1995) provides an interesting case example of a middle-class Sikh woman who runs a small store in a manner that blurs the lines between work and domestic life; she cooks meals in the store for her children and does paperwork for the business at home.

Regardless of standard of living, prejudices invade the lives of Asian Indian Americans. In the early 20th century, Asian Indians were seen as "the least desirable race of immigrants, ragheads, a tide of turbans [both references to Sikhs], and 'the Hindu menace' " (Sheth, 1995, p. 181). More recently, ethnic name-calling and urban violence has included anti-Indian gangs in New Jersey and sporadic "Dot Buster" incidents (*dot* refers to the mark on Hindu women's foreheads).

Vietnamese Americans and Other Indochinese Peoples

The presence of Vietnamese and other Indochinese peoples in the United States represents a unique story among the Asian immigrant groups. The Indochinese peoples had virtually no history in the United States prior to U.S. involvement in the Vietnam War, and few came to the United States until after the U.S. withdrawal from Vietnam and the fall of Saigon in 1975. The Communist takeover and U.S. "peace with honor," as it was called, marked the beginning of a long and wrenching process through which Indochinese refugees would leave their devastated homelands. The refugees' arrival (along with a smaller number as immigrants) created an Indochinese diaspora in the United States, which was essentially a "ground zero" situation for the Indochinese people. Compared to Cuban refugees, the Indochinese group were different in view of the violent and prolonged atrocities to which they had been subjected, their economic circumstances, limited contact with the U.S. culture, and a younger age distribution.

The refugee and immigrant situation for Vietnamese, Laotian, Cambodian, and Hmong (an ethnic minority largely from the rural highlands of Laos but spread throughout Indochina) is historically complex. Only basic information is given here, but Ruben Rumbaut (1995) provides an excellent, information-packed account.

In 1990, the U.S. Census counted the Vietnamese American population at about 600,000, the Cambodian and Laotian populations each near 150,000, and the Hmong at over 94,000 (see Table 7.10). Some ethnic Chinese likely identified themselves in the census as Chinese rather than Vietnamese. Vietnamese continue to be a substantial source of U.S. immigrants, with over 40,000 arriving annually in recent years.

Vietnam's history is permeated with Chinese domination. Vietnam was a colony of China from 938 A.D. to 1776. The French ruled southern Vietnam and what was termed French Indochina from 1867 to 1945. The Japanese overthrew France in World War II and granted independence to the French Indochinese countries, but France once again took control of the region after the Japanese were defeated in the war. The French-Indochinese War ensued,

TABLE 7.10   Asian American Speakers of Languages Other Than English:
Speakers 5 Years of Age and Older From Top 15 Ancestry
Groups: 1990

Ancestry Group	Population	Speakers of Other Languages (Percentage of Population)	Limited English Proficiency[a] (Percentage of Speakers of Other Languages)
Chinese	1,574,918	1,230,235 (84)	739,995 (84)
Taiwanese	73,778	64,140 (92)	37,447 (58)
Filipino	1,419,711	900,675 (68)	318,305 (35)
Japanese	866,160	360,415 (44)	206,213 (57)
Korean	797,304	593,529 (82)	375,527 (63)
Asian Indian	786,694	561,247 (78)	169,363 (30)
Vietnamese	593,213	510,240 (94)	330,837 (65)
Pacific Islander	350,592	98,014 (31)	34,614 (35)
Polynesian	283,885	65,372 (31)	22,265 (34)
Hawaiian	205,501	18,601 (10)	5,032 (27)
Cambodian	149,047	124,211 (96)	90,614 (73)
Laotian	147,375	126,136 (97)	88,347 (70)
Hmong	94,439	71,891 (97)	56,152 (78)
Thai	91,360	69,421 (81)	40,078 (58)
Pakistani	81,691	65,188 (89)	22,017 (34)
Samoan	57,679	33,165 (66)	10,933 (33)

SOURCE: U.S. Bureau of the Census (1994b).
a. Counted as those who report on the census form that they "do not speak English very well."

in which France lost its claim to the region. Independence was gained for
Vietnam, Cambodia, and Laos in 1953, and Vietnam was divided into North
and South in 1954. In complex ways, the language systems have retained the
long-standing influence of other Asian cultures and the more modern influence of French colonial presence.

About 18,000 Indochinese people were in the United States prior to 1975,
most of whom came between 1970 and 1974 (Rumbaut, 1995). The refugee
process began with the enactment of the Refugee Act of 1975, leading to
three waves of Indochinese arrivals in the United States (Cheng, 1987;
Chung, 1988; Rumbaut, 1995): (a) 1975 to 1979, (b) 1979 to 1982, and
(c) 1982 and the years following. Through the refugee process, incoming
Indochinese received special financial support from the government.

The first wave occurred immediately after the fall of Saigon and included
mainly educated Vietnamese who were affiliated with the U.S. government.
Close to 100,000 came between 1975 and 1978, with some 88,500 in 1978
alone.

The second wave, beginning in 1979, followed a border war between Vietnam and China and included a large number of ethnic Chinese and Hmong (many of whom are ethnic Chinese) as well as Cambodians and Laotians. The second wave group was much more diverse and numbered over 300,000 people.

The third wave of refugees came to the United States under the conditions of the Refugee Act of 1980, which provided for entry through the Orderly Departure Program (ODP). This act also brought a number of Amerasian children who were the offspring of Vietnamese women and U.S. soldiers. Prior to arriving in the United States, refugees received orientation and training in "re-education" and resettlement camps, which included cultural overviews and "survival English" skills (Chung, 1988; Rumbaut, 1995). Placements in the United States often located Indochinese Americans in challenging urban sites "on the margin" between larger groups of whites and blacks (Somekawa, 1995).

Based on information compiled by Rumbaut (1995), in the 10 years from 1982 through 1992, 637,544 Indochinese entered the United States, 483,204 as refugees and 154,340 as immigrants. Many of the children who came during this period had experienced one or more years of school interruption, which put them at a great disadvantage in entering their new peer and school environments in the United States.

The refugee process virtually stopped during the 1990s, but a substantial number of Indochinese now enter the United States as immigrants, especially under the family reunification provisions. From 1993 to 1995, the Vietnamese immigrant total neared 143,000 (see Table 7.3).

Although the regional distribution of Indochinese Americans varies more than for other Asian groups, clusters have emerged over time. The highest concentration is located in California (40%), mainly in the Southern California metropolitan area (Rumbaut, 1995). Other states with proportionally high numbers are Texas, Virginia, Massachusetts, Washington, Wisconsin, and Minnesota.

The standard of living for Indochinese Americans has, for obvious reasons, been low. Disadvantaged by lack of facility in English, the trauma of war, and the dramatic differences between their native cultures and life in the United States, the Indochinese people have found their new home challenging in many ways. The majority of arrivals did not come from advantaged backgrounds. At the extreme, the rural Hmong people lived in a preliterate society until the 1950s, when their language was first put into written form.

Per capita incomes for Indochinese groups fall well below, and percentage of families in poverty well above, the U.S. average: about $9,000 per capita for Vietnamese and $5,000 for Cambodians in 1990, with 24% of Vietnamese families and 42% of Cambodian families below the poverty level (see Table 7.9).

But with more experience and time in the United States, this situation is slowly improving. Overall, the college education rates for Vietnamese men come close to matching those for the U.S. population in general, although women still lag far behind (see Table 7.7). The prospects for movement "upward" can be found in the characterization of Vietnamese in southern California offered by Alejandro Portes and Ruben Rumbaut (1996), who report a broad array of data from studies conducted on minority groups: "They form a tightly knit community that, in recent years, has become increasingly entrepreneurial. . . . The resources of family and community appear sufficiently strong to anticipate solid upward mobility among the Vietnamese second generation" (p. 256).

Confucian notions of hierarchy dominate Indochinese social organization leading to "profound inequality between men and women and strict seniority by age" (Hein, 1991, p. 156). This accounts for the differential education rates between men and women and is the source of marital stress. As Vietnamese American women become more central as wage earners and more aware of advances for women in the United States, they desire more independence from their husbands and more equality (Espiritu, 1997; Luu, 1989). The family structure is one of extended family and extensive kinship ties.

Asian American Cultural Themes

As we have seen in the Asian American group profiles, diversity abounds beneath the aggregate ethnic label normally used to designate these peoples. Histories, languages, and particular experiences as immigrants combine distinctively for each group. Diversity also exists in the cultural practices of the groups we have considered. In this section, I examine those cultural threads that align the particular Asian American groups more with one another than with Eurowhite culture(s) in the United States. The usefulness of this sort of generalizing allows comparison to non-Asian ethnic groups but is not intended to universalize Asian American cultural patterns.

I consider (a) the general notion of pan-Asian identity, (b) the role of Confucian influence in most Asian American cultures, and (c) a set of specific Asian American cultural orientations.

Pan-Asian Cultural Identity

To the extent that there is something we can designate as an Asian American cultural identity, its roots are in what Espiritu (1992) calls "Asian American panethnicity" and Pyong Gap Min (1995) calls "Pan-Asian unity." Using the Language-Centered Perspective on Culture, pan-Asian cultural identity would be located at a level superordinate to any particular Asian culture as a unifying set of cultural abstractions that give rise to the particular cultural practices of different groups.

To make the notion of pan-Asian identity concrete, Min (1995) identifies nine value similarities:

1. Group rather than individual orientation
2. Filial piety
3. Respect for authority
4. Self-control and emotional restraint
5. Educational achievement
6. Shame as a source of control
7. Virtue associated with middle position
8. High status for the elderly
9. Centrality of family relationships

These are designated as pan-Asian and not pan-Asian American themes, but their coherence in the U.S. context is significant for two reasons. First, the vast majority of Asian Americans are not U.S.-born, which means that their enculturation was likely in an Asian national context. Second, even in the context of multicultural influences and change over generations of Asians in the United States, many of these patterns stand out. Many acquaintances of Asian background, for example, comment on the importance of filial piety in their families.

Confucianism

One strong link connecting many Asian Americans stems from Confucian influence. With the exceptions of Filipinos and Asian Indians, Confucianism is important to Asian peoples and their migration and adaptation to the American scene. Confucius was a Chinese philosopher who lived from 551 to 479 B.C. Confucianism spread to Japan and Korea as well as to other Asian countries and cultures. Confucianism emphasizes human nature and propriety in human relationships, organized around four human natures (Chen & Chung, 1994; Yum, 1987, 1988): (a) *jen,* which is the cardinal principle of humanism governing benevolence in relationships; (b) *i,* faithfulness and righteousness related to common good; (c) *li,* propriety through an etiquette for relationships, and (d) *chih,* or wisdom that is attainable through education. June-Ock Yum (1988) isolates *"proper* [italics added] social relationships and their maintenance" (p. 375) as the foundations for this way of thinking. As such, Confucianism is a pragmatic philosophy, devoid of religious aspects.

Much of Confucianism relies on ethical principles, called the Five Codes of Ethics. These guide different types of relationships in a very complex manner:

> (1) loyalty between king and subject [binding mutual obligation], (2) closeness between father and son [obligating the son to the father above all else], (3) distinction in duty between husband and wife, (4) obedience to orders between elders and youngsters, and (5) mutual faith between friends. (Yum, 1987, p. 75)

We can see in these five ethics a map for principles of hierarchy, of gender relations, of status accorded to age, and of peer relations. The Confucian ideal, as discussed by Hui-Ching Chang and G. Richard Holt (1991), puts social relations in the center of human action in a particular way; *kuan-hsi* (meaning *relations*) "implies a special connection between people, a connection which brings along with it interactants' special rights and obligations" (p. 256).

The cultural themes derived from Confucianism show heavy emphasis on social relations, propriety in discourse, and education. Yum (1988) explains that "Confucian philosophy views relationships as complementary or asymmetrical and reciprocally obligatory. . . . A person is forever indebted to others, who in turn are constrained by other debts" (p. 379). Society rests in this view on proper maintenance of five basic relationships: (a) father-son love, (b) emperor-subject righteousness, (c) husband-wife chaste conduct, (d) elder-younger order, and (e) friend-friend faithfulness (Chang & Holt, 1991). Guo-Ming Chen and Jensen Chung (1994, p. 98) note that "the perfectibility and educability of human beings" are cornerstones in Confucianism. In the Confucian worldview, the goal of education, as expressed by Aimin Li (personal communication, July 8, 1997), is to achieve *"nei sheng wai wang*—sageness within and kindness without."

Cultural Orientations

The specific cultural themes outlined in the next section represent cultural retentions of varying degree, much the same as those existing among other migrant and diaspora groups. The retentions are more direct for foreign-born individuals but also pertain to the U.S.-born.

I highlight five themes of importance: (a) collectivism, (b) social and gender hierarchy, (c) family centeredness, (d) harmony, and (e) education. Each theme defines cultural abstractions that give rise to language practices. As cultural abstractions, some express broad value orientations, some reflect ethical principles, and still others look more like cultural perceptions of natural laws.

Each theme also holds implications for the production of cultural artifacts, although such artifacts are more particularized to specific Asian American groups than would be manifested in pan-Asian expression. The most prominent of all Asian crossovers is Chinese food, which is in most cases Americanized. The "real thing" is available in Chinatowns and increasingly in other locales, as Americans become more adventuresome about their eating habits. Japanese architectural influence is evident in most urban areas, especially those that have prospered in the past 20 to 30 years. Depending on where one lives, the influences are more or less visible and integrated into daily life. Such is the case for San Francisco, which is the home of many Asian Americans. Richard Rodriguez (Postrel & Gillespie, 1995) goes so far as to say that living in San Francisco is making him (a Mexican-American) "more Chinese."

Literature is one artifact domain where Asian American voices are increasingly part of mass American culture, but even here the impact remains limited. Maxine Hong Kingston's (1976) acclaimed autobiography *The Woman Warrior: Memoirs of a Girlhood among Ghosts* was the first book to move successfully into the mass market domain; in this novel, Hong Kingston tells her story of growing up as a second-generation Chinese American in California. Novelist Amy Tan's (1989) successful book, *The Joy Luck Club,* a story primarily about mother-daughter relations among China-born mothers and U.S.-born daughters, is the best known, undoubtedly because it crossed over into the Hollywood movie genre. A younger generation of Asian American writers also appears to be coming into the public sphere with their narratives of identity and cultural multiplicity. Gish Jen (featured at the beginning of this chapter) is one such writer. Korean American Chang-Rae Lee (1995) is another; his book, *Native Speaker,* focuses on the cultural identity struggles of a young man—American born of Korean immigrants—

named Henry Park. Nora Okja Keller (of Korean and U.S. white back-
ground), Patricia Chao (of Chinese and Japanese background), and Nina
Revoyr (of Japanese and Polish-American background) were featured in
Time magazine (Farley, 1997). More emerge each year.

Not all of the Asian Americans groups orient to the cultural themes
discussed here in the same ways. Differences will be found based on specific
ancestry, socioeconomic status, and generation. In some instances, cultural
values and orientations brought from other countries persevere more rigidly
in the new migrant environment than they do in the ancestral location, where
changes continuously occur.

Collectivism

The most frequently noted cultural orientation among Asians and Asian
Americans is the emphasis on collectivism more than individualism. Two
basic ideas guide collectivist thinking: (a) Identity is situated in various loci
of group status and (b) people do things for the common or group good rather
than for individual recognition or gain. One way to understand the collectivist orientation is to think of it as engaging the antithesis of ego orientation
(Chen, 1993), which is much more prominent among Western cultures,
especially Eurowhite America.

Collectivist values affect family and community activities, political orientations, and attitudes toward work and success. Examples abound. Ivan
Light's (1987) examination of "rotating credit associations" in the historical
development of Asian American communities provides one kind of evidence
of how this orientation manifested itself when conventional bank credit was
difficult to obtain. In Chinese, these are called *hui* and in Japanese, *tanomoshi*
or *mujin.*

Collectivism, then, defines the social unit and contrasts with the strength
of individualism in U.S. society. The balance is relative, but notions related
to freedom for the individual contrast sharply with the cultural systems to
which most Asian Americans trace their roots (Cushman & Kincaid, 1987).

Social Hierarchy and Gender Hierarchy

The second cultural theme among Asian groups reflects retention of social
and gender hierarchy traceable to Confucianism. Contrasted to the American
ideology of social mobility, the "self-made person," and "equality of opportunity," cultures stressing social and gender hierarchy locate people in
positions ascribed as part of the social order. The Confucian principle of

li—propriety through relational etiquette—gives elders status over younger people, parents over children, teachers over students, and managers over employees. Publicly discrediting parents, which is a common practice on today's "tell all" television talk shows, would be unthinkable and undoable in most Asian American groups. Hierarchy in the Asian traditions requires knowledge (communicative competence) about appropriateness rules for discourse, which must be acquired.

Ascribed gender hierarchy among Asian Americans has been especially resistant to the U.S. trend toward greater gender equity. Analyses of every Asian American group, save Filipinos, include characterizations of patriarchal control, even in cases where women are well educated (Espiritu, 1997).

Filipinos, who are not influenced by Confucianism, do evidence respect for family elders (Agbayami-Siewert & Revilla, 1995) but practice greater gender equality than other Asian groups. The Filipino version of the creation story, for example, tells much about the power of cultural narratives to construct gender ideology. Unlike Judeo-Christian stories of Eve springing from Adam's side and being created through one of Adam's ribs, the Filipino Adam-and-Eve legend locates both "emerging simultaneously from a large bamboo tube" (Agbayami-Siewert & Revilla, 1995, p. 160).

Family Centeredness

Contrasted with prevailing non-Hispanic white patterns of nuclear family structure, which move children into adult independence, Asian Americans are notable for their orientation toward family centeredness, especially through extended family structures entailing reciprocal obligations over a lifetime. Family disruption tends to be frowned on, as evidenced in substantially lower divorce rates among Asians compared to the U.S. population in general (U.S. Bureau of the Census, 1995b). Consistent with extended family structure, more people live in Asian American households than in non-Hispanic white households (U.S. Bureau of the Census, 1995b).

Embedded in the family centeredness among Asian American cultures is the cultural attitude and practice of filial piety, which refers to fidelity and natural obligation of sons and daughters. Filial piety arises from the ascribed status of parents, which obligates sons and daughters in ways much more carefully delineated and controlled than is the case in most American families. Yum (1987) traces this to the Confucian nature of *jen,* which places parents in a primary position for the definition of all relationships.

Family focus also extends beyond the immediate family: "concepts such as loyalty, obedience, and filial piety practiced in the family are transferred to social organizations in which habits of disciplined subordination and acceptance of authority are fostered" (Chen & Chung, 1994, p. 96).

Harmony

Sustaining harmony and human accord in family and social affairs holds great value in Asian cultures. Cushman and Kincaid (1987) isolate the value placed on spiritual harmony as historically important to Eastern perspectives on the communication process. In the American context, this value continues to be manifest among Asian peoples, implying particular patterns for language use that minimize overt conflict. Agbayani-Siewert and Revilla (1995) describe the importance of "smooth interpersonal relationships" among Filipino Americans who value *pakikisama*—"which means going along with others, even if one must contradict one's own desires" (p. 160). Vietnamese Americans stress the repression of negative feelings to promote family relations (Luu, 1989).

Ideas related to the concept of "face" and dignity are directly related to the value of harmony. Face as an Asian cultural notion is something that every person has; it is not a facade but rather the core of self-dignity. In most Asian cultures, it is important to ensure that others are not embarrassed, humiliated, or shamed by the actions of others—even if this means not telling the absolute truth.

Education

To repeat a point made previously, Asian Americans in aggregate are the best-educated ethnic group in the United States, although educational attainment does vary both between and within specific ancestral groups. Asian people possess no greater inherent intelligence than others, but they do emphasize education of children and educational attainment in general, especially for men. As early as third grade, the son of Chinese American friends, for example, spent over 3 hours each evening studying, with most of his homework supplied by his parents to supplement school work.

For some Asian Americans, the value for education arises from the Confucian nature *chin,* emphasizing wisdom and the importance of perfecting the mind. The educational status of Asian Indian Americans is more attached to class and the legacy of caste; the majority of Indians who migrate to the United States are from the highest levels of Indian cultural hierarchy.

Conclusions

The great variability in national ancestry and history makes generalizing across Asian Americans difficult. Yet there seem to be strands showing the tendency to bring into the U.S. cultural mix a set of specific ethnic cultural systems that include several pan-Asian qualities. Like other cultural patterns, those identified as Asian dynamically interact with other cultures in the United States. Even in the context of limited research, what is available augments the reductive stereotype of Asians as model minority.

Language Context and Discourse Dimensions

In this section, I examine the language situation for Asian Americans from four different perspectives. The first looks broadly at the nature of language complexity and diversity within the Asian American population, specifically at Asian languages used in the United States and the balance of these with English among Asian American peoples. The second perspective offers a glimpse at the language situation from which Asian immigrants come, focusing on some linguistic and communicative features of selected Asian languages and on the national language contexts for the major Asian immigrant groups. The third considers attitudes about Asian languages and Asian-accented English. The fourth section focuses on aspects of the pragmatics of language use that are notable for Asian Americans.

Asian Language Complexity in the American Context

About 65% of those age 5 years and older with Asian ancestry speak a language other than English at home, and about 52% of these possess limited English proficiency (LEP); the LEP percentage represents 34% of the entire Asian American population. Language data for the 15 most populous ancestry groups are displayed in Table 7.10, which shows both the numbers and percentages of speakers of non-English languages.

Asian American "at home" languages. The differences among ancestral groups in terms of language profiles reflect the different histories of these groups in the United States. The large proportion of Chinese Americans who are foreign-born (69%) contributes to the high vitality of the Chinese language as seen in the large proportion (84%) of Chinese Americans who speak Chinese in the home environment.

TABLE 7.11   Asian American With Limited English Proficiency (LEP),
by Age Group: 1990

Age Group	Percentage of Asian Population	Percentage of Age Group with LEP
5 to 17 years	18	44
18 to 64 years	74	55
65+ years	8	72

SOURCE: U.S. Bureau of the Census (1993c).

Understandably, those groups with a short history in the United States and a history dominated by refugee conditions use their native languages as the primary mode of communication in the home environment (94% of Vietnamese, 96% of Cambodians, 97% of Laotians, and 97% of the Hmong). Japanese Americans stand out for their lower rate of people who speak a language other than English in the home. The low immigration rate and high rate of the U.S.-born account for this pattern. The Japanese American experience during World War II also exerted pressure to fit into U.S. society and to prove loyalty; speaking English was one way to do just that.

LEP speakers. In aggregate, about 40% of all Asian Americans are LEP speakers (U.S. Bureau of the Census, 1994a). By family unit, about one quarter of Asian American households are "linguistically isolated," which means that no person age 14 or older speaks English with proficiency (Rumbaut, 1995). The rate of linguistically isolated units is especially high for Indochinese groups, where the percentages are about twice that of the overall Asian American population. As the generations of Indochinese Americans progress and there are more U.S.-born, we would expect linguistic isolation to recede.

The largest percentages of LEP speakers are in the Indochinese refugee groups. It is likely, however, that the LEP percentages shown in Table 7.11 have already decreased slightly, especially for Vietnamese, simply because of the longer experience of these refugee groups in the United States

Sizable percentages of LEP speakers occur in other Asian American groups as well. Close to two thirds of Korean Americans who speak Korean at home consider themselves LEP; this represents 47% of the entire Korean American population. Close behind are the mainland Chinese Americans, a group in which 60% of those who speak Chinese at home consider themselves LEP (47% of the entire Chinese mainland group). The Taiwanese American group is even slightly higher, with 51% of the entire group claiming to be LEP. These statistics compare to the lower 24% of Japanese Americans who consider themselves LEP.

Understandably, LEP rates relate to age. As demonstrated in Table 7.11, close to three quarters of those 65 years of age and older in 1990 reported themselves to be LEP speakers, compared to one fifth of those age 5 to 17 (U.S. Bureau of the Census, 1993b); the school-age group consists of young-sters born in the United States who have much more exposure to English and those who have moved with varying levels of success through bilingual education programs.

An informative case study of English proficiency is available for the younger cohort in research on 80,000 high school students in the San Diego school system (Rumbaut, 1995, reported in Portes & Rumbaut, 1996). In 1990, the following percentages of LEP students (in descending order) were found for the major Asian American groups: 78% Cambodian, 66% Laotian, 57% Hmong, 44% Vietnamese, 33% Korean, 21% Chinese, 13% Japanese, and 7% Filipino (the Hispanic number was 20%). These data result mainly from different length of experience in the United States. Obviously, the implications point to priorities for bilingual education (see Chapter 9).

Consistent with the profiles on occupational clustering associated with the different Asian American groups, patterns of work also account for the degree to which English is or is not mastered. Several illustrations show the lan-guage-work connection. Chinese Americans often run small businesses (res-taurants, dry cleaners, etc.), both for Chinese American clientele and for others; even in the latter situation, Chinese language vitality remains high in the day-to-day operations of these businesses because employees tend to be Chinese and the interaction with customers requires a limited set of verbal exchanges. Even among Chinese Americans working in professional fields, engineering and technology jobs dominate; these jobs require the least English relative to other professional positions. In contrast, Asian Indian Americans are more likely to be in professional jobs requiring substantial use of English—for example, jobs in health care and related fields.

Major Asian languages in the U.S. context. Data on speakers of specific languages conform to the overall profile presented in Table 7.10. In descend-ing order, the languages spoken in the home (Bruno, 1993) are Chinese, Tagalog (the major language of the Philippines, virtually identical to the national language which is called Pilipino), Korean, Vietnamese, Japanese, Hindi (from India), Thai (Laotian), and Mon-Khmer (Cambodian). Table 7.12 shows the number of speakers of each. The differences in the numbers

TABLE 7.12 Most Frequent Languages Spoken at Home by Asian Americans in the United States: 1990

Language	Number of Speakers
Chinese[a]	1,249,213
Tagalog	843,251
Korean	626,478
Vietnamese	507,069
Japanese	427,657
Hindi	331,484
Thai	206,266
Mon-Khmer	127,441

SOURCE: Bruno (1993).
a. Includes all dialects, which may be mutually unintelligible, as is the case for Cantonese and Mandarin.

here and in the column for "Speakers of Other Languages" in Table 7.10 occur because the language spoken at home does not always correspond to the location of ancestry; every country has minority language speakers and/or complex multilingual situations.

The linguistic demography of Asian Americans, then, is one of considerable complexity. Added to the diversity introduced by many different languages are the approximately 35% of Asian Americans who are monolingual English speakers or have limited proficiency in an Asian language. Looking ahead, this complexity is certain to continue simply because Asian immigration will drive Asian American population growth.

Language Context of Asian Countries of Origin

In the context of a general tendency for U.S. youth to shy away from foreign language study, there is especially great fear about trying to learn Asian languages because they are perceived as so radically different from English. Language difficulties work in the other direction, too. Asian immigrants must learn the rules for American English—a significant challenge at every level of language system. Because language systems symbolize culture-based meanings, the burdensome transition involved for Asian immigrants in the United States reaches far beyond translation. Immigrants must learn wholly new cultural linguistics.

In this section, each of the ancestral countries focused on in earlier sections is examined for its overall language situation. In a number of cases, aspects of the linguistic system, per se, are considered.

The Chinese American language context. The prevailing dialect situations for mainland China, Taiwan, and Hong Kong offer a useful starting point. About 90% of the population of mainland China is from the Han ethnic group, 70% of whom speak varieties of a single language called *Beifanghua*; its standard version, *Putonghua*, is usually referred to as *Mandarin* (Asher & Simpson, 1994). Mandarin is the national language, but it is not used uniformly in education, especially in rural areas. Mandarin is also the national language of Taiwan, where it prevails in schooling, but it is not the native dialect of most of the population, who speak *Taiwanese* in private (Wong, 1988). Linguistically, Taiwanese is a variety of the Min dialect (Minnan), but the political importance of designating it as Taiwanese has gained momentum as a nationalistic symbol. In Hong Kong, the standard spoken variety of Chinese has been Cantonese, although Mandarin has been taught more in the past decade because of Hong Kong's return to China in July 1997 after 150 years as a British colony. One indication of the move toward Mandarin was reported just days before Hong Kong's reunification with China. A popular music group, the Canto Pop, described by a journalist as "sugary Cantonese-language singers," had started to do recordings in Mandarin (Lakshmanan, 1997).

Whereas this three-location situation for spoken Chinese may look straightforward in terms of its implications for immigrants, it is not. In fact, the large majority of early Chinese immigrants to the United States spoke Cantonese because they were predominantly from the Guangdong province. This "edge" for Cantonese in the formation of Chinese American immigrant linguistic identity has been bolstered by immigrants from Hong Kong, and more recently by ethnic Chinese immigrants, most of whom are Cantonese speakers (Wong, 1988). Mandarin, however, has increased rapidly in the United States as a result of the opening of immigration from mainland China. Many monolingual English speakers are shocked to learn that Mandarin and Cantonese speakers cannot understand one another. Added to this, the Chinese dialects have adapted to the U.S. environment, changing according to the needs of everyday expression. Succinctly put, the spoken Chinese language situation in the United States is complex.

Across the varieties of Chinese, certain linguistic characteristics stand out as sharply contrasted to English. First, Chinese is a tone language, meaning that the pitch level in which syllables are uttered carries meanings, usually at the morphemic and lexical level. Second, unlike English and other Indo-European languages, Chinese morphemes are mostly one syllable. Third, Chinese lacks grammatical inflections (such as the -*ed* marking past tense in

English or the -*s* marking plural); word order carries the meaning. Fourth, and most interesting for its cultural implications, nouns are not marked singular and plural. They can be modified by what the English speaker would construe as singular and plural adjectives, but the noun itself does not change: for example, "one *volume* of book" and "two *pieces* of table" (examples provided by Li, personal communication, July 8, 1997).

Against the great diversity in spoken varieties of Chinese, the written characters are a constant. Characters are essentially syllables, most of which are morphemes: "many characters represent phonetically identical morphemes (homonyms)," and there are approximately 8,000 characters (Asher & Simpson, 1994, p. 517). These characters endure despite differences and change over time in oral forms, making the situation quite different from English.

The status of English in the three locations of Chinese immigrants varies (Wong, 1988). In Hong Kong, English is taught from kindergarten or first grade forward because of Hong Kong's history as a British colony. In Taiwan, English training does not begin until the junior high school/middle school years. Against a 20th-century history in China that placed emphasis on Russian as the most important second language, interest in English has grown subsequent to the establishment of diplomatic relations with the United States in the late 1970s. College students are required to study English. The implication of all three language situations is that the more educated the person, the more likely he or she is to be relatively fluent in English, especially written English.

The Filipino American language context. The 20th-century history of the Philippine Islands as a U.S. colony has resulted in English being one of two official languages along with Pilipino. This accounts for the high English fluency rate among Filipino Americans.

In the Philippines, the language situation is one of complexity alongside the official languages. With a population spread over many islands, there are some 75 languages, 8 of which have been "designated major languages because they were spoken natively by the eight largest ethnic groups in the Philippines" (Galang, 1988, p. 234). These eight languages are not mutually intelligible, which gives a pragmatic boost to official languages.

Multilingualism dominates among educated people, many of whom are trilingual. Galang (1988) refers to studies regarding the development of a Filipino variety of English as well as a mixture of Tagalog and English "called variously Taglish (if Tagalog predominates), Engalog (if English predominates), Halo-Halo, or Mix-Mix (a Pilipino term with pejorative connotations)" (p. 238). Mass media use either English or Tagalog.

Among Filipino immigrants, the vast majority are speakers of Tagalog (see Table 7.12). The Tagalog language uses the Roman alphabet but has major syntactic differences from English. First, nouns are inflected for neither gender nor number. Second, there are no articles (English *a, an, the*). Third, the usual syntactic order places the verb in first position, in contrast to English, which is a subject-verb-object order language.

All things equal, the language transition of Filipinos into the English-dominant United States is less difficult than for most Asians. The status of English in the Philippines gives an advantage, even if the variety differs from those encountered in the United States.

The Japanese American language context. For those Japanese Americans who are Japan-born and whose first language is Japanese, the language background varies with generation. More recent immigrants are likely to be better educated than those who came earlier (Nishi, 1995). And even though cultural patterns tend to be retained, English has been the dominant language for the three generational cohorts born in the United States.

As context for Japanese Americans whose native or first language is Japanese, it is useful to consider several aspects of the Japanese language. There are many, often mutually unintelligible dialects of Japanese, but there is both a standard writing system and a standard variety of spoken language drawn from the Tokyo dialect. Thus, the national language situation is less complex than some others.

Several linguistic aspects of Japanese are interesting in contrast with English. First, although Japanese is not a tone language, its speakers learn to be more sensitive to pitch and tone variations than do speakers of English, because pitch and tone mark certain work meanings. Second, the Japanese syntactic structure differs from English because it follows subject-object-verb order. Third, Japanese lexicon uses many *mimetic* words to correspond to perceptions of the sounds of things and beings in nature and also to more abstract mental states (Asher & Simpson, 1994). Fourth, the use of pronouns in Japanese differs from English both because pronouns are less frequently used overall and because they can be omitted in some contexts. Finally, Japanese employs an elaborate set of *honorifics,* which are linguistic markers used to indicate respect, politeness, and humbleness. The many distinctions in how to talk, how to address others, and how to refer to oneself imply a vastly more complex system of discourse registers than would be the case among typical monolingual English-speaking Americans.

The Japanese writing system is based on Chinese characters but also includes what are called *syllabary*. A Roman alphabet orthography has made its way into the language for certain place names and abbreviations based on English (e.g., airport names and abbreviations such as VCR).

The Korean American language context. The language situation for Koreans in their home country provides yet another example of why it is important to consider the distinctive aspects of each Asian American group. Koreans who emigrate into the United States bring a language context that helps explain Korean language vitality in the migrant context. Homogeneity characterizes Korea both ethnically and linguistically (Asher & Simpson, 1994). Korea does have regional dialects, but these are mutually intelligible. Korea also boasts an amazingly high literacy rate of 98% (*National Geographic Atlas,* 1995). Common language and ethnicity/nationality thus help establish cultural identity once in the United States.

Linguistically, Korean contrasts with English in many ways, just a few of which are noted here. First, Korean is a polysyllabic language that uses a system of elaborate markers. These markers are used "to indicate the role of a word within the sentence . . . , mood, tense, location, and the social relationship between the speaker, listener, and person spoken about" (Asher & Simpson, 1994, p. 1869). Second, like Tagalog, Korean does not use articles. Third, like Japanese, Korean employs a system of honorifics that are both self- and other-referential. Kim (1988) observes that the lack of an honorific system in English often impedes the use of English among Koreans, who feel uncomfortable in conversation without clear honorific markers of social relationships. Fourth, both the vowel and consonant systems in Korean are much more complex than in English. Fifth, Korean does not require the same kinds of grammatical agreement between sentence elements as does English. Sixth, like Japanese, Korean uses subject-object-verb order.

The Korean system of writing is based on Chinese characters, which can be mixed with Korean script using the Korean alphabet, called *Han-gul,* which dates from the 15th century. About half of all Korean words are borrowed directly from Chinese, although the Korean pronunciation is distinctive (Kim, 1988).

The Asian Indian American language context. The most important factor about language issues for Asian Indian Americans is that, compared to other immigrant groups, Asian Indians possess advanced English skills. Advanced education in India is in English, and Asian Indians in the United States are by far the best educated of all American groups for which data are available by ethnicity (see Table 7.7). For those born in the United States, there is strong likelihood of English monolingualism—more so than for Asian Indian immigrant groups in other countries (Sheth, 1995).

Historically, British colonial rule in India established English as the language of the elite, of government, and of advanced education. After independence from Britain in 1947, the constitution of India provided for 15 major national languages, reflecting the right of each state to have an official language (Khubchandani, 1983). English continues to dominate as the language of educated people, who are in most cases bilingual or trilingual. The dominant Indian language is Hindi, which is the mother tongue of more than 180 million people and second language to another 300 million (Hindi, 1997). As a nation, India is vastly multilingual, with roughly 200 separate languages and many more dialects. The literacy rate of India is only 52% (*National Geographic Atlas,* 1995). About 13% of the Indian population is bi- or trilingual (Asher & Simpson, 1994).

Because the large majority of Asian Indian immigrants to the United States after 1965 were college educated, the likelihood that they came with fluency and literacy in Indian English was also high. In one study conducted in New York in the mid-1980s (Sridhar, 1988), over 80% reported that English was the language of their high school education in India, and 95% reported that English was the main language of their college education. Those Asian Indian Americans with limited or no English proficiency are likely to be family members who immigrated into the United States under family reunification priorities.

The Indochinese language context. The Vietnamese, Laotian, Mon-Khmer (spoken in Cambodia), and Hmong languages carry distinctive political legacies that have permeated the linguistic systems. Some of the major distinctive features of each of the Indochinese languages give a sense of their character and of their contrast with English (much of this information is drawn from Cheng, 1987, and Chung, 1988).

Vietnamese is a monosyllabic, tonal language. It has no consonant blends, and final sounds tend to be dropped. Vietnamese is an uninflected language and thus does not distinguish such aspects as singular and plural or past, present, and future in the way in which words are structured within sentences; this feature places emphasis on context much more so than is the case for English. Many Vietnamese words originated in other languages, including French, Chinese, and English. In the early part of the 20th century, the written version of the language was transformed from a system based on Chinese characters to a new system making use of a Roman-type alphabet augmented with diacritical marks that indicate tone qualities.

Lao, too, is a tonal language, and its standard dialect uses six tones as a basis for varying meaning. Lao lexicon is elaborately differentiated according to the addressee. Contrasted to most languages, Lao uses no stress, which makes learning the stress patterns in other languages difficult for native speakers of Lao. Other contrasts with English are that words usually end in vowels, tense is conveyed with words rather than syntactic markers, and adjectives follow rather than precede nouns.

Mon-Khmer, which is the language spoken by most Cambodians, was influenced by India. The Mon-Khmer alphabet was adapted from Sanskrit and Pali, the languages of Hinduism and Buddhism, respectively. The influence of French rule is evident in the lexicon of Mon-Khmer. It differs from other Indochinese languages in that it is not a tonal language. The intonation pattern stresses the end of sentences. Noteworthy in Mon-Khmer are its four different registers: language used with ordinary people, formal language, language of the clergy, and a form considered royal language (Cheng, 1987). A broad array of honorifics is also used.

Hmong, as already noted, was an oral language until recently. Oral legends and folk tales are thus a distinctive part of this language of rural mountain dwellers. Like many other Asian languages, Hmong is tonal, using a seven-tone system. Of special interest is the existence of two varieties of Hmong, called White and Blue/Green.

The literacy rates in the Indochinese countries provide some indication of the ways in which war can affect education. At 92%, Vietnam's literacy rate is high. The Laotian rate is far below, at 64%, and the Cambodian rate is an astonishingly low 35% (*National Geographic Atlas,* 1995). Clearly, those without literacy in their native languages will find both learning English and adapting to a English-dominant culture difficult.

Complex diversity. For native speakers of all Asian languages, substantial challenges arise in the process of learning English. The six language contexts described above should make clear why it is inappropriate to lump together language issues for all Asian Americans and why it is imperative that more be learned about specific language situations within this aggregate grouping. Added to the contextual complexity outlined here are groups not even mentioned—Thai, Pakistani, and Samoan to name some—plus bi- and multiethnic individuals whose cultural experiences are developed in families of, say, Filipino fathers and Japanese mothers or Korean mothers and non-Hispanic white fathers.

Language Attitudes Associated With Asian Americans

Language attitudes—toward both particular varieties and particular speakers—often function to shape or to reinforce beliefs about whole groups of people. I have already examined, for instance, the prejudice against African American Vernacular English (AAVE). There is little research available to document how such attitudes function in relation to Asian languages. The main liability associated with Asian languages is the negativity of foreignness sometimes leading to ridicule (Chen, 1995). It is not unusual to hear American English monolinguals characterize Chinese or Japanese, for example, as choppy, fast, or sing-song, or to mimic Chinese speakers with phrases like "ah sooo" or "no tickie no washie."

In its most simple application, the "foreign language assumption" anticipates that a person who appears "oriental," Asian, or even of some specific Asian ancestry will speak "in one of those languages": Chinese/Japanese/Korean/Vietnamese, and so on. Nakayama's (1997) response to being asked if he speaks English is instructive of how deeply seated the foreignness notions are: Responding to the question by saying " 'Of course I do' does not usually dis/orient the questioner's assumption that one needs European ancestors to be 'American' " (p. 17). Many Asian American students—native speakers of English as well as those for whom English is a second or third language—comment that white Americans often speak slowly in their presence, communicating their sense that Asian Americans cannot understand normally paced English.

One recent study that investigated non-Asian American California college students' judgments about English spoken with a Japanese accent offers an intriguing vantage point on the issue of language attitudes. Aaron Cargile and Howard Giles (1998) found that more Japanese-accented speech leads to judgments that the speaker is less friendly, kind, enthusiastic, and active but has little impact on judgments of intelligence and literacy. There may be some diffuse type of judgment being made when hearing a Japanese accent that relates to dominant ideology about the specter of the Orient or to associations of Japanese people (and perhaps most Asians) with sinister motives, suspicion, impersonalness, and reserve.

Pragmatic Aspects of Asian American Discourse

Scholarly commentary, autobiographies, creative literature, and anecdotal evidence all imply the possibility of pan-Asian American discourse pragmatics that are related to the pan-Asian American cultural themes discussed in an earlier section of this chapter. What is written about here should be taken as a general sense of the contours of Asian American discourse but certainly not as a definitive or universal characterization. We would also expect individuals to have differing degrees of communicative competence. Youths who rebel, for example, against traditional cultural practices of their Asian American parents may know the particular ethnic discourse practices of their cultural heritage but choose not to use them.

Confucian applicability to Asian diasporas. Confucian influence offers one reasonable starting point for positing pan-Asian discourse pragmatics. For Chinese, Japanese, Korean, and Vietnamese Americans, the cultural legacy of this philosophical system plays an important role in what is learned as appropriate language-in-use.

Fortunately, for our purposes, Hui-Ching Chang (1997) has systematically examined references regarding "words and speaking" in the Confucian tradition as recorded in the *Analects*. She characterizes the many comments about language into four orientations: "(a) words define and reflect moral development, (b) beautiful words lacking substance are blameworthy, (c) actions are more important than words, and (d) appropriate speaking relies on rules of propriety" (p. 110). This viewpoint cautions against excesses in language—certainly a view different than found in some cultures, where eloquence and artful discourse are valued. Translated from the *Analects* (Chang, 1997), "language is only a means to express oneself. As long as language is sufficient for clear meaning, whether it is ornate or not is unimportant" (p. 116).

For foreign-born Asian Americans, the influence of Confucianism implicates a process in which cultural attitudes about language migrate to communication in the United States. But U.S.-borns reared in relatively traditional households may learn these cultural attitudes about language as well.

Politeness and process orientation. The dimensions of politeness and process orientation complement each other in pan-Asian American pragmatics of language use. Cheng (1987) describes several specific manifestations of politeness that usefully demonstrate the contrast with prevalent communication patterns in the United States. Her first is of Laotian students, who are reluctant to respond to a teacher's questions with answers such as "I don't know" or to almost any question by saying "no"; such answers violate respect rules. Her second example deals with the ease with which Chinese Americans will ask questions about age, marital status, and job precisely because the answers give information about social status, which in turn guides discourse. One can imagine how difficult it is to explain to Chinese newcomers to the United States why questions about age and marital status are illegal in the workplace, or why some American women consider their age to be nobody's business.

Many Asian Americans feel discomfort with the fluidity of discourse in the American English mainstream cultural context. Situations where informality is encouraged pose special difficulties because the discourse markers accompanying differences in social relationships disappear or become minimized. Addressing those of higher social status by their first names is an increasingly common practice in the United States but is considered in complete violation of rules for hierarchy and politeness that are deeply embedded into the cultural abstractions of most Asian American groups. Encouragements for open, honest communication pose similar difficulties.

Asians have also been characterized as being more concerned for the appropriate and smooth process of communication than the outcome. Yum (1987), for example, describes Koreans as oriented to accommodation rather than confrontation. Speaking more broadly about Asiatic modes of communication, Jan Servaes (1988) says,

> In interpersonal communication, Asians will try to assess the feelings and state of mind of those present. They do not want to bring the harmony of the group into danger, and thus will give their opinion in an indirect way. Not the product, or the message, but the process is of importance. (p. 68)

This emphasis on process is oppositional to the typical American preoccupation with "rugged individualism," "speaking your mind," "making your point," "arguing logically and forcefully," and "being assertive."

The language of silence and strategic indirection. Silence is not considered desirable in most typical American contexts of communication, but Asians/Asian Americans may prefer silence to spoken language in situations where interpersonal disagreement is evident or conflict incipient. Simply put, silence is better than disharmony, and its meaning is much more than nothing. Traise Yamamoto (1995), a Japanese American, explains the choice *not* to speak, especially by Asian American women: "There is no use in it, *shikata ga nai,* no use to calling so much attention to oneself, to one's family; no use to shame others" (p. 139). Silence in this sense is active.

A related concept affecting language use is that of indirection. Consistent with the importance of maintaining social relationships as well as the face and dignity of others, elaborate indirect measures are likely to be used in situations where non-Asian Americans would be more direct, assertive, and even confrontational. Linda Wai Ling Young's (1982) fascinating examination of Chinese discourse strategies sheds light on this discourse element. Her analysis of the ways in which Chinese use a "steady unravelling and build-up of information before arriving at the important message" (p. 77) is accompanied by a report on Americans' judgment that such verbal reasoning lacks clarity and persuasive impact. Ringo Ma (1992) documents another type of discursive indirection in his research on the role of unofficial intermediaries in conflict situations. These intermediaries facilitate problem solving by ensuring that the parties involved need not address one another.

Emotional restraint. Different cultural systems place varying degrees of emphasis on the appropriateness of expressing emotions and feelings. The Asian cultures, and by implication the Asian American cultures, favor restraint when it comes to emotional expression.

Across differences among the Asian American groups in specific language and cultural background, including groups that are and are not directly influenced by Confucianism, the tendency toward emotional restraint in language stands out. Min (1995) defines it as Asian American "self-control and restraint in emotional expression" (p. 30). Considering specific cultural groups, Nishi (1995) notes that Japanese Americans strive for control of private feelings. Luu (1989) comments on the Vietnamese "repression of negative or aggressive feelings" (p. 71), such that any emotional problem is likely to be held within oneself or, if communicated at all, expressed within one's family. Yum (1987) discusses the tradition in Korea for little emotional expression, spanning personal expression and the arts. Describing Filipinos' concerns for harmony in relationships, Cheng (1987) says that openly expressing emotions is considered "rude and uncultured" (p. 59).

Restraint in expressing emotions is definitely part of what leads non-Hispanic whites to describe Asian Americans as the model minority. The simple fact that Asian Americans will not openly express their emotions can lead others to conclude wrongly that problems do not exist and that the absence of emotional expression equates with the lack of emotion and assertiveness. As a kind of corollary, Eurowhites often react negatively to Asian Americans' expressions of emotion or acts of assertion, seeing these verbal acts in violation of what they expect to be model minority conduct.

Implications

In this chapter, I have looked at a range of Asian American histories, languages, and circumstances in the United States. The perspective developed here stresses that in the mix of cultures that make up the United States, pan-Asian cultural themes and language practices can be found. Yet alongside these aggregate notions are many particularized situations of Asian ethnic groups. Some Asian Americans fare well economically, and some do not. Some are multilingual, and some are not. Some live in ethnic enclaves and linguistic isolation, and some do not. In short, not all Asian Americans compete for admission to UC Berkeley or earn high incomes.

Unfortunately, there are few studies of Asian American speech communities or discourse practices, although demographic analysis increasingly offers important contextual information. Scholarship examining cultural themes is more readily available. As a result, the perspective taken emphasizes the demographics of Asian language use in the United States and the relationship between Asian languages and English. In general, Asian language vitality is high, even where English fluency exists.

Like all migrant groups, Asian Americans demonstrate dynamic mixing of cultural retentions and cultural adaptations to the new national context and local settings in which they find themselves. The balance of cultural retentions and adaptations rests delicately on the core worldviews deeply enculturated into Asian newcomers to the United States and steadfastly practiced by many of Asian descent who have long histories in the United States. In the coming years, opportunities will expand to learn much about the large number of Asian immigrants whose arrival followed the major immigration policy reforms of 1965. More generational cohort studies will be possible for the different Asian American immigrant groups. It will also be important to focus on the diaspora experience of Indochinese refugees. What will be the balance of cultural and language retention for these groups? Will they come to resemble other Asian American groups more or less? For all Asian Americans, pervasiveness of mass culture, frequency of intermarriage, and increase in educational and workplace mixing will affect the cultural identities and discourse practices that evolve. Just how or how much, we do not know.

The other side of the coin shows the face of Asian Americans who are U.S.-born, native English speakers—those who show but do not tell their ethnicity. Yet the presumption too often locates these individuals as foreign immigrants. For this group of Asian Americans, race and ethnicity matter, but they may matter differently. Attitudes of others powerfully circumscribe possibilities; this is the influence from without. Family histories—with immigration, with racism, with language—give focus to identities; this is the influence from within.

Of major significance for all Americans is the prevailing judgment that Asians constitute the model minority. The model minority idea draws from academic success stories and educational attainment so often reported in the news and from observations about the hard work and well-earned achievement of many Asian Americans. But the model minority idea misses much of the reality of Asian American life. It misses the fact that Asians too experience poverty, that economic circumstances among Asian Americans often resemble camels' backs—highs and lows with not much in the middle, that highly educated Asia Americans earn less than their white counterparts, that Asian Americans experience racist epithets and behaviors despite the idea in mainstream society that they are models of how minorities should behave. At a deeper level, the model minority myth likely persists because white Americans feel comfortable with the relative silence of Asian Americans. Because Asian Americans eschew "in your face" behavior, white Americans can comfortably believe all is well. As the Asian American population grows, it will be increasingly important for all Americans to understand the realities of Asian cultural complexity and the inherently racist foundation of the model minority myth. In a society overwhelmed with self-absorption and a corresponding loss of community, all U.S. citizens would benefit from a better understanding of the cultural themes and discourse practices of their Asian American neighbors.

PART III

Language Consequences and Controversies

8

Discourse Consequences: Where Language and Culture Matter

In this chapter, I discuss the consequences of cultural and language diversity, and how aspects of discourse deeply embedded in cultural systems make a difference in domains of substantial consequence. Most Anglo Americans are only occasionally if ever aware of the ways in which dominant American ideology displaces other meaning systems. Most people of color and other marginalized groups often see their displacement clearly but can also be unaware of its daily consequences.

Each of the cultural groupings considered in this book experiences linguistic consequences differently, although some patterns cut across groups. Different kinds of invisibility and inaudibility exist for African Americans, Hispanic Americans, Asian Americans, and all the diverse groups represented in these categories, including women and men. What cuts across marginalized groups is the likelihood that their members rarely have the power to define what discourses will prevail in those situations of greatest consequence.

In preceding chapters, I looked at the ways in which language expresses cultural meanings. I now extend that analysis to consider the implications of language diversity in four different sites of consequence: (a) health care, (b) the legal system, (c) schools, and (d) the workplace. Because of its importance and timeliness as a language policy issue, bilingual education is addressed in the chapter that follows. The aim of this chapter is to identify major issues arising in these sites and to suggest critical needs that should be addressed.

In addressing these different sites of consequence from the perspective of diversity in discourse, we necessarily engage the workings of dominant ideology and the ways in which ideology implicates power in discourse. Freedom of expression is less free within the cultural discourses considered so far in this book because cultural power relations include the power to define appropriate registers for language use and the power to disregard any articulation formulated in some different manner. To speak freely within a discourse different from the expectations for speaking in mainstream American institutions and public life is to speak with constraint, to have less voice, to have less chance in the marketplace of ideas.

Institutional Discourses

Discourses of power, that is, those of the dominant ideology, permeate society most noticeably through what are called *institutional discourses* associated with education, law, medicine, the mass media, religion, government, and corporate business. Teun van Dijk (1993) describes these as elite discourses because of their lodging in power centers. Elites use these discourses to "manufacture the consent needed for the legitimation of their own power" (p. 8). In the United States (and other Western countries), these discourses belong historically and presently to whites, even when they are used by non-whites. When any of us enter institutional contexts—to see a doctor, to enroll in a class, to go to work, to appeal a parking ticket—we enter into expectations for certain pre-established discourses. The power of the relevant institutional discourse prevails because this discourse has been repetitively taught through public, formal processes reinforced in many quasi-public situations until the discourse becomes "second nature" to its learner. A visit to a physician at a health maintenance organization might be ruled by 20-minute appointment slots, prohibition against calling the doctor by first name, limits on talk extraneous to the purpose of the visit, question-answer sequences between doctor and patient, and so forth.

The power of dominant ideology in constraining discourse exists partly because most people take discourse for granted, at least in contexts where they perceive everyone to be speaking with the same rules and codes. For monolinguals in situations where the discourses of dominant ideologies prevail, the taken-for-granted nature of talk and text is especially pernicious because communication is not understood to be cultural, especially at its microdiscourse levels. Without acknowledging that all communication is cultural and possessing at least some level of intercultural communicative competence, those operating with discourse systems elaborated through dominant ideology prevail and exert discursive power over those whose discourse systems differ from the dominant ideology. Often, the contrasts and differences go completely unnoticed, arising as they do out of well-honed ideological practices rather than any conscious intent to discount the role of discourse differences. In some cases, the discourses of dominant ideology become at least superficially apparent because they are questioned or challenged, or because notice is taken of "others'" inability to perform in these discourses or of their choice to speak in registers judged to be inappropriate. When this happens, the "others" involved might be characterized as naive, uneducated, unfamiliar with how things are done, troublemakers, and even crazy. They can also be harshly dealt with. I vividly recall observing a judge who was dealing with a Hispanic speaker of limited English proficiency (LEP) who had no language interpreter. The man was standing in the wrong place and was asked to move. When he did not move to the right place, the judge said, "Please follow my direction Mr.—or I will cite you for contempt of court." When the man replied, "I don't know contempt," the judge's volume rose as he told the man again that he would cite him for contempt unless he did what he was told. The judge said nothing to clarify what "contempt of court" meant, and the situation was resolved when the judge instructed a court officer to lead the man to the proper place, which he did by literally taking his arm and propelling him.

As we look to the consequences of language diversity in the four institutional sites I discuss in this chapter, we will see more clearly the role of discourses in reproducing and reinforcing ideology. We will see, too, some surprising outcomes that result when specific linguistic features and broader discourse strategies are brought from one cultural framework into another.

Consequences of Language
Diversity for Health Care

Health care has been a major topic of discussion and news reports in the United States in recent years. Concerns about rising costs, the growth of health maintenance organizations (HMOs), uneven coverage, quality of coverage, access to specialists, and access to new treatment and medicine top the list of health-related topics. Yet headline news rarely touches on differences in access to health care that are accounted for by financial constraints, nature of health problems, or differences in cultural background or cultural practices. We never read about the ways in which a person's culturally based language practices affect both access to and experience with medical care. Although we hear more about women's health topics, such as mammography and estrogen replacement therapy, little focus is given to the ways in which women experience the medical professions differently than do men. Language and communication problems face patients and medical specialists every day (see West & Frankel, 1991, for a useful overview), even for individuals whose native language is English and whose race and class present no particular bias. Yet the study of health and medical communication struggles for its place against the prevailing prestige of medicine and its specialties.

In discussing how language and culture come into play for health care, four issues are examined: (a) language barriers in health communication, (b) relationship hierarchies and communication in U.S. medical practice, (c) cultural constructions of *health* and *medicine,* and (d) cultural notions of the "speakable." A group of experts on medical communication see the implications of culture as far-reaching for health care: "Implicit rules and attitudes regarding how relationships are established and maintained, what is spoken and is left unspoken, and how differences are negotiated are often culturally derived, raising the possibility of problems in the cross-cultural situation" (Sharf et al., 1990, p. 9).

Language Barriers in Health Communication

Those who watch the popular television program *ER* (Emergency Room) may recall episodes in which the medical personnel are yelling requests for someone who can translate, or when the translator for a patient is a close family member. These television situations resemble what can transpire in medical facilities facing the challenges of an increasingly multilingual U.S. population. Non-English speakers and LEP speakers have no legal right to medical interpreters, so they must rely on a combination of (a) family members and others who can translate and (b) the hope that the medical scenes they find themselves in both employ bilingual personnel and have access to appropriate translators who can intervene in the absence of bilingual personnel or family members.

Clarity in language use and mutual understanding are vitally important in describing symptoms, detailing narratives about medical emergencies or the antecedents to symptoms, making decisions about treatment, consenting to medical procedures, and understanding what one is to do after leaving the hospital or doctor's office. Medical terminology and the orientation of many physicians toward obfuscation often leave even the proficient native speaker of English bewildered. Indeed, nurses and pharmacists often "translate" medical language into more common English so that patients can better understand their condition. But the English speaker's problems pale in comparison to those encountered by the non-English speaker, who encounters enormous obstacles in trying to communicate about simple descriptive matters (how long an operation will take, how to get a lab test, etc.) and more serious matters involving clarity in understanding medication and consent for medical treatment.

On a recent trip to the pharmacy, I overheard a difficult transaction between a pharmacist and a Spanish-speaking woman who was there with her sick child. The pharmacist began giving instructions for the prescribed medication. When the woman said "No English," the pharmacist first restated the instructions slowly. That failing, she asked a colleague if anyone was around who spoke Spanish. The answer was, "No, I think she left the building." The woman was asked (by pointing to a watch) to wait, and I suspect she was there for a long time. This situation may be among the better ones facing the LEP speaker.

The consequences of no English or LEP mount as the health situation becomes more serious. Those who write about medical communication for non-English speakers and LEPs stress the importance of interpretation and translation services for basic, quality medical care. (In this chapter, translation is used in association with written communication and interpretation with oral communication; this usage conforms to that in the legal system.) Writing about Asian Americans and Pacific Islanders, Reiko Homma True and Tessie Guillermo (1996) stress the importance of trained interpreters for non-English speaking individuals and call attention to the problems of relying on family members and especially on the children of patients: "Such substitutions could lead not only to errors and misunderstandings but also to strained family dynamics (e.g., role reversal between parents and children" (p. 116). Relying on children (whose facility with English often far surpasses that of their parents) for translation and interpreting can result in special strain for Asian Americans, in particular those whose cultural background stresses filial piety. Writing about Spanish-speaking Hispanics, Aida Giachello (1996) offers similar cautions, in this case stressing the difficulty of translating terms and ideas from one language and cultural system into another. Deborah Martinez, Elizabeth Leone, and Jennifer Sternbach de Medina (1985) cite a court case in 1978 involving language and cultural barriers that led to "nonconsenting sterilization" of 10 Mexican-American women. These authors argue that without knowledge of English, health care in the United States is seriously compromised.

Many urban health centers and hospitals in the United States now offer at least some basic level of interpreter and translation services for languages common to the area. Bilingual health providers are also somewhat more available than in the past. Hospitals, health clinics, and pharmacies often post signs in Chinese or Spanish, with a few even posting the notice "*Se habla Espanol.*" Yet for most speakers of languages other than English the situation often comes down to either family translators or the possibility that someone can be found in the health facility who speaks Korean, Mandarin, Portuguese, Lao, and so forth. The risks are substantial: risks that there will be no interpreter at all, that the interpreter services will be inadequate, and that interpreter services may overlook important discourse pragmatics that represent meanings not on the surface. There is also the risk that health care providers harbor negative attitudes about patients who need language interpreters.

Dialect use may also play an important role in triggering particular attitudes in physicians and other health care providers—attitudes that may be negative, insidious influencers of the quality of care given. The wealth of research about language and attitude does not include research sufficient to make any claims about medical situations, but there is no reason to assume that language attitudes functioning in other domains disappear in the medical situation. Perceptions of low social status based on degree of nonstandardness in accent (see Giles & Powesland, 1975) coupled with information gathered in medical interviews may well combine to the detriment of those already in marginal positions.

Relationship Hierarchies and Communication in Medical Practice

Of all professions in the United States, medicine is the one afforded the greatest degree of consistent public status. One clear example of the status accorded doctors is the use of the honorific title *Dr.* in front of the name of physicians and surgeons, even outside the context of their medical practice. Medical doctors use and receive the honorific title for personal mail, for hotel and dinner reservations, for their names on credit cards, and for a variety of other purposes. Dentists, too, maintain relatively strict practices in terms of the honorifics due them. A faculty friend told about the nonplused reaction of a dentist she had gone to for the first time when she responded to his "Hello Karen, I'm Dr. Jordan" with "Hello Richard, I'm Dr. Swaine." Individuals with the Ph.D. degree are likewise entitled to use the title of *Dr.* for general use but usually reserve that title for professional situations.

The relative rigidity of the honorific system for medical doctors in the United States is significant because it stands out so clearly as an exception to the more general trend to de-emphasize honorifics. Young children, for example, no longer address all adults unknown to them by *Mr., Mrs.,* or *Ms.* but frequently use first names instead. Some doctors attempt to make themselves less scary to children by using their first names after *Dr.,* but they still announce their professional titles. A medical resident introduced himself to one of my children as "Dr. Eric" (but not "Eric") and another's orthodontist first greeted him with a cheerful "Hello, I'm Dr. Barbara" (but not "Barbara"). In sum, maintenance of the honorific system for those practicing medicine symbolizes the social status of doctors in general.

The more general implications of the status accorded medical doctors occur in the structure of interactions between doctor and patient. Not surprisingly, the medical profession teaches doctors—often implicitly—to maintain the status boundaries between themselves and patients. This is why transforming the everyday communication practices of doctors toward a more communication-oriented, patient-sensitive model occurs at a snail's pace.

As an outcome of hierarchy in medical practice, the structure of conversational interactions between doctor and patient in the United States typically follows a pattern of extreme imbalance. John Wiemann and Howard Giles (1988) summarized the typical characteristics of this imbalance: Doctors talk much more than patients (initiating 99% of the utterances), set the topic agenda, decide when the medical appointment is over, ask a large majority of the questions (90+%), often barrage patients with questions, and (male but not female doctors) interrupt patients much more than patients interrupt them. Consistent with the patterns typical of women's communication and the cultural abstractions from which those patterns arise, evidence points to the greater likelihood for female physicians to be less dominant in controlling the discourse than their male counterparts (Ainsworth-Vaughn, 1992; West, 1990).

The asymmetries in doctor-patient relationship are culturally reinforced through the type of reasoning prevalent in U.S. (and most Western) medicine. Medical practice rests on fundamental principles related to scientific reasoning, cause-effect relationships, and knowledge hierarchies. These notions are deeply seated in the cultural abstractions guiding treatment of illness and physical malfunction. Diagnoses and the prescription of treatment are targeted to the specific ailment, with little regard for holistic or systemic consideration. This scientific orientation has led to elaborate medical specialization, complex medical testing, and the proliferation of prescription drugs. In a given year, a typical U.S. family of three generations (children, parents, and grandparents) with health insurance might make visits to a general practitioner, a pediatrician, a gynecologist, a dermatologist, a cardiologist, a urologist, and an oncologist—and, of course, a dentist and an orthodontist. That family will also likely have experience with many different medications, both prescription and across-the-counter. In short, physical and emotional problems are "medicalized." This orientation leaves little room for alternative perspectives (see the section below on cultural constructions of medicine); doctors simply do not like it when their patients refuse to follow orders or contest their diagnoses and treatment regimens.

The effect of the hierarchical properties of U.S. medical practice almost always places patients in a one-down position, hopeful that they will get what idiomatically is described as a good "bedside manner." Thus, even in situations of cultural similarity, the doctor-patient relationship is based on status and power differentials coupled with the orientation toward technical medical diagnosis and treatment, the particulars of which are not accessible to most people. Patients are expected to "follow the doctor's orders." This "normal" health care situation accentuates how added cultural complexities in the medical situation can further complicate the relationship between doctor and patient.

Women who see male doctors, regardless of their ethnicity or race, enter medical situations with all the gender imbalances in language use that occur in society at large. These broader gender patterns compound the inequities built into doctor-patient relationships. African American women and women from other cultural minority groups experience a kind of triple jeopardy in medical situations: gender asymmetries, medical asymmetries, and cultural asymmetries—because they are, respectively, women, patients, and members of marginalized cultural groups. Social class further compounds the cultural collision in medical encounters because so many cultural minorities either are or are judged to be socially and economically marginal. The situation is especially stacked against the cultural minority when some form of state or federal medical assistance pays the bill. Imagine facing an already hierarchy-ridden medical system as a Hispanic woman on Medicaid who is a LEP speaker.

Individuals from cultural backgrounds that stress hierarchy and proper relationships more heavily than prevailing American practice may find themselves in special jeopardy in the face of medical hierarchy. Most Americans are reticent to talk back to their doctors, but there is some expectation that things like ineffective treatment should be confronted and second opinions should be sought when there is a degree of doubt about diagnosis. Challenging the authority of doctors or even contacting an ombudsperson may represent far too serious a cultural infraction for some Asian immigrant groups in particular.

Cultural Constructions of Health and Medicine

Many times, medical situations for individuals with marginalized cultural backgrounds become problematic because of the very nature of what occurs in the semantic system to represent notions of health and medicine. The U.S. orientation toward scientific analysis, as well as treatment of parts of the body through medication and surgical intervention, is itself culturally based, which means that individuals who identify with different cultural systems may find this orientation alien.

Based on cultural identity, individuals think about health in culturally nuanced ways. In their book on communication in multicultural health settings, Gary Kreps and Elizabeth Kunimoto (1994) stress the importance of culturally based health beliefs in multicultural medical situations. These beliefs, which are part of the system of cultural abstractions, directly influence discourse pragmatics by structuring what is normative and what is not in the medical situation. *Health, illness,* and *medicine* are all semantic notions subject to vastly different interpretative processes depending on an individual's cultural anchoring.

Interpersonal and personal aspects of medical practice arise from cultural beliefs about health, illness, and treatment through cultural artifacts and culturally based discourse. Hospital practices, for instance, are designed to enforce barriers between patients and visitors (which can include family members). Designated visiting hours, the arrangement of patient rooms, and the lack of chairs in them convey these barriers. Only recently have rooms been designed to accommodate overnight stays by spouses or partners of women giving birth or by parents of children who are hospitalized; even this level of family presence is not routine, and extended family members are rarely welcome. If one's cultural milieu stresses family for decision making, as is the case for most Asian American groups, both patient and family member may experience extreme displacement and stress in dealing with the taken-for-granted barriers between patient and visitors.

Discourse practices, too, are deeply culturally based. In situations of surgery or dire medical conditions, the relatives of the patient usually have limited interaction with the specialists who are treating the patient. Unless the family members are persistent (and sometimes aggressive), the medical specialist may be unavailable to answer their questions or to provide a status report on the patient. Regardless of whether or not English language proficiency is an issue, for cultural groups valuing restraint and the importance of proper relationships, hours may pass with little or no sense of what is happening.

The most basic starting point for cultural notions about health and medicine is the baseline for what I term *default medicine,* or the approach to medical practice and treatment that is taken for granted and institutionally supported. One test for what constitutes default medicine can be found in the coverage offered through medical insurance plans. Forms of medicine common in cultural systems other than that which dominates in the United States are lumped under the terms *alternative medicine* and *complementary medicine* (both relatively new terms). More everyday terms include "quackery" or "witch doctor methods." Alternatives would include various holistic healing practices like acupuncture, homeopathy, herbal remedies, and certain folk medicine approaches. Western medicine has been reluctant to acknowledge the effectiveness of any of these methods, even in the face of growing interest among the non-Hispanic white population beginning in the 1970s. Some limited recognition is recently evident—especially in locales with high concentrations of cultural groups for whom these alternatives are common practice.

We can estimate who might be most affected by default definitions for health and medicine by considering which alternatives correspond to which ancestral groups. For substantial numbers of Chinese immigrants, their offspring, and other Asian peoples, acupuncture is default medical practice. Dating back at least 2,000 years, acupuncture emphasizes balance in the flow of energy (*chi*) throughout the body. Balance is restored and achieved through the use of needles inserted into the skin in combination with herbs, heat, and pressure. For those who believe in acupuncture, discourse presents a major difficulty. No satisfactory conversation can occur about drug treatments or about the relationship between symptoms and causes if the patient's cultural system includes neither.

Native American approaches to health and healing also emphasize wholeness. The importance of ceremony among all Native American tribes is key to perpetually establishing harmony among all things. The medicine men and women of native tribes not only conduct healing ceremonies but also dedicate their time to activities aimed at keeping the people healthy. In contrast to drugs used in Western medicine, Native American healing relies on natural substances such as cedar, sage, and sweet grass. In one description of Native American healing (Berkeley Holistic Health Center, 1978), the importance of the Earth Mother is explained as follows:

> The relationship to one's environment—the earth, trees, animals, sun, and sky —is intimately involved in healing. Accordingly, whenever possible, healing is done in a natural setting. The Earth has an electromagnetic vibration that is able to assist the medicine man or woman in extracting the imbalanced energy existing within the person being healed. (p. 65)

Given these culturally based health beliefs, it is easy to understand why U.S. medicine with its sterile interior hospital rooms and artificial intrusions into the body is feared and suspected of evil by many native peoples. Clearly, it would be difficult to have meaningful discourse aimed at merging the two systems because the deeper cultural abstractions about what constitutes health and healing are incompatible.

Many Hispanics, too, depart from default U.S. medical practice in their beliefs about healing. Giachello (1996), for example, summarizes a number of research studies on the health attitudes and practices of Hispanics in the United States, concluding that Hispanics are often skeptical of modern medical techniques and diagnoses, preferring instead home remedies, folk medicine, and patent medicines for ailments that would lead most insured Americans to their health care center. Although not isomorphic to all Hispanics, these practices run counter to both the emphasis on hierarchy and physician authority in U.S. medicine and the orientation toward medical diagnosis and prescription.

The overall impact on discourse of culturally based diversity in semantic notions associated with health and medicine is complex. Fear, distrust, intimidation, skepticism, and powerlessness are only some of the responses that culturally marginalized minorities might have to default U.S. medical practice. Communication in medical situations rarely explores the deeper cultural foundation of doctor and patient perspectives, leaving substantial room for misunderstanding of motive, symptom, and follow-through.

The "Speakable" in Health Care

One of the main issues for health care in a multicultural society is the variability from culture to culture in what is considered appropriate for discussion, that is, what is speakable. The American preoccupation with individuality and self-disclosure, as well as greater attention to issues of health in the mass media, produces a cultural readiness to speak openly about many health and medical conditions that even 25 years ago were still taboo. Hemorrhoids, jock itch, stomach gas, hair loss, breast implants, diarrhea, and yeast infections as well as more serious medical issues such as contraception, infertility, alcoholism, breast cancer, menopause, prostate cancer, anorexia, and obesity are commonly discussed. The expectation is that patients should feel free to talk about these health issues; yet these emerging norms for the appropriate use of language (lexically, semantically, and pragmatically) often conflict with the norms of marginalized cultural systems. Likewise, the medical preference for technical terms may lead to negative judgments by patients who use vernacular terms.

One example of a language-based concern related to the speakable is provided by True and Guillermo (1996) in their discussion of Asian women's health issues. Asian women, say these authors, often avoid medical care because of "their modesty and reserve about their bodies, particularly about such anatomical areas as the breasts, vagina, and cervix" (p. 115). One course of action is to educate Asian women about the importance of routine medical examinations, but health care providers also need education so that they can respond with sensitivity to their patients.

One area that is especially culturally laden related to the speakable is mental health and psychological therapy. Not only do many people now experience therapy, often of several varieties, but therapy has become a normative way to handle individual and family problems. Children with behavioral problems are often sent to therapists. Couples experiencing marital difficulty go to marriage counseling. Depression, anxiety, job dissatisfaction, and antisocial behavior are often dealt with through therapy. Group counseling abounds for people with chemical or alcohol dependencies, terminal or serious illnesses, and eating disorders as well as for those who have been sexually abused or are experiencing grief. The use of what are called *psychoactive medications* (antidepressants, tranquilizers, and mood stabilizers) has also skyrocketed.

With what essentially amounts to a therapism movement comes also a particular construction of the human being as a potential locus for mental and emotional flaws that can be fixed/mended/healed through the therapy process. An ever-expanding array of "problems" are reified by naming them, leading to an ever-expanding pool of clients for therapy who can be served by the ever-expanding pool of therapy specialists. Although many readers of this book may view therapy in a positive light, therapy is nonetheless a cultural practice steeped with cultural abstractions and culturally defined discourse patterns.

Although both women and men engage in therapy, women participate in more therapy and drug intervention than do men (Rodin & Ickovics, 1994). The most plausible explanation for the genderization of therapy and psychoactive medication rests in women's cultural definition as being more emotional than men; their problems are thus more likely to be diagnosed (or dismissed) as originating from emotional and psychological causes rather than from physical or environmental causes.

Robin Lakoff (1990) dubs therapy "the talking cure" because it uses language for both diagnosis and treatment—a problem for people whose primary cultural systems do not view talk as either appropriate or useful for such purposes. Verbal elaborations related to the self simply do not comport with the cultural beliefs of individuals in collectivist cultures and cultures suspicious of excess in emotional expression. Min (1995) explains the greater reticence of Asian Americans to seek out mental health services as stemming from their cultural beliefs that communicating emotional and personal problems outside the family brings shame to them and their families. In one example that I am familiar with, the Korean wife of a U.S.-born white man refused to attend marriage counseling because she felt this would cause humiliation for her family.

Looking to another group, Indochinese refugees are frequently identified as the victims of severe psychological stress, often what has been labeled *post-traumatic stress syndrome* (PTS). PTS has been especially prevalent among Cambodians who witnessed human brutalities of monstrous proportions. Yet their culturally based rules for discourse keep them away from mental health interventions. Research conducted by Rumbaut in the mid-1980s (reported in Portes & Rumbaut, 1996) documented significantly higher levels of depressive symptoms (especially for women) among Indochinese groups compared to the general U.S. population. In general, stress and depressive symptoms combined with cultural beliefs regarding appropriateness in personal disclosure imply the likelihood of difficulties in the discourse demands of therapies designed to assist victims of war. The very speech acts and registers required for therapy may themselves induce additional stress resulting from the sense of shame.

Another potential issue in the cultural dimensions of therapeutic discourse concerns the imposition of semantic notions and labels from one culture onto another. The naming of psychological, emotional, and mental health problems stabilizes the reality of these problems and simultaneously defines the person involved. U.S. psychiatry and clinical psychology diagnose mental health problems in a fashion similar to physical health problems. Having a *bipolar personality,* being *paranoid, depressive,* or *manic-depressive* all imply factors within the individual that are part of his or her identity. The labels themselves may unwittingly function as a kind of cultural assault and disconfirmation. Cathryn Houghton (1995), for example, analyzed the discourse in group therapy sessions for Latina adolescents in state-funded facilities to show how the discourse of these girls served to resist the dominant discourse of their therapy. Of particular interest was Houghton's insight about the labeling of these girls' relationships with their mothers as "co-dependent." For these girls, mother-daughter relationships "are among the most significant" (p. 122). Understood within the cultural framework of the therapy sessions, labeling them *co-dependent* is essentially a linguistic act of intimate assault. In this case, therapy leads to resistant discourse, but the outcome could be shame or guilt in another cultural context.

Critical Needs

When language diversity founded in cultural pluralism meets matters of health and well-being, problems can range from insufficiency of translation and interpreter services to much deeper issues related to beliefs, values, morals, and ethics that rest in cultural abstractions and are manifested in discourse. Race, ethnicity, and socioeconomic standing not only affect access and quality of health care but also shape language attitudes that guide practice.

All patients and clients using any aspect of the health care system must confront the alienating and power-distancing implications of *medicalese.* Medical language is jargon-ridden and often cryptic, even for those in the mainstream. Patients and clients whose cultural backgrounds and patterns of language use differ from default U.S. medical practice may have even more difficulty with medicalese. Moreover, the many health care services that people can come in contact with are enacted through registers for language use with which patients and clients may be more or less familiar. Lack of or partial communicative competence for appropriate use of language in the medical context, through what can be designated medical register, can lead to misunderstandings.

Many health care facilities, especially in large urban areas, are working to establish better multicultural services, but progress is slow. The following five critical needs for addressing language diversity in the health care setting should guide priorities for improving health care in a multicultural, multilingual society:

1. The need for more trained language interpreters and translators to assist those who do not speak English or are LEP speakers;

2. The need for better training of medical personnel in the cultural dimensions of language use for both non-native and native speakers of English;

3. The need for easily accessible educational information about the health care system that is produced not only in different languages but also contains content about cultural dimensions that may be important to patients and clients in medical encounters;

4. The need for outreach programs stressing the importance of acquiring English language proficiency for accessing and understanding the health care system and its components;

5. The need for more trained medical personnel who are bi- or multilingual and bi- or multicultural in their backgrounds.

Consequences of Language Diversity in the Legal System

We live in an increasingly litigious society. The formal legal and court system is stressed beyond its capacity to dispose of cases, and informal "out of court" mediations, agreements, and resolutions are legion. There are criminal and civil cases; city courts, county courts, district courts, grand juries, appellate courts, and Supreme Courts. All are peopled by lawyers, judges, clerks, paralegals, mediators, arbitrators, and more. The legal system is knotted with complexity and specialization in its structure, rules, and personnel such that understanding the system is beyond the capacity of many a citizen.

Every legal system operates from its own code of justice. The code of legal principles that underlies the U.S. justice system contains many linguistically familiar phrases, each dense with semantic notions: "Justice is blind," "innocent until proven guilty," "equal protection under the law," "the scales of justice," "the punishment fits the crime," "the right to trial by a jury of one's peers." Each phrase symbolizes principles of fairness and equality. The U.S. code of justice is attractive to people from many countries where legal principles are more arbitrary, where punishments are based more on politics than on the unfolding of reasoning and evidence, and where cultural notions such as legal rights have no meaning.

In many cases, the U.S. legal system does exactly what it claims in principle to do: render justice fairly through systematic processes. In some cases, the reality differs from the principle. In recent years, there has been greater recognition of systematic biases in the legal system related to gender, ethnicity, and race.

Among legal scholars, a branch of analysis called *critical race theory* has emerged to target the ways in which race distorts legal principles and practices. Feminist legal theory does the same related to gender. The broader field of legal scholarship from which these have emerged is *critical legal studies,* where the focus is on the influence of culture (more specifically of race and gender) on legal ideas and process (see, e.g., Boyle, 1994; Epstein, 1993; Leonard & Ashe, 1995).

A number of states have conducted studies of their court systems to determine what kinds of bias exist; these are usually called gender bias or race bias studies. Massachusetts, to use an illustration familiar to me, conducted a gender bias study published in 1989 (Massachusetts Gender Bias Study Committee, 1989), which included an entire section on "Gender Bias in Courthouse Interactions." Among the findings reported in this document was substantiation for the following: "As litigants and witnesses, women are subjected to inappropriate terms of address, suggestive comments, unwanted touching, yelling, and verbal harassment" (p. 9). The Massachusetts gender study was followed by one focused on race, titled "Equal Justice: Eliminating the Barriers" (Massachusetts Commission, 1994). This report documents the bias against speakers of languages other then English both because of negative attitudes toward the speakers and because of insufficient translation and interpreter services for them. These two state court documents (and others like them) provide a glimpse into the ways in which the legal system fails to apply with cultural consistency the very principles on which it is founded.

Among the many ways in which race, ethnicity, and gender skew the legal process, language, not surprisingly, dominates. Language expresses legal beliefs and laws and is relied on to weigh the evidence presented in cases through witness testimony. Judges and other court personnel use language to give instructions and render judgments. Out of court processes (settlements, mediations) are conducted using language as the vehicle to reach resolution. American law, moreover, draws heavily on written English, which biases its oral register. Karin Aronsson (1991) in discussing the "recycling" of legal evidence observes, "The legal trial is circumscribed by written documents, the written law, the summons, the final judgment, as well as the verbatim trial record. Hence, interrogations are intimately linked to written documents, both in police interrogations and in the courtroom" (p. 217). The justice system, then, makes sense within its own culturally elaborated discourse, which is a peculiar, formal variety of written Standard American English to express certain notions of justice.

To see how language diversity often disadvantages particular cultural minorities and marginalized cultural groups, we will examine four issues: (a) the impact of varieties of English that differ from the standard American English expected in legal proceedings, (b) language translation and interpreters in the legal process, (c) the impact of cultural beliefs on legal discourse, and (d) matters of blatant racist and sexist discourse practices in legal proceedings. Although there is not a vast amount of direct evidence linking certain language features to specific legal outcomes, various case studies offer compelling analyses of the consequences of discourse in legal proceedings, and a considerable number of mock jury studies point to likely outcomes with real juries.

The issues discussed here strongly implicate discourse practices common in legal and quasi-legal contexts as undermining some of the foundational principles of the American justice system. Furthermore, recent analyses of court cases by Rosina Lippi-Green (1994) show that patterns of language use and evidence thereof are rarely given the kind of weight and consideration by judges that is extended to other forms of evidence. In cases where "language-trait-focused discrimination" is a central issue in allegations of discrimination in the workplace, Lippi-Green finds reasoning about language to be lacking in sophistication and overshadowed by simplistic ideology regarding good communication skills: "The judges who wrote these opinions are willing to depend on their own expertise in matters of language in a way they would never presume to in matters of genetics or mechanical engineering or psychology" (p. 177). With few exceptions certainly, linguists do not prevail as convincingly as do experts in other fields. It seems that the prevalence of monolingualism perpetuates an ideology in the courts that, while acknowledging language difference, (a) oversimplifies its impact and (b) may place undue burdens on the person for whom Standard American English (SAE) is not the mother tongue.

Varieties of English and Legal Processes

It is difficult to gauge the impact of using a variety of English in court that is other than what the court expects, which is some version of SAE appropriately tuned to the register of the courtroom. Flagrant violations (such as obscenities) can lead to contempt of court charges, but most stylistic matters have no such immediate and obvious consequences. Imagine, for example, the speaker of African American Vernacular English (AAVE) who systematically uses the syntactic *be* for habitual action. In the following hypothetical sequence, an attorney interrogates a witness about what time it was when she turned out the light on a particular night:

Q: On the night of June 17, what time did you turn out the light in your bedroom?
A: I be turnin it out at 11:30.
Q: But isn't it possible that you turned out the light at 11:15 or 11:45?
A: No, I be turnin out the light at 11:30.
Q: How can you be sure?

The witness might appear to be evasive or obstinate in not answering the question directly, when in fact the witness reiterates through the *be* construction that she always turns out the light at 11:30, so on the night of June 17, that is the time she turned out the light.

One of the most interesting studies of the consequences of language variety for legal outcomes was conducted by John Gumperz (1982b), who investigated the case of a Filipino doctor who was indicted for perjury based on his initial testimony following the death of a child he attended in the emergency room. The child had been brought to the emergency room for burn treatment (the child's parents said it was "sunburn"), released, and then brought back later with much more serious symptoms that led to death. The child's stepfather was charged with first-degree murder, and the doctor was one of the witnesses for the prosecution at the trial. The perjury indictment against the doctor occurred subsequent to the trial and was based on the allegation that the doctor had not told the truth in his original testimony (even though that testimony was corroborated by others working in the emergency room with him). The doctor spoke Aklan as his native language and was also fluent in Tagalog and in English, a multilingual proficiency profile typical of an educated, professional Filipino. No one ever questioned the English fluency of this man. The case, however, hinged on various features of the variety of English that he spoke. Gumperz describes the variety as having "grammatical characteristics of its own that ultimately derive from local languages such as Tagalog and Aklan" (p. 173). He cites unpublished research by P. B. Naylor, who analyzed linguistic aspects of testimony given by two Filipina nurses indicted for conspiracy and murder; the case involved their alleged improper administration of medication that caused patient deaths from respiratory failure. Naylor explains that the nurses' testimony was misunderstood because they frequently used present tense verbs when speaking about the past; Tagalog, unlike English, does not mark tense at the verb, which explains the grammatical interference.

Using this grammatical foundation, Gumperz examined the trial transcript to show how the doctor's use of verb tense created the impression that he had contradicted himself. Specifically, questions indicating the past tense are answered by the doctor in the present tense. For example:

Q. At the end when you released the child to the parents, did you feel that the cause of the injuries was sunburn or thermofluid burn?

A. I still feel it was due to sunburn.

Q. Did you suspect that it was thermofluid burn?

[after which there is an objection that the question has already been answered, which is sustained by the judge] (p. 174)

Gumperz explains that the use of the construction "I still feel" leads to the interpretation that this is what the doctor not only believed at the time but continues to believe was the cause. A more typical MAE construction would have been "I felt at the time that . . . ." Not marking past tense is, according to the linguistic interference argument, a carryover from Tagalog and other languages of the Philippines. The doctor's attorney made the case in the perjury trial that a number of such constructions had been misunderstood, thus leading to the perjury charge; fortunately for the doctor, this argument prevailed, and he was cleared of all charges.

The most important point to be drawn from the Filipino English case study is that even fluent speakers of English whose advanced professional education has been in English may use certain constructions that are misunderstood in an American English context. The implications for less fluent speakers are obvious.

Both the AAVE example and the Filipino English case study deal with syntax, but other aspects of language can also be the source of interference from one variety to another. Culturally based beliefs about the appropriateness of verbal elaboration versus restraint, for example, could be of consequence.

One domain of discourse style that has been investigated in the legal context is the impact of what William O'Barr (1982) terms "powerless" speech style. O'Barr was initially interested in Robin Lakoff's early formulations about women's style of speaking (see Chapter 4). O'Barr and his colleagues approached their study by first conducting ethnographic analysis of testimony and then designing experiments to assess the effects of certain aspects of language style on matters of consequence in the legal situation. The investigators (O'Barr & Atkins, 1980) first analyzed the testimony of three men and three women to determine the degree to which they spoke using attributes of "women's language": hedges, superpolite forms, tag questions, hesitation forms, and so forth. Although there are serious validity problems with the study as an examination of gender-related language style (sample size, confounding of the role of the witness with gender), the study is useful in outlining contrasts between powerless and powerful language styles.

The experiments used to assess the impact of these style markers placed undergraduate students in mock trial situations. In these mock trial situations, the powerful speech style proved to enhance the credibility of the speaker and make a more favorable impression on the students. O'Barr (1982) concludes from his research and related findings that "there is little question that presentational form of testimony does indeed matter and is ultimately consequential in the legal process" (p. 121).

To the extent that the powerless style of presentation is more likely to be used by cultural groups who are marginalized, members of those groups may be at a disadvantage in the legal process. Many women, for example, may be more likely to use this style for reasons related to their greater preference for collaborative discourse. O'Barr's research is simply too limited to draw conclusions one way or the other. Yet, those with restricted facility in English would likely use more of the powerless markers.

The register of the courtroom and other venues for legal process privilege some litigants over others. We would expect certain varieties of English to have negative consequences because either the dialect features or register features of those varieties mesh poorly with the expectations of court personnel and the majority of jury members.

Language Translation in Legal Proceedings

No issue in the domain of language and the legal process more clearly shows the ideological presumptions of a dominant power structure born and bred with monolingualism than does the use of language interpreters and translators. Even when interpreters are available, those without command of English enter legal proceedings at great risk.

The most basic issue for non-English speakers in the U.S. legal process is the presumption by default that legal proceedings are conducted in English. Court records contain only what is said in English; thus, statements, before they are interpreted into English, have no legal status. This practice alone renders non-English statements nonexistent. One cannot go back and read what was said in Spanish or Korean or Farsi. In some instances, court personnel do strive to recognize the language needs of those who are brought into the legal process for one reason or another. An attorney friend shared the example of a judge in an urban housing court who gives general instructions at the beginning of a court session first in English and then "in the best Spanish he can manage." His efforts probably make a difference, but even if judges or other court personnel show good faith in making their courtrooms more "language friendly" by giving general instructions in more than one language, the record inscribes only English (except for certain cases in Puerto Rico).

Overall, progress has been made regarding language translation in the justice system, but glaring insufficiency continues. Federal law provides for translation in federal criminal cases, but neither civil cases nor courts of lower jurisdiction are compelled by federal law to provide translators. Many states also have regulations, as do some counties and municipalities, but they vary greatly.

The landmark federal legislation affecting court interpreters came in 1978 with passage of Public Law No. 95-539, the Court Interpreters Act, which applies to both criminal and civil cases initiated by the government. This act "establish[ed] a program to facilitate the use of interpreters in courts of the United States" at the discretion of the presiding judicial officer for any party in a legal case or witness who "(1) speaks only or primarily a language other than the English language; or: (2) suffers from a hearing impairment" (Court Interpreters Act, 1978, reprinted with amendments in Berk-Seligson, 1990). Since passage of the Court Interpreters Act, the presence of interpreters has become more commonplace. In 1987, there were 46,477 court interpreter appearances, 93% (43,166) of which were in Spanish (Berk-Seligson, 1990).

The process relies on certification procedures for interpreters (Arjona, 1985), but judicial officers can appoint other competent interpreters. Judgments about what constitutes a competent interpreter have provided the fodder for some notorious news items. Massachusetts, for instance, passed a court interpreters law in 1986, but the lack of sufficient interpreters and certified interpreters prompted the *Boston Globe* newspaper to do an investigative report of the situation. One front-page profile described Sylvester Fortes, a Cape Verdean who still "struggles with English"; he "sweeps the floors and cleans the bathrooms at the Brockton District Court, but at a moment's notice, he may be summoned into court to become the official interpreter" (McKim, 1994, p. 1). The court's defense is that the state does not provide sufficient funds to hire certified interpreters. As of 1996 (McKim, 1996), the problem continues to exist despite harsh reports from both the Supreme Judicial Court and a special committee of the state legislature. These shortcomings in providing adequate interpreter services are not unique to Massachusetts—at least the state does have an interpreter law.

Limited or no facility with English poses problems even when interpreters are available. Some arise from the role of the interpreter, and others because of the ways in which interpreters tend to modify language in the interpretation process.

Impartiality and fairness are threatened by three problems related to court interpreters. The first problem arises from the prescribed role of the interpreter. The interpreter, as a matter of court rules, must be unbiased and refrain from giving advice. For a non-English speaking litigant, the interpreter is in the peculiar position of being the center for everything that is said and done in court but also at the same time being required to maintain appropriate distance from the litigant. The fact that the interpreter is an employee of the court adds a further complication. Thus, an elaborate construction of impartiality surrounds the interpreter, which is ultimately so artificial as to be impossible in practice.

A second problem occurs because of the court's priority for exactitude in language. The view of language that guides the interpreter process rests on the proposition that languages are directly translatable one to another, a view likely to cause problems for the people who the Court Interpreter Law is designed to protect. As presented in Chapter 3, universal viewpoints on culture characterize language as a vehicle for meaning rather than as symbolic action that creates meaning. Berk-Seligson (1990) says of this process,

> Court personnel assume that the interpreter is nothing short of a machine that converts the English speech of attorneys, judges, and English-speaking witnesses into the mother tongue of the non-English-speaking defendant or witness . . . [and vice versa] for the benefit of the court." (p. 2)

A court interpreter is also situated as a kind of *nonentity* in the legal proceeding. Litigants and witnesses are supposed to answer questions by directing their testimony to the person who asked the question, which would be an attorney or judge in most cases, and not to the interpreter, who is the person from whom they actually hear meaningful discourse. Berk-Seligson (1990) cites examples from her ethnographic studies in which peculiar aspects in the pragmatics of language use occur because the witness or litigant does, in fact, talk to the interpreter rather than the questioner; one example occurs with confused politeness forms, in which case interpreters sometimes add politeness forms when they translate and at other times translate politeness forms intended for them that are inappropriate when directed to the questioner.

The third type of problem results from the ways in which language interpreters shape the discourse used in the courtroom. Because of the emphasis on literal translations from one language to another, the interpreter process stresses lexicon at the expense of both semantic and pragmatic aspects of language use. Interpreters may sacrifice culturally important meanings in the process of working with the surface structure of words. Berk-Seligson's (1990) research with Spanish-English interpretation documents how interpreters silence witnesses, how judges and attorneys speak directly to interpreters rather than to the witnesses, and how clarification procedures used by interpreters change and redirect meaning. One especially significant insight about interpreter effect has to do with "powerless" testimony style, in the sense in which O'Barr (previously discussed) described that style. Interpreters, Berk-Seligson found, tend to lengthen Spanish testimony statements by witnesses into longer English statements and in so doing create the kind of fragmented style that contains powerless speech attributes: "Specifically, hedges, hesitation forms (pause fillers and meaningless particles), and polite forms have been shown to be elements that interpreters add to their English rendition of witness testimony" (p. 142). Follow-up experimental research using mock juries from a heterogeneous sample in their late teens and 20s revealed that the language manipulations of interpreters significantly alter juror perceptions of witnesses. For example, verbal hedges in the interpreter's rendering of the witness's testimony led all but Hispanic members of the sample to judge the witness as less competent and less intelligent than when no hedges were present; rendering the English version in "hyperformal" rather than more casual style led the mock jurors to judge the witness as more competent, more intelligent, and more trustworthy.

Based on the research available, it appears that language interpreters have the linguistic power to alter court proceedings through their interpreter practices. At the very least, non-English speaking litigants and witnesses need to be aware of this. Ideally, court personnel should be more aware of the ways in which linguistic impositions intrude into the construction of meanings when interpreter services are used.

Cultural Beliefs and Legal Discourse

The U.S. legal system, like any other legal system, is a culture within the larger framework of dominant national ideology. Those familiar with it can identify its cultural artifacts: the blindfolded statue of justice holding the balance scales, the bible on which the oath of truthfulness is sworn, the raised judge's bench (represented in the common synecdotal phrase, "appointed to the bench"), the jury box placed to the side of the courtroom to represent impartiality. Some changes occur over time (e.g., the introduction of computers on judges' benches), but the justice system is resilient to much remodeling. Abstractions and discourse patterns, too, retain their character over time. When changes occur, they are seldom dramatic or fast-paced. The court personnel of today, for instance, are more gender mixed and culturally diverse. Yet many retentions minimize the impact of change: Lawyers tend to dress conservatively, judges still wear black robes, and the opening dictum "Order in the court, all rise . . . " remains default practice. Although specific laws and interpretations of those laws change, the legal process (itself heavily defined by language) changes little over time. Much more mediation occurs today than in previous years, and Court TV (extended by Cable News Network to give the world the now-famous living room trial of O. J. Simpson) is a reality in states allowing live coverage of legal proceedings. Yet more stays the same than changes—especially in the domain of legal principles and discourse.

As children are acculturated through their speech communities and mass culture, they learn aspects of the legal system. Children learn what constitutes illegal behavior. They are exposed to a full cast of justice and legal characters by watching everything from cartoons to the local and national evening news. Many experience for themselves different aspects of the justice or legal process: crime scenes, arrests, court proceedings related to child custody, and so forth. Children often act out scenes and play games related to law and order, which are their approximations of the ideas and appropriate language for the legal context. I recall one of my children at about age 8, for example, pacing back and forth, hands clasped behind his back, addressing "Ladies and gentlemen of the jury" as part of a make-believe game that had something to do with going to court. The humor to an adult observer was that the person addressing the jury in this make-believe scene then proceeded to proclaim "I find you guilty and sentence you to jail." Capsule phrases, together representing several different core semantic notions about justice, were bundled together into the role of one person with the powers of lawyer, jury, and judge.

Unfortunately, there is no body of scholarship directly relevant to understanding the impact of one's culturally based beliefs on discourse in the legal context, nor on the more material outcomes of legal proceedings. We can, however, speculate and draw tentative inferences based on other domains of knowledge.

Gender is one area where cultural beliefs may be important in the legal process. To the extent that women's cultural orientations lead them to be more concerned about personal and interpersonal matters, they may speak differently in a legal proceeding than their male counterparts. In research conducted in small claims court (Johnson, 1987), where the norm is for litigants to speak for themselves rather than through attorneys, we found evidence that women present their side of the case through narrative logic, or the kind of logic that rests in understanding the specifics of the situation rather than through a logic more reliant on abstract rules, which was typical for male litigants. In one case, for example, a Mrs. P was claiming that she was owed money by Ms. D, who was overpaid for care provided to her sick mother. Mrs. P had paid in advance because of an arrangement with a home care agency. The sick mother recovered more quickly than expected, ending the employment before the anticipated number of hours had been worked.

Mrs. P wanted the balance returned to her, and Ms. D believed that the money was rightfully hers because of the understanding they had about the work situation. At one point in the proceeding, the judge indicates that he is likely to order that the money be returned to Mrs. P because it was not earned. The following dialogue ensues:

Judge: From all the facts that I've heard so far and all the information I've solicited that I now say it's more than likely I will not make a finding urr for the defendant for these hours but I would make it out for the plaintiff for all the reasons that I've already stated [about the money not having been earned].

Ms. D: But isn't it a matter of principle? This was our agreement and I expected the money. You'd give it to her even as a matter of principle?

Judge: No, No. Principles are—I can't do that. If if I were to make decisions based upon principle then we might as well throw all the law books out the window. I'm guided by the law. The law, but you can't do things on principle.

Ms. D attempts several more times to plead on the basis of the situational principle involved, but she is unsuccessful against the legal principles that guide the judge. We are reminded here of Carol Gilligan's insights about the different ways in which women and men think about what is right and wrong. Ms. D looks for recognition of the line of responsibility flowing from her employer to her based on their personal understanding. The court looks to a principle in contract law to resolve the case. This is a small matter in the site of small legal claims, but to the extent that this type of reasoning is more common among women than men, gendered cultural beliefs would have an impact on the legal process.

In another vein, research on various communication strategies common to Chinese people points to a possible connection between cultural beliefs and the legal process. Ringo Ma's (1992) analysis of the use of intermediaries to deal with informal conflict situations among Chinese highlights a method for resolving disputes that differs from default legal practice in the United States. One can imagine the reluctance of individuals whose beliefs eschew direct, face-to-face conflict in favor of the use of intermediaries to voluntarily enter legal situations where one must offer explicit statements about the conflict which are heard by the other party. Thus, some Chinese Americans might avoid the legal system because its discourse demands are perceived to violate cultural integrity. It would be of interest to know if Asian Americans initiate legal actions in small claims court or take other legal actions requiring formal legal process less often than would be expected given their presence in the population. Those who are used to informal intermediaries may also find themselves at a disadvantage when accused of illegal behavior or sued by someone else; even formal mediation, which is increasingly used to resolve legal disputes, could be problematic because of the lack of structural distance between disputants that is provided in the courtroom. The Chinese preference for discourse indirection strategies (see Young, 1982) similarly implicates the possibility for problems in the legal context where direct statements and decisiveness are highly valued aspects of discourse.

The larger point to be drawn from these examples related to gender and ethnicity is that a person's primary cultural belief system and its expression in discourse will often play a larger role in situations of conflict than may be apparent on the surface. Beliefs about family life, the nature of the individual in the larger social system, discourse rights and obligations, face-to-face conflict, and so forth provide the invisible foundation for surface structures of speaking that may lead to misunderstanding and differential use, equity, and benefits from a legal system designed on the tenets of equality and fairness.

Racist and Sexist Discourse in the Legal Process

Unfortunately, racist and sexist discourse still can be heard in the legal context. State court studies have reported that women lawyers, litigants, and witnesses occasionally experience comments from men that put them in their place: comments from a judge such as "you look pretty today" or references to her as a "lady lawyer"; or opposing attorney references to adult females as "girls" or questions that attack a woman's maternal virtues because she works full-time. African Americans and other marginalized groups are often referred to as "you people," and it is not uncommon for opposing lawyers and judges to refuse to use terms such as *African American, Chicano, Latino, gay,* or *lesbian,* choosing instead to refer to *blacks, Spanish,* or *homosexuals.*

A survey study of a sample of over 1,200 lawyers in Massachusetts (Massachusetts Gender Bias Study Committee, 1989) gives concrete details of blatant discourse discrimination in the legal process. More female attorneys compared to male attorneys reported such things in the past 5 years as being addressed by their first names, receiving comments about their appearance, and being the recipient of suggestive sexual comments. Table 8.1 shows a selected set of findings from this study.

TABLE 8.1   Attorneys' Self-Report of Language Bias, by Gender of Attorney and Source of Comment

Question	Percentage of Women	Percentage of Men
Addressed by first name or term of endearment when surname or title expected, by:		
judges	20	7
counsel	59	16
employees	32	12
Asked if you were an attorney, by:		
judges	30	10
counsel	68	14
employees	63	29
Received inappropriate comments about your personal appearance, from:		
judges	5	—
counsel	30	2
employees	15	2
Subjected to inappropriate comments of a sexual or suggestive nature, from:		
judges	5	—
counsel	27	1
employees	12	1

SOURCE: Massachusetts Gender Bias Study Committee (1989). Used by permission.

Remarks by other attorneys constitute the largest share of offenses in each of the four categories. The gap in the breach of honorific use is consistent, with the more general trend for women to be first-named more than are men in comparable situations. Comments about personal appearance and suggestive or sexual remarks were reported by over one quarter of the female attorneys. What is startling about these data is that the study was conducted after such language had been commonly discussed as inappropriate, and prohibitions against sexual harassment had become a matter of law. If female attorneys experience this kind of sexist language, we would expect female litigants and witnesses to be even more vulnerable as targets of similar linguistic sexisms.

There are more subtle ways in which racism and sexism mark the discourse of the legal process. Legal proceedings and quasi-legal processes engage strict rules and cultural conventions. A person in command of standard educated English is in a much better position to match the requirements of the legal register than is a person whose primary language variety differs from the standard. By definition, speaking AAVE or ChE in a legal situation may evoke a racist interpretation with negative consequences analogous to those suggested by the O'Barr studies discussed earlier; that is, the speaker may be the target of racist interpretations by dint of dialect. If an opposing party or a juror or anyone else involved in the process associates speaking AAVE or ChE with less credibility or intelligence, then the response involves racism.

Racism and sexism can also work their way into the kinds of microlevel aspects of discourse seldom noticed by anyone other than a trained linguist. A fascinating case of such micro aspects is found in Norma Mendoza-Denton's (1995) analysis of the U.S. Senate confirmation hearings for Supreme Court Justice Clarence Thomas. In the transcript of the Hill-Thomas case, Mendoza-Denton found ample evidence of racist and sexist patterns of language use by the all-male, all-white Senate committee. Three of her main findings are described here. First, Mendoza-Denton measured the time length of the gap (that is, silence) between the end of Hill's and Thomas's statements and the beginning of the next question. The gaps were significantly longer after Thomas spoke, effectively giving time "to underscore the import of his words and allow the weight of his response to 'sink in' with the audience"; Hill, in contrast, was treated to "rapid questions in succession . . . giving her little time to think" (p. 55). Second, the majority of the questions directed to Thomas were in yes/no form, whereas for Hill, the majority were tag questions. The impact was for Hill's answers to seem more disjointed because she was often in the position of dealing with leading questions or questions with premises that she wanted to dispute. Third, when answers were nonconcise, Thomas received overt acknowledgment 50% of the time, but not once did Hill receive this kind of overt acknowledgment. Instead, following close to half of her nonconcise answers, the questioner changed the subject. Overall, these findings reveal a deep structure of sexist discourse that was likely outside the awareness of many involved but that nonetheless powerfully shaped the discursive direction of the hearings. The racist dimensions of the hearings are complex, but the main element of racism turned on the topic itself, that is, on placing an African American man and an African American woman on public display to deal with matters of sexual conduct dealt with in a discursively graphic manner. The sex and race drama (see the analyses in Chrisman & Allen, 1992) gained intensity because it was televised for all to hear and see. The Hill-Thomas ordeal did spark greater consciousness in the American public about sexual harassment but at the expense of exploiting stereotypes about black sexuality.

Probably the most important implication to be drawn from Mendoza-Denton's (1995) analysis of the Thomas-Hill case is that the discriminatory aspects of the discourse are not ones that are either likely to be noticed or, if they are, likely to be acknowledged as significant. This is precisely the issue raised by Rosina Lippi-Green (1994) in her point that language variety is not accorded serious consideration in U.S. legal cases. In significant cases involving language variety, usually accent, she found that "the judges who wrote these opinions are willing to depend on their own expertise in matters of language in a way they would never presume to in matters of genetics or mechanical engineering or psychology" (p. 177). If this is true for aspects of language that are, in fact, the reason for the legal case, the situation is likely worse for micro aspects of discourse, whether part of the case itself or important to the legal processes through which cases are dealt.

Critical Needs

Justice in the United States, definitely more blind and more equitable than that in many other places in the world, nonetheless carries with it discursive prejudices that are culturally seated. Entering the justice system or processes modeled after it carries very different implications for people of cultures not in the center of public American life. The formative cultural abstractions and discourse patterns guiding U.S. legal processes are, like everything else, neither universal nor culturally neutral. Greater awareness of the discourse ramifications of cultural diversity in the legal process would be a first step in providing more equitable access and less culturally biased experience with institutionalized legal systems. That awareness could be facilitated through focused analysis of the cultural aspects of language use in the context of legal education. Laypeople too could benefit from informational booklets that clearly specify the kinds of language issues that may arise in the legal system.

Language Diversity at School

As would be expected from the demographic shifts occurring in the United States, schools increasingly reflect racial, ethnic, and language diversity. Diverse student bodies bring with them a broad range of language and cultural backgrounds. Public schools in urban areas are the most ethnically, racially, and linguistically diverse, with many in fact belying the national statistical reality of their students as minorities. African Americans and Hispanics predominate in these schools because they are ghettoized by the racially and ethnically compounded economics of the country, but in some areas of the country, Asian students are found in large numbers as well. All public schools and most private schools enroll both boys and girls, which adds another layer of cultural complexity.

In this section, I consider several consequences of language diversity at school. Two related aspects of language are critical in the school context: the explicit development of language skills and literacy as a subject matter and the language-in-use that is part of all learning and activities in school. Whether literacy is the subject or language in its more everyday oral usage, the language variety of the student can carry consequences in many school situations. What happens to students who use AAVE, ChE, or any other variety of English associated with marginalized peoples? Does language symbolically construct boys and girls differently in the classroom? What if children's cultural background clashes with that of the educational system and their teachers? What if children enter school with no or limited proficiency in English? These and related questions will be addressed through four topics, each providing a different angle for thinking about the multiple consequences of language diversity in schools: (a) tacit culture in schools, (b) the roots of diversity awareness in schools, (c) marginalized cultures and language varieties in the context of teacher-student interaction, and (d) gender and discourse in schools. The most important current language policy issue in schools is bilingual education, and that topic is the subject of Chapter 9.

Tacit Culture in Schools

When a youngster enters school from a cultural and language system markedly different from the culture and discourse of schooling, that youngster faces much more than the normal challenges of learning. More and more children, for instance, must learn the primary language of U.S. schooling (English) as a second language. For many children whose native language is English, language is a problem in school because their dialects and discourse styles do not mesh well with the language of schooling. Students, regardless of their native language, often struggle with learning the values and norms about relationships that are implicit in the whole process of "doing school." To "do school" effectively demands a command of not just the appropriate language variety (the best approximation of Standard English possible for the individual student) but command as well of the value system on which the discourse of school builds—in short, communicative competence for school and mastery of the school register for speaking.

As U.S. society becomes more culturally complex, the dimensions of communicative competence for school also become more complex. One compounding factor in this complexity results from the racial and cultural differences between students and school personnel. In contrast to the cultural demographics of students in America's schools, the administrators and teachers are still primarily Eurowhite, monolingual English speakers, most of whom would claim to speak a standard variety of American English, even if that variety is regionally marked.

More hidden but even more significant for the cultural asymmetries that characterize most schools are the culturally steeped discourses through which education proceeds. These discourses carry long-standing cultural traditions about legitimate knowledge, motivation, teacher-student relationships, individualism, competition, and effective communication. These traditions are taught and reinforced in the organization and administration of schools, forming the tacit culture of schools. In practice, these traditions constitute what Basil Bernstein (1990), an eminent British sociolinguist and classroom researcher, terms *invisible pedagogies,* a concept that has become important to the work of certain scholars of discourse and schooling (see Cazden, 1994).

Most discourses of education proceed as though they are either compatible with or hostile to life outside of school but not as though they must strive to be well integrated into daily life as lived. Any working parent, regardless of race or class, can talk at length about the ways in which school practices are oblivious to the realities of parents: School schedules are erratic, with the school day sometimes ending as early as noon; before-school and afterschool programs often do not have enough spaces to meet demand; half-day kindergarten still exists in many school systems; teacher-parent conference times require that parents take vacation time to attend; and the list goes on.

The compatibility perspective on schooling assumes that school is integrated into and compatible with the rest of life. For activities such as homework, school is viewed as so important that everything else recedes into the background. Students receive lengthy assignments with little lead time, projects involve field research or parental involvement, and so forth. Succinctly, the pedagogical assumption is that school idles all else, displacing events, routines, and family plans.

In contrast, the hostility perspective on schooling assumes that school competes with the daily lives of its students and their families. Many teachers and school administrators are quick to blame television and video games for what they see as errant behavior in their students. Implicitly blaming women who work for not being home to supervise their children's homework is one kind of sexist hostility that places gender economics and politics as competitors. Drugs and alcohol as hostile competitors against school enter the scene at some point, earlier in the cities than the suburbs, and earlier in some suburbs than others. Violence will compete in some schools, usually those in the inner city, where violence has become a way of life.

When those who teach and administer schools see schooling as either compatible with life outside the classroom or as competing with a hostile external environment, they likely miss much of what the child brings to school that can be made part of the learning process. Children who come to school from cultural backgrounds, life circumstances, and language varieties not compatible with the discourses of schooling are, then, constantly placed in situations of conflict and incommensurate meanings with the schools and most of its teachers.

Faced with the diverse students populating today's classrooms but thinking within the prevalent invisible pedagogies, it is not surprising that so many teachers fantasize about classes filled with homogeneous students reared in the tradition of American middle-class values. The children in these fantasized classes come from homes where televisions and video games are turned off or closely monitored and where the family reads together each evening. These fantasized classrooms are filled with students who come to school not only well rested and well fed but speaking SAE or a regional version thereof as their native language, with values oriented toward success in school and later life, with a disposition to care about effort and citizenship, with parents who are educationally able to assist them in their learning and cocurricular activities, and with families materially privileged enough to own home computers and to buy books. In these fantasized spaces, the job of the teacher is indeed to teach and to help youngsters develop academically and morally and not—as so often seems to be the case—to struggle for disciplinary control of students in the context of an environment antithetical to learning.

Although many of today's current and prospective teachers yearn for the conditions described above, we need to think carefully about what is judged "ideal" about these conditions and who is making that judgment. Many images of the ideal classroom are also images of homogeneous cultural background. Adding cultural complexity to any situation makes it more challenging for students and teachers alike. Obviously, everyone likes their work to be rewarding and to spend most of their time doing those aspects of their jobs that are central rather than peripheral. When I enter a college classroom as a professor, for example, I want to focus completely on the topic for the day, to count on my students having done the assigned reading in advance, and to engage in lively, challenging discussion. I do not want to spend my time reading announcements, taking attendance, dealing with temperature control in the classroom, or trying to adapt to students who have not completed the assigned reading. Schoolteachers want the same type of experience, but there are additional issues that function to shape their sense of the ideal. One of those issues has to do with the cultural values and assumptions undergirding education's invisible pedagogies: Teaching becomes more difficult to the degree that common cultural ground is absent. Another issue is shared language, or more precisely, shared variety and sense of appropriate discourse: If the difference in language practices between teacher and student is more than generational, then either the communication system of the classroom is challenged or the students who differ become even more marginalized than when they entered. These issues are at the core of language and cultural diversity as manifested in the lower schools and carried forward into successive levels of education.

How can we better understand language and culture in the site of American schooling? One approach has been to see the schools for what they are: sites of cultural complexity that cannot and should not be forcibly submerged or minimized.

Cultural Studies of Discourse and Schooling

Most theories of learning and curricular design have been based on emphasizing the ways in which children cognitively develop and function (the student side) and on philosophical notions about what the results or outcomes of education should be (the curriculum side). A more recent approach being developed by some educators places the realities of cultural diversity at the center of pedagogy. This approach deals with matters of cognitive functioning, motivation, and curriculum in the context of how children "do school" in many different discourses arising from multiple cultures.

Cultural studies of discourse and schooling is a perspective on how to look at schools and schooling. As such, this approach explicitly asks questions about the cultural system through which school is owned, organized, and operated: the organization of power relations in schools, the values underlying curriculum and rules for conduct, methods used for decision making in schools, criteria for evaluating student progress in academic subjects, and so forth. Key questions differ from those conventionally posed about schooling. Why is it that so many teachers think that the administration of their schools impedes their ability to teach? Why do so many students think school is totally useless to their life? The cultural studies approach attempts to answer these questions by looking to factors other than how well teachers and students can channel their abilities and behaviors into the preestablished discourses of school. As such, this approach confronts both (a) the discourse used to conduct school and (b) the content and pedagogy of the "language arts" curriculum.

The cultural studies approach is compatible with a broader perspective that goes under the name of *critical studies of education.* Most of this work grows out of the pathbreaking ideas of a Brazilian educator named Paulo Freire (Freire, 1968, 1973; Freire & Macedo, 1987; Shor, 1992), who throughout his life has advocated the importance of taking the critical view (that is, questioning rather than taking things for granted) about why and how things happen as they do.

The critical studies approach uses terms such as "critical literacy" and "critical language awareness." By focusing on language in its cultural context and on schools as sites of cultural multiplicity, critical literacy scholars aim to better understand the consequences of language diversity in school. Norman Fairclough (1992), an important British thinker in the area of discourse and schooling, describes critical language study as a particular orientation toward language:

> It highlights how language conventions and language practices are invested with power relations and ideological processes which people are often unaware of. It criticises mainstream language study for taking conventions and practices at face value, as objects to be described, in a way which obscures their political and ideological investment. (p. 7)

The cultural study of discourse in education directly confronts, then, default pedagogy, just as critical legal theory questions default legal practices perpetuated through discourse practices.

Marginalized Language Varieties Come to School

Although sociolinguists long ago established that Standard English is not required for logical or intelligent expression (see Labov, 1972a, section on "The Vernacular in Its Social Setting"), the attitudinal resistance to varieties marked for race, ethnicity or nationality, and class continues to keep SAE ensconced as the dialect of educated people and the register of important places. As we know from the long tradition of research on language and attitude, just sounding a particular way can carry liabilities because of the judgments associated with particular patterns of speaking. This process of making nonlinguistic judgments about a person based on linguistic cues is the most basic way in which language diversity can have consequences in schooling. It is all too easy to conclude that the student who uses AAVE or ChE is not "well spoken" or uses "sloppy English" or that the student who uses Korean- or Chinese-accented English speaks with "broken English." Broken English represents a fascinating metaphor because it suggests that English-as-a-thing has been broken and is now of lesser value because the speaker has in his or her possession only shards of the whole language. Furthermore, the metaphor suggests that this broken thing does not work very well, but there might be something like "repaired English" that can transform it into a workable (although less than totally valuable) language.

Beyond the attitudinal responses triggered by certain language varieties, a deeper consequence looms. Because marginalized language varieties usually express marginalized cultural systems, more is at stake than the conventional notions associated with dialects as different ways of saying the same thing. The model of culture used throughout this book makes clear the profound connections of thinking, social relationships, and the expression and interpretation of what one thinks, wants, believes, and so forth to language variety. One can imagine the African American child who has been taught the value of artful expression being labeled as a "show off" or a "smart aleck" or the Chinese American child who has been taught the importance of restraint in expression and respect for hierarchy being labeled reticent. More generally, any child from a culture where individualism is not prominent will experience difficulty participating in U.S. schooling.

To the extent that the "foreign" discourses of the school are learned by its students, the result will likely be stress between school and the outside life of home and community environments. Some children can manage the demands of bidialectal, bilingual, and bicultural daily life, but others experience difficulty.

Analyses of what happens in circumstances of cultural incompatibility are beginning to surface in a particular stream of work within critical pedagogy. Those interested in multiple literacies and schooling locate many of the problems associated with failure in schools (most prominent in urban schools) more in discourse than other factors frequently cited. Sarah

Michaels (Michaels & O'Connor, 1990), for example, who founded an urban education center, says the following:

> Children from different backgrounds come to school with different discourse assumptions and styles—different ways of interpreting a question, giving an explanation, or telling a story. . . . These students are not gaining access to what we have called school-based discourses. They are not gaining mastery of the particular ways of using language, and integrating and extending knowledge that are valued and privileged in school—ways that are required to enter higher education and many other professional spheres of life. In this sense, they are not developing control over the literacies that are the cornerstones of success in academic disciplines. (p. 12)

From a pragmatic perspective, students are ill served unless the pedagogies through which they learn facilitate the kind of cornerstone literacies to which Michaels and O'Connor (1990) refer. The challenge, then, is not to replace the traditional discourses of schooling with marginalized discourses but to actively draw on the discourses that students bring to school to develop facility in understanding and using a range of discourses. Michaels and O'Connor demonstrate the subtle power of discourse with an example from a science lesson about balance that Michaels observed in a combined third- and fourth-grade multiethnic class. She shows text from a series of attempts to get a Haitian Creole-speaking girl to explain how she arrived at the answer to a balance problem. After much probing by Michaels (the teacher had given up) of the girl's reasoning for what is a "correct" answer, the girl explains exactly in both Creole and English how she arrived at her answer. She did not—unlike many of her classmates—understand the demands of "why questions" in the context of science, yet she knew how to do the problem and, ultimately, how to explain the process she went through. Her teacher, however, passed over her answer as the result of a good guess.

Another type of case study of the cultural dimensions of teacher-student discourse shows how cultural and language code switching by a teacher can facilitate classroom process. Michele Foster (1995) focuses on the discourse of an African American teacher in a classroom of African American students. Although the site for the research is a community college, the points made suggest broader applicability to K–12 education. Foster explicates text in which segments of the teacher's presentation incorporate African American discourse features. The teacher is described as "break[ing] into performance" at various times during the class to make points more clearly or engage the students. "The talk during performances," remarks Foster, "is embellished by a number of African American stylistic devices: manipulation of grammatical structure, repetition, use of symbolism and figurative language, and intonational contours, including vowel elongation, and changes in meter, tempo, and cadence" (pp. 335-336). The features Foster describes go beyond phonological and syntactic markers of African American English to engage a pragmatic discourse style with long-standing cultural foundations. What this teacher does is use many of the markers of African American discourse that were discussed in Chapter 5.

Students and teachers cannot, of course, be matched one-to-one for cultural background. Not only is such matching unrealistic, but it would defeat some of the broader purposes of education in the context of multicultural society. However, teachers' understanding of students' cultural backgrounds and their accompanying discourses can and should be engaged in school systems.

Gender and Discourse in Schools

Ironically, the metaphor often used to describe efforts to make education more equitable for females in comparison to their male age cohorts is that of a "level playing field"—a metaphor inherently masculinized because of its rootedness in field sports. Without question, compared to my generation, girls today may in fact be beneficiaries of a more level playing field. Despite "girl power," however, girls still make up most of the cheerleaders who yell, jump, and dance at high school football games; are less likely to pursue science, advanced math, and computer classes; and must worry about both sexual harassment at a young age and the cultural pressures to conform to relentless beauty and femininity standards. Boys, on the other hand, find many aspects of school to be entailed with cultural notions of masculinity. Strength in sports, independence, and autonomy are all desired characteristics to be cultivated as a way of proving that one is not feminine. Boys who fail the test, though, suffer greatly in adolescence and teen years.

Both implicitly and explicitly, the organization of schools and the cultural practices of schooling teach appropriate gender relations and construct meanings for gender, womanhood, and manhood. Public schools and most private schools today are coeducational, bringing together boys and girls in classroom learning and numerous cocurricular activities. Even in the few same-sex private school contexts that remain, the cultural messages of gender speak volumes about gender relations and genderized conditions for learning.

The persistence of women's colleges provides one of the strongest indicators that something happens through the discourse of schooling to favor boys over girls. In a broadly circulated and influential paper published by the Association of American Colleges and Universities (Hall & Sandler, 1982), the collegiate classroom situation for women is captured in the metaphor of a "chilly climate." The authors discuss factors such as the tendency of faculty (women and men alike) to call on and recognize men students more often than women students, to provide more encouraging feedback to men than women, and to interrupt women students more than men. Some of these patterns are reciprocally constructed between teachers and students because of the gender styles in language use that have developed throughout the gendered enculturation process. In my own observations, I have found that even in classes where women students are in the majority, the men almost always provide a disproportionate number of comments. In other words, they have more "clock time" in proportion to their numbers. I have also noted that men often are looked to (by faculty and students alike) for the "last word" or last comment on a subject.

The "chilly climate" paper includes recommendations for creating greater gender equity in classroom interaction and student-faculty discourse. The paper has been used in many colleges and universities as a vehicle for understanding the ways in which gender inequity in interaction can occur in classrooms and to formulate strategic steps to achieve greater gender parity. Yet, none of the recommendations really address deeper cultural explanations for the differences that are observed. The complexities of race, ethnicity, and ancestral background also add entirely different dimensions to the complexity.

The national focus on ways in which the language of classrooms is genderized in the K-12 grades came after the AACU initiative on the college classroom. Educators have long observed the trend for the academic performance of girls to surpass that of boys in the elementary grades but for boys to catch up and surpass girls as the shift is made from junior high/middle school into high school. Girls, in fact, hold their own in school up to the point of pubescence. We know that sex-role models for behavior in general and language in particular take hold as early as preschool (recall the section on children's gendered discourse in Chapter 4). The result shows clearly in the voluntary sex segregation of girls and boys. Starting in the first or second grade, same-sex groupings become the basis for peer relations and the foundations for attitudes about school and talk at school. A friend whose 11-year-old son is a fifth grader commented, for example, that at about the end of third grade, the boys in her son's class clearly had established that getting top grades was not the thing to do. Her son, whose teachers tried to encourage him to work up to his "A" potential, thought "B" grades were just fine. Young girls are much more likely to define school as important and to do what is expected of them, which usually leads to better academic performance.

Even though this sex segregation continues after elementary school, the added gender dynamic of boy-girl relations, romance, and sexual attraction becomes important to gender discourses subsequent to elementary school. The kind of bias found in the college classroom shows up in lower schools as well. A major report published in the early 1990s by the American Association of University Women (AAUW; 1992) galvanized attention to the classroom gender environment in American schools. One of the major findings of this report was that the discourse in high school classes especially is systematically skewed such that boys become the beneficiaries. Because boys are often more reluctant to openly embrace learning, more unruly in class, and less compliant in school, teachers tend to focus on them both to curb undesired behavior and to encourage behaviors considered appropriate to the classroom context. The many boys who fit this pattern receive substantially more verbal attention from teachers than do the girls.

While this gendered language cycle is building, so too are the still-present cultural notions about gender relations: Girls have learned that they should not one-up boys or appear too smart, and boys have learned that they need to assert themselves. Not all boys and girls conform to these cultural notions, but the pressure to do so is substantial, and the implications for discourse reach far beyond the classroom. For those interested in this process, Penelope Eckert and Sally McConnell-Ginet (1995) offer an eye-opening field study account of the intersections of gender and class divisions in an urban high school.

Teachers at all grade levels can make strategic efforts to create more patterns of equity in their classroom discourse. Four high school teacher-researchers (Allen, Cantor, Grady, & Hill, 1997) report on one such effort. Their analysis is of particular interest because they focus on classroom discourse in a private high school context where boys attend classes at a girls' school as part of a cooperative arrangement between the two schools. They were able, thus, to compare the all-girl classes with the coeducational classes conducted on the girls'-school turf. Among their observations were that girls sustained more student-oriented, lively discussion in the single-sex context than in the coed context and that boys were more likely to respond to questions of fact compared to open-ended questions. They also found ample evidence for the kind of gendered behaviors that have an impact on teachers' discourse strategies:

> Girls come into a classroom, settle down, and chat among themselves. . . . Boys often come in noisily, bantering and horsing around. Their energy is tangible. The teacher often engages in banter to establish rapport and to begin to bring the boys into the class. . . . The boys' behavior and the teacher's response heighten students' and teachers' awareness of gender differences. (p. 45)

At an abstract level, the cultural message to teachers is that boys need more attention to entice them into the class agenda. More attention directed to boys may unwittingly create perceptions among boys and girls alike about their relative status and ability. Allen and associates (1997) do, however, draw positive implications from their research. In their classroom observations, they saw girls who continued to participate in class even when boys were present, and they saw teachers who creatively worked to overcome the kind of gender patterns that solidify the classroom discourse into gendered polarities.

The many ways in which gender shapes classroom discourse suggest the need for more awareness about the subtleties of this process. The first step is for teachers and parents to be better informed about how education practices function to uphold broad scale cultural constructions of gender.

A second step requires continued vigilance about gender biases in American English. In many schools, for example, the marital status of women teachers is easily determined by sorting through which ones are listed as *Mrs.* and which *Ms.* Even though every person has the individual right to choose her or his address title, a policy regarding such work-based titles would be no more intrusive than having a policy (either implicit or explicit) that teachers are to be addressed by their title plus last name. Another bias in language use still prevalent in many school settings is the use of generic male reference: *he/him/his* for male and female alike and *man/mankind* for all people. Many parents teach their children to use the nonsexist constructions, only to find that what the kids hear and are told to do in school contradicts what they were taught at home.

Critical Needs

Schools as cultural institutions structure education around tacit cultural practices and invisible pedagogies. The impact of these practices and pedagogies on students from cultural groups outside the mainstream of education and on the definitions of gender cultivated in school settings can carry consequences far beyond what even the well-intentioned teacher ever imagined. Although it would not be desirable or workable for schools to be sites of cultural anarchy where every conceivable cultural practice is embraced and taught, it is not unreasonable to aim toward having schools that more effectively acknowledge and make use of complex cultural practices to advance student development and learning. In some cases, this will mean little more than preparing teachers to recognize when a cultural system different from default schooling likely underlies a particular student's approach to learning and displaying that learning through discourse. In other cases, more dramatic changes in pedagogy will be required.

Minimally, educators, parents, and students alike need better grounding in the reality that schools are cultural institutions. If the purpose of schooling is to facilitate the learning potential of all students and not to screen students for cultural differences, then education specialists and citizens alike will need to better understand both the tacit culture of schooling and the cultural diversity brought into the school setting. Two specific strategies would be starting points. First, more emphasis should be placed on critical and cultural studies of education and on analyzing the default cultural practices of U.S. schooling. Such studies are necessary to create pedagogies suitable to multicultural learning environments. Second, teachers must be trained in at least some basic linguistics and in the discourse dimensions of culture so that they can understand the meaning of discourse practices in the classroom and other school site venues. Unless teachers are knowledgeable about the cultural and linguistic backgrounds of their students, they will understandably be limited in pedagogical and curricular options. Most teachers would welcome such knowledge but are impeded because of deficient college training as well as entrenched school practices.

Language Diversity at Work

Contrary to the futurist visions of the 1970s, which predicted an increase in leisure time, Americans work more than in the past: Many work more than one job at a time, many work overtime in their jobs to earn additional money, and many find themselves in jobs where the expectation is that work pushes far beyond the conventional 9-to-5 day. As a fact of life, work holds the key to many characteristics of well-being. Disposable income but also health insurance, prospects for a financially secure retirement, child care, family leave opportunities, and vacation time all pivot on one's type of job and place of employment.

We usually think of job qualifications as directly related to training or education, with better-paying jobs and higher-status professions belonging to those who possess certain credentials—usually specific preparation and/or prior experience. Apart from the ubiquitous qualification of "effective communication skills" found in many job descriptions and the occasional necessity for fluency in a language other than English, we seldom think about the specific role of language in qualifying a person for a job or as an attribute of consequence in the work situation. Yet language use carries important consequences when it comes to work.

The most obvious situations where language has consequences for work are those in which particular varieties and styles of language use become de facto criteria for whether or not one can perform a particular job. Without command of a good approximation of SAE (or a regional variety thereof), it would be difficult, for example, to be a language arts or history teacher but probably less difficult to be an art teacher or athletic coach. A journalist must have an excellent command of written English, although that person's spoken variety may be less important. A politician, on the other hand, benefits from excellent oral communication skills but might rely on others to prepare written statements. Sales and customer service are language intensive, whereas jobs in computer graphics and dry cleaning are not. The role of language use in job performance, then, varies greatly across jobs and professions.

In this section, I consider three different types of consequences: (a) consequences linking language to occupations, (b) consequences arising because of attitudes about language in the workplace, and (c) consequences arising from conflicts between culturally defined discourse pragmatics and the discourse of work.

Language-Linked Occupations

The linking of language to occupation can be strong or weak. Strong language-linked occupations are those requiring extensive command and use of particular language registers. The occupation of lawyer in the United

States, for example, requires fluency in English. Weak language-linked occupations are those requiring no particular language variety or fluency. Many repetitive labor jobs are in this category because the work itself is primarily hand and/or machine related, training can be done in any language, and new workers can be taught the job through a combination of explanation from coworkers and observation. Carpentry, farm work, and factory jobs fall into this category.

In a country dominated by monolingual English speakers, individuals without substantial proficiency in English have narrowly channeled work opportunities, often leading to either ethnic-language work ghettos or ethnic-identified occupations.

Ethnic-language work ghettos exist when one or more of the following conditions describe the workers: LEP, lack of job training and skills, and temporary or illegal immigration status. Migrant farm and sweat shop work are the most notorious employment ghettos of this type. In these situations, LEP may be the main factor accounting for what type of job the person can get. Once in the job, language limitations often interfere with negotiation over working conditions or employee grievances.

In some instances, the combination of language, ethnicity, and gender form the conditions of employment ghettoization. The concentration of women in the circuit assembly jobs for the microelectronics industry in California is a case in point. About half of the women working in these jobs are recent immigrants from Korea, Vietnam, the Philippines, or Southeast Asia (Espiritu, 1997). Pay is low, the work tedious and stressful, and little or no facility with English is required. A similar situation exists for Asian immigrant women employed in the garment industry on a piecework basis. Sometimes, however, ghettoized employment also provides certain advantages for workers. Williams's (1989) case study of Punjabi Sikh women employed in California canneries (described in Chapter 7) demonstrates how poor working conditions can be counterbalanced by meeting family and cultural needs. The Sikh women's options are few because of their LEP status, but the cannery jobs give them the opportunity to earn extra money for their families, break out of their domestic sex-roles by working outside the home, and both speak in their native language and resist certain types of communication with their employers.

Limitations with fluency in English also lead in some cases to ethnic clustering in certain types of jobs. As noted in Chapter 7, a combination of factors including overt racism, geographic location, and constraints imposed by LEP account for the clustering of Chinese immigrants into laundries, dry cleaning businesses, restaurants, and small stores. Grocery store ownership and jobs among Korean immigrants evolved similarly. Although such clustering often provides a viable economic foundation for immigrants, it can also fuel ethnic stereotypes. Non-Asians easily draw the inference from the occasional spelling or grammatical error on the menu at a Chinese restaurant that all Chinese people have difficulty with the fundamentals of English.

A different type of job consequence related to language is linked to attitudes about varieties of oral English other than the standard type of speech considered to come "from nowhere." A person's language variety can essentially serve as a screening factor for some jobs. The most obvious example comes from the field of news broadcasting. The broadcasting code's long-standing requirement for newscasters to speak "accentless speech" canonizes one variety of American English as superior. The desirable "speech from nowhere" is actually based on the standard, midwestern variety, stigmatizing even standard varieties of southern or eastern dialects. Those with marked regional, ethnic, or social class dialects who aspire to be on-air newscasters are advised indirectly by the broadcasting code and directly by teachers to undergo speech therapy to achieve "accent reduction."

Language Attitudes in the Workplace

Many of the consequences of language diversity in the workplace are traceable to attitudes. The workplace can become an enforcement zone for language attitudes in many ways: by screening out potential employees at the interview stage, by using language as a factor in performance evaluations and promotions, by citing language problems as cause for dismissal, and by using language to marginalize some employees.

Even among those who are tolerant of language diversity, work-related language attitudes sometimes surface because of ideas about the appropriate discourse register for work. The broadcasting code for news reporters is a case in point. In a *Time* article several years ago, a speech therapist who runs a thriving dialect reduction business in Tennessee is described as speaking "perfect television-anchor talk" (Conniff, 1988). The therapist/entrepreneur was quoted as saying "there is nothing wrong with sounding Southern—just that it may not be the most suitable sound for the business world" (p. 12): pure attitude.

The most obvious way in which work-related language attitudes surface is in allegations that using a language variety that differs from the norm impedes effective communication with colleagues, customers, or clients.

Communication often is not the problem, but rationalizing negative attitudes by pointing to communication effectiveness gives the attitudes at least some superficial merit. The case of a Chinese-born college professor who was not promoted illustrates this line of reasoning (*Hou v. Pennsylvania Department of Education*, cited in Lippi-Green, 1994). In finding against the professor in his case against his employer, the judge cited accent as one contributing factor: "He is at a decided disadvantage in the classroom because of his natural accent . . . he has a difficult time overcoming this handicap. The obvious grammatical errors on his application attest to his communication problems" (Lippi-Green, 1994, p. 179).

Work-related language attitudes can also be founded in cultural notions about national, class, or ethnic privilege. Even characterizing the United States as "an English speaking country" presumes the privilege of not mentioning that millions of its residents speak languages other than English. A person with this sense of language privilege believes in the right not to be subjected to varieties other than his or her own. The most common example of this occurs in work situations where bilingual or LEP employees choose to use a language other than English in situations among coworkers (for example, speaking Spanish while making sandwiches at a luncheonette) or with clients and customers who share the same language background (e.g., speaking Mandarin Chinese with customers in a computer store). The example at the beginning of the book of the Puerto Rican women in a corporate lavatory being shouted at to speak English or go back home shows precisely this underlying attitude of privilege. In another example reported in an urban newspaper, a Spanish-speaking hotel worker reported that a supervisor told her not to speak Spanish "because it gives her a headache" (Lewis, 1997, p. B3).

When a low-prestige variety of English (ChE for example) is the target of negative language attitudes, many of the same assumptions about cultural privilege are at work. In addition, the demand not only for fluent American English but for a variety of it that approximates the ideal of standardization reveals an assumption about communicative responsibility and language privilege: Language privilege includes the right to listen to others without making any effort to understand the linguistic features of their variety. Many times when a monolingual English speaker claims to not understand a person who is speaking English as a second language, the problem is that no effort was made. Even worse, an individual's negative attitudes toward a language variety might lead to claims about unintelligibility when that is not the case; this is similar to the Parisian who refuses to "hear" the French of a foreigner.

Job Interviews and Language Screening

Anyone who has gone through a job interview knows how stressful the situation can be. The applicant for the job wants to make the best impression possible, and the employer wants to determine as much as possible about the candidate's qualifications. If you have gone through this process yourself, you also know that communication in the interview differs from normal conversation. The format is question-answer, with most of the questions coming from the interviewer, and speech is usually carefully monitored, especially by the candidate, for both content and style.

The stakes are high when a person enters any interview, and the interviewee's particular variety of language is one factor that can make a difference. Judgments based on language variety can be negative, positive, or any combination of the two; the point is that linguistically based judgments play a role in impression formation and assessment of qualifications. For many jobs involving substantial contact with the public, anything but being thought of as "well spoken" may lead to negative judgments (Hopper & Williams, 1973). Negative judgments are most likely in situations where the interviewee uses a dialect of English associated with marginalized status or speaks with an accent judged to be foreign and low prestige (AAVE, for instance, might cause more problems than Norwegian-influenced English). A particular dialect might not determine the destiny of the interviewee, but it may introduce a barrier to be overcome. Summarizing a broad range of research on language and attitude, Giles and Coupland (1991) say that "listeners can very quickly stereotype others' personal and social attributes on the basis of language cues and in ways that appear to have crucial affects on important social decisions made about them" (p. 58).

The pragmatics of language use can also be the source of problems in the interview process itself. Following from the comparative cultural profiles I have presented, we would expect that the employment interview might be understood differently by two people from two different cultural backgrounds. If the interviewer expects questions to be answered directly and factually, failure to do so will have negative consequences. This was the case in the example I cited in Chapter 5, in which an African American used narrative style in his interview for a university department head position. One can easily imagine the difficulties in an interview situation when a Chinese American or Japanese American is essentially asked to boast about his or her accomplishments and strengths. Responding indirectly and without clearly creating a picture of oneself as an individual might lead to the judgment that the person has been evasive. There is scant research directly showing how these larger, pragmatic discourse differences affect employment interviews, but Akinnaso and Ajirotutu's (1982) analysis of mock interviews with African Americans in a job training program offers instructive insights. Based on evaluations of these interviews, the researchers were able to show distinctions in language use between a successful and unsuccessful interviewee; inability to shift from conversational African American speech to formal "interview talk" led to incorrect inferences about the interviewee's experience and abilities.

English-Only "Outlaws"

One of the harshest consequences of language diversity in the workplace occurs when a person finds his or her native language banned or strongly discouraged. Normally, employees would expect to speak English when they are in contact with English-speaking people or when the job itself requires or assumes English as the language of communication. But what happens when the customers in a store, diners in a restaurant, or residents of a nursing home share a native language other than English with the employee in question? Or if several employees are conversing among themselves and share a language other than English? These are the kinds of situations where employees can become—sometimes by surprise—language outlaws.

At its extreme, language outlaw policies can be the basis for firing an employee. This was the case for Jordania Reed, an immigrant from the Dominican Republic and native Spanish speaker, who worked at a convalescent hospital in California (Foster, 1992). The hospital imposed an "English only" policy banning the use of languages other than English in the workplace. Reed's second offense of speaking Spanish to colleagues led to her dismissal. Similar cases have occurred in factories, fast-food restaurants, and retail stores. The policies usually carry some rationale related to the specific workplace, and when challenged in court, such policies have often been upheld (Foster, 1992). The scales tipped heavily toward workplace English-only policies when the Supreme Court in 1994 declined to hear the case of an employee who had been fired from a California meat and poultry factory (*Priscilla Garcia v. Spun Steak Co.*, as reported in Savage, 1994) for speaking Spanish. By not hearing the case, the Supreme Court let stand the federal district judge's ruling in favor of the company and its policy.

Although some language policies in the workplace may be justified based on working conditions or the position itself, the ambiguous areas pose employment risks and identity consequences for many speakers of languages other than English. What might seem natural, logical, and ethical to the employee may turn out to be against company policy—written or unwritten—about language on the job. Even if the outcome of an infraction is not dismissal, the consequences can be substantial for self-esteem, for workplace morale, for promotions and pay increases, and for relations with one's supervisors and coworkers.

The most insidious policies are those that are implicit. An unwritten policy might be communicated "between the lines" of a supervisor's suggestion to bilingual employees that "English is always appropriate in the workplace." In other instances, supervisors might clearly convey that "English only" is the rule even when the employer has no formal policy. At an upscale hotel in Boston, "several hotel employees interviewed said that although the hotel doesn't have a written English-only policy, workers were told not to speak any other language but English in public areas" (Lewis, 1997, p. B3). Similar anecdotal reports are frequent around the country.

Cultural Discourses and Work Life

Much of what underlies how any employee will fare at work has to do with how well that employee fits into the work environment. Assuming that an employee is appropriately trained for the job and is able to comply with an organization's rules and procedures for things such as punctuality, lunch breaks, and so forth, fit can still be elusive.

Workplace fitness sometimes depends on factors related to the particular person as a member of a cultural group. How an individual's language use and communication style are culturally marked influences a host of factors—retention, promotion, pay increases, peer relations, superior-subordinate relations, and employee satisfaction.

The pragmatic dimension of language use associated with cultural identity often presents obstacles in the workplace. When a woman is advised to learn about sports, especially football, so she can join in Monday morning conversation about the weekend games, she is being advised to learn a cultural discourse not her own. When a Korean American man is advised to be assertive and to advocate his ideas more forcefully, he is being advised to use cross-cultural discourses. When an African American woman is advised to be less assertive or to speak more quietly, the implications may also be cultural. Because the dominant roles in workplaces historically belong to white men, the cultural practices in most organizations reflect the ideology encoded by this group over a long period of time (Ferguson, 1984; Fine, 1995). When workers use language and communicative strategies based in different cultural systems, they risk being misunderstood, disliked, or isolated.

When cultural aspects of language use create difficulties at work, the discourse mechanisms are often subtle. Outside-of-awareness aspects of cultural patterning at the microdiscourse level may result in negative consequences. Young's (1982) analysis of how native English speakers respond to discussions among Chinese businessmen is illustrative of how this can occur. Young explicated transcripts to show how aspects of discourse pattern provided the basis from which native English speakers negatively judged Chinese businessmen to be "beating around the bush" (p. 79). To the extent that a Chinese immigrant or native-born Chinese American follows Chinese cultural patterns of communication, the same judgment likely meets them in the workplace. Another illustration—this time in the domain of gender— comes from Edelsky's (1981/1993) research, which was discussed in Chapter 4. She demonstrated that even though men and women both actively participated in a series of meetings devoted to a particular project the men accounted for all of the "singly developed floors," that is, the long, monologue-type segments of the group meetings. There are no other studies similar to Edelsky's, but every time I assign the reading in a class or mention its focus to working professionals who spend considerable time in meetings, the nods of affirmation abound.

The consequences of cultural diversity for language in the workplace deeply penetrate the surface level of language. Incommensurate discourse strategies lie at the root of at least some situations where poor communication skills are cited. My own research with Marlene Fine and Sallyanne Ryan (Fine, Johnson, & Ryan, 1990) in a federal agency employing a large number of scientists, engineers, and lawyers brought to light the hidden reality behind the assumption that men, women, and cultural minorities experience the "same" work environment differently. We found that cultural background accounted for vastly different perceptions of the workplace:

> [Our] results suggest that men, women, and minorities do not share a common
> culture of organizational life; rather, each group identifies, defines, and orga-

nizes its experience in the organization in unique ways . . . and [workers] are often unable to see or understand the experience of others. (p. 317)

These "different realities" contrasted so sharply that when we presented the results of both survey and interview research to senior management—all of whom were white males—they countered by first questioning the accuracy of our reporting and then expressing disbelief at what women and people of color had told us. The Asian Americans' complaint about their absence from management positions despite their positive job performance was at first denied by management but later confirmed by analyzing the personnel database. In the same discussions in which management denied that the communication styles of women and Asian Americans influenced promotion decisions, comments about those very same styles were offered as "constructive" suggestions to enhance promotability.

Critical Needs

The consequences of different realities for different cultural groups in the workplace obviously weigh heavily on the negative side for employees who are in someway marginalized or encounter barriers to their retention and advancement. But the negative consequences weigh on the side of the employer too because of the loss of potential productivity for the organization. Following from the cultural abstractions and communicative practices considered in earlier chapters, a host of consequences can ensue: consequences for many Hispanic and Asian Americans, whose family orientations and culturally defined family responsibilities are viewed as indicators of low job commitment; consequences for women, whose commitment to more egalitarian styles of communication is viewed as indicating lack of decisiveness and leadership potential; consequences for all members of marginalized cultural groups who cope with cultural stress in the workplace by seeking out those of similar gender and cultural identity, only to be accused of cliquishness and inability to "fit in"; consequences for Hispanics of being perceived as too emotionally expressive and for Asian Americans of being too reserved; and so forth.

Unfortunately, the lack of cultural mindedness too frequently underlies cultural tensions and misunderstandings in the workplace. Marlene Fine (1995), in her analysis of culture and U.S. organizations, terms unacknowledged or misunderstood diversity "dysfunctional." Fortunately, some workplaces are responding in positive ways both to make effective use of diversity for organizational purposes (the bottom line) and to assist workers in better understanding the cultural foundations of language use that are part of everyday talk at work.

Implications

In this chapter, I have considered four important contexts in which the cultural dimensions of language use are of consequences. Some of the language consequences mentioned follow from the imposition of ideology, as when a doctor believes he (or she) is above being held responsible for clear communication with patients or when a judge feels free to impose his (or her) views about language for those of linguistic experts. Some consequences are less obviously a product of ideology and more the outcome of misinterpretations due to modes of cultural communication that may not be mutually intelligible; language interpreters can influence testimony, borrowings from one language to another can lead listeners to draw inappropriate conclusions, and cultural beliefs about communication can trouble the waters of medical or workplace discourse.

The contexts and consequences discussed in this chapter are not exhaustive, of course. Almost any situation where people find themselves in interaction with one another or in the position to make sense of discourse produced by a person operating from a different cultural system can be problematic. In some situations, the consequences weigh heavier than in others, but the sources of difficulty usually emanate from the same complex of symbolic meanings that attend multiple discourses in a multicultural society. In Chapter 9, I look at one of the most critical and hotly debated language issues facing the United States: What should be done educationally in response to the many different native languages children of the United States speak? This is the question of bilingual education. The bilingual education question is not, however, substantially different from questions about the relationship of mainstream culture to marginalized ethnic culture and about the relationship of Standard English to varieties bearing labels such as Ebonics. Thus, the Ebonics and bilingual questions demand integrated consideration because they similarly challenge the place of SAE at the linguistic ideological apex of American life.

9

Bilingual Education, Ebonics, and the Ideology of "Standard English"

No language policy issue so clearly exposes the conflicting impulses about cultural diversity in the United States as bilingual education. Advocates believe bilingual education is critical both to preserve the integrity of marginalized cultural populations and to ensure English language literacy, but they also lament its frequent ineffectiveness in accomplishing either goal. Opponents attack it for eroding the status of the United States as "an English-speaking country" and for squandering scarce fiscal resources on programs that fail, they say, to deliver literate students. Embedded in the controversies about bilingual education, then, are political, fiscal, cultural, and pedagogical issues.

The mass media fuel the firestorm over bilingual education by focusing on extreme cases and abuse within school programs. Regardless of one's position on the issue, reactions of alarm and anger are likely when headline news reads:

Newsweek: Classrooms of Babel (Leslie, 1991, p. 56)

The Boston Globe: Latinos, others blame it [bilingual education] for illiteracy (Gorov, 1997, p. A12)

Los Angeles Times: More schools shunning bilingual methods (Anderson, 1997, p. A3)

The New York Times: Trapped in the bilingual classroom—After six years, David still couldn't read (Jimenez, 1996, p. 23, Op-Ed.)

Wall Street Journal: The bilingual ed trap (González, 1995, p. A20)

Many of the news stories recount failed pedagogy, forced placement in bilingual classes against the will of parents, and language ghettos in the schools. Few of these exposés provide comprehensive analyses of the situations under scrutiny, and even fewer help clarify the intent of bilingual education, what laws govern its operation, how its effectiveness is gauged, or the broader issues of bilingual education in the context of language education in the United States. As Geoffrey Nunberg (1992) observes, "Questions about the effectiveness of bilingual education can be fairly discussed in an academic forum or a legislative hearing, but not in the popular press or in thirty-second sound bites" (p. 483). The problem, of course, is that public opinion forms mainly in relation to mass media representations and not in relation to academic research or the full text of legislative debates.

The debates over bilingual education will be with us for the foreseeable future because, as Giles and Coupland (1991) concisely state it, "bilingualism is endemic to modern society" (p. 156). The presence of more than one language among more than a smattering of people living within a national border will provide the conditions for differences of opinion about what the status of minority languages should be, especially in sites of public education.

In everyday conversations, as well as in more focused decision- and policy-making situations, certain questions reoccur: Should bilingual education exist at all? If so, who should be taught, when, and for how long? What methods are most effective? How should effectiveness be measured? These questions usually reference what should or should not be done with students whose first language is not English; the questions rarely broach the larger reference point of *all* citizens, regardless of native language. In theory, bilingual education is just as important to monolingual English speakers as it is to the native speaker of Spanish, Tagalog, or French—a point to which I return at the end of the chapter.

My intent in this chapter is to provide a context for understanding the linguistic, political, and policy dimensions of the bilingual education debate. Although most people treat bilingual education as a discrete educational and policy domain, the core questions differ only in degree from those posed about varieties of English, such as African American Vernacular English (AAVE), that are prevalent in the multiple discourses of the school environment.

In the pages that follow, four topics are addressed that are relevant to the specific policy status of bilingual education and the more general issue of multicultural discourse: (a) the flawed view of language and communication inherent to monolingualism, (b) the legal policy status of bilingual education in American schooling, (c) the strange case of Ebonics in language education, and (d) Standard English and bilingual education in the context of cultural multiplicity and multicultural discourse. The efficacy of bilingual education is not the central topic here, but studies abound from which both supporters and detractors have drawn evidence to bolster their case. The National Research Council (1997) recently issued a report prepared by an independent assessment panel, the conclusions of which point to a number of years of research finding effectiveness of native language instruction for young children, some support for what are essentially "sink or swim" approaches to teaching English, but largely politicized and rarely comparable research studies. Setting the efficacy issue aside, bilingual education as an approach can be assessed for its broader purposes related to enriching the cultural and linguistic resources of the nation. The core issue ultimately hinges on the value accorded cultural and linguistic pluralism. As this chapter unfolds, the discussion builds toward the conclusion that although Standard English fluency and literacy are essential for full participation in U.S. society, the development of bilingualism for all citizens is of equally compelling importance.

Monolingualism and Flawed Conceptions of Language

Monolingualism begets false conceptions of the role of language and communication among humans. This is a bold statement, but its validity rests on assumptions that underlie almost every theory of cognition: Humans organize and make sense of much of their world through comparisons and contrasts that are made salient in the process of enculturation. Children learn culturally salient opposites at preschool age through visual presentations in books and activities of concrete differences between long and short, fat and skinny, full and empty, big and small, up and down, in and out, and so forth. Within a cultural context, more abstract contrasts are developed on dimensions such as *good-bad, beautiful-ugly, kind-cruel, right-wrong, moral-immoral,* and the culturally loaded *black-white* dimension. In learning these opposites and contrasts, attention is drawn to their "reality"—reality that varies across cultural contexts.

Much of what we learn becomes taken for granted as part of reality. When monolingualism prevails, language is taken for granted much more than it would be in situations where public contexts (mass media, political discourse, banking terms, and mass mailings) include more than one language or where a language or languages other than the dominant one are taught in school. For example, in comparison to the United States, a particular language would be less taken for granted in northern Italy, where proximity to France and Germany means that television programs occur in Italian, French, or German; and less taken for granted anywhere in India, a country where native languages vary tremendously, 15 official languages exist that correspond to the Indian states, and English is the language of higher education. Where multilingualism is present, the symbolic nature of language and the communication process in which language predominates must at least be acknowledged by those who are not themselves bi- or multilingual. For those who are bi- or multilingual, the contrasts of worldview and communicative practices as they relate to specific languages are simply parts of daily life. One language might be used in the home and immediate community with certain connotations and domains of expression, whereas another might be used elsewhere with quite different connotations and domains of expression; such functional distinction by use is called *diglossia.*

The absence of multilingualism and the force of monolingual American English in the United States has resulted in cultural views of language far removed from notions of language as symbolic, connotative, and selectively suited for certain domains of experience. This situation is complicated by the general ineffectiveness of U.S. schools in teaching foreign languages. Although many states require some foreign language in high school, the instruction is insufficient in both duration and pedagogy to provide fluency for more than a few. Many bachelor's degree-granting colleges and universities require foreign language as well, but again, the results rarely warrant acclaim.

Scientism and Language

A seemingly unrelated force propelling the particular views associated with monolingualism in 20th-century U.S. society has been the preoccupation with science and scientific principles. The scientific method of discovery depends on certain ideas about knowledge, the main ones of which are objectivity rather than subjectivity, observation rather than introspection, and detachment rather than direct involvement of the investigator in what he or she studies. These ideas have seeped into everyday life in domains far removed from formal scientific inquiry, and American English contains ample semantic notions that are evidence of *scientism* in worldview such that sciencelike ideas form the basis for beliefs about reality in everyday life. We often implore one another to be objective, or we look for a person who can be objective about some issue; we endeavor "to separate fact from fiction," to "get down to the facts," or sometimes to factualize opinion to give it more credibility. *Bias* is a word frequently used to describe *in a pejorative manner* the viewpoint or opinion that a person has developed because of that person's experience; in other words, we encode through American English a semantic dimension indicating distrust in personal experience and opinion.

We do not usually see science as intimately connected to language-in-use or communication, but a brief look at the very vocabulary we use to describe communication shows scientism's force. The dominant vocabulary for communication in the second half of the 20th century features terms suggesting a mechanical/mechanistic metaphor: *Senders* and *receivers* transmit messages to and receive *feedback* from one another. Although such a vocabulary can accommodate problems in meaning by referring to communication breakdowns, the mechanical metaphor remains intact with no hint of the deeply cultural and symbolic nature of all communication. With such terminology forming the dominant cultural conception of communication, it is not difficult to understand why simplistic notions about the significance of language to thought and worldview would prevail or why the rationale for bilingual education could be so thoroughly trivialized as it often is. If a person believes that learning a language is only a matter of translating words and learning certain rules, then expenditures on long-term bilingual education would seem wasteful. Likewise, what goes into learning a second language would be underestimated. Yet most monolingual English speakers probably do have a good idea of how difficult it is to learn another language because they themselves cannot do it. Contrary to the idea that children absorb new languages quickly, there is ample evidence suggesting that it can take up to 12 years to become fluent in a language (Crawford, 1997).

Monolingualism as "Taken for Granted"

Monolingualism, even when benevolent, fosters the idea that language is a culturally neutral instrument used to relate ideas and information to others. Not surprisingly, this idea underlies the language interpretation policy found today in the judicial system: Understanding is construed as merely a matter of getting the words translated properly. Berk-Seligson (1990), whose research on the bilingual courtroom was reviewed in Chapter 8, notes that even matters of tone and style of discourse are reduced by the requirements for court interpreters to focus on "lexical equivalence" (p. 40). By making vocabulary the center of language translation, the viewpoint of language as instrument and conduit for expression can be maintained.

The impact of dominant monolingualism at a society level positions languages other than English as a problem. The problem, says Richard Ruíz (1988), has particular consequences:

> Not only are we not developing language skills in the population to any great extent; we are doing almost nothing to encourage non-English language maintenance. The result could well be a pattern of language loss over just a few generations. (p. 15)

An alternative focus sees language as a resource to be developed as well as conserved.

U.S. Policy on Bilingual Education

Bilingual education, as it is commonly called, was first initiated not in California, New York, or in the Texas towns bordering Mexico, and not for the benefit of Mexican-Americans or Puerto Ricans. The first bilingual education program to be offered in a public school in the United States was in Dade County, Florida, at the Coral Way Elementary School. The year was 1963 (3 years after arrival of the first group of Cuban refugees), and the program began at the urging of Cuban parents, who wanted their children to maintain and further develop their Spanish while learning English. Recall from Chapter 6 that many in the first group were well-educated social elites; they assumed that Castro's reign would be short-lived and their status as sojourners temporary. Thus, these parents did not want their children's Spanish language and literacy development to be halted or displaced by English. The program, however, was open to both native Spanish and native English speakers, with the aim of producing fluent bilingualism among all of its students (Crawford, 1989). The Coral Way program continues today as an example of effective bilingual education, serving as the model for Miami's new initiative requiring bilingual education for *all* students (Mears, 1998).

As the Hispanic, Spanish-language speaking population of the United States grew in the 1960s, so did the more general interest in providing educational programs to assist in the development of English and simultaneously to enhance native-language abilities. Teachers in certain areas of the country were confronted with increasing numbers of students who entered school with little or no English background. The Civil Rights Act of 1964 provided a compelling rationale for ensuring that minorities and the poor received special protection through national laws and policies to compensate for uneven treatment from state to state. It was in this context that legislation was introduced at the federal level that would shape bilingual education for many years to come.

Bilingual Education Act of 1968

The Bilingual Education Act (BEA) of 1968 was an addition to the Elementary and Secondary Education Act of 1965. The 1965 act established a federal role in education for the first time, and the BEA became Title VII of that act. Although various versions of the initial proposal circulated through the congressional process, the principal sponsorship for the legislation is credited to Senator Ralph Yarborough from Texas, who had attended a conference sponsored by the National Education Association focused on the teaching of English to Spanish-speaking children (Crawford, 1992). As a Texan, he was acutely aware of the growing Spanish language-speaking population. Yarborough's bill proposed that financial assistance be available to support a range of bilingual programs in schools with sizable numbers of Spanish-speaking Mexican-American or Puerto Rican students. The final version of the BEA approved in 1968 contained broader language with no restrictions to the Spanish language.

There are many misconceptions about the purpose and scope of the BEA. Despite its name, perceptions persist that the act empowers schools to offer alternative education programs in languages other than English and to minimize the emphasis on English in the process. Nothing is further from the truth, although some programs of instruction may be ineffective in moving children quickly enough into mainstream English education. Specifically, the BEA as passed in 1968 focused on

1. providing "financial assistance to local educational agencies to carry out new and imaginative elementary and secondary school programs designed to meet these special educational needs [of LEP students]" (PL 90-247, Sec. 702); and

2. requiring that programs of instruction include native language instruction along with instruction in English.

The BEA itself did not require that programs be created for LEP students, nor did it specify what method of instruction should be used for programs that would be offered.

The BEA was made increasingly specific through interpretive guidelines and court cases, both of which defined more exact requirements for states to use in meeting requirements for federal assistance in teaching LEP students. In this way, the executive and judicial branches of the government became critical in defining what began as legislative policy.

In the executive branch, the Office of Civil Rights (OCR)—part of the Department of Health, Education, and Welfare (DHEW)—was to become the major federal agency to articulate the requirements of the BEA. In 1970, the head of the OCR issued a memorandum to school districts, published in the *Federal Register,* indicating that "where inability to speak and understand English excludes national origin minority group children from effective participation in the educational program . . . the district must take affirmative steps to rectify the language deficiency" (35 *Federal Register,* 11595; guidelines became known as the Health, Education and Welfare Department Guidelines). The memorandum did not specify pedagogy but did disallow placement of LEP students into classes for children with retardation or learning problems.

Lau Remedies and Transitional Bilingual Education

The year 1974 stands as the landmark for defining the requirements of public schools in the area of bilingual education. That year, the case of *Lau v. Nichols* (1974) came before the U.S. Supreme Court. The suit was filed on behalf of Kinney Kinmon Lau and 12 other Chinese American students in the San Francisco school system (there were about 1,800 non-English speaking Chinese students in San Francisco at the time) against the school district for failing to offer special English classes with bilingual teachers. Based on the Civil Rights Act of 1964 and the 1970 OCR guidelines related to "affirmative steps," the Court overturned a decision in the federal appeals court that had upheld San Francisco's right to follow state laws regarding English as the language of instruction. The Court required the school district to fashion "appropriate relief," arguing that

> students who do not understand English are effectively foreclosed from any meaningful education. Basic English skills are at the very core of what these public schools teach. Imposition of a requirement that, before a child can effectively participate in the educational program, he must already have acquired those basic skills is to make a mockery of public education. We know that those who do not understand English are certain to find their classroom experiences wholly incomprehensible and in no way meaningful. (*Lau v. Nichols,* 1974)

Following the 1974 *Lau* case, the OCR issued a memorandum that has become known as the Lau Regulations or Lau Remedies. For the first time, a particular method was prescribed for achieving English proficiency among LEP students: *transitional bilingual education* (TBE). TBE is bilingual in the sense that teaching is done using both the students' native language and English. It is transitional in that the emphasis gradually shifts over time from instruction in the native language to instruction in English. Crawford (1989) describes TBE goals:

> [TBE] provides a portion of instruction in LEP children's native language to help them keep up in school subjects, while they study English in programs designed for second-language learners. *The goal is to prepare students to enter mainstream English classrooms, a transition usually completed within two to three years* [italics added]. (p. 175)

A model of TBE is shown in Figure 9.1 to illustrate the shifting balance of native language (NL) and English (ENG) based instruction.

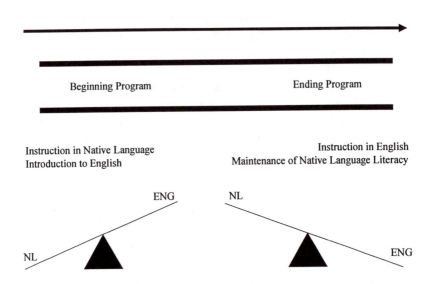

Figure 9.1. Transitional Bilingual Education Model for Shifting Balance Between Native Language (NL) and English (ENG).

The impact of the Lau Remedies has been two-fold. First, many school systems have used the Remedies as an advisory blueprint for setting up their programs, which yields many TBE programs in places where they are not mandated. Second, in the absence of other guidelines, the Lau Remedies have often been used by the federal government in consent decrees with school systems judged not to be in legal compliance. There was a proposal in the early 1980s to reformulate the Lau Remedies as official rules, but the proposal was withdrawn as one of the first acts of President Ronald Reagan's administration. The irony from the perspective of those opposed to bilingual education is that withdrawing the proposal let stand guidelines more rigorous than what had been proposed (Malakoff & Hakuta, 1990).

In the Lau Remedies, as everywhere in government statements, bilingual education exists to facilitate the learning of English language skills both oral and written. Where states or individual school systems have gone beyond that goal to include bicultural education or maintenance of the native language, they have done so without the requirement of federal government. Yet, in the main, bilingual pedagogy emphasizes a path away from the student's native language and toward mainstream education conducted in English.

Modifications to the Bilingual Education Act

The BEA has been modified in successive reauthorizations by the legislative branch of the federal government. Before *Lau,* the 1974 reauthorization dropped the low-income requirement for the target clientele of programs to be funded through federal grants. The 1978 reauthorization amended the provision for instruction in a child's native language by qualifying it to mean that this was necessary only to the extent that it would assist children in achieving competence in English. The 1984 reauthorization even opened the door in a limited way for programs that did not use any native language instruction, but the 1994 reauthorization stipulated that such programs were appropriate only when the particular population of students was small or no qualified teacher could be found. Yet all of these changes must be understood within the context of the many cases adjudicated and the many school programs modeled following the Lau Remedies.

The BEA received a boost for its rationale through one other legislative action: passage in 1974 of the Equal Educational Opportunities Act (EEOA). Following shortly after the *Lau* decision, this act extended the role of the federal government to public schools that did not receive federal aid. The EEOA prohibited states from denying "equal educational opportunity to an individual on account of his or her race, color, sex, or national origin" and required school districts to "take appropriate action to overcome language barriers that impede equal participation by its students in its instructional programs" (20 U.S.C. Sec. 1703f). In a 1981 appellate court case on behalf of a group of Mexican-American students and their parents in Raymondville, Texas (*Castañeda v. Pickard*), three criteria were stated as the test for whether or not a school district's approach would be judged "appropriate action": (a) that the "program [be] informed by an educational theory recognized as sound by some experts in the field," (b) that the program should be "reasonably calculated to implement effectively the educational theory adopted," and (c) that there must be "results indicating that the language barriers confronting students are actually being overcome" (*Castañeda v. Pickard,* 1981, pp. 1009-1010). These criteria outline only general parameters, all of which are open to interpretation by education experts, practitioners, and government officials.

As with many federal mandates, states have substantial authority in implementing and monitoring policies, and states in turn set requirements for school districts. States and school districts have responded in many different ways to the needs of students with limited or no English language proficiency. Massachusetts, for example, was the first state to enact its own requirements for TBE when its legislative body passed the Transitional Bilingual Education Act of 1967, which was implemented in 1971. This act, still in force today, required school districts with 20 or more children of the same non-English language group to offer the TBE approach. Other states have similar program requirements, although the threshold numbers differ from state to state.

Because pedagogical requirements for bilingual education have arisen based on court cases rather than through clear legislative action, uniformity is not assured. Students in different states and even in different school districts within the same state experience varied approaches. For example, if a Vietnamese student lives in a state where policy mandates bilingual education if 12 or more students with the same language background reside in the district and that student's family then moves to a state where the numerical threshold is 20, the reality could be an abrupt change in pedagogical approach.

As the federal government and states become increasingly embroiled in controversies over the education of America's LEP youth, the number of LEP students grows. According to the National Center for Education Statistics (1995), by 1993-1994, 3.07% of all public school students were participating in a bilingual education program, with another 3.97% in ESL programs (the combined total close to 3 million students). That number continues to move upward, and estimates put the number of different languages spoken by school-age children at 150 (Office of Bilingual Education, 1998).

The California Challenge

The most heated controversy over bilingual education programs has occurred in California, the state with the largest number of LEP students. In 1998, 1.4 million students received some type of bilingual education in California (Murr, 1998). Battles in this state over bilingual education heated up in 1997, when a citizen initiative to end California's current bilingual education programs was initiated. Called "English Language Education for the Children in Public Schools," the referendum was sponsored by Ronald

Unz, a wealthy software developer turned politician, with Gloria Matta Tuchman, a classroom teacher, as cosponsor.

On June 2, 1998, Proposition 227 was approved by 61% of the voters. It mandates the replacement of bilingual education with "sheltered English immersion"—meaning conventional English language classroom methods. Text of the referendum question stated that

> all children in California public schools shall be taught English by being taught in English. . . . Children who are English learners [meaning that their native language is not English and they are LEP] shall be educated through sheltered English immersion during a temporary transition period not normally intended to exceed one year. Local schools shall be permitted to place in the same classroom English learners of different ages but whose degree of English proficiency is similar. Local schools shall be encouraged to mix together in the same classroom English learners from different native-language groups but with the same degree of English fluency. (Unz & Tuchman, 1997, p. 2)

The referendum question spells out policy in such a way that parents who want their children in bilingual education must petition the school. If the parents do nothing—either because they choose not to or because they lack information and confidence to do so—their children are to be taught in an essentially English-only educational environment. Proposition 227 stipulates not only that parents must petition but that there must be petitions on behalf of at least 20 students in the same grade level at the same school for a bilingual class to be provided. Yet even though the proposition's stipulations are official policy, many parents have petitioned for bilingual services, and some school districts have found ways to provide bilingual education while abiding by the legal requirements. As of this writing, there is some indication that the views of the new governor of California, Gray Davis (a Democrat), may lead to a more positive climate for bilingual education. There is ample educated opinion not only to allow but to support such pedagogy and its underlying philosophy. One expert on language learning and bilingual education, Stephen Krashen (1997), countered Proposition 227 by saying,

> Bilingual education is sensible. . . . Bilingual education gives children subject-matter knowledge and thus speeds their English language development. Also, children who develop literacy in their primary language have a much easier time developing literacy in English. (p. 6)

Whether or not Proposition 227 fuels similar measures elsewhere or remains peculiar to California is an open question. With California a bellwether, we can expect prolonged debates about public language policy to occupy citizens throughout the country for many years to come.

Methods and Mind-Sets
for Teaching LEP Students

Analysis of the debate over bilingual education requires understanding of both (a) the variations in pedagogies that have been developed and implemented and (b) the attitudes and mind-sets associated with different positions on the issues involved. The debates over effectiveness, whether waged by academics or nonspecialists, typically involve both substantive and political/value-oriented perspectives. Unfortunately, the political discourse and mass media coverage of bilingual education too often focus on superficial or biased presentation of the substantive issues to support more elaborated viewpoints regarding politics and attitudes toward diversity. In this section, the main methods for instructing LEP students are described, followed by commentary on the ways in which political, legislative, and media treatments reduce the complexities involved.

As outlined in the previous section, the BEA and the move toward TBE resulting from it operationally define what most educators designate as bilingual education, meaning education using both native and English language instruction with the balance shifting from the native language to English and normal, mainstream classes. Other pedagogies exist, the most common five of which are described below.

Immersion

Immersion programs are familiar in the U.S. context mainly as alternatives offered in many suburbs and some urban schools for English speakers to learn Spanish or French, beginning at the kindergarten level. The model for these programs comes from Canada, where this approach was initially developed to teach French to native English-speaking children. Where used for LEP children, the method is the same, that is, to place the children with teachers who are bilingual but in a classroom context where English is the medium of instruction. One particular method used in this approach is designated *structured immersion*. As described by McKay (1988), English is used for instruction, but students can ask questions and make comments in their native language if they are having difficulty in the target language. The teacher, however, "will respond only in English" (p. 354).

Concurrent Translation

Concurrent translation literally means to shift back and forth in the classroom between English and the native language of students. As such, it is a bilingual method by virtue of the emphasis placed on both languages and the grouping of students together by native language group. Yet most commentators on the method fault it because students can easily avoid the target language (English in this case) in favor of their native language, and teachers often emphasize one language over the other (Crawford, 1989).

English as a Second Language (ESL)

ESL pedagogy can be found in almost any school with LEP students. The common threads across ESL approaches are the presence of students from different language backgrounds in the same classroom and the "pullout classes" for which these students leave their regular classroom instruction. Although methods for ESL instruction vary, the ESL classroom is the site for English language instruction using methodology developed for teaching English as a foreign language. Early approaches to ESL emphasized grammar, but the more common approach today is based on content and task requirements of academic subjects; in this approach, the English language training is articulated to the rest of the student's school curriculum. Ideally, instructors of ESL are certified, but they will not usually possess fluency in the native languages of those being instructed. Literally, ESL is not a method of bilingual education but, rather, a method of English education for those with no or limited proficiency; as such, the ESL method relies completely on assimilationist assumptions.

Developmental Bilingual Education

In many ways, developmental bilingual education (also called "maintenance" bilingual education) is the only genuinely *bi*lingual method because its purpose is to develop the student's native language fluency and literacy while teaching English. Developmental pedagogies emphasize the importance of bilingualism and often include cultural as well as language education. In some cases, this approach is termed *bilingual/bicultural* education. By fostering bilingualism, these programs are structured to achieve what is called *additive bilingualism* rather than *subtractive bilingualism,* which is the more common programmatic approach, in which a student's native language is gradually replaced in school by English.

Two-Way Bilingual Education

The two-way approach employs a range of methods through which bilingualism is developed in all children, including those reared in monolingual English environments. Two-way bilingual education takes the philosophy of developmental programs a significant step further by emphasizing the educational priority for a bilingual citizenry. One method for this type of instruction is language immersion, in which all students are immersed in a second language until they develop sufficient fluency to be able to deal in a common classroom environment conducted in both languages. Another method puts children from two different language backgrounds together so that the students are part of the two-way teaching process. Two-way bilingual education programs are uncommon, with their cost cited as the major reason. I will return to this approach in the final section of this chapter.

The Fulcrum of Attitudes

Evaluating the effectiveness of different programs and methods for teaching English to LEP students should be the critical factor in making policy decisions for the future. Attitudes about languages and cultures, however, shape many of the perspectives on program evaluation and often underlie the policy debates that are raging in localities, states, and the federal government. Unfortunately, evaluation of bilingual education and ESL methods has been just as controversial and political as the subject matter at issue. At least on the surface, many research results are inconclusive or even contradictory, with studies sometimes framed in ways that guarantee a politically expedient outcome. The case can be made one way or another based on many different approaches to assessment (see, for example, Ambert, 1991; August & Hakuta, 1997; Chavez, 1991; Crawford, 1997; Porter, 1996; Ramirez, Yuen, Ramey, Pasta, & Billings, 1991). The root issue for those against bilingual education—academics, politicians, and members of the general public alike—has more to do with beliefs about cultural pluralism and cultural assimilation than about teaching effectiveness. If teaching effectiveness were the main issue, then the debates would center on pedagogy rather than on ideology and policy—that is, how to improve the language abilities and linguistic competitiveness of *all* children regardless of their native language. As a comparison, imagine abolishing math instruction in the face of dismal math performance by students.

What tends to happen in the attitudinal insertions to language policy questions mirrors what happens in many public policy debates: The issues become polarized around falsely drawn alternatives. The most common in the domain of language is to equate allegiance to English with patriotism and American behavior; in such a polarization, those who wish to retain and develop their native language are seen as divisive, unpatriotic, and unwilling to accommodate to the American way of life. One outspoken Hispanic critic, Linda Chavez (1991), who was staff director of the U.S. Commission on Civil Rights during President Reagan's administration, typifies this line of reasoning when she pits bilingual education—construed as part of affirmative action—against immigrant assimilation:

> Previous immigrants had been eager to become "American," to learn the language, to fit in. But the entitlements of the civil rights era encouraged Hispanics to maintain their language and culture, their separate identity, in return for the rewards of being members of an officially recognized minority group. Assimilation gave way to affirmative action. (p. 5)

A variation on the line of reasoning developed by Chavez makes cultural pride oppositional to the ideology of "one people with a common language." Former Secretary of Education William Bennett (1988) takes this position in his views about common culture. Bennett asserts that bilingual education, as a vehicle for instilling cultural pride in children, detracts from national unity and the discourse of democracy.

Whether at the federal, state, or local level, it is impossible to talk about bilingual education without understanding the attitudinal understructure that polarizes discussion and debate. This is not to suggest that reasoned arguments are devoid of attitudes; they are not.

Those who support bilingual education hold attitudes that shape the particular pedagogies they favor. One can support the letter of the law regarding bilingual education while still maintaining the goal of eventual fluency in English, diminution of the native language, and embracing an attitudinal posture of melting pot ideology; in this case, bilingual education is a path to one public discourse conducted in English. One can also support cultural pluralism if bilingual education is taken to mean fluency and literacy in two languages; in this case, bilingual education is a path to multiple discourses in the public as well as the private domain.

For all the criticisms that have been leveled against bilingual education, one fact remains. There has never been an anti-English movement in the United States, nor have voices been raised to counter the proposition that English is essential to both opportunity and citizen participation. Advocates for bilingual education recognize the difficulty of second-language learning and see benefits for both the individual and the larger society of diverse cultural practices and the cultural identities embedded in those practices. Opponents more often than not oversimplify what is involved when a child must learn a second language and overstate the status of English as a common world language (Fishman, 1998).

No one would expect the question of how best to educate speakers of languages other than English to be controversy-free. Different programs exist for teaching most school subjects, and controversies abound when it comes to choices between, for instance, structured versus open classrooms, graded versus ungraded assessment of student performance, or "whole language" versus phonics as a way to develop basic language skills. Some states, in fact, have incorporated the controversies over bilingual education into their regulations. Florida offers the option of structured immersion or bilingual education (unfortunately referred to as "fast track" and "slow track"). Like most subjects, development of English language fluency and literacy likely cannot be accomplished by a "one size fits all" model. The weighing of alternatives, however, should openly articulate both the ideological positions implied within certain pedagogies and the complex connections between language as an expressive system of culture and the less visible cultural dimensions giving shape to language practice. Failure to articulate either amounts to the assertion that language is culturally neutral.

Is Bilingual Education a Threat to American English?

No evidence exists that English in the United States is being eroded or displaced by other languages, including Spanish. The presence of speech communities in which languages other than English are spoken indicates the coherence of cultural groups, just as does the presence of speech communities where particular varieties of American English can be heard.

The cultural practices and beliefs packed into bilingual education as a semantic notion are complex. Perspectives range from uninformed wide angles to telescopic detail out of context. The term itself is confusing and misleading. *Bi-* means *two,* yet the *bi-* in *bilingual* is only preparatory to English language education. Catherine Snow and Kenji Hakuta (1992) make this point bluntly: "Bilingual education in its present form may be one of the greatest misnomers of educational programs. What it fosters is monolingualism; bilingual classrooms are efficient revolving doors between home-language monolingualism and English monolingualism" (p. 390). A more literal meaning of the term suggests an approach in which fluency and literacy are developed in two languages.

U.S. educational practices offer little aimed at preserving cultural diversity. The most dramatic examples come from policies for dealing with Native Americans and their languages. Only a fine line divides those who supported the eradication of native languages and those who oppose bilingual education. The line is also fine between policy positions on "foreign languages" and policies addressed to marginalized, culturally marked varieties of English, which brings us to the recent controversy over the status of African American English in educational practice.

The Strange Case of Ebonics

On December 18, 1996, the Oakland, California, School Board passed a resolution the effect of which would be to educate speakers of AAVE in a manner similar to students in bilingual education programs. This action—the outcome of a local school district's struggle with how best to confront the poor academic performance of its African American students—immediately skyrocketed into national headline news. In what developed as a media frenzy, Oakland's action was quickly denounced, often in a manner that denigrated and poked fun at what Oakland had chosen to term *Ebonics.*

The Oakland Ebonics case provides an intense national episode evidencing everything from overt racism to irresponsible articulation of opinion devoid of even the most superficial knowledge of the issues involved. As the case saturated the mass media during the 1996 yuletide season and into early 1997, its strangeness became increasingly pronounced. Three aspects of the case show just how strange it was, seeming to come from a zero-context situation. First, the Oakland Ebonics case played out as an ahistorical episode completely disconnected from the 30-odd years of research on African

American language varieties and pedagogical initiatives to teach Standard American English (SAE) to AAVE users. Second, it surfaced every manner of racist and sometimes self-contradictory discourse. Third, it demonstrated just how deeply intolerant (and perhaps fearful) many Americans are of language diversity. Linguistic experts were virtually absent from mainstream media coverage, whereas experts in other fields, political figures, and star-quality African American artists and writers took center stage to have their say—most of which was negative. To better understand the strangeness of this case, I look first at the Oakland policy and then at the way the news media shaped the issues to set the national agenda heavily against what the Oakland School committee had proposed.

Much Ado About "What?"

The resolution passed by the Oakland School Board was intent on address-ing the disproportionate failure of its African American students. The board appointed a special task force and, based on its recommendations, considered a policy the primary purpose of which was "to improve the English language acquisition and application skills of African American students" ("Resolu-tion," 1996). Citing research on African American language as the foundation for viewing Ebonics as a distinctive language, the board voted the following policy:

> that the Superintendent . . . shall immediately devise and implement the best possible academic program for imparting instruction to African American students in their primary language *for the combined purposes of maintaining the legitimacy and richness of such language* [italics added] whether it is known as "Ebonics," "African Language Systems," "Pan African Communication Behaviors" or other description, *and to facilitate their acquisition and mastery of English language skills* [italics added].

The original resolution, then, appeared very similar to bilingual education policies in taking a dual focus on maintaining native language variety and developing facility in Standard English. Opponents and those aware only of the sound-bite media coverage of the issue seized on the first purpose only, that is, the teaching of Ebonics *rather than SAE* to African American stu-dents. This, combined with an ill-chosen definition of Ebonics as "genetically-based," precipitated a firestorm of reaction, which will be discussed in this section.

By mid-January 1997, *Ebonics* and *Oakland* were seared into the public mind through a flurry of media spotlights. Oakland's School Board responded to many of the criticisms in the form of a revised resolution. The amended resolution ("Resolution," 1997) reworded the purpose of the policy:

> *The combined purposes [will be] facilitating the acquisition and mastery of English language skills, while respecting and embracing the legitimacy and richness of* [italics added] the language patterns . . . known as *Ebonics* [etc.].

In a separate document ("Resolution," 1997), the first recommendation for dealing with the problems of African American students stated, "African American students shall develop English language proficiency as the foundation for their achievements in all core competency areas"—a statement that hardly suggests replacing Standard English with Ebonics!

Media Representations

If the mass media had highlighted the Oakland School Board's official statements about Ebonics and the scholarly research on African American language, "Ebonics in Oakland" would have been a significantly different issue in the public mind than it turned out to be. For the most part, however, journalistic accounts (both "news" and "feature" stories) created a tone of ridicule toward Ebonics and ignored expert linguistic opinion. Ebonics quickly became shorthand for a host of stereotypic notions about African American English and for a deeper-seated expression of racism, sometimes disguised in rhetoric proclaiming to be in the best interest of African American urban youth. Not surprisingly, when the final report of Oakland's task force was issued in May 1997, the word (but not the ideas behind) *Ebonics* had been dropped because of its volatility.

A sampling of statements made in the days following December 18, 1996, demonstrates how the scale of legitimacy quickly weighed heavily against Ebonics. News stories hit most of the nation's papers on December 20 or 21, 1996. Close to Oakland, the *Los Angeles Times* carried a front-page article on December 20 (Woo & Curtis, 1996) and another article on December 21 (Woo & Moore, 1996) that reported the story with reasonable accuracy.

These stories did not use the term Ebonics in their headlines, but the first one did imply that the policy emphasized teaching Ebonics rather than using Ebonics as a foundation to teach Standard English. On the other side of the continent, where the story became national news, the *New York Times* began its coverage on December 20 (Applebome, 1996) with an article titled "School District Elevates Status of Black English"—again no *headlined* Ebonics.

The story might have died down had not Jesse Jackson appeared on *Meet the Press* on Sunday, December 22. In his typically forceful manner, Jackson criticized the decision as "an unacceptable surrender bordering on disgrace. . . . It's teaching down to our children, and it must never happen" (in Lewis, 1996, p. A18). Newscasters around the country quoted Jackson, yet no one called attention to the fact that Jackson himself frequently uses communicative forms clearly marked by African American style. Jackson softened his views after meeting with school officials and sociolinguists, but the power of his initial statement, as it saturated the news, set the public agenda for what to think about Ebonics.

Following quickly after Jackson's denouncement, U.S. Secretary of Education Richard Riley informed the nation on Christmas Eve that federal funds would not be available to assist Oakland. He pronounced Black English to be slang rather than a language, "a nonstandard form of English" that the federal government would not elevate to "the status of a language" (Harris, 1996, p. A15).

Newspapers continued to feature the Oakland Ebonics story. For example, one story in mid-January (Zernike, 1997, p. A1) described a program using Ebonics in South Central Los Angeles, which had been ongoing for 6 years. The article began with a student's answer in Ebonics to being asked the meaning of *justice,* followed by the teacher's translation of it for the class:

If somebody get somethin' an' you don't give nothin' to somebody else, that ain't justice. (Ebonics)

If someone gets something and someone else doesn't, that's not justice. (Standard English)

The portion of the article appearing on the front page ends with the statement that there is no "hard evidence" that the pedagogy works, whereas there is plenty of evidence of other ills in the schools that need addressing; the implication to be read between the lines is that Ebonics diverts both resources and priorities.

The editorial pages also contained a number of strongly worded position statements. There were some positive pieces, but the quantity and tone of negative statements overwhelmed them. Where the negative response came from African Americans, the effect was especially potent. Leonard Pitts, Jr., an African American columnist writing for *The Miami Herald,* characterized the use of Ebonics in education as "absurd, asinine, imbecilic and moronic . . . most of all though . . . deeply, profoundly insulting." One of the more vitriolic assaults on Ebonics came in an opinion piece by James Shaw (1996), an African American consultant for the Los Angeles County Office of Education. Published in the *Los Angeles Times* on December 27, Shaw's editorial characterizes Ebonics as "nothing more than a linguistic sham that, with porcupine gluttony, vacuum-sucks every verbal deformity from plantation patios to black slang, from rap to hip hop, from jive to crippled English, and serves up the resultant gumbo as 'black English' " (p. B9).

Mass circulation magazines also had their say. Consider these headlines. *Newsweek* led with "Hooked on Ebonics: A muddled plan to teach black English in the schools made outraged headlines, but the actual teaching methods may make sense" (Leland & Joseph, 1997, p. 78). Although the headline focus of the story is relatively balanced, "Hooked on Ebonics" as a play on "Hooked on Phonics" trivializes the topic, and the assertion of a "muddled plan" undermines Oakland's entire approach. Writing in *Forbes,* economist Thomas Sowell (1997, p. 48) reduced the issue to one of funding with his title "Ebonics: Follow the Money" (a play on the often quoted "show me the money" from the then popular film *Jerry Maquire*). Venturing far from his field, Sowell felt comfortable concluding that Ebonics is just the product of various British influences. *The New Republic,* known for its conservative leanings, headlined its story "Speech Therapy: Ebonics—It's Worse Than You Think" (Heilbrunn, 1997, p. 216). Even *The Nation,* a largely liberally focused magazine, positioned the issue with the headline "Classroom Rap" (Verdelle, 1997, p. 264). The article is written by an African American statistical consultant/recently published novelist who argues with some complexity that teaching through an Ebonics methodology is racist. She concludes that "the ebonics idea seems a faulty simplification, an approach that lacks analysis, a freezeframe of schools and teachers and children teetering on the precipice of total collapse and failure" (Verdelle, 1997, p. 265). In *The New*

Yorker, Louis Menand (1997) double puns with his title "Johnny Be Good: Ebonics and the Language of Cultural Separatism" (p. 5)—calling on the sophisticated readership's associations with both the older headline "Why Johnny Can't Read" and the syntactic use of habitual *be* in the AAVE variety.

Perhaps the most blatantly racist press representation of the Ebonics issue appeared in cartoons. In the January 13, 1997 issue of *Newsweek,* a Bevis and Butthead cartoon by Nick Anderson showed the two characters with a sign reading "Moron + Phonics = Moronics" which they were carrying into the U.S. Department of Education's funding office. On January 5, 1997, the *New York Times* ran a cartoon depicting a parody of Hamlet's famous soliloquy, with the cartoon character exclaiming "I Be, or I Don't Be Dat's Whuzzup." Without even mentioning the word Ebonics, which had become a household term, a cartoon in the January 20, 1997 issue of the *Boston Globe* characterized the Middle East conflict by showing two men sitting at a table; above one a sign reads "Speaks only Palestinics," and above the other a sign reads, "Speaks only Hebronics." This kind of biting wordplay was a likely stimulus for the Internet joke page on Ebonics that included among its parody terms: Jewish-American Speak—Zionics; Native-American Speak—Kimosabics; Chinese-American Speak—Won-tonics; and Eskimo-American Speak—Harpoonics ("New Languages," 1997). The home page that displayed this list also invites readers to submit their Ebonics jokes.

In all this vitriolic media opinion, it was difficult to find the voice of linguistic scholarship, or a substantive discussion of African American English, or anything related to the history of pedagogy used to teach Standard English to speakers of AAVE. Occasional quotes appeared from black language experts such as William Labov, John Baugh, or Geneva Smitherman, but they were usually buried deep in the article. A few magazine articles offered supporting arguments for Oakland's proposal, but they were few and seldom mainstream. One of the best series of pieces ("Ebonics," 1997) appeared in the January 14, 1997 issue of *The Village Voice* (hardly a mainstream magazine). *Essence,* a magazine marketed to a black readership, included a thoughtful analysis by Khephra Burns (1997), who concisely pointed out that "Ebonics would never have inspired such controversy and concern if Black English were not so influential" (p. 150). In the various "samplers" of Ebonics, one rarely encountered anything amounting to a general description of what a language variety is from a linguistic point of view, or what rules govern AAVE that make it more than a bad approximation of SAE. In the absence of clear information about the linguistic integrity of varieties such as AAVE, the force of terms like *slang* and *street language* became central in identifying the character of Ebonics.

The Missing Link of Ann Arbor

One of the strangest aspects of the Oakland Ebonics case was the conspicuous absence in almost all accounts of information of a precedent-setting court case in Ann Arbor, Michigan. In 1979, a U.S. district court judge ordered the school board in Ann Arbor to rectify its teaching approach for African American children at the Martin Luther King, Jr. Elementary School (*Martin Luther King, Jr., Elementary School Children v. Ann Arbor School District Board,* 1979). A class action suit had been brought on behalf of 15 children whose parents were concerned about their lack of progress in school. The case for the plaintiffs was developed by using expert witnesses who detailed the linguistic profile of what was known at the time about Black English Vernacular. Geneva Smitherman offered extensive evidence based on the analysis of BEV features evident in tape recordings of the students involved in the case. William Labov (1982) credits her testimony for favorable news accounts of the case and "the only informed and accurate accounts of Black English that have appeared in the press so far" (p. 171).

The judge in the case, Charles Joiner, ordered the Ann Arbor School Board to institute a program to train teachers in Black English so they could more effectively teach their students for whom BEV was a native language variety. The case rested on arguments related to the failure of the school to take action to "overcome linguistic barriers that impede equal participation by its students in its instructional programs" (Title 20 of the U.S. Code, Section 1703, as cited in Labov, 1982, p. 169).

The case was a landmark for educational pedagogy related to the teaching of children whose first language variety is AAVE, but it was all but erased as relevant for Oakland. When Ann Arbor was mentioned, the references were brief and never prominently placed.

Oakland Ebonics as Sign

Taken together, the representations of the Oakland Ebonics case lead to disturbing conclusions because of what those representations surfaced about racist attitudes and about both attitudes toward and basic knowledge regarding human language. One conclusion to be drawn from the strange case of

Ebonics is that knowledge played little role in how the issue developed in the public domain. The many media representations and the general level of public misunderstanding of the case revealed total disconnection from both scholarly inquiry into the history and current characteristics of varieties of American English spoken by African Americans and the very nature of language use in a diverse, culturally complex society. Geneva Smitherman and Sylvia Cunningham (1997) summed up what occurred in late December 1996 and early January 1997 by saying "Today's negative pronouncements on Ebonics reveal a serious lack of knowledge about the scientific approach to language analysis and a galling ignorance about what Ebonics is and who speaks it" (p. 227).

For several generations of people, Ebonics will likely remain a sign for negative conceptions of the language of African Americans, a conception associated with verbal deprivation, improper English, rap, and gutter talk. That conception bears startling similarity to the prevailing views that existed prior to the growth of linguistic scholarship on this subject beginning some 30 years ago. If my own students are any indication of what happens when lack of knowledge about an issue is replaced by careful analysis, they are a good barometer of public opinion. At the beginning of a course on language policy issues, most of my students leaned toward the negative side in their attitudes about the Oakland resolution on Ebonics. After a semester during which they read relevant scholarship and considered Oakland as a case study of language policy in the making, the weight of opinion swung heavily. The combination of assigned readings about the history and current status of African American communication and analyses of media constructions of the case left everyone quite certain that the public "information" available about the Ebonics case seriously misrepresented what was at issue. Politics, glib reporting, and opinions masquerading as information displaced substantive coverage and analysis of the case. The lessons about the mass media are sobering, but the deeper national ignorance about language and language policy suggest a seriously flawed approach to language education. One avenue for addressing the deeper national problem regarding language is to consider the role of Standard English alongside both enhanced linguistic literacy and universal bilingual education. Both linguistic literacy and universal bilingual education could serve the larger needs of a citizenry increasingly multicultural and multilingual in a world of complexly connected discourses.

"Standard English" and Universal Bilingual Education

The furor over Ebonics and proposals to curtail bilingual education for LEP students share in common an intolerance for language diversity. Both also reveal national attitudes about language deeply lodged in an education system that embraces American English monolingualism. The American educational system has by most accounts failed to teach the majority of students how to write and speak effectively. Although there are no simple solutions to these ills of language education, it is fair to say that few students grasp even the basics of what languages are all about and how they relate to personal and cultural identities. In the quest to teach all students what the prescriptive grammarians have moved into traditional language arts basics, there is no glimpse of the language forest comprising all the grammatical trees. Hammering the rules of Standard English (usually known to students simply as "language" or "writing" or "speech") while disregarding languages other than English until later in the educational process—and then only for some students—inflicts young learners with limited ideas about the power of language. Students are not taught to reflect on their own way of speaking as a marker of identity nor on the processes of cultural reasoning expressed through language. Students virtually never possess sufficient knowledge of descriptive linguistics to even think about what a dialect is or why the verb system works so differently in a language other than English; even more serious is the likelihood that the vast majority of teachers, including those who teach English, lack elementary knowledge of linguistics or language as a cultural resource.

One approach to better preparing youth for the discourses of a multi-cultural society would include both clarifying the nature and role of Standard English—partly to facilitate its development in individual learners and partly to demystify it—and initiating an approach to language education stressing universal bilingual education. I consider each part of this agenda in the sections that follow.

Why and Whither "Standard English"?

Throughout this book, Standard English has been presented as one variety of English among many. Standard English is neither descriptive of what most people speak and write, nor is the conception and modeling of it everywhere the same. The latter point demands that the qualification of *American* or *U.S.* be made to distinguish one national variety from another from another, thus the term *Standard American English* (SAE). One standard linguistics text defines SAE as "an idealized dialect of English that is considered by some prescriptive grammarians to be the proper form of English" ((Fromkin & Rodman, 1998, p. 537). In this definition, the words *idealized, dialect,* and *proper* all convey special aspects of SAE as a language variety: (a) Ideals are often not realized but become important because they are models, (b) a dialect is one of many forms of a language, and (c) speaking proper English conveys the notion of prestige. Thus, SAE is an idealized notion of proper dialect. Another text's author adds something regarding contexts for the standard variety: "There is a variety of English [called Standard English] in the U.S. used widely on the public media (movie, radio, television) and in schools and other public institutions" (Gee, 1993, p. 334). This broad definition pivots on the proposition that public language reflects standard features. Another way to think about "standard" varieties of any language is to construe standardness as a product of education and superimposition, that is, as a variety consciously superimposed on spoken and written language through an explicit process of teaching and learning for the purpose of cultivating usage deemed to reflect education and at least some degree of decorum.

We expect to hear SAE when we speak to a teller or officer at a bank, when we interact with court officials, when we turn on the television for the evening news, when we talk on the telephone to a customer service representative for a utility company; and we expect to read SAE when we scan a newspaper or a magazine, look over a bank's terms and conditions for credit cards, study a proposal made by someone at work, or try to follow the instructions for how to put together a child's toy or a computer system. In other words, SAE as a common, public, formalized variety serves many purposes. Having said that, we all know of many exceptions to the "proper ideal" we expect, and depending on where one lives, spoken SAE sounds a certain way because of the regional varieties.

SAE as a prescriptive ideal accounts for why so much attention is paid to its improvement. It is just that: an ideal. Few people speak in the prescriptively ordained ideal variety. Even the most polished writers occasionally depart from the formally taught standard variety.

More than occasional departures from the ideal (what some call lapses) are evident as well. We have all heard successful politicians use varieties so heavily marked for regional identity that those outside the person's region find their speech humorous. Some judges speak with pronounced ethnic-regional dialects. Store owners feature themselves in local advertisements for their products or services using patterns of speech that are characterized as everything from regional to folksy to lower class. Yet these people are all successful in their respective areas of work.

SAE has such symbolic force, however, that failure to approximate it can function as one of the main gatekeepers for success in school, work, and community. When the gatekeeping function is largely a sign for attitudes about race, ethnicity, ancestry, and the like, its legitimacy is questionable. When the gatekeeping function is pragmatically tied to communication, the standard variety takes on a role analogous to a *lingua franca*—or a common language used to facilitate communication among diverse peoples. In this sense, SAE is a commonly agreed-on variety that binds together those involved in a particular activity or function.

SAE as both touchstone for attitudes and as *lingua franca* will likely become more rather than less important in the United States in the near future. Just as English continues to be the common national language (and will remain so), an idealized standard variety will continue to guide the development of reading, writing, and speaking in the educational process. What is critical, however, is elaborating for students a much better understanding of what a standard variety is and how it functions. Linguistic minorities, whether native English speakers whose primary speech communities lie outside the well-educated Eurowhite population or native speakers of languages other than English, understand the role of the standard variety better than do monolingual Anglos. But this understanding needs to go beyond what speakers of nonprestige varieties believe about their language use, that is, their judgment that they speak "incorrectly." All students, and the general public as well, deserve to know what linguists know, which is that

SAE is an idealized dialect, imposed on native speech, that is judged by grammarians from a particular cultural background to be proper written and oral usage.

We can agree that a common variety has many useful functions and that advantages accrue to those who use the variety deemed standard. Yet we can also teach people that deviations from the standard weigh negatively when their users are judged to be marginal, minority, working or underclass, and not well educated, but they matter little and can even enhance prestige when their users are judged to be of high social status, dominant, powerful, and well educated. No one would ever have proposed, for example, that President John Kennedy enroll in a therapeutic program of dialect reduction, but this is the prescription for many African Americans and white working-class individuals who aspire to professional success.

For those who maintain the fussiest and most stubborn attitudes about what they perceive SAE to be, linguistically oriented explanations of the range of Englishes spoken and written around the world are also in order. English may be growing as the world language and as the *lingua franca* of business and trade, but divergent systems of English are also evident as the cultural identities of regionally different populations influence the phonology, lexicon, syntax, and pragmatics of English language use. Including at least basic information about world Englishes in the language curriculum of U.S. students would provide a useful context for understanding both the variability among varieties deemed "standard" around the world and the nature of language as a contextual, cultural system.

Universal Bilingual Education

For several decades, the United States has explicitly acknowledged the dismal failure of its schools in teaching foreign language. In the late 1970s, then-President Jimmy Carter appointed the special Commission on Foreign Language and International Studies to investigate how the nation could better teach its students to move beyond monolingualism (Burn, 1980). The rationale for appointing the Commission acknowledged the growing need for Americans to be aware of the world around them and to move beyond their U.S.-centered views. President Carter achieved international recognition, for example, when he served as a model for bilingual competence by delivering a speech in Mexico in both Spanish and English.

In describing the foreign language problem in the United States, Barbara Burn (1980), the Commission's executive director, cited "poor teaching . . . too little teaching and too short an exposure to the language [being learned]" (p. 50). The Commission provided many soundly crafted recommendations, and, for a brief period of time at least, guarded optimism existed among educators that progress might be made. Various states established guidelines for high school curricula, and state-supported colleges and universities outlined minimal levels of foreign language study to be required for admission to their institutions. The results of these initiatives, however, barely made a dent in the monolith of monolingualism. More students were exposed to languages other than English, but learning remained rudimentary and rote. Furthermore, introduction of languages other than English continued to be put off until after the elementary school years, which, by implication, sent the wrong message about the priority for second-language learning. On the teaching side of the problem, little progress was evident a decade later when a 1987 survey (Thompson, Christian, Stansfield, & Rhodes, 1990) revealed that among teachers providing instruction in languages other than English, 44% of those in elementary schools and 63% of those in secondary schools were not native speakers of the languages they were teaching, and half in elementary schools were not certified.

The situation today is no better. The ramifications of the ideology and reality of monolingualism loom even more intensively, however, than they did two decades ago when the presence of languages other than English was just beginning to become part of the contemporary national scene. With few exceptions, the rote learning pedagogies of yesteryear continue to be used in today's schools. Students find little motivation to learn a language other than English, and emphasis on conversational skills is limited. Comprehensive foreign language instruction has also been deemed too costly to contemplate, a judgment seated in short- rather than long-term impact. Clearly, little progress has been made, resulting in the need to once again examine national policy ("Foreign Language Policy," 1994).

What differs for the United States, as we enter the new century, from the conditions even 20 years ago is the certainty that languages other than English and cultures differing from mainstream America will be more rather than less common in the foreseeable future. The stability of the Hispanic population and its growth through immigration, coupled with the ever-increasing stream of immigrants from Asian countries, ensure, as we have seen in earlier chapters, a linguistic climate of diversity in the United States. Developments in technology and transportation also ensure continued globalization and widen the prospects for human contacts across cultures and languages.

The best solution to the dual problems of effective bilingual education for LEPs and effective second-language instruction for monolingual English speakers is a comprehensive program of universal, two-way bilingual education in the United States. If bilingual education were to be universal in the United States—just like education in math, science, and social studies—all students would have a chance to develop both competency in a second language and more complex appreciation for the nature of language and its role in personal and cultural identity.

Several features of universal bilingual education make it an attractive option for the United States. Most important, such an approach would shift the perspective on language diversity from that of problem to that of resource. Second, as a resource, bilingual facility offers the possibility for a new generation of American youth who are better equipped that those educated in the 20th century to understand people both in the United States and throughout the world. There is probably no better way to appreciate distinctively different worldviews than to learn a second language. Third, universal bilingual education would contribute pragmatically to the prospects of those who will come to adulthood in the 21st century. Because of global connections, the demand for fluent speakers and writers in languages other than English continues to grow. The person who has command of both English and another language, especially if that second language is Spanish, will have many more options as the next century unfolds. Finally, universal bilingual education will destigmatize bilingual education for students whose native languages differ from English. In some instances, students will be able to assist and coach one another. Ideally, they will develop mutual respect for the difficulty and promise associated with learning a language different from one's native tongue.

Universal bilingual education is no panacea for the ills of the U.S. educational system or for the attitudes underlying racism and cultural elitism. It will work only if investments are sufficient and long term and if the commitment includes incorporating new pedagogies into the curriculum. Even more important to this project will be the challenge of building national support for multilingualism. Sandra McKay's (1988) observation that "two-way bilingual programs . . . [where they are successful] reflect a social belief that multilingualism is beneficial for both dominant and minority language groups" (p. 358) identifies a component essential to considering a shift to universal bilingual education. In addition to educators, politicians and the mass media will need to contribute more than they have in the past to thoughtful analysis and public service information about language education.

As the metaphor of the melting pot becomes more inadequate to describe the reality of the U.S. population, new avenues to national identity become more pressing. From being a nation of immigrants and mature cultural communities, the United States has the potential to be a nation of cultures woven together to complement one another. Because language functions so centrally in defining individual and social identities, greater investment in language training for all students promises at least some positive impact on the broader challenge of establishing coherence and interconnectedness among the diverse cultural groups populating the United States.

Implications

Bilingual education may on the surface appear to be a policy issue directed clearly and simply to the best interests of school children in the United States for whom English is not a native language. As tempting as it might be to see the issue so sharply focused, we miss much of the complexity associated with debates over methods and outcomes by reducing the issue to one mainly about pedagogy. Rather, bilingual education has become a site for a host of issues related to language and cultural diversity, but often the deeper issues go unvoiced and unacknowledged—especially in mass media accounts. The ideological hold of monolingualism coupled with the illusion that the United States is or ever was monocultural produce discourse about bilingual education that rarely addresses the full story.

National ideology about both the melting pot and the separation of public and private life has exerted considerable influence on the discourse about language diversity in the United States. Attitudes about bilingual education, about the vitality of languages other than English, and by implication about varieties of English associated with cultural minorities arise in a complex way from the seemingly simple ideological notion that commonly adhered-to mixing processes can eliminate differences by bringing them into a blend of common consistency. The melting pot metaphor has long been a slogan for this process, even though the slogan glosses over the harsh imagery of its root metaphor. Although the resulting product of the literal melting pot may be strong, the heat needed to break down the properties and borders of its ingredients destroys the identity of those ingredients. Melting pot ideology, as a recurring affirmation for the possibility of a monoculture nation with "one language," just as surely results only from harsh force on the distinctive identities and discourses that supposedly will flow into oneness. In this ideology, SAE holds prominence as the essential dynamic of that monoculture.

The ideology of public-private life also lies beneath much of the debate about bilingual education and American English diversity. This aspect of

U.S. national ideology allows for a convenient separation of languages other than English from English and of marked varieties from the "standard" by relegating the former in each pair to the private domain and the later to the public domain. The argument frequently made is that all languages are welcome in the United States, as long as they are kept in the private domain, and that all dialects such as AAVE belong in their place—a place apart from the public mainstream.

Ironically, even in the context of support for bilingual education and dialect diversity, such support is rarely joined with more expansive concerns for the cultural systems from which language varieties arise. Cultural studies have not been evident in school curricula except for those studies of culture exotically focused or placed into the context of learning about different countries around the world. When culture is central, its meaning is usually left implicit, as in the case of literature courses where African American or Hispanic authors are required reading but often without sufficient cultural education to make cultural (rather than sociological) points about subject matter and narrative development. Even the most general aspects of cultural orientation associated with, for instance, Latino/a concepts of spirituality or Confucian foundations of much Asian thought are missing in school curricula. Likewise, traditions in African American culture for verbal artistry remain invisible when the language of urban black youth is at issue.

I began this book by juxtaposing the richly expanding terrain of languages and cultures in the United States with examples of white Anglo hostility targeted at language diversity. Language-targeted hostility usually erupts when language diversity is seen as a problem rather than a resource. The more complex target of culture in what the mass media have dubbed "culture wars" also represents diversity as a problem rather than resource. In some situations, language diversity *is* a problem, and in others, it *is* a rich resource. To assume as a principle that language diversity poses a problem, indeed a threat, to the United States such that we need ways to minimize this diversity fails to account both for the cultural underpinnings of marginalized language varieties and for the potential of cultural and language complexity to enhance knowledge and options for addressing complex problems in the context of globalization.

Issues of national identity are also central to the range of perspectives on language diversity that underlie policy discussions on issues such as bilingual education and Ebonics. Just as negotiations are difficult between nations with different histories, religious practices, educational systems, and systems of justice, so too are the everyday transactions between and among groups within culturally complex national borders. Although some advocate English as the "social glue" holding together diverse peoples, speaking English does not in itself resolve problems more deeply seated in cultural identities. A more productive approach is to consider the ways in which varieties of language-in-use engage systems of meaning and how the power relations of dominant and marginalized groups often erase whole systems of meaning by failing to recognize their existence. In such an approach, cultures and language varieties must be understood relative to one another, which requires understanding significant dimensions of distinctiveness and enabling marginalized groups to speak. Yet the dimension of integration across cultural and language groups is equally important: Knowledge of the cultural dimensions of language use offers possibilities to communicate more effectively in those situations where problems need to be understood and resolved and where ideas and insights must be maximized. In short, when it comes to issues of national identity and national resources, rampant relativism is no better than monolithic monoculturalism. The important challenge is to probe deeply enough in both education and policy formation to understand the cultural foundations of language and the linguistic dimensions of culture.

As presented in the beginning of this book, a cultural approach to understanding language diversity has many advantages over the more conventional analysis common to sociolinguistics. If we think of language not just as a social process but as a cultural resource, we will attend in more complex ways to what may otherwise seem exotic nuances of linguistic manifestation—verb patterns, manifestation of agency in utterances, turn-taking systems in conversation, and the reading of intent. Grasping the cultural systems of meaning and expression characteristic of different identities—in short, developing cultural mindedness—may help in exploding the rationalistic explanations often given for what is deeply ideological. Today's cultural and linguistic complexity is but a preview for what everyday life will engage in the 21st century, a century before us in which we will all need to be increasingly aware of the implications of speaking culturally.

References

Abrahams, R. D. (1963). *Deep down in the jungle: Negro narrative folklore from the streets of Philadelphia.* Hatboro, PA: Folklore Associates.

Agbayani-Siewert, P., & Revilla, L. (1995). Filipino Americans. In P. G. Min (Ed.), *Asian Americans: Contemporary trends and issues* (pp. 134-168). Thousand Oaks, CA: Sage.

Ainsworth-Vaughn, N. (1992). Topic transitions in physician-patient interviews: Power, gender, and discourse change. *Language in Society, 21,* 409-426.

Akinnaso, F. N., & Ajirotutu, C. S. (1982). Performance and ethnic style in job interviews. In J. J. Gumperz (Ed.), *Language and social identity* (pp. 119-144). Cambridge, UK: Cambridge University Press.

Allen, S., Cantor, A., Grady, H., & Hill, P. (1997). Classroom talk: Coed classes that work for girls. *Women and Language, 20,* 41-46.

Alvarez, L. (1997, March 25). It's the talk of Nueva York: The hybrid called Spanglish. *New York Times,* pp. A1, B4.

Ambert, A. N. (Ed.). (1991). *Bilingual education and English as a second language: A research handbook: 1988-1990.* New York: Garland.

American Association of University Women. (1992). *How schools shortchange girls.* Washington, DC: Author.

Andersen, E. S. (1986). The acquisition of register variation by Anglo-American children. In B. B. Schieffelin & E. Ochs (Eds.), *Language socialization across cultures* (pp. 153-161). Cambridge, UK: Cambridge University Press.

Anderson, C. A., Fine, M. G., & Johnson, F. L. (1983). Black talk on television: A constructivist approach to viewer perceptions of Black English Vernacular. *Journal of Multilingual and Multicultural Development, 4,* 181-195.

Anderson, N. (1997, April 14). More schools shunning bilingual methods. *Los Angeles Times,* pp. A3, A14.

Andrews, W. (1986). *To tell a free story: The first century of Afro-American autobiography, 1760-1865.* Urbana: University of Illinois Press.

Anzaldúa, G. (1987). *Borderlands/La Frontera: The new mestiza.* San Francisco: Aunt Lute Books.

Applebome, P. (1996, December 20). School district elevates status of black English. *New York Times,* p. A9.

Aries, E. (1976). Interaction patterns and themes of male, female, and mixed groups. *Small Group Behavior, 7,* 7-18.

Aries, E. J. (1982). Verbal and nonverbal behavior in single-sex and mixed-sex groups: Are traditional sex roles changing? *Psychological Reports, 51,* 127-134.

Aries, E. J., & Johnson, F. L. (1983). Close friendship in adulthood: Conversational content between same-sex friends. *Sex Roles, 9,* 1183-1196.

Arjona, E. (1985). The court interpreters certification test design. In L. Elías-Olivares, E. A. Leone, R. Cisneros, & J. R. Gutiérrez (Eds.), *Spanish language use and public life in the United States* (pp. 181-200). New York: Mouton.

Aronsson, K. (1991). Social interaction and the recycling of legal evidence. In N. Coupland, H. Giles, & J. M. Wiemann (Eds.), *"Miscommunication" and problematic talk* (pp. 215-243). Newbury Park, CA: Sage.

Asante, M. K. (1980). *Afrocentricity: The theory of social change.* Buffalo, NY: Amulefi.

Asante, M. K. (1987). *The Afrocentric idea.* Philadelphia: Temple University Press.

Asante, M. K. (1990). *Kemet, Afrocentricity, and knowledge.* Trenton, NJ: Africa World Press.

Asante, M. K. (1991, September 23). Putting Africa at the center [cover story]. *Newsweek, 118,* p. 46.

Asher, R. E. (Ed.-in-Chief), & Simpson, J. M. Y. (Coordinating Ed.). (1994). *The encyclopedia of language and linguistics* (Vols. 2-4, 6, 9). New York: Oxford/Pergamon.

Asimov, N. (1998, June 3). Big victory for measure to end bilingual education—Opponents say they'll file suit today. *San Francisco Chronicle.* [On-line]. Available: http://ourworld.compuserve.com/homepages/jwcrawford [1998, July 2, 1998].

Attinasi, J. (1979). Language attitudes in a New York Puerto Rican community. In R. V. Padilla (Ed.), *Bilingual education and public policy in the United States* (pp. 408-460). Ypsilanti, MI: Department of Foreign Languages and Bilingual Studies.

August, D., & Hakuta, K. (Eds.). (1997). *Improving schooling for language-minority children: A research agenda.* Washington, DC: National Academy Press.

Austin, A. M., Salehi, M., & Leffler, A. (1987). Gender and developmental differences in children's conversations. *Sex Roles, 16,* 497-510.

Austin, J. L. (1962). *How to do things with words.* Oxford, UK: Oxford University Press.

Bailey, G., & Maynor, N. (1987). Decreolization? *Language in Society, 16,* 449-473.

Barringer, H. R., & Kassebaum, G. (1989). Asian Indians as a minority in the United States: The effects of education, occupations, and gender on income. *Sociological Perspectives, 32,* 501-520.

Baugh, J. (1983). *Black street speech.* Austin: University of Texas Press.

Belenky, M. F., Clinchy, B. M., Goldberger, N. R., & Tarule, J. M. (1986). *Women's ways of knowing: The development of self, voice, and mind.* New York: Basic Books.

Bem, S. L. (1993). *The lenses of gender.* New Haven, CT: Yale University Press.

Benhabib, S. (1995). Feminism and postmodernism: An uneasy alliance. In L. Nicholson (Ed.), *Feminist contentions* (pp. 17-34). New York: Routledge.

Bennett, W. J. (1988). *Our children and our country: Improving America's schools and affirming the common culture.* New York: Simon & Schuster.

Berkeley Holistic Health Center. (1978). *The holistic health handbook.* Berkeley, CA: And/Or Press.

Berk-Seligson, S. (1990). *The bilingual courtroom: Court interpreters in the judicial process.* Chicago: University of Illinois Press.

Bernstein, B. (1990). *Class, codes, and control: Vol. 4. The structuring of pedagogic discourse.* London: Routledge.

Bernstein, C. (1988). A variant of the "invariant" *be. American Speech, 63,* 119-124.

Bhachu, P. (1985). *Twice migrants: East African Sikh settlers in Britain.* London: Tavistock.

Bodine, A. (1975). Androcentrism in prescriptive grammar: Singular "they," sex-indefinite "he," and "he or she." *Language in Society, 4,* 129-146.

Boswell, T. D., & Curtis, J. R. (1983). *The Cuban-American experience: Culture, images, and personality.* Totowa, NJ: Rowan & Allanheld.

Boyle, J. (Ed.). (1994). *Critical legal studies.* New York: New York University Press.

Bruno, R. (1993). *Languages spoken at home and ability to speak English for United States regions, and states: 1990* ([CPH-L-133]/Microfiche ASI 1993 2328-92). Washington, DC: U.S. Department of Commerce News CB93-78.

Bucholtz, M. (1995). From mulatta to mestiza: Passing and the linguistic reshaping of ethnic identity. In K. Hall & M. Bucholtz (Eds.), *Gender articulated: Language and the socially constructed self* (pp. 351-373). New York: Routledge.

Burn, B. B. (1980). *Expanding the international dimension of higher education.* San Francisco: Jossey-Bass.

Burns, K. (1997, March). Yakkity yak, don't talk black! *Essence,* p. 150.

Butler, J. (1990). *Gender trouble: Feminism and the subversion of identity.* New York: Routledge.

Butler, J. (1993). *Bodies that matter: On the discursive limits of "sex."* New York: Routledge.

Calloway, C. (1938). Cat-alogue: A hepster's dictionary. On *At the clam-bake carnival* [disc]. New York: Vocalion.

Cameron, D. (1992). *Feminism and linguistic theory* (2nd ed.). New York: St. Martin's.

Carbaugh, D. (Ed.). (1990). *Cultural communication and intercultural contact.* Hillsdale, NJ: Lawrence Erlbaum.

Cargile, A. C., & Giles, H. (1998). Language attitudes toward varieties of English: An American-Japanese context. *Journal of Applied Communication Research, 26,* 338-356.

Carmichael, S., & Hamilton, C. (1967). *Black power.* New York: Vintage.

Carver, C. M. (1989). *American regional dialects: A word geography.* Ann Arbor: University of Michigan Press.

Casteñeda v. Pickard, 648 F. 2nd 989 (5th Cir. 1981).

Cazden, C. B. (1994). Visible and invisible pedagogies in literacy education. In P. Atkinson, S. Delamont, & B. Davies (Eds.), *Discourse and reproduction* (pp. 161-174). Creskill, NJ: Hampton Press.

Chang, H.-C. (1997). Language and words: Communication in the *Analects* of Confucius. *Journal of Language and Social Psychology, 16*(2), 107-131.

Chang, H.-C., & Holt, G. R. (1991). More than relationship: Chinese interaction and the principle of *Kuan-Hsi. Communication Quarterly, 39,* 251-271.

Chavez, L. (1991). *Out of the barrio: Toward a new politics of Hispanic assimilation.* New York: Basic Books.

Chen, G.-M. & Chung, J. (1994). The impact of Confucianism on organizational communication. *Communication Quarterly, 42,* 93-105.

Chen, L. (1993). Chinese and North Americans: An epistemological exploration of intercultural communication. *Howard Journal of Communications, 4,* 342-357.

Chen, V. (1995). Chinese American women, language, and moving subjectivity. *Women and Language, 18,* 3-7.

Chen, V. (1997). (De)hyphenated identity: The double voice in *The Woman Warrior.* In A. González, M. Houston, & V. Chen (Eds.), *Our voices: Essays in culture, ethnicity, and communication* (2nd ed., pp. 3-13). Los Angeles: Roxbury.

Cheng, L.-R. L. (1987). *Assessing Asian language performance: Guidelines for evaluating limited-English-proficient students.* Rockville, MD: Aspen.

Chicago, J. (1979). *The dinner party: A symbol of our heritage.* Garden City: Anchor Books.

Chomsky, N. (1965). *Aspects of the theory of syntax.* Cambridge: MIT Press.

Chomsky, N. (1966). *Cartesian linguistics.* New York: Harper & Row.

Chomsky, N. (1968). *Language and mind.* New York: Harcourt, Brace, Jovanovich.

Chrisman, R., & Allen, R. L. (Eds.). (1992). *Court of appeal: The black community speaks out on the racial and sexual politics of Clarence Thomas vs. Anita Hill.* New York: Ballantine.

Chuh, K. (1995). Race, gender, and the law: Asian American women and rape. In G. Y. Okihiro (Ed.), *Privileging positions: The sites of Asian American studies* (pp. 233-243). Pullman: Washington State University Press.

Chung, C. H. (1988). The language situation of Vietnamese Americans. In S. L. McKay & S. C. Wong (Eds.), *Language diversity: Problem or resource?* (pp. 276-292). Boston: Heinle & Heinle.

Coates, J. (Ed.). (1998). *Language and gender: A reader.* Oxford/Malden, MA: Blackwell.

Code, L. (1993). Taking subjectivity into account. In L. Alcoff & E. Potter (Eds.), *Feminist epistemologies* (pp. 15-48). New York: Routledge.

Collins, P. H. (1990). *Black feminist thought: Knowledge, consciousness, and the politics of empowerment.* New York: Routledge.

Condon, J. C. (1985). *Good neighbors: Communicating with the Mexicans.* Yarmouth, ME: Intercultural Press.

Conniff, R. (1988, March 7). In Chattanooga: Anchor talk. *Time,* pp. 12-13.

Cook, A. S., Fritz, J. J., McCornack, B. L., & Visperas, C. (1985). Early gender differences in the functional usage of language. *Sex Roles, 12,* 909-915.

Cott, N. (1977). *The bonds of womanhood: "Women's sphere" in New England, 1780-1835.* New Haven, CT: Yale University Press.

Cran, W. (Producer). (1986). Black on white [videotape from PBS series *The Story of English*]. (Available from MacNeil/Lehrer Productions, PMI/Films, Inc., Chicago)

Crawford, J. (1989). *Bilingual education: History, politics, theory, and practice.* Trenton, NJ: Crane.

Crawford, J. (1997). *Best evidence: Research foundations of the Bilingual Education Act.* Washington, DC: National Clearinghouse for Bilingual Education.

Crawford, M. (1995). *Talking difference: On gender and language.* London: Sage.

Cushman, D. P., & Kincaid, D. L. (1987). Introduction and initial insights. In D. L. Kincaid (Ed.), *Communication theory: Eastern and Western perspectives.* London: Academic Press.

D'Andrade, R. G. (1984). Cultural meaning systems. In R. A. Shweder & R. A. LeVine (Eds.), *Culture theory: Essays on mind, self, and emotion* (pp. 88-119). Cambridge, UK: Cambridge University Press.

Daniel, J. L., & Smitherman, G. (1976). How I got over: Communication dynamics in the black community. *Quarterly Journal of Speech, 62,* 26-39.

Daniel, J. L., & Smitherman-Donaldson, G. (1990). How I got over and continue to do so in our mothers' churches. In D. Carbaugh (Ed.), *Cultural communication and intercultural contact* (pp. 41-44). Hillsdale, NJ: Lawrence Erlbaum.

Day, J. C. (1993). Population projections of the United States by age, sex, race, and Hispanic origin: 1993 to 2050. In *Current population reports* (P25-1104). Washington, DC: Government Printing Office.

Dhaliwal, A. K. (1995). Gender at work—the renegotiation of middle-class womanhood in a South Asian-owned business. In W. L. Ng, S. Chin, J. S. Moy, & G. Y. Okihiro (Eds.), *Reviewing Asian America: Locating diversity* (pp. 75-85). Pullman: Washington State Univeresity Press.

Dillard. J. L. (1972). *Black English: Its history and usage in the United States.* New York: Vintage.

Dillard, J. L. (1976). *Black names.* The Hague, Netherlands: Mouton.

Dillard, J. L. (1977). *Lexicon of Black English.* New York: Seabury.

Dillard, J. L. (1985). *Toward a social history of American English.* New York: Mouton.

Dorian, N. C. (1982). Defining the speech community to include the margins. In S. Romaine (Ed.), *Sociolinguistic variation in speech communities* (pp. 25-33). London: Edward Arnold.

Du Bois, W. E. B. (1961). *Souls of black folk.* New York: Fawcett. (Original work published 1903)

Dyson, M. E. (1993). *Reflecting black: African American cultural criticism.* Minneapolis: University of Minnesota Press.

Ebonics—Everything you ever wanted to know but were afraid to ax. (1997, January 14). *Village Voice* [four articles].

Eckert, P., & McConnell-Ginet, S. (1995). Constructing meaning, constructing selves: Snapshots of language, gender, and class from Belten High. In K. Hall & M. Bucholtz (Eds.), *Gender articulated: Language and the socially constructed self* (pp. 469-507). New York: Routledge.

Edelsky, C. (1993). Who's got the floor? In D. Tannen (Ed.), *Gender and conversational interaction* (pp. 189-227). New York: Oxford University Press. (Original work published 1981)

Edwards, T. M., Lafferty, E., Monroe, S., & Rainert, V. (1997, May 5). I'm just who I am. *Newsweek,* pp. 32-36.

Elías-Olivares, L., Leone, E. A., Cisneros, R., & Gutiérrez, J. R. (Eds.). (1985). *Spanish language use and public life in the United States.* New York: Mouton.

Enloe, C. (1989). *Bananas, beaches, and bases: Making feminist sense of international politics.* London: Pandora.

Epstein, C. F. (1993). *Women in law* (2nd ed.). New York: Basic Books.

Espiritu, Y. L. (1992). *Asian American panethnicity: Bridging institutions and identities.* Philadelphia: Temple University Press.

Espiritu, Y. L. (1997). *Asian American women and men.* Thousand Oaks, CA: Sage.

Esposito, A. (1979). Sex differences in children's conversation. *Language and Speech, 22,* 213-220.

Fainaru, S. (1997, April 27). From a sense of injustice to a rebel's death. *The Boston Globe*, pp. A1, 14.

Fairclough, N. (1992). Introduction. In N. Fairclough (Ed.), *Critical language awareness* (pp. 7-29). New York: Longman.

Falmagne, R. J. (1997, April). *Toward a feminist theory of inference: Exploration of a cross-disciplinary methodology.* Paper presented at the EnGendering Rationalities Conference, University of Oregon, Eugene.

Farley, C. J. (1997, May 5). No man's land: Three new novelists take on Asian American life. *Time*, pp. 64-65.

Fasold, R. (1990). *Sociolinguistics of language.* Cambridge, UK: Basil Blackwell.

Ferguson, K. E. (1984). *The feminist case against bureaucracy.* Philadelphia: Temple University Press.

Fernandez, R. G. (1983). English loanwords in Miami Cuban Spanish. *American Speech, 58,* 13-19.

Fine, M. G. (1995). *Building successful multicultural organizations: Challenges and opportunities.* Westport, CT: Quorum Press.

Fine, M. G., Johnson, F. L., & Ryan, M. S. (1990). Cultural diversity in the workplace. *Public Personnel Management, 19,* 305-319.

Fishman, J. A. (1998, Winter). The new linguistic order. *Foreign Policy,* pp. 26-40.

Floyd, M. B. (1985). Spanish in the Southwest: Language maintenance or shift? In L. Elías-Olivares, E. A. Leone, R. Cisneros, & J. R. Gutiérrez (Eds.), *Spanish language use and public life in the United States* (pp. 13-26). Berlin: Walter de Gruyter.

Folb, E. (1980). *Runnin' down some lines: The language and culture of black teenagers.* Cambridge, MA: Harvard University Press.

Ford, M. B. (1985). Spanish in the Southwest: Language maintenance or shift? In L. Elías-Olivares, E. A. Leone, R. Cisneros, & J. R. Gutiérrez (Eds.), *Spanish language use and public life in the United States* (pp. 13-26). Berlin: Mouton.

Fordham, S. (1993). "Those loud black girls": Black women, silence, and gender "passing" in the academy. *Anthropology and Education Quarterly, 24,* 3-32.

Foreign language policy: An agenda for change. (1994). *Annals of the American Academy of Political and Social Science* (Vol. 532 002-7162). Thousand Oaks, CA: Sage.

Forgas, J. P. (1988). Episode representations in intercultural communication. In Y. Kim & W. Gudykunst (Eds.), *Theories in intercultural communication.* Newbury Park, CA: Sage.

Foss, K. A., & Foss, S. K. (1991). *Women speak: The eloquence of women's lives.* Prospect Heights, IL: Waveland Press.

Foster, D. (1992, September 2). Worker battles brew over the official language. *The Boston Globe,* p. 3.

Foster, M. (1995). "Are you with me?": Power and solidarity in the discourse of African American women. In K. Hall & M. Bucholtz (Eds.), *Gender articulated: Language and the socially constructed self* (pp. 329-350). New York: Routledge.

Freire, P. (1968). *Pedagogy of the oppressed.* New York: Seabury.

Freire, P. (1973). *Education for critical consciousness.* New York: Seabury.

Freire, P., & Macedo, D. (1987). *Literacy: Reading the word and the world.* South Hadley, MA: Bergin & Garvey.

Fromkin, V., & Rodman, R. (1998). *An introduction to language* (6th ed.). Fort Worth, TX: Harcourt Brace College Publishers.

Galang, R. (1988). The language situation of Filipino Americans. In S. L. McKay & S. C. Wong (Eds.), *Language diversity: Problem or resource?* (pp. 229-251). Boston: Heinle & Heinle.

Gangotena, M. (1994). The rhetoric of *la familia* among Mexican Americans. In A. González, M. Houston, & V. Chen (Eds.), *Our voices: Essays in culture, ethnicity, and communication* (pp. 69-80). Los Angeles: Roxbury.

García, O., Evangelista, I., Martínez, M., Disla, C., & Paulino, B. (1988). Spanish language use and attitudes: A study of two New York City communities. *Language in Society, 17,* 475-511.

García, O., & Otheguy, R. (1988). The language situation of Cuban Americans. In S. L. McKay & S. C. Wong (Eds.), *Language diversity: Problem or resource?* (pp. 166-192). Boston: Heinle & Heinle.

Garner, T. (1983). Playing the dozens: Folklore as strategies for living. *Quarterly Journal of Speech, 69,* 47-57.

Garner, T. (1994). Oral rhetorical practice in African American culture. In A. González, M. Houston, & V. Chen (Eds.), *Our voices: Essays in culture, ethnicity, and communication* (pp. 81-91). Los Angeles: Roxbury.

Gaudio, R. P. (1994). Sounding gay: Pitch properties in the speech of gay and straight men. *American Speech, 69,* 30-57.

Gee, J. P. (1992). *The social mind: Language, ideology, and social practice.* New York: Bergin & Garvey.

Gee, J. P. (1993). *An introduction to human language.* Englewood Cliffs, NJ: Prentice Hall.

Geertz, C. (1973). *The interpretation of cultures.* New York: Basic Books.

Geertz, C. (1983). *Local knowledge: Further essays in interpretive anthropology.* New York: Basic Books.

Giachello, A. L. (1996). Latino women. In M. Bayne-Smith (Ed.), *Race, gender, and health* (pp. 121-171). Thousand Oaks, CA: Sage.

Giles, H., & Coupland, N. (1991). *Language: Contexts and consequences.* Pacific Grove, CA: Brooks/Cole.

Giles, H., & Powesland, P. F. (1975). *Speech style and social evaluation.* New York: Academic Press.

Gilligan, C. (1982). *In a different voice: Psychological theory and women's development.* Cambridge, MA: Harvard University Press.

Gilmore, D. D. (1990). *Manhood in the making: Cultural concepts of masculinity.* New Haven, CT: Yale University Press.

Gilroy, P. (1995/November). *The black Atlantic and changing same.* Paper presented at the Henry R. Luce Lecture Series, Clark University, Worcester, MA.

Godinez, M., Jr. (1984). Chicano English phonology: Norm vs. interference phenomena. In J. Ornstein-Galicia (Ed.), *Form and function in Chicano English* (pp. 42-48). Rowley, MA: Newbury House. (Reprinted 1988, Malabar, FL: Robert E. Krieger)

Goffman, E. (1972). The neglected situation. In P. P. Giglioli (Ed.), *Language and social context* (pp. 61-66). Baltimore, MD: Penguin.

Gómez-Quiñones, J. (1979). Toward a concept of culture. In J. Sommers & T. Ybarra-Frausto (Eds.), *Modern Chicano writers* (pp. 54-66). Englewood Cliffs, NJ: Prentice Hall.

Gonzales Velásquez, M. D. (1995). Sometimes Spanish, sometimes English: Language use among rural New Mexican Chicanas. In K. Hall & M. Bucholtz (Eds.), *Gender articulated: Language and the socially constructed self* (pp. 421-446). New York: Routledge.

González, M. (1995, October 18). The bilingual ed trap. *Wall Street Journal,* p. A20.

Goodenough, W. H. (1981). *Culture, language, and society* (2nd ed.). Menlo Park, CA: Benjamin/Cummings.

Goodwin, M. H. (1990). *He-said she-said: Talk as social organization among black children.* Bloomington: Indiana University Press.

Gorov, L. (1997, August 31). In Calif., a fight against bilingual classes—Latinos, others blame it for illiteracy. *The Boston Globe,* p. A12.

Gumperz, J. (1972). The speech community. In P. P. Giglioli (Ed.), *Language and social context* (pp. 219-231). Baltimore: Penguin. (Original work published 1968)

Gumperz, J. J. (1982a). *Discourse strategies.* New York: Cambridge University Press.

Gumperz, J. J. (1982b). Fact and inference in courtroom testimony. In J. J. Gumperz (Ed.), *Language and social identity* (pp. 163-195). Cambridge, UK: Cambridge University Press.

Gunzburger, D. (1996). Gender adaptation in the speech of transsexuals: From sex transition to gender transmission? In Berkeley Women and Language Group (Ed.), *Gender and belief systems: Proceedings of the Fourth Berkeley Women and Language Conference* (pp. 269-278). Berkeley, CA: Berkeley Women and Language Group.

Haas, A. (1979). Male and female spoken language differences: Stereotypes and evidence. *Psychological Bulletin, 86,* 616-626.

Hagan, W. T. (1961). *American Indians.* Chicago: University of Chicago Press.

Hall, K., & Bucholtz, M. (1995). Introduction: Twenty years after *Language and women's place.* In K. Hall & M. Bucholtz (Eds.), *Gender articulated: Language and the socially constructed self* (pp. 1-22). New York: Routledge.

Hall, R., & Sandler, B. (1982). *The classroom climate: A chilly one for women?* (Project on the Status and Education of Women). Washington, DC: Association of American Colleges.

Halliday, M. A. K. (1978). *Language as social semiotic: The social interpretation of language and meaning.* Baltimore MD: University Park Press.

Hannerz, U. (1989). Culture between center and periphery: Toward a macroanthropology. *Ethnos, 54,* 200-216.

Harding, S. (1991). *Whose science? Whose knowledge? Thinking from women's lives.* Ithaca, NY: Cornell University Press.

Harding, S. (1993). Rethinking standpoint epistemology: What is "strong objectivity"? In L. Alcoff & E. Potter (Eds.), *Feminist epistemologies* (pp. 49-82). New York: Routledge.

Harris, J. F. (1996, December 25). Federal funds ruled out for black English. *The Boston Globe,* p. A15.

Hatchett, S. J., Cochran, D. L., & Jackson, J. S. (1991). Family life. In J. S. Jackson (Ed.), *Life in black America* (pp. 46-83). Newbury Park, CA: Sage.

Haugen, E. (1950). The analysis of linguistic borrowing. *Language, 26,* 210-231.

Heath, J. G. (1984). Language contact and language change. *Annual Review of Anthropology, 13,* 367-384.

Heath, S. B. (1981). English in our language heritage. In C. A. Ferguson & S. B. Heath (Eds.), *Language in the USA* (pp. 6-20). Cambridge, UK: Cambridge University Press.

Hecht, M. L., Collier, M. J., & Ribeau, S. A. (1993). *African American communication: Ethnic identity and cultural interpretation.* Newbury Park, CA: Sage.

Heilbrunn, J. (1997, January 20). Speech therapy: Ebonics—It's worse than you think. *New Republic,* pp. 216-217.

Hein, J. (1991). Indochinese refugees' responses to resettlement via the social welfare system. In S. Hune, H.-C. Kim, S. S. Fugita, & A. Ling (Eds.), *Asian Americans: Comparative and global perspectives* (pp. 153-167). Pullman: Washington State University Press.

Held, V. (1993). *Feminist morality: Transforming culture, society, and politics.* Chicago: University of Chicago Press.

Herskovits, M. J. (1958). *The myth of the Negro past.* Boston: Beacon. (Original work published 1941)

Higginbotham, E. B. (1992). African American women's history and the metalanguage of race. *Signs, 17,* 251-274.

Hiller, M., & Johnson, F. L. (1996, November). *Gender and generation in conversational topics: A case study of two coffee shops.* Paper presented at the annual meeting of the Speech Communication Association, San Diego, CA.

Hindi: The language of songs. (No date). [On-line]. Available: http://www.malaiya@cs.colostate.edu [1997, June 12].

Holloway, J. E. (1990). The origins of African American culture. In J. E. Holloway (Ed.), *Africanisms in American culture* (pp. 1-18). Bloomington: Indiana University Press.

Holloway, J. E., & Vass, W. K. (1993). *The African heritage of American English.* Bloomington: Indiana University Press.

Hoover, M. R. (1978). Community attitudes toward Black English. *Language in Society, 7,* 65-87.

Hopper, R., & Williams, F. (1973). Speech characteristics and employability. *Speech Monograph, 46,* 296-302.

Houghton, C. (1995). Managing the body of labor: The treatment of reproduction and sexuality in a therapeutic institution. In K. Hall & M. Bucholtz (Eds.), *Gender articulated: Language and the socially constructed self* (pp. 121-131). New York: Routledge.

Houston Stanback, M. (1985). Language and black woman's place: Evidence from the black middle class. In P. A. Treichler, C. Kramarae, & B. Stafford (Eds.), *For alma mater: Theory and practice in feminist scholarship* (pp. 177-193). Urbana: University of Illinois Press.

Hudson, R. A. (1980). *Sociolinguistics.* Cambridge, UK: Cambridge University Press.

Hurston, Z. N. (1995). Characteristics of Negro expression. In *Zora Neale Hurston: Folklore, memoirs, and other writings* (pp. 830-846). New York: Penguin. (Original work published 1934)

Hymes, D. (1971). Competence and performance in linguistic theory. In R. Huxley & E. Ingram (Eds.), *Language acquisition: Models and methods* (pp. 3-28). New York: Academic Press.

Hymes, D. (1972). Models of the interaction of language and social life. In J. J. Gumperz & D. Hymes (Eds.), *Directions in sociolinguistics: The ethnography of communication* (pp. 35-71). New York: Holt, Rinehart & Winston.

Jackson, J. (1981). The black American folk preacher and the chanted sermon: Parallels with a West African tradition. In C. Card, J. Cowan, S. C. Helton, C. Rahkonen, & L. K. Sommers (Eds), *Discourse in ethnomusicology II* (pp. 205-222). Bloomington, IN: Ethnomusicology Publishing Group.

Jacobs, G. (1996). Lesbian and gay male language use: A critical review of the literature. *American Speech, 71,* 49-71.

James, D., & Clarke, S. (1993). Women, men, and interruptions: A critical review. In D. Tannen (Ed.), *Gender and conversational interaction* (pp. 231-280). New York: Oxford University Press.

James, D., & Drakich, J. (1993). Understanding gender differences in amount of talk: A critical review of research. In D. Tannen (Ed.), *Gender and conversational interaction* (pp. 281-312). New York: Oxford University Press.

Jimenez, A. (1996, February 3). Trapped in the bilingual classroom. *New York Times* (Op-ed), p. 23.

Johnson, F. L. (1979). Communicative competence and the Bernstein perspective. *Communication Quarterly, 26*(4), 12-19.

Johnson, F. L. (1987). *Women's language on trial: Styles of discourse in small claims court.* Unpublished manuscript.

Johnson, F. L. (1989). Women's culture and communication: An analytical perspective. In C. M. Lont & S. A. Friedley (Eds.), *Beyond boundaries: Sex and gender diversity in communication* (pp. 301-316). Fairfax, VA: George Mason University Press.

Johnson, F. L. (1996). Friendships among women: Closeness in dialogue. In J. Wood (Ed.), *Gendered relationships* (pp. 79-94). Mountain View, CA: Mayfield.

Johnson, F. L., & Aries, E. J. (1983a). Conversational patterns among same-sex pairs of late-adolescent close friends. *Journal of Genetic Psychology, 142,* 225-238.

Johnson, F. L., & Aries, E. J. (1983b). The talk of women friends. *Women's Studies International Forum, 6,* 353-361.

Johnson, F. L., & Buttny, R. (1982). White listeners' responses to "sounding black" and "sounding white": The effects of message content on judgments about language. *Communication Monographs, 49,* 33-49.

Johnson, F. L., & Fine, M. G. (1985). Sex differences in uses and perceptions of obscenity. *Women's Studies in Communication, 8,* 11-24.

Jordan, J. (1985). *On call: Political essays.* Boston: South End Press.

Kachru, B. B. (1981). American English and other Englishes. In C. A. Ferguson & S. B. Heath (Eds.), *Language in the USA* (pp. 21-43). Cambridge, UK: Cambridge University Press.

Kanellos, N. (Ed.). (1993). *The Hispanic-American almanac.* Detroit: Gale Research.

Kellner, B. (Ed.). (1989). *The Harlem Renaissance: A historical dictionary for the era.* Westport, CT: Greenwood.

Kennedy, C. W., & Camden, C. (1983). A new look at interruptions. *Western Journal of Speech Communication, 47,* 45-58.

Khubchandani, L. M. (1983). *Plural languages, plural cultures: Communication, identity, and sociopolitical change in contemporary India.* Honolulu: University of Hawaii Press.

Kim, B.-I. (1988). The language situation of Korean Americans. In S. L. McKay & S. C. Wong (Eds.), *Language diversity: Problem or resource?* (pp. 252-275). Boston: Heinle & Heinle.

Kim, Y. Y. (1991). Intercultural communication competence: A systems-theoretic view. In S. Ting-Toomey & F. Korzenny (Eds.), *Cross-cultural interpersonal communication* (pp. 259-275). Newbury Park, CA: Sage.

Kimmel, M. S. (1994). Masculinity as homophobia. In H. Brod & M. Kaufman (Eds.), *Theorizing masculinities.* Thousand Oaks, CA: Sage.

Kincaid, D. L. (Ed.). (1987). *Communication theory: Eastern and western perspectives.* London: Academic Press.

Kingston, M. H. (1976). *The woman warrior: Memoirs of a girlhood among ghosts.* New York: Knopf.

Kipers, P. S. (1987). Gender and topic. *Language and Society, 16,* 543-557.

Kochman, T. (1972). *Rappin' and stylin' out: Communication in urban black America.* Chicago: University of Illinois Press.

Kochman, T. (1981). *Black and white styles in conflict.* Chicago: University of Chicago Press.

Kolchin, P. (1993). *American slavery, 1619-1877.* New York: Hill & Wang.

Kozol, J. (1991). *Savage inequalities: Children in America's schools.* New York: Crown.

Kozol, J. (1995). *Amazing grace: The lives of children and the conscience of a nation.* New York: Crown.

Kramarae, C. (1989). Redefining gender, race, and class. In C. M. Lont & S. A. Friedley (Eds.), *Beyond boundaries: Sex and gender diversity in communication* (pp. 317-329). Fairfax, VA: George Mason University Press.

Kramarae, C., & Jenkins, M. M. (1987). Women take back the talk. In J. Penfield (Ed.), *Women and language in transition* (pp. 137-156). Albany: State University of New York Press.

Kramer, C. (1977). Perceptions of female and male speech. *Language and Speech, 20,* 151-161.

Kramer, M. H. (1995). *Critical legal theory and the challenge of feminism: A philosophical reconception.* Lanham, MD: Rowman & Littlefield.

Krashen, S. (1997). A researcher's view of Unz. [On-line]. Available: http://ourworld.compuserve.com/homepages/JWCRAWFORD [1997, October 30].

Kreps, G. L., & Kunimoto, E. N. (1994). *Effective communication in multicultural health care settings.* Thousand Oaks, CA: Sage.

Labov, W. (1970). The logic of nonstandard English. In F. Williams (Ed.), *Language and poverty: Perspectives on a theme* (pp. 153-189). Chicago: Markham.

Labov, W. (1972a). *Language in the inner city: Studies in the Black English vernacular.* Philadelphia: University of Pennsylvania Press.

Labov, W. (1972b). *Sociolinguistic patterns.* Philadelphia: University of Pennsylvania Press.

Labov, W. (1982). Objectivity and commitment in linguistic science: The case of the Black English trial in Ann Arbor. *Language in Society, 11,* 165-201.

Labov, W. (1987). Are black and white vernaculars diverging? (Papers from the NWAVE XIV panel discussion). *American Speech, 62,* 5-12.

Labov, W. (1998). Co-existent systems in African American Vernacular English. In S. S. Mufwene, J. R. Rickford, G. Bailey, & J. Baugh (Eds.), *African American English: Structure, history, and use* (pp. 110-153). New York: Routledge.

Labov, W., Cohen, P., Robins, C., & Lewis, J. (1968). *A study of non-standard English of Negro and Puerto Rican speakers in New York City.* New York: Columbia University.

Labov, W., & Harris, W. A. (1986). De facto segregation of black and white vernaculars. In D. Sankoff (Ed.), *Diversity and diachrony* (pp. 1-24). Philadelphia: John Benjamins.

Lakoff, R. (1975). *Language and woman's place.* New York: Harper Colophon.

Lakoff, R. T. (1990). *Talking power: The politics of language.* New York: Basic Books.

Lakoff, G., & Johnson, M. (1980). *Metaphors we live by.* Chicago: University of Chicago Press.

Lakshmanan, I. A. R. (1997, June 17). Waving flags for China. *The Boston Globe,* pp. A1, A14.

Lau v. Nichols, 414 U.S. 563 (1974).

Leap, W. L. (1981). American Indian languages. In C. A. Ferguson & S. Brice Heath (Eds.), *Language in the USA* (pp. 116-144). Cambridge, UK: Cambridge University Press.

Leap, W. L. (Ed.). (1995). *Beyond the lavender lexicon.* Amsterdam: Gordon & Breach.

Leap, W. L. (1996). Fruit loops and naughty places: How the language of *gay city* reflects the politics of urban gay experience. In *Gender and belief systems: Proceedings of the Fourth*

Berkeley Women and Language Conference (pp. 411-423). Berkeley, CA: Berkeley Women and Language Group.

Lee, C.-R. (1995). *Native speaker.* New York: Riverhead Books.

Lefkowitz, M. R. (1997). *Not out of Africa: How Afrocentrism became an excuse to teach myth as history.* New York: Basic Books.

Leland, J., & Joseph, N. (1997, January 13). Hooked on Ebonics. *Newsweek,* pp. 78-79.

Leonard, J., & Ashe, M. (Eds). (1995). *Legal studies as cultural studies: A reader in (post)modern critical theory.* Albany: State University of New York Press.

Leonard, K. (1982). Marriage and family life among early Asian Indian immigrants. *Population Review, 25,* 67-75.

Lerner, G. (1979). *The majority finds its past: Placing women in history.* Oxford, UK: Oxford University Press.

Leslie, C. (1991, February 11). Classrooms of Babel. *Newsweek,* pp. 56-57.

Levinson, S. C. (1983). *Pragmatics.* Cambridge, UK: Cambridge University Press.

Lewis, D. E. (1997, March 29). 5 hotel workers quit, cite English-only demand. *The Boston Globe,* pp. B3-B4.

Lewis, N. (1996, December 23). Black English is not a second language, Jackson says. *New York Times,* p. A18.

Liebow, E. (1967). *Talley's corner: A study of Negro street-corner men.* Boston: Little, Brown.

Light, I. (1987). Ethnic enterprise in America: Japanese, Chinese, and blacks. In R. Takaki (Ed.), *From different shores: Perspectives on race and ethnicity in America.* New York: Oxford University Press.

Lincoln, C. E., & Mamiya, L. H. (1990). *The black church in the African American experience.* Durham, NC: Duke University Press.

Lippi-Green, R. (1994). Accent, standard language ideology, and discriminatory pretext in the courts. *Language in Society, 23,* 163-198.

Lourie, M. A. (1978). Black English Vernacular: A comparative description. In M. A. Lourie & N. F. Conklin (Eds.), *A pluralistic nation: The language issue in the United States* (pp. 78-93). Rowley, MA: Newbury House.

Luu, V. (1989). The hardships of escape for Vietnamese women. In Asian Women United in California (Ed.), *Making waves: An anthology of writings by and about Asian American women* (pp. 60-72). Boston: Beacon.

Ma, R. (1992). The role of unofficial intermediaries in interpersonal conflicts in the Chinese culture. *Communication Quarterly, 40,* 269-278.

Major, C. (1970). *Dictionary of Afro-American slang.* New York: International Publishers.

Major, C. (1994). *Juba to jive: A dictionary of African American slang.* New York: Viking.

Malakoff, M., & Hakuta, K. (1990). History of language minority education in the United States. In A. M. Padilla, H. H. Fairchild, & C. M. Valadez (Eds.), *Bilingual education: Issues and strategies* (pp. 27-43). Newbury Park, CA: Sage.

Maltz, D. N., & Borker, R. A. (1982). A cultural approach to male-female miscommunication. In J. J. Gumperz (Ed.), *Language and social identity* (pp. 196-216). Cambridge, UK: Cambridge University Press.

Martin, E., & Martin, J. (1978). *The black extended family.* Chicago: University of Illinois Press.

Martin Luther King Junior Elementary School Children v. Ann Arbor School District Board, 451 F. Supp. 1324 (E.D.Mich 1978); 463 F. Supp 1027 (E.D. Mich 1978); 473 F. Supp 1371 (E.D. Mich 1979).

Martin, S., & Wolfram, W. (1998). The sentence in African American vernacular English. In S. S. Mufwene, J. R. Rickford, G. Bailey, & J. Baugh (Eds.), *African American English: Structure, history, and use* (pp. 11-36). New York: Routledge.

Massachusetts Commission to Study Racial and Ethnic Bias in the Courts. (1994). *Equal justice: Eliminating the barriers.* Boston: Supreme Judicial Court.

Massachusetts Gender Bias Study Committee of the Supreme Judicial Court. (1989). *Gender bias study.* Boston: Supreme Judicial Court.

McKay, S. L. (1988). Weighing educational alternatives. In S. L. McKay & S.-L. C. Wong (Eds.), *Language diversity: Problem or resource?* (pp. 338-366). Boston: Heinle & Heinle.

McKay, S. L. & Wong, S.-L. C. (Eds.). (1988). *Language diversity: Problem or resource?* Boston: Heinle & Heinle.

McKim, J. (1994, December 13). Barrier in the courts. *The Boston Globe,* pp. 1, 22.

McKim, J. (1996, February 13). Report hits speech barrier. *The Boston Globe,* pp. 17, 22.

McMahon, A. M. S. (1994). *Understanding language change.* Cambridge, UK: Cambridge University Press.

Mead, G. H. (1934). *Mind, self, and society.* Chicago: University of Chicago Press.

Mears, T. (1998, April 12). Saying "si" to Spanish. *The Boston Globe,* p. A2.

Meier, A., & Rudwick, E. M. (1966). *From plantation to ghetto: An interpretive history of American Negroes.* New York: Hill & Wang.

Menand, L. (1997, January). Johnny be good—Ebonics and the language of cultural separatism. *The New Yorker,* pp. 4-5.

Mencken, H. L. (1980). *The American language.* New York: Knopf.

Mendoza-Denton, N. (1995). Pregnant pauses. In K. Hall & M. Bucholtz (Eds.), *Gender articulated: Language and the socially constructed self* (pp. 51-66). New York: Routledge.

Merriam-Webster's collegiate dictionary, tenth edition. (1995). Springfield, MA: Merriam-Webster, Inc.

Michaels, S., & O'Connor, M. C. (1990). *Literacy as reasoning within multiple discourses: Implications for policy and educational reform.* Paper presented at the Council of Chief State School Officers Summer Institute.

Min, P. G. (Ed.). (1995). *Asian Americans: Contemporary trends and issues.* Thousand Oaks, CA: Sage.

Molesky, J. (1988). Understanding the American linguistic mosaic: A historical overview of language maintenance and language shift. In S. L. McKay & S. C. Wong (Eds.), *Language diversity: Problem or resource?* (pp. 29-68). New York: Newbury House/Harper & Row.

Morgan, M. (1998). More than a mood or an attitude: Discourse and verbal genres in African American culture. In S. S. Mufwene, J. R. Rickford, G. Bailey, & J. Baugh (Eds.), *African-American English: Structure, history, and use* (pp. 251-281). New York: Routledge.

Morgan, R., & Wood, K. (1995). Lesbians in the living room: Collusion, co-construction, and co-narration in conversation. In W. L. Leap (Ed.), *Beyond the lavender lexicon* (pp. 235-248). Amsterdam: Gordon & Breach.

Moulton, W. G. (1976). The sounds of Black English. In D. S. Harrison & T. Trabasso (Eds.), *Black English: A seminar* (pp. 149-170). Hillsdale, NJ: Lawrence Erlbaum.

Mufwene, S. S. (1997). The ecology of Gullah's survival. *American Speech, 72,* 69-83.

Mufwene, S. S. (1998). The structure of the noun phrase in African American vernacular English. In S. S. Mufwene, J. R. Rickford, G. Bailey, & J. Baugh (Eds.), *African American English: Structure, history, and use* (pp. 69-81). New York: Routledge.

Mufwene, S. S., Rickford, J. R., Bailey, G., & Baugh, J. (Eds.). (1998). *African American English: Structure, history, and use*. New York: Routledge.

Murr, A. (1998, April 27). English spoken here—or else. *Newsweek*, p. 65.

Myhill, J. (1988). The rise of *be* as an aspect marker in Black English Vernacular. *American Speech, 63*, 304-325.

Myhill, J. (1995). The use of features of present-day AAVE in the ex-slave recordings. *American Speech, 70*, 115-147.

Nakayama, T. (1997). Dis/orienting identities: Asian Americans, history, and intercultural communication. In A. González, M. Houston, & V. Chen (Eds.), *Our voices: Essays in culture, ethnicity, and communication* (pp. 14-20). Los Angeles: Roxbury.

National Center for Education Statistics. (1995). *Digest of education statistics 1995* (Table 57). Washington, DC: Government Printing Office.

National Geographic atlas of the world (1995, rev. 6th ed.). Washington, DC: National Geographic Society.

National Research Council. (1997). *Improving schooling for language-minority children: A research agenda*. Washington, DC: National Academy Press.

New languages being taught in Oakland, California. (1997). [On-line]. Available: http://www.makeyoulaugh.com/Ebonics/newlanguages.shtml [1997, September 22].

Nichols, P. C. (1983). Linguistic options and choices for black women in the rural south. In B. Thorne, C. Kramarae, & N. Henley (Eds.), *Language, gender, and society* (pp. 54-68). Rowley, MA: Newbury House.

Nishi, S. M. (1995). Japanese Americans. In P. G. Min (Ed.), *Asian Americans* (pp. 95-133). Thousand Oaks, CA: Sage.

Nunberg, G. (1992). The official English movement: Reimagining America. In J. W. Crawford (Ed.), *Language loyalties: A source book on the official English controversy* (pp. 479-494). Chicago: University of Chicago Press.

Nye, A. (1988). *Feminist theory and the philosophies of man*. New York: Routledge.

Oaks, E., & Taylor, E. (1995). The "Father Knows Best" dynamic in dinnertime narratives. In K. Hall & M. Bucholtz (Eds.), *Gender articulated: Language and the socially constructed self* (pp. 97-120). New York: Routledge.

O'Barr, W. M. (1982). *Linguistic evidence: Language, power, and strategy in the courtroom*. New York: Academic Press.

O'Barr, W. M., & Atkins, B. K. (1980). "Women's language" or "powerless language"? In S. McConnell-Ginet, R. Borker, & N. Furman (Eds.), *Women and language in literature and society* (pp. 93-110). New York: Praeger.

Office of Bilingual Education and Minority Languages Affairs. (1998). *Today's students* [On-line]. Available: http://www.ed.gov/offices/OBEMLA [1998, March 21].

Ono, K. A., & Sloop, J. M. (1995). The critique of vernacular discourse. *Communication Monograph, 62*, 19-46.

Ornstein-Galicia, J. (Ed.). (1984). *Form and function in Chicano English*. Rowley, MA: Newbury House. (Reprinted 1988, Malabar, FL: Robert E. Krieger)

Ortego, P. D. (1970). Some cultural implications of a Mexican American border dialect of American English. *Studies in Linguistics, 21*, 77-82.

Osborne, P., & Segal, L. (1994). Gender as performance: An interview with Judith Butler. *Radical Philosophy, 67*, 32-39.

Otheguy, R., García, O., & Fernández, M. (1989). Transferring, switching, and modeling in West New York Spanish: An intergenerational study. *International Journal of the Sociology of Language, 79*, 41-52.

Pedraza, P. (1985). Language maintenance among New York Puerto Ricans. In L. Elías-Olivares, E. A. Leone, R. Cisneros, & J. R. Gutiérrez (Eds.), *Spanish language use and public life in the United States* (pp. 59-71). Berlin: Mouton.

Peñalosa, F. (1980). *Chicano sociolinguistics.* Rowley, MA: Newbury House.

Peñalosa, F. (1985). A world-system perspective for Chicano sociolinguistics. *International Journal of the Sociology of Language, 53*, 7-19.

Penelope, J. (1990). *Speaking freely: Unlearning the lies of the fathers' tongues.* New York: Pergamon.

Penfield, J. (1984). Prosodic patterns: Some hypotheses and findings from fieldwork. In J. Ornstein-Galicia (Ed.), *Form and function in Chicano English* (pp. 49-59). Rowley, MA: Newbury House. (Reprinted 1988, Malabar, FL: Robert E. Krieger)

Penfield, J., & Ornstein-Galicia, J. L. (1985). *Chicano English: An ethnic contact dialect.* Philadelphia: John Benjamins.

Pennington, D. L. (1979). Black-white communication. In M. Asante, E. Newmark, & C. Blake (Eds.), *Handbook of intercultural communication* (pp. 383-402). Beverly Hills, CA: Sage.

Pérez Firmat, G. (1994). *Life on the hyphen.* Austin: University of Texas Press.

Philips, S. J., & Reynolds, A. (1987). The interaction of variable syntax and discourse structure in women's and men's speech. In S. U. Philips, S. Steele, & C. Tans (Eds.), *Language, gender, and sex in comparative perspective* (pp. 71-94). New York: Cambridge University Press.

Philipsen, G. (1975). Speaking "like a man" in Teamsterville: Culture patterns of role enactment in an urban neighborhood. *Quarterly Journal of Speech, 61*, 13-22.

Phillips, M. A. (1994). Develop a female voice. *Tapestry Journal*, pp. 25-28.

Pitts, L. (1996, December 25). Support for using "slanguage" marginalizes children. *Miami Herald.* [On-line]. Available. http://www.herald.com [1998, March 2]

Pitts, W. (1989). West African poetics in the black preaching style. *American Speech, 64*, 137-149.

Poplack, S. (1981). Quantitative analysis of a functional and formal constraint on code switching. In R. Duran (Ed.), *Latino language and communicative behavior.* Norwood, NJ: Ablex.

Poplack, S. (1982). "Sometimes I'll start a sentence in Spanish *y termino en espanol*": Toward a typology of code-switching. In J. Amastae & L. Elías-Olivares (Eds.), *Spanish in the United States: Sociolinguistic aspects* (pp. 230-263). Cambridge, UK: Cambridge University Press.

Porter, R. P. (1996). *Forked tongue: The politics of bilingual education, 2nd ed.* Brunswick, NJ: Transaction.

Portes, A. & Rumbaut, R. G. (1996). *Immigrant America: A portrait* (2nd ed.). Berkeley: University of California Press.

Postrel, V., & Gillespie, N. (1995, March-April). On borders and belonging: A conversation with Richard Rodriguez. *UTNE Reader, 68*, 76-79.

Ramirez, J. D., Yuen, S. D., Ramey, D. R., Pasta, D. J., & Billings, D. K. (1991). *Final report: Longitudinal study of structured immersion strategy, early-exit, and late-exit transitional bilingual education programs for language-minority children* (Executive Summary). San Mateo, CA: Aguirre International.

Raymond, J. G. (1986). *A passion for friends: Toward a philosophy of female affection.* Boston: Beacon.

Resolution of the Oakland Board of Education [On-line]. (1996). Available: http://ourworld. compuserve.com/homepages/JWCRAWFORD [1997, October 30].

Resolution of the Oakland Board of Education [On-line]. (1997). Available: http://ourworld. compuserve.com/homepages/JWCRAWFORD [1997, October 30].

Rickford, J. R. (1998). The creole origins of African American Vernacular English: Evidence from copula absence. In S. S. Mufwene, J. R. Rickford, G. Bailey, & J. Baugh (Eds.), *African American English: Structure, history, and use* (pp. 154-200). New York: Routledge.

Risch, B. (1987). Women's derogatory terms for men: That's right, "dirty" words. *Language in Society, 16,* 353-358.

Rodgers, B. (1972). *The queens' vernacular: A gay lexicon.* San Francisco: Straight Arrow Books.

Rodin, J., & Ickovics, J. R. (1994). Women's health: Review and research agenda as we approach the 21st century. In P. R. Lee & C. L. Estes (Eds.), *The nation's health* (4th ed., pp. 373-382). Boston: Jones & Bartlett.

Rodriguez, R. (1982). *Hunger of memory: The education of Richard Rodriguez.* Toronto: Bantam Books.

Romaine, S. (1982). What is a speech community? In S. Romaine (Ed.), *Sociolinguistic variation in speech communities* (pp. 13-24). London: Edward Arnold.

Romaine, S. (1994). *Language in society: An introduction to sociolinguistics.* New York: Oxford University Press..

Romero, M. (1988). Chicano discourse about language use. *Language Problems and Language Planning, 12,* 110-129.

Rose, T. (1994). *Black noise: Rap music and black culture in contemporary America.* Hanover, NH: Wesleyan University Press.

Ross, K. (1993, January 29). Puerto Rico, amid dissent, raises standing of English. *The Boston Globe,* p. 3.

Ruddick, S. (1989). *Maternal thinking: Toward a politics of peace.* Boston: Beacon.

Ruíz, R. (1988). Orientations in language planning. In S. L. McKay & S. L.-C. Wong (Eds.), *Language diversity: Problem or resource?* (pp. 3-25). Boston: Heinle & Heinle.

Rumbaut, R. G. (1995). Vietnamese, Laotian, and Cambodian Americans. In P. G. Min (Ed.), *Asian Americans: Contemporary trends and issues* (pp. 232-270). Thousand Oaks, CA: Sage.

Ryan, E. B., & Giles, H. (Eds.). (1982). *Attitudes toward language variation.* London: Edward Arnold.

Sachs, J. (1987). Preschool boys' and girls' language use in pretend play. In S. U. Philips, S. Steele, & C. Tanz (Eds.), *Language, gender, and sex in comparative perspective* (pp. 178-188). New York: Cambridge University Press.

Sacks, H., Schegloff, E. A., & Jefferson, G. (1974). A simplest systematics for the organization of turn-taking in conversation. *Language, 50,* 696-735.

Said, E. W. (1979). *Orientalism.* New York: Random House.

Santa Ana, O. A. (1993). Chicano English and the nature of the Chicano language setting. *Hispanic Journal of Behavioral Sciences, 15,* 3-35.

Savage, D. G. (1994, June 21). High court lets English-only jobs rule stand. *Los Angeles Times,* pp. A1, A14.

Saville-Troike, M. (1989). *The ethnography of communication: An introduction* (2nd ed.). New York: Basil Blackwell.

Schiffrin, D. (1984). Jewish argument as sociability. *Language in Society, 13,* 311-335.

Schneider, E. W. (1989). *American earlier Black English: Morphological and syntactic variables*. Tuscaloosa: University of Alabama Press.

Schultz, E. A. (1990). *Dialogue at the margins: Whorf, Bakhtin, and linguistic relativity.* Madison: University of Wisconsin Press.

Scott, K. (1995a, October). *Bridging cultural borders: The role of "girl" and "look" in black women's talk about language use.* Paper presented at the meeting of the Organization for the Study of Communication, Language, and Gender, Minneapolis, MN.

Scott, K. (1995b). Identity and ideology in black women's talk about their talk: A report of research in progress. *Women and Language, 18,* 8-10.

Searle, J. (1969). *Speech acts: An essay in the philosophy of language.* London: Cambridge University Press.

Searle, J. (1974). Chomsky's revolution in linguistics. In G. Harman (Ed.), *On Noam Chomsky: Critical essays* (pp. 3-33). Garden City, NY: Anchor Books.

Servaes, J. (1988). Cultural identity in East and West. *Howard Journal of Communications, 2,* 58-71.

Seymour, H. N., & Seymour, C. M. (1979). The symbolism of Ebonics: I'd rather switch than fight. *Journal of Black Studies, 9,* 397-410.

Shapiro, L. (1997, May 12). The myth of quality time. *Newsweek,* pp. 62-69.

Sharf, B. F. (1997). Breast cancer on-line: Support and empowerment on the Internet. *Women and Health, 26,* 63-82.

Sharf, B. F., Kahler, J., Foley, R. P., Grant, D., Bomgaars, M., & Harper, S. (1990). *A shared understanding: Bridging racial and socioeconomic differences in doctor-patient communication.* (Available from the Department of Medical Education, The University of Illinois College of Medicine, Chicago).

Shaw, J. (1996, December 27). Don't self-inflict another obstacle. *Los Angeles Times,* p. B9.

Sheldon, A. (1990). Pickle fights: Gendered talk in preschool disputes. *Discourse Processes, 13,* 5-31.

Sheldon, A. (1992). Conflict talk: Sociolinguistic challenges to self-assertion and how young children meet them. *Merrill-Palmer Quarterly, 38,* 95-117.

Sheldon, A. (1993). Preschool girls' discourse competence: Managing conflict. In M. Bucholtz, K. Hall, & B. Moonwomon (Eds.), *Locating power: Proceedings of the 1992 Berkeley Women and Language Conference* (Vol. 2, pp. 528-539). Berkeley, CA: Berkeley Linguistic Society.

Sheldon, A. (1996). You can be the baby brother but you aren't born yet: Preschool girls' negotiation for power and access in pretend play. *Research on Language in Social Interaction, 29,* 57-80.

Sheth, M. (1995). Asian Indian Americans. In P. G. Min (Ed.), *Asian Americans: Contemporary trends and issues* (pp. 169-198). Thousand Oaks, CA: Sage.

Shor, I. (1992). *Empowering education: Critical teaching for social change.* Chicago: University of Chicago Press.

Shweder, R. A. (1984). Anthropology's romantic rebellion against the enlightenment, or there's more to thinking than reason and evidence. In R. A. Shweder & R. A. LeVine (Eds.), *Culture theory: Essays on mind, self, and emotion* (pp. 27-66). Cambridge, UK: Cambridge University Press.

Siegler, D. M., & Siegler, R. S. (1976). Stereotypes of males' and females' speech. *Psychological Reports, 39,* 167-170.

Silva-Corvalán, C. (1994). *Language contact and change: Spanish in Los Angeles*. New York: Oxford University Press.

Singapore: After the caning, "Mike's in pain." (1994, May 16). *Newsweek*, p. 41.

Smitherman, G. (1977). *Talkin' and testifyin': The language of Black America*. Boston: Houghton Mifflin.

Smitherman, G. (1994). *Black talk: Words and phrases from the hood to the Amen corner.* Boston: Houghton Mifflin.

Smitherman, G., & Cunningham, S. (1997). Moving beyond resistance: Ebonics and African American youth. *Journal of Black Psychology, 23*, 227-232.

Smith-Rosenberg, C. (1985). *Disorderly conduct: Visions of gender in victorian America*. New York: Knopf.

Snow, C. E., & Hakuta, K. (1992). The costs of monolingualism. In J. W. Crawford (Ed.), *Language loyalties: A source book on the official English controversy* (pp. 384-394). Chicago: University of Chicago Press.

Somekawa, E. (1995). On the edge: Southeast Asians in Philadelphia and the struggle for space. In W. L. Ng, S. Chin, J. S. Moy, & G. Y. Okihiro (Eds.), *Reviewing Asian America: Locating diversity* (pp. 33-47). Pullman: Washington State University Press.

Sowell, T. (1997, January 27). Ebonics: Follow the money. *Forbes*, p. 48.

Spears, A. K. (1982). The Black English semi-auxiliary *come*. *Language, 58*, 850-872.

Spears, A. K. (1987). Are black and white vernaculars diverging? (Papers from the NWAVE XIV Panel proceedings). *American Speech, 62*, 48-55, 71-72.

Spears, A. K. (1992). Reassessing the status of Black English (review article). *Language in Society, 21*, 675-682.

Speicher, B. L., & McMahon, S. M. (1992). Some African American perspectives on Black English Vernacular. *Language in Society, 21*, 383-407.

Spender, D. (1980). *Man-made language*. London: Routledge.

Spivak, G. C. (1996) Subaltern studies: Deconstructing historiography. In D. Landry & G. MacLean (Eds.), *The Spivak reader* (pp. 203-235). New York: Routledge. (Original work published 1985)

Sridhar, K. K. (1988). Language maintenance and language shift among Asian-Indians: Kannadigas in the New York area. *International Journal of the Sociology of Language, 69*, 73-87.

Stavans, I. (1995). *The Hispanic condition: Reflections on culture and identity in America*. New York: HarperCollins.

Stewart, W. (1970). Continuity and change in American Negro dialects. In F. Williams (Ed.), *Language and poverty* (pp. 362-379). Chicago: Markham.

Stewart, W. C., & Bennett, M. J. (1991). *American cultural patterns: A cross-cultural perspective*. Yarmouth, ME: Intercultural Press.

Stuckey, S. (1987). *Slave culture: Nationalist theory and the foundations of black America*. New York: Oxford University Press.

Sutton, L. A. (1995). Bitches and skankly hobags: The place of women in contemporary slang. In K. Hall & M. Bucholtz (Eds.), *Gender articulated: Language and the socially constructed self* (pp. 279-296). New York: Routledge.

Takaki, R. (1993). *A different mirror: A history of multicultural America*. Boston: Little, Brown.

Tan, A. (1989). *The joy luck club*. New York: Ivy Books.

Tannen, D. (1990a). Gender differences in topical coherence: Creating involvement in best friends' talk. *Discourse Processes, 13*, 73-90.

Tannen, D. (1990b). *You just don't understand: Women and men in conversation.* New York: William Morrow.

Taylor, J. C., Gilligan, C., & Sullivan, A. M. (1995). *Between voice and silence: Women and girls, race and relationship.* Cambridge, UK: Harvard University Press.

Taylor, R. J., & Chatters, L. M. (1991). Religious life. In J. S. Jackson (Ed.), *Life in black America* (pp. 105-123). Newbury Park, CA: Sage.

Thompson, L., Christian, D., Stansfield, C. W., & Rhodes, N. (1990). Foreign language instruction in the United States. In A. Padilla, H. H. Fairchild, & C. M. Valadez (Eds.), *Foreign language education: Issues and strategies.* Newbury Park, CA: Sage.

Thompson, R. F. (1990). Kongo influences on African American artistic culture. In J. E. Holloway (Ed.), *Africanisms in American culture* (pp. 148-184). Bloomington: Indiana University Press.

Time's most influential Americans. (1997, April 21). *Time,* pp. 41-66.

Torres, L. (1989). Mood selection among New York Puerto Ricans. *International Journal of the Sociology of Language, 79,* 67-77.

Traugott, E. C. (1976). Pidgins, creoles, and the origins of Vernacular Black English. In D. S. Harrison & T. Trabasso (Eds.), *Black English: A seminar* (pp. 57-93). Hillsdale, NJ: Lawrence Erlbaum.

Tröemel-Plöetz, S. (1991). Selling the apolitical. *Discourse and Society, 2,* 489-501.

Trudgill, P. (1974). *Sociolinguistics: An introduction.* Middlesex, UK: Penguin.

True, R. H., & Guillermo, T. (1996). Asian/Pacific Islander American women. In M. Bayne-Smith (Ed.), *Race, gender, and health* (pp. 94-120). Thousand Oaks, CA: Sage.

Turner, L. (1968). *Africanisms in the Gullah dialect.* New York: Arno Press. (Original work published 1949)

Uchida, A. (1992). When "difference" is "dominance": A critique of the "anti-power-based" cultural approach to sex differences. *Language in Society, 21,* 547-568.

Unz, R., & Tuchman, G. M. (1997). *English language education for children in public schools* [On-line]. Available: http://ourworld.compuserve.com/homepages/jwcrawford [1997, October 30].

U.S. Bureau of the Census. (1993a). Hispanic Americans today. *Current population reports* (Series P23-183). Washington, DC: Government Printing Office.

U.S. Bureau of the Census. (1993b, 1994, 1995, 1996, 1997). *Statistical abstract of the United States.* Washington, DC: Government Printing Office.

U.S. Bureau of the Census. (1993c). *We the American Asians.* Washington, DC: Government Printing Office.

U.S. Bureau of the Census. (1994a). *1990 census of population: Asian and Pacific Islanders in the United States* (CP-3-5, ASI 1994 2531-4.5). Washington, DC: Government Printing Office.

U.S. Bureau of the Census. (1994b). *1990 census of population: Characteristics of American Indians by tribe and language* (CP-3-7, 2 vols.). Washington, DC: Government Printing Office.

U.S. Bureau of the Census. (1995a). *The Hispanic population* (P23-189). Washington, DC: Government Printing Office.

U.S. Bureau of the Census. (1995b). Population profile of the United States. *Current population reports* (Series P23-189). Washington, DC: Government Printing Office.

U.S. Bureau of the Census. (1996a). *Black population in the U.S., March 1996.* [On-line]. Available: http://www.census.gov/population/socdemo/race/black [1998, February 8].

U.S. Bureau of the Census. (1996b). Educational attainment level by race-ethnicity age 25 and over. *March 1996 current population survey.* [On-line]. Available: http:www//census.gov [1998, June 2].

U.S. Bureau of the Census. (1996c). *Estimates of the population of states by age, sex, race, and Hispanic origin: July 1, 1996.* [On-line]. Available: http://www.census.gov [1998, March 18].

U.S. Bureau of the Census. (1996d). Family income in previous year by race-ethnicity. *March 1996 current population survey.* [On-line]. Available: http:www//census.gov [1998, June 2].

U.S. Bureau of the Census. (1996e). Money income in the United States: 1996. *Current population survey* (Series P60-197). [On-line]. Available: http://www.census.gov [1998, February 8].

U.S. Bureau of the Census. (1996f). *Population and housing, county and city data book: Black population.* [On-line]. Available: http://www.census.gov [1996, February 22].

U.S. Bureau of the Census. (1996g). Population projections of the United States by age, sex, race, and Hispanic origin: 1995-2050. *Current population reports* (Series P25-1130). [On-line]. Available: http://www.census.gov/prod/www/titles.html#popest [1998, February 8].

U.S. Bureau of the Census. (1996h). *Selected economic characteristics of all persons and Hispanic persons, by type of origin: March 1996* [On-line]. Available: http://www.census.gov [1998, June 2].

U.S. Bureau of the Census. (1997a). *Asian and Pacific Islander population in the United States: March 1996* [On-line]. Available: http://www.census.gov/population/socdemo/race/api96 [1998, May 14].

U.S. Bureau of the Census. (1997b). Historical income tables. *Current population survey* [On-line]. Available: http://www.census.gov [1998, May 21].

U.S. Bureau of the Census. (1998). *POPClock projection* [On-line]. Available: http://www. census.gov [1998, February 8].

U.S. Bureau of the Census. (1999). *Resident population estimates of the United States by sex, race, and Hispanic origin, April 1, 1990 to April 1 1999* [On-line]. Available: http://www. census.gov/population/estimates/nation/intfile1-3. http://www.census.gov/population/estimates/nation/intfile1-3.— Text [1999, June 6].

U.S. Department of Commerce. (1994). *Characteristics of American Indians by tribe and language* (U.S. Census of Population 1990, CP-3-7). Washington, DC: Government Printing Office.

U.S. Immigration and Naturalization Service. (1998). *Illegal alien resident population* [On-line]. Available: http://www.ins.usdoj.gov/stats/illegalalien/index.html

Valdés, G. (1988). The language situation of Mexican Americans. In S. L. McKay & A. C. Wong (Eds.), *Language diversity: Problem or resource?* (pp. 111-139). Boston: Heinle & Heinle.

van Dijk, T. A. (1987). *Communicating racism: Ethnic prejudice in thought and talk.* Newbury Park, CA: Sage.

van Dijk, T. A. (1993). *Elite discourse and racism.* Newbury Park, CA: Sage.

Vass, W. (1979). *The Bantu speaking heritage of the United States.* Los Angeles: UCLA Center for African American Studies.

Verdelle, A. J. (1997, January 27). Classroom rap. *The Nation,* pp. 264-265.

Walker, A. (1982). *The color purple.* New York: Washington Square Press.

Watzlawick, P., Beavin, J. H., & Jackson, D. D. (1967). *The pragmatics of human communication: A study of interactional patterns, pathologies, and paradoxes.* New York: Norton.

West, C. (1990). Not just doctor's orders: Directive-response sequences in patients' visits to women and men physicians. *Discourse and Society, 1,* 85-112.

West, C. (1993a). *Keeping faith: Philosophy and race in America.* New York: Routledge.

West, C. (1993b). *Race matters.* Boston: Beacon.

West, C., & Frankel, R. M. (1991). Miscommunication in medicine. In N. Coupland, H. Giles, & J. M. Wiemann (Eds.), *"Miscommunication" and problematic talk* (pp. 166-194). Newbury Park, CA: Sage.

West, C., & García, A. (1988). Conversational shift work: A study of topical transitions between women and men. *Social Problems, 35,* 551-575.

West, C., & Zimmerman, D. H. (1983). Small insults: A study of interruptions in cross-sex conversations between unacquainted persons. In B. Thorne, C. Kramarae, & N. Henley (Eds.), *Language, gender, and society* (pp. 102-117). Rowley, MA: Newbury House.

Whorf, B. L. (1956). *Language, thought, and reality: Selected writings of Benjamin Lee Whorf* (J. B. Carroll, Ed.). Cambridge: MIT Press. (Original work published 1940)

Wiemann, J. M., & Giles, H. (1988). Interpersonal communication. In M. Hewstone, W. Stroebe, J. P. London, & G. M. Stephenson (Eds.), *Introducing social psychology* (pp. 199-221). Oxford, UK: Blackwell.

Wilkes, P. (Producer and Director). (1977, Spring). *Six American families* [six-part documentary film]. Broadcast by Westinghouse and PBS.

Williams, G. (1992). *Sociolinguistics: A sociological critique.* London: Routledge.

Williams, M. (1989). Ladies on the line: Punjabi cannery workers in central California. In Asian Women United of California (Ed.), *Making waves: An anthology of writings by and about Asian American women* (pp. 148-159). Boston: Beacon.

Wolfram, W. (1969). *A sociolinguistic description of Detroit Negro speech.* Washington, DC: Center for Applied Linguistics.

Wong, M. G. (1995). Chinese Americans. In P. G. Min (Ed.), *Asian Americans: Contemporary trends and issues* (pp. 58-94). Thousand Oaks, CA: Sage.

Wong, S. C. (1988). The language situation of Chinese Americans. In S. L. McKay & S. C. Wong (Eds.), *Language diversity: Problem or resource?* (pp. 193-228). Boston: Heinle & Heinle.

Woo, E., & Curtis, M. (1996, December 20). Oakland school board recognizes Black English. *Los Angeles Times,* p. A1.

Woo, E., & Moore, S. (1996, December 21). School decision on Black English stirs up a storm of commentary. *Los Angeles Times,* p. A24.

Worldmark encyclopedia of the states. (1998). Detroit: Gale Research.

Yamamoto, T. (1995). Different silence(s): The poetics and politics of location. In W. L. Ng, S. Chin, J. S. Moy, & G. Y. Okihiro (Eds.), *Reviewing Asian America: Locating diversity.* Pullman: Washington State University Press.

Yang, A. (1996). *The mail-order bride industry.* Unpublished student paper, Clark University, Worcester, MA.

Yim, S. B. (1989). Korean immigrant women in early twentieth-century America. In Asian Women United of California (Ed.), *Making waves: An anthology of writings by and about Asian American women* (pp. 50-60). Boston: Beacon.

Young, L. W. L. (1982). Inscrutability revisited. In J. J. Gumperz (Ed.), *Language and social identity* (pp. 72-84). Cambridge, UK: Cambridge University Press.

Yum, J.-O. (1987). Korean philosophy and communication. In D. L. Kincaid (Ed.), *Communication theory: Eastern and western perspectives* (pp. 71-86). London: Academic Press.

Yum, J.-O. (1988). The impact of Confucianism on interpersonal relationships and communication patterns in East Asia. *Communication Monographs, 55,* 374-388.

Zentella, A. C. (1985). The fate of Spanish in the United States: The Puerto Rican experience. In N. Wolfson & J. Manes (Eds.), *Language of inequality* (pp. 41-59). New York: Mouton.

Zernike, K. (1997, January 16). LA schools embrace Ebonics. *The Boston Globe,* p. 1A.

Zimmerman, D. H., & West, C. (1975). Sex roles, interruptions, and silences in conversations. In B. Thorne & N. Henley (Eds.), *Language and sex: Difference and dominance* (pp. 105-129). Rowley, MA: Newbury House.

Index

About the Author

Fern L. Johnson, Ph.D., is Professor of English and Director of the Interdisciplinary Communication and Culture Program at Clark University in Worcester, Massachusetts, where she also participates in the Women's Studies Program. She teaches courses on language and culture in the United States, language policy, conmunication and culture, and discourse and gender. She has published numerous articles in communication, sociolinguistics, psychology, and women's studies journals, and has contributed chapters to many books. Her current scholarship on verbal imaging in advertising continues a long-term interest in the ways in which language in the mass media offers subtle but persistent ideological codes.